Managing Professionals
and
Other Smart People

CW01497180

Managing Professionals and Other Smart People

Dermot Duff

with

Dr Mary Collins
Hannah Carney
Mary Goulding
Dr James M. Sheehan

and

Nick Koumarianos
Gerry Prendergast
Colm Russell

Chartered Accountants Ireland

Published in 2014 by
Chartered Accountants Ireland
Chartered Accountants House
47–49 Pearse Street
Dublin 2
www.charteredaccountants.ie

This publication is designed to provide accurate and authoritative information in regard to the subject matter covered. It is provided on the understanding that The Institute of Chartered Accountants in Ireland is not engaged in rendering professional services. The Institute of Chartered Accountants in Ireland disclaims all liability for any reliance placed on the information contained within this publication and recommends that if professional advice or other expert assistance is required, the services of a competent professional should be sought.

ISBN   978-1-908199-26-3

Typeset by Compuscript
Printed and bound by CPI Group (UK) Ltd, Croydon, CR0 4YY

To my beloved Mary and Seán

and to smart people everywhere,
especially the Colorado Cannonball Club.

Contents

Contributors

Dr Mary Collins

Dr Mary Collins is Senior Executive Development Specialist for the Royal College of Surgeons in Ireland (RCSI) Institute of Leadership. She has worked in the field of organisation development/talent management for over 14 years. She was Head of Talent Development at Deloitte from 2006–2013, having had a range of different OD roles in the telecommunications sector. She lectures part-time on a range of OD/HR topics at Dublin City University, NUI Maynooth and also inputs as a guest lecturer for the RCSI Institute of Leadership. Mary supervises research at doctoral and masters level.

Mary completed the Professional Doctorate Programme in DCU in 2010. Her research focus was on enhancing the psychological contract of 'Generation Y' in the professional services sector to enhance performance and engagement levels. She is an accredited coach with the Association of Coaching and is qualified in the use of a range of psychometric and personality assessment instruments. Mary is also a licensed Business NLP Practitioner and holds an Advanced Diploma in hypno-psychotherapy.

Hannah Carney

Hannah Carney is an independent consultant offering consultancy services and leadership, talent and team development interventions. In consulting and designing to clients' needs, Hannah works with a range of coach/ mentoring, facilitation and skills development processes. She has a special interest in the areas of communication and interpersonal/team dynamics. Prior to her work in organisation and individual development, Hannah's professional background was legal. She was a partner in a leading Dublin law firm, specialising in contentious scenarios and dispute resolution. She is also qualified, and practiced for a number of years, in New South Wales, Australia.

Mary Goulding

With over 30 years' experience in senior executive, CEO and consulting positions, Mary Goulding is a strategic business consultant, facilitator and business coach to entrepreneurs and CEOs of early-stage and high-growth companies. She has seen many companies flourish from start-up to mature business phase or successful buy-out, and has also seen the flipside of floundering CEOs and companies failing.

In 1991, having worked at senior management level in various software start-ups, Mary set up her own company, Synaptics, which successfully provided global data communications software products and services to clients in Europe, the US and Canada. Subsequently, she ran Rapid Technology Group Plc before establishing her own consultancy business in 2000.

Mary holds a BSc Degree in Computer Science, a Postgraduate Diploma in Executive Coaching, and a Diploma in counselling, therapy and NLP.

Dr James M. Sheehan

Jimmy Sheehan is a retired orthopaedic surgeon. Graduating from University College Dublin in 1963 with Gold Medals in medicine, surgery and obstetrics, he then trained in Ireland, the UK and France. He was appointed Consultant Orthopaedic Surgeon to St. Vincent's Hospital and Cappagh Orthopaedic Hospital, Dublin, in 1970. He established the Joint Replacement Unit at Cappagh and introduced the Swiss AO System for internal fixation of fractures at St. Vincent's.

Jimmy also qualified as an engineer in order to develop his understanding of the intricacies of artificial joint design and went on to develop his own artificial knee and hip joint replacements. As a surgeon, engineer, businessman and entrepreneur, he has also spent decades at the forefront of hospital development in Ireland. Passionate about the delivery of healthcare and frustrated with the slow development of Ireland's health services and severe cutbacks in public funding in the early 1980s, he set out with three colleagues to found the Blackrock Clinic. Many years later, the success of this venture was followed by the Hermitage and Galway Clinics.

Nick Koumarianos

Nick Koumarianos has many years' experience in technology, mainly in the communications sector. As MD of his own company he merged with Cable & Wireless Plc and became C&W MD for Ireland and Portugal. During his 12 years with C&W, he was Director of C&W Europe and sat on the board of each of the C&W European subsidiaries. He was promoted to MD of C&W Caribbean and Atlantic Islands division, the second largest division of C&W and which held the exclusive licence for telecommunication services on 14 islands from Bermuda through the Caribbean Islands and as far south as the Falkland Islands.

Following his retirement from C&W, Nick has taken up a number of advisory positions and shareholdings in Irish companies, including chairmanships of Dome Telecom Ltd, Soft-ex Ltd and Saadian Ltd, and non-executive directorship of SLT Global Credit Solutions. He is also on the advisory board of ICC Venture Capital, a division of Bank of Scotland and has served on the boards of Irish public companies, including Alphyra Plc and Calyx Plc. Nick is past President of the American Chamber of Commerce in Ireland and is an active member of a number of business groups and associations.

Gerry Prendergast

Gerry Prendergast (Msc Mgt., B. Tech. Eng.) is a highly experienced manager, with an excellent track record in such areas as lean manufacturing, operational excellence, and project management. Gerry has worked for a variety of leading manufacturing companies, mainly in the pharmaceutical and medical devices sectors. He has taken a pioneering approach to continuous improvement and has a passion for involving, developing and coaching people, especially in engineering and in knowledge management activities.

Acknowledgements

Knowledge is in the end based on acknowledgement.

Ludwig Wittgenstein

It takes a village to raise a child, so perhaps it is not surprising that it took a whole community to produce this book. Certainly, I am indebted to all my fellow authors: Dr Mary Collins, Dr Jimmy Sheehan, Hannah Carney, Mary Goulding, Nick Koumarianos, Gerry Prendergast, Colm Russell, and unnamed others, for their wonderful contributions and emotional support. The book rests on the deep foundations of their expertise.

Without the endless patience and encouragement of our publishers, Michael Diviney, Liam Boyle and the dedicated team at Chartered Accountants Ireland, this book would have remained a mere concept, so a deep and sincere thanks to them for their professionalism and precision. As editors, they provided the perfect balance of literary freedom and academic rigour, and proved ideal partners in bringing this text to life.

Many others, knowingly or otherwise, made significant contributions: Micheline Egan of HeadStrong for her work on building self-confidence; Greg Byrne of The Three Little Pigs Co. for his original piece on marketing professional firms; Sheila Fanning for her insights on behaviour; and Peter O'Connor for his expertise in personality profiling.

Still others provided intellectual support – and actual help: all my colleagues in Trinity College, Dublin, but especially Dr Louis Brennan on cognitive productivity, Mary-Rose Greville on psychology, John Quilliam on organisation design, Michael Flynn on business strategy, Paul Coghlan on operations management, Joe McDonagh on project leadership, Jim Quinn on management development and David Coghlan on learning.

Many of the practical examples included were influenced by the management development programmes in the Irish Management Institute and I am especially thankful to all the staff and associates, but particularly to Siobhan McAleer, Fabio Grassi, Mike Feeney, Cathy Winston, Moira Creedon, Ashley Hughes, Georgina Corscadden, Julia Rowan, Fergus Barry, Liz Norris, Tim Wray, Andrew McLoughlin, Derek Fox, Catherine Goodman, Mary Hogan, Ronan McNamara, Jonathon Westrop, Simon Boucher and Alistair Tosh.

My colleagues in the University of Nottingham brought perspectives: sincere acknowledgement is due to Simon Boucher, Andrew Greenman, Yasmin Holmes, Andrea O'Mahoney and all the Growth 100 team.

Special thanks to close friends and mentors such as Dr Sean Brady for his unending support, strategic insights literary criticism and generosity; Sean

Sweeney for being such a wonderful sounding board; and John McDonald of MediaTeam for his business sense.

Enterprise Ireland, in association with Dublin City University and the IMI, provided me the opportunity to engage as an advisor to many wonderful companies, and a note of thanks is due to Wesley McGrath, Clare Power, Richard Keegan, Julie Sinnamon, Patrick Flood, Finian McGrath, John Loughran and John McMackin.

Entrepreneurs and professionals such as: Chris Kilpatrick of KCC Architectural; Fionan Dunne of CFO Services: Bernard McGlade and Gary Browne of CIDP, David Horan and Martin Horan of Biotector; Brian Stephens of Design Partners; Simon Keogh and Barry O'Loughlin of CKSK; Michael Brophy, John Ryan and Elena Moreno of Certification Europe; Linda Mellerick of GXP Systems; Stephen Kelly, Gary McElroy and Michael McElduff of Headcount Engineering Services; Essam Basheer of GSM Exchange; and their colleagues, are due sincere thanks for the many stimulating conversations we had. They might even detect some echoes of those conversations in these pages!

Acknowledgment is due to the pioneers in this area: David Maister, Gareth Jones, Rob Goffee, Otto Scharmer, Dan Pink, Malcolm Gladwell, Chris Argyris and a host of other iconic giants of learning.

Above all, I want to thank my wife Mary English (a consummate professional) and my son Seán (one of the smart people) for allowing me the freedom – and the space – to write.

Last and not least, I beg forgiveness of all those who have assisted me over the years and whose names I have failed to mention.

I would maintain that thanks are the highest form of thought, and that gratitude is happiness doubled by wonder.

Gilbert K. Chesterton

Chapter 1

Introduction

The empires of the future will be the empires of the mind.

Winston Churchill

Intelligence matters, now more than ever, and the aim of this book is to help managers develop the full potential of smart people, especially modern professionals engaged in high-intellect work.

For the purposes of this book, *smart* means those especially talented people who have the capability to achieve disproportionate value for an organisation.

Knowledge is now perhaps the most strategically important of an organisation's resources, and the central question is how to create and transfer knowledge efficiently. The foundation of organisational advantage has shifted from natural resources to intellectual assets. The reward for managing knowledge astutely has been dramatically amplified. Releasing the tacit knowledge of people is crucial to success, and creativity creates its own prerogative.

Managing smart people, and especially professionals, therefore requires new insights and this book attempts to provide a framework for managing such smart professionals. It particularly tries to shed new light on the nature of professionals and their different types of work, and to suggest means of motivating them to optimum performance.

Bright light creates dark shadows: intelligence creates the potential for high achievement, but it can also cast a dark shadow over an organisation if that tremendous mental power cannot be harnessed in the social context of the workplace. Often, the so-called solution is to isolate or quarantine the 'troublesome' genius, undermining both the brilliant individual and the organisation he or she needs as the vehicle for achievement.

The undoubted potential of the gifted performer invariably needs skilful management if it is to be fully realised, and this book aims to provide the understanding (and useful advice) that is sorely needed, despite the abundance of standard management tracts on managing mainstream performers.

Intellectual work was once the preserve of the few, but now it is the responsibility of many, in fields as diverse as accounting, medicine, science and engineering. Management theory for traditional manual and clerical work abounds yet, until recently, little was formulated in navigating the murky channels of work performed largely in the brain. Such 'tacit' work was considered, with some justification, to be impenetrable, yet the modern organisation, from Amgen to Zara, depends on this elusive brain capacity.

The co-ordination of this tacit knowledge requires the collaboration of talented individuals who stereotypically have low regard for hierarchical structures or even for emotional intelligence and social niceties.

One of the foundational thinkers in this area is Daniel Pink (who evolved the concept of 'whole brain' thinking as a means of understanding how to combine analytical (left-brain) thinking with the more creative (right-brain) side.[1] The essence of achieving high performance in professionals is in combining the best of both worlds – left and right brain. Professionals may tend to overuse a thinking style, at the expense of other modes of thinking, becoming, for example in the case of a 'classic' accountant, overly analytical and perhaps ignoring emotional intelligence. They may similarly tend, over time, to become more pronounced in their personality type, especially if their professional formation encourages, for example, conservative, introverted and analytical approaches.

Similarly, an abstract thinker may fail because of their lack of pragmatism, or the academic may become a caricature, favouring brain activity over all other forms of activity (the academic is invariably the one at the party who can't dance!).

Seeing the full picture means taking different perspectives. Resolving these 'either–or' dilemmas requires the professional to combine the 'Ying and the Yang', so to speak. Becoming a more rounded, capable professional requires understanding of the non-cognitive, emotional aspects of human behaviour, especially if that professional aspires to management or leadership roles.

In this book, therefore, attention is paid to developing intelligence of various forms, including emotional intelligence and different thinking styles. This is intended to benefit both the professional and those who must manage such talented and "smart" individuals. It is truly tragic to allow the high potential of the smart professional to be undermined by correctable flaws in behaviour: this book aims to raise awareness of personality factors and to provide implementable means of achieving high levels of social and emotional intelligence in addition to the smart professional's inherent cognitive intelligence.

Ever-increasing specialisation requires smart people to dedicate themselves to resolving complex problems or designing elegant solutions on an unprecedented scale. The professions, especially in medicine, engineering and accounting, are relentlessly subdividing into narrower specialisations to achieve the necessary precision and depth of knowledge. New knowledge areas, particularly in information technology, science and business, are spawning new professions: many other disciplines, from executive coaching to economists, aspire to earn the elevated rank of a profession.

What is a Profession?

A profession arises when any trade or occupation transforms itself through "the development of formal qualifications based upon education, apprenticeship, and examinations, the emergence of regulatory bodies with powers to admit and discipline members, and some degree of monopoly rights."[2]

Professions enjoy a high social status, regard and esteem conferred upon them by society. This high esteem arises primarily from the higher social function of their work, which is regarded as vital to society as a whole and thus of having a special and valuable nature. All professions involve technical, specialised and highly skilled work, often referred to as 'professional expertise'. Training for this work involves obtaining degrees and professional qualifications without which entry to the profession is barred.

The original professions were in divinity, law and medicine (interestingly, they came to signify their distinct identity through red robes, black cloaks and white coats, respectively). The list of recognised professions now includes: accountants, academics, actuaries, architects, dentists, engineers, economists, lawyers, librarians, nurses, nutritionists, pharmacists, physicians, physiotherapists, psychologists, scientists, social workers and veterinarians. Many other occupations (such as computer science) have many similar characteristics of dedicated work, continuous development, barriers to entry and accredited membership criteria, and are regarded as professions, although some of these newer professions lack the vocational and social responsibility aspects of the classic professions, and may require lower levels of trust between the client and the professional.

Characteristics of a Profession

A profession is distinguished by three important characteristics:

1. The professional expects to have autonomy in decision-making regarding their professional work, by virtue of their training, qualifications and personal integrity. A professional such as a doctor, lawyer, teacher or accountant is expected to *be* a professional, not merely *do* professional work. Their identity is inherently linked to their profession and their ties to their professional association are strong, both in the economic and social senses.

2. The professional is expected to have an orientation of service to society that goes beyond immediate self-interest: a doctor, for example, takes the Hippocratic Oath, promises to "first, do no harm", and has a duty of care to patients. Other professionals, such as accountants, similarly have a fiduciary duty of trust to their clients (individual or corporate) and are expected to meet specified codes of behaviour, at the risk of expulsion from their professional association.

3. Every profession engages in the practical application of the underlying theory, converting abstract knowledge into skilful service.

These characteristics are illustrated in the figure below:

FUNDAMENTAL QUALIFYING CHARACTERISTICS OF A PROFESSION

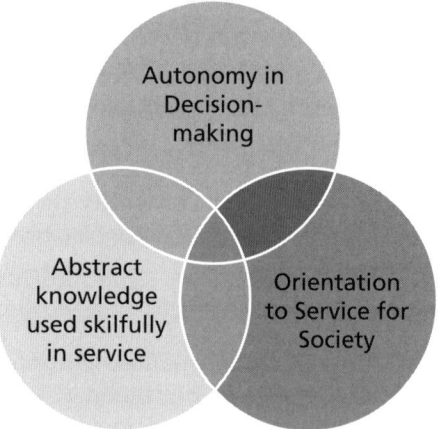

PROFESSIONALS AND AMATEURS

A '**professional**' is a member of a vocation founded upon specialised educational training, and traditionally means a person who has obtained a degree in a professional field. The term commonly describes highly educated, mostly salaried workers, who enjoy considerable work autonomy and are usually engaged in creative and intellectually challenging endeavours.

Because of the personal and confidential nature of many profession-al services and thus the necessity to place a great deal of trust in them, most professionals are held up to strict ethical and moral regulations.

Everett Hughes, a sociologist, suggests that "in return for access to their extraordinary knowledge in matters of great human impor-tance, society has granted them a mandate for social control in their fields of specialization, a high degree of autonomy in their practice, and a license to determine who shall assume the mantle of professional authority".[3]

Cameron Winklevoss: ultimate amateur, Olympic rower,
entrepreneur and social network progenitor.

The term '**amateur**' is derived from the French word for 'lover'. An amateur is a lover of a particular pursuit, study, or science, without pay and often without formal training. The true amateur is considered noble, enjoying the pursuit entirely for its own sake, without pay, in the true Olympic spirit. Whereas 'professional' is usually a compli-ment, 'amateur' is often used pejoratively.

The Nature of Intelligence

"I think intellect is a good thing, unless it paralyses your ability to make decisions because you see too much complexity. Presidents need to have what I would call a synthesising intelligence."

Bill Clinton, Former US President and Rhodes Scholar

Work requiring complex interactions and a high level of expertise now accounts for some 40% of the US labour market, and a staggering 70% of the jobs created since 1998.[4]

Synthesis is the essence of managing; putting things together, in the form of coherent strategies, unified organizations, and integrated systems. That is what makes managing so difficult – and so interesting. It's not that managers don't need analysis; it's that they need it as an input to synthesis. Where to find synthesis in a world so decomposed by analysis?[5]

Intelligent, Clever or Smart: Key Distinctions

While 'intelligent' seems an internationally accepted non-judgemental adjective for those with superior capacities for abstract thought, reasoning, planning, and problem-solving, usage the term of 'smart' versus 'clever' differs radically. In the USA, 'smart' usually conveys both cleverness and wisdom (e.g. "that was a smart move"). In other English-speaking countries, such as Ireland, Australia and the UK, however, 'smart' often carries negative connotations (e.g. stop your "smart remarks"). In this book, 'smart' is used to define those with high academic or technical intelligence, which is frequently not matched by commensurate social intelligence.

Exceptional Intelligence: Born or Made? Genes and Genius

'Genius' is a widely used term that is hard to define absolutely. A genius is generally regarded as someone embodying exceptional intellectual ability, creativity or originality, leading to unprecedented insight.

The term is commonly used to denote scholars, whether in a single area (e.g. Nicola Tesla in physics) or in multiple areas (e.g. Leonardo da Vinci, renowned for his many intelligences).

Albert Einstein, 20th-Century genius

Popular opinion has it that geniuses are born, not made, but recent research by Malcolm Gladwell (quoting psychologist Anders Ericsson) indicates that mastery (perhaps even genius?) is achieved by those who first practice intensively enough, with 10,000 hours of purposeful practice considered the magic basis for out-performance.[6] Gladwell's book, *Outliers*,[7] shows that some elements of chance play a role in the creation of a genius, including the so-called self-reinforcing 'Matthew Effect' (e.g. 'the rich get richer').

The 'Halo Effect' is a similar, self-fulfilling prophesy, where encouragement primes a cycle of achievement leading to further encouragement. Similarly, while high-achieving academics, for example, may indeed produce similarly gifted offspring (promoting the 'genes' theory), the role of a suitable home environment in promoting mastery must be recognised (the nurture theory). Geniuses, it seems, may well be born but they can also, to a degree, be made. Similarly, as will be explained in later chapters, leadership can actually be developed significantly through intellectual stimulation. In fact, the key criterion for such development, according to Dr John Antonakis of the University of Lausanne, is a certain threshold of intellectual ability.[8] As Malcolm Gladwell explains, it is safe to say that dedication and hard work play a role.

Anders Ericsson, who is an "expert in expertise", claims that mentors play an important role in attaining mastery.[9] Many of a genius's skills may be tacit or implicit, making it a challenge to articulate (i.e. make explicit) how they do what they do, and this aspect is considered in the later chapters on developing intuition and fostering innovation, especially collectively.

It is not yet scientifically known what makes some brains smarter than others. Is it that intelligent people are physically better at the fundamentals of brainwork – storing and retrieving memories? Perhaps their 'brain-speed' helps them make quicker or better connections, therefore creating new combinations of ideas? Perhaps their ability to link seemingly unrelated ideas provides the spark of genius?

The currently accepted view among scientists is that there are basic types of intelligence – analytic, linguistic, practical and emotional – but there is disagreement whether these are linked or independent.

Psychologist Howard Gardner promotes the 'Theory of Multiple Intelligences', postulating eight distinct types of intelligence and claiming that there need not be a correlation among them; in other words, a person could have high emotional intelligence but lack, for example, analytical intelligence.[10] Psychologist Robert Sternberg argues that current definitions of intelligence are too narrow because they are predicated on intelligences that can only be assessed in IQ testing.[11]

Different Types of Intelligence

Intelligence comes in many forms, including some barely recognised talents as Howard Gardner explains, below. The key categorisations of intelligence according to Daniel Goleman are[12]:

- Rational intelligence – this is the classic kind, at the centre of academic education.
- Creative intelligence – much lauded and simultaneously often sneered at, possibly due to its non-explicit form which makes it hard to describe or to teach.
- Emotional intelligence – that ability to read and respond in real time to the nuances of human behaviour.
- Social intelligence – highly evolved self- and social awareness and an ability to manage complex social change.

Howard Gardner's theory of multiple intelligences[13] proposes at least eight different components of intelligence:

- Logical
- Linguistic
- Spatial
- Musical
- Kinesthetic
- Interpersonal
- Intrapersonal
- Naturalistic
- Existential.

Goleman argues that psychometric tests address only linguistic and logical plus some aspects of spatial intelligence. His theories have gained wide recognition and are worthy of consideration, even though they lack absolute scientific proof.

Emotional Intelligence

Howard Gardner claims that evolution has developed the various forms of intelligence, suggesting that:

> "as history unfolds, as cultures evolve, of course the intelligences which they value change. Until a hundred years ago, if you wanted to have higher education, linguistic intelligence was important. I teach at Harvard, and 150 years ago, the entrance exams were in Latin, Greek and Hebrew. If, for example, you were dyslexic, that would be very difficult because it would be hard for you to learn those languages, which are basically written languages."

Emotional intelligence is now ever more important in society:

> "While your IQ, which is a sort of language logic, will get you behind the desk, if you don't know how to deal with people, if you don't know how to read yourself, you're going to end up just staying at that desk forever or eventually being asked to make room for somebody who does have social or emotional intelligence."[14]

While professionals typically excel in cognitive intelligence, only the truly outstanding performers seem to manage to also display high social and emotional intelligence, either by nature or by nurture (the formation of particular beliefs and/or the neglect of certain interpersonal aspects as a result of rigorous education and training). This dichotomy is explored at many points throughout this book.

"I know that I am intelligent, because I know that I know nothing."
                                                                    Socrates

---

Defining Characteristics of Smart Professionals

Smart people share a number of common defining characteristics, particularly those especially talented and driven performers:

1. They have a disdain for the very act of management itself, associating it with controls that will inhibit their autonomy and impede their progress. Truth to tell, **they don't want to be managed** at all!

    However, they do want to be led, but not in the conventional sense. Rather than a typical hierarchical boss, they appreciate a leader who is their intellectual equal (but preferably in a different sphere, so as to get the benefit of high intellect without the risk of being upstaged). Such a leader must also help their cause by clearing a path towards their goal; their ideal leader is not a hierarchical superior but a Shackleton-type of expedition leader.

2. They **crave autonomy** in pursuit of their chosen goals, believing (often rightly) that they know where to go and how to get there; they also crave recognition and get their satisfaction from being the smartest kid on the block.

    They will often be cleverer than the boss, and despise hierarchy, even to the extent of disdaining promotion, preferring to stay close to their core work.

    However, they do covet the power to get resources, and need recognition for their accomplishments. Feeding these ego needs is therefore crucial, even if the recipients may sometimes claim to disdain awards and other forms of public recognition. As Napoleon wisely noted, "men will die for ribbons", so use this maxim in driving recognition systems: dispense awards and accolades that recipients actually esteem.

3. Respect their corporate capability. Despite their intolerance for hierarchy and bureaucracy, they are politically savvy enough to know where the levers of power are located, and they are not afraid to use these levers to further their work.

    The best of them will understand the dynamics of their markets, and the need to have a defined goal, enervating vision and a viable strategy, if only so that their goals can be realised. Indeed, they will strenuously test the rationale behind any strategy, and can provide valuable insights in the form of acerbic critique. Never expect them to endure endless vacuous meetings or deathly PowerPoint presentations.

4. Though they have high levels of drive, their energy (and confidence) is not infinite, and they can flip between obsession and indifference, especially if they encounter failure. As failure is inevitable, even for the brightest, be prepared to pour balm on their wounds, and show that the light at the end of the tunnel is not just an on-coming train.

    In dealing with their failures, it is not sympathy they want, but understanding; understanding of the effort expended. Smart people thrive on tough love, not indulgence.

5. They are different in that they need higher mountains to climb. Use their intense need to achieve (and to have achievements recognised) to set them very challenging targets; soft targets, for them, are counter-productive and demotivating. In fact, by their very nature, they will often set higher targets than you might think reasonable.

THE FALLACY OF CONVENTIONAL BELIEFS ABOUT MOTIVATION

Standard management beliefs about motivating workers centre on these four elements:

- Recognition – to have excellence in one's work recognised appropriately
- Incentives – to have appropriate reward and remuneration
- Interpersonal – to have good peer relationships and friendships at work
- Clear goals – to understand what the aim is, and why it matters.

While these beliefs are not, in themselves, incorrect, they do not fit well with the in-depth research of Professor Teresa Amabile of Harvard Business School, who has discovered that the biggest motivational factor for high-performers is simply progress itself.[15] The satisfaction for high-achievers lies fundamentally in progress. This straightforward but startling discovery will be explored more fully later (see **Chapter 7**), as it has tremendous implications for both professionals and those who manage them.

6. Smart people need a 'loose–tight' arrangement. A good boss will be close to them at key moments, to help deal with disappointment; otherwise the good boss would be well advised to preserve a distance:
    - be available, but not on hand;
    - help, when asked, but don't intrude;
    - lead, but don't micro-manage;
    - trust, but verify, if you must;
7. The smartest people detest bureaucracy as it takes them away from their mission. They have low regard for those who represent the classic 'punishment' bureaucracy, where rules are dictated by dominant control groupings. They need protection from this kind of organisational harassment; give them dispensation from bureaucracy, or devise a work-around solution, because there truly are better uses of their talent than filling in redundant information or irrelevant forms.

Note that smart people can have some respect for so-called 'representational' bureaucracy, where the rules exist for a clearly useful reason (an example being high-performing sports teams accepting tactical orders).

THE MODERN DILEMMA – MANAGING SMART PEOPLE

According to economist and philosopher Malcolm Gladwell, author of *Blink* and the *Tipping Point*, the greatest challenge managers face in modern organisations is managing smart people, because in today's environment a manager is not necessarily the best professional. Those days are over. He or she no longer has the ultimate knowledge and the ability to understand all issues of the business, department, or sometimes even the team. His or her staff often know more about specific things than he or she does and have skills that he or she does not. They are indeed smart, and in more ways than pure IQ.

8. While talented people have an inherent drive that compels them to engage with their chosen field, they are less easily engaged with the organisation itself. As far back as 1969, behavioural scientist Frederick Herzberg noted that the factors that motivate people differ markedly from those factors that demotivate them: they are not two sides of the same coin, so to speak, but are fundamentally different.[16]

Motivation, Herzberg's research revealed, is essentially intrinsic and difficult to stimulate from 'outside' the person (e.g. by bosses, or through higher remuneration).

Demotivation occurs much more easily, and is often triggered by so-called 'hygiene' factors, such as stifling bureaucracy or chafing restrictions. While many such petty irritations should be easily discarded, in practice they are found to persist.

While this lack of engagement is, of course, not confined to the intelligent, they could be more prone to disengagement because they have more critical faculties and a higher disregard for hygiene items that impede their path to progress.

PROFESSIONALS AND DISENGAGEMENT

Prominent management strategist Gary Hamel's studies show that less than 20% of employees worldwide are highly engaged in their work.[17] This is a potentially debilitating handicap for organisations competing in today's 'creative economy'.

Disengaged employees may be obedient, industrious and smart, but they are unlikely to bring initiative, creativity and passion to their work – even though, as individuals, they may be richly endowed with these valuable capabilities.

The right tools, a compelling sense of mission, access to information, the freedom to chose one's work, high calibre colleagues, a stimulating physical environment – these are just a few of the things that help amplify individual accomplishment.

9. The brightest 'stars' often have an unconscious ability to produce results that they cannot effectively articulate. This is partly due to their intuitive ability, and partly due to being so closely wound up in their work that they cannot separate conscious and unconscious steps. Similarly, they can resent others' lack of comprehension of what steps are involved or lack of appreciation of the nuance.

    It is generally prudent to tolerate their lack of process orientation; they simply cannot explain their own subconscious creative processes. In any case, all the evidence is that innovation emerges from a messy 'process', so chaotic as to be beyond description. Note that innovation emerges from a sort of purposeful mess. It is a loose assembly of ideas and fragments put together over time, with the essential elements gathered along the way.

10. High-achievers want to be lone rangers, but not to be all alone; they want to plough their own furrow, yes, and are often in competition with others in their sphere. They respect ability, not mere likeability, so don't expect charm or obsequiousness from pioneering staff.

CLEVER PEOPLE AND THEIR DISDAIN FOR AUTHORITY

Clever people, at their most difficult, have the following characteristics, according to Gareth Jones and Robert Goffee of the London Business School[18]:

- They take genuine pleasure when they break any rule.
- They tend to trivialise the importance of non-technical people.
- They suffer heavily from 'knowledge is power' syndrome and seldom share their knowledge or contribute to knowledge management systems.
- They are never happy with the review/evaluation process to which their projects are subject.
- They are over-sensitive about the projects they are working on and almost never agree to kill projects they know are not leading anywhere.

It must be emphasised that cleverness is not automatically a cause of awkward behaviour. Intelligence may well be linked with greater powers of analysis and with speed of thought, but of course it is not inextricably linked to aggression or truculence. Many critics of intelligent people (depicting them as arrogant or socially inept, for example) fail to realise that such relationships depend on both sides, and a surgeon's arrogance, an accountant's dispassion or an architect's abstractedness are often just essential demeanours of the trade.

DISPROPORTIONATE VALUE: OUTSTANDING TALENT IS WORTH ITS WEIGHT IN GOLD

> Top talent will produce innovations and breakthroughs beyond the capability of a legion of average performers. Moreover, these will invariably emerge from a messy process, helped by having a loose community of like-minded, dedicated talent.
>
> Ruben Vardanian, founding president of the Moscow School of Management, asserts: "The main struggle in the nineteenth century was about the land. In the twentieth century, it was about industrial assets and natural resources. In the twenty-first century, the main challenge is to attract the best people."[19]

Talent attracts talent, and it is from such clusters of thought-leaders that useful innovations emerge. This is partly because talented people compete and simultaneously collaborate, and partly because the diversity of the community brings different perspectives and different ingredients.

> Despite the common view that intelligence tends to detract from 'soft skills', such as leadership, the opposite may be true. In his book *Executive Intelligence*,[20] Justin Menkes asserts that too much emphasis has been placed on personality and style and too little on types of intelligence that enhance leadership performance. He argues that: "when it comes to predicting work performance, cognitive ability tests have been demonstrated to be approximately ten times as powerful as personality assessments … Personality is not a differentiator of star talent. It is an individual's facility for clear thinking or intelligence that largely determines their leadership success." Menkes proclaims that 'executive intelligence' is the key differentiator; the ability to digest information and make key decisions that produce useful action with the right amount of deliberation is paramount.

Information, Knowledge, Wisdom and Learning

It is 50 years since the great management authority Peter Drucker coined the term 'knowledge worker' to express the prevalence of intellectual work. This is a very loose term, much derided by the anti-hero Dilbert, the Everyman of the modern IT world. Knowledge work remains the corner-stone of the modern economy, yet it remains a domain that is only vaguely understood.

There is an important distinction between *information* (facts or data) and *knowledge* (the synthesis of the meaning of those facts).

Furthermore, there is a marked difference between such *knowledge* and *wisdom*; wisdom knows not just the answer but can also pose the pertinent question.

Similarly, *education* differs from the more practical *training,* and of course actual student *learning* does not necessarily follow simply from the *teaching* of a particular subject.

Ultimately, it is this ability to learn that distinguishes the smart person. Intelligence involves the ability to reason, plan, solve problems, think abstractly, comprehend complex ideas, but especially to learn from experi-ence. It is not just book learning, but a capacity for comprehending one's sur-roundings and making sense of things. Such 'action learning' is fundamental both for daily progression and for the occasional breakthrough thinking so characteristic of the smart professional.

Developing the Reflective Practitioner: Action Learning

Organisation theorist Donald Schön extensively researched how people actually learn.[21] Using examples from diverse areas such as architecture, music performance and psychotherapy, he discovered how people in these very different professions learn. He concluded that while one can provide the opportunity, the environment, the encouragement ... **the learning belongs ultimately to the learner**.

Schön gave the example of how designers learn, and help others to do so:

> "Designing, in its broader sense, involves complexity and synthesis. In con-trast to analysts or critics, designers put things together and bring new things into being, dealing in the process with many variables and constraints, some initially known and some discovered through designing. Almost always, designers' moves have consequences other than those intended for them. Designers juggle variables, reconcile conflicting values, and manoeuvre around constraints – a process in which, although some design products may be superior to others, there are no unique right answers."

You discover more about the problem even as you try to solve the problem. You choose a course of action, only to find yourself surprised at some con-sequence. You adjust, you manoeuvre ... but basically you synthesise in a world of complexity.

You, as the manager or 'master', must make your thinking transparent to the learner. Schön says:

> "It is as though the studio master had said to him, 'I can tell you that there is something you need to know, and with my help you may be able to learn it. But I cannot tell you what it is in a way you can now understand. I can

only arrange for you to have the right sorts of experiences for yourself. You must be willing, therefore, to have these experiences. Then you will be able to make an informed choice about whether you wish to continue. If you are unwilling to step into this new experience without knowing ahead of time what it will be like, I cannot help you. You must trust me.'"

The 'master' has a repertoire of options, drawing from them as appropriate. The master responds to the learner's actions by re-framing, listening, reflecting, engaging in dialogue and trying again. In so doing, the master exposes his or her own thinking. Having herself learned at some point in the past, she is now called upon to think aloud, making explicit her reasoning in order to clarify it as much for herself as for the learner.

The question for the manager is not how much he or she knows, but how much he or she can help someone to learn successfully: this is fundamental to effective leadership of professionals and other smart people.

The theme of 'action learning' is threaded throughout this book, and is developed more explicitly in later chapters. The barriers to learning for professionals and other smart people are often not cognitive, but are psychological, rooted in previously successful and now ingrained modes of behaviour, or in social blindness. As Bill Gates said: "Success is a lousy teacher. It seduces smart people into thinking they can't lose." On the other hand, it is through smart thinking that the world progresses, and the 'care and feeding' of smart people is crucial to success on so many levels. According to Steve Wozniak, Bill's predecessor in personal computing: "wherever smart people work, doors are unlocked". This book is dedicated to unlocking those doors for the benefit of all, professionals and managers alike.

Summary

This introductory chapter highlights the need to manage professionals and other smart people differently. The foundational belief is that smart people have great potential and that conventional forms of management fail to realise their disproportionate value. High intellect workers, such as accountants, engineers or surgeons, may sometimes have deficiencies in emotional or social intelligence, but it is a tragic waste to sideline such people when remedies and counter-measures are available. Indeed, awareness itself (exposing a professional to the man in the mirror) may be enough to ignite the change, but this book also offers tools, techniques and insights that will assist smart people in their personal and professional development.

Management guidelines have been outlined to help release this potential in professionals and other smart people. The upcoming chapters explore these themes in detail, revealing the keys of motivating and leading high intelligence performers, particularly those whose 'blind spots' limit their potential. For example, in **Chapter 6** Dr Mary Collins provides a framework for managing professionals, particularly the next generation of accountants and consultants, and in **Chapter 4**, Dr Jimmy Sheehan describes his principled approach to leading talented people such as doctors and surgeons.

How to Manage Professionals and Other Smart People

	Do
1	Lead, but **don't** manage (clear a path, then clear off)
2	Be a guardian angel, not a ministering devil
3	Set real challenges and give just enough resources
4	Open doors to key people
5	Be close to them, at appropriate times
6	Let them fail – often
7	Never let them like failure, but help them understand it
8	Stay away when you're not needed – maintain distance and perspective
9	Show tough love, not indulgence
10	Help them create community and assemble a cluster of talent

How Not to Manage Professionals and Other Smart People

	Don't!
1	*Don't* micro-manage or tell people exactly what to do; encourage initiative
2	*Don't* prescribe precisely how a task is to be done; allow latitude
3	*Don't* let administrative aspects delay the work; let the most suited do these tasks
4	*Don't* meddle; allow some failure
5	*Don't* let hierarchy prevail; let merit influence decisions
6	*Don't* fail to give proper feedback; avoid sycophancy, but give real encouragement
7	*Don't* let the political sharks corner their prey: provide staff with a safe environment
8	*Don't* put talent on a pedestal; bright people are people first, bright second
9	*Don't* quarantine staff; allow contact with the real world, avoiding toxic elements

10	*Don't* hire bright stars in isolation; realise that stars shine in a particular firmament
11	*Don't* ever hog the credit; the quality of giving is twice blest, and repays the giver

Further Reading and Acknowledgements

The foundations of this book were laid by Daniel Pink, Daniel Goleman, Gareth Jones and other authorities in their respective fields, as listed below. Interested readers are encouraged to explore their writings further, and I express my personal gratitude to them for their endeavours, especially Gareth Jones, Daniel Goleman and Malcolm Gladwell, whom I encountered on their exhilarating presentations to the Irish Management Institute.

Whole-brain Thinking	Daniel Pink
Emotional Intelligence	Daniel Goleman
Authentic Leadership	Gareth Jones
Intuition and Innovation	Otto Scharmer
Teaching Smart People to Learn	Chris Argyris
Motivation and Talent	Teresa Amabile
Crucial Conversations	Nancy Dixon
Systems Thinking	Peter Senge
Managing Knowledge Work	Ikajura Nonaka
Knowledge Work	Thomas Davenport
The Knowing/Doing Gap	Jeffrey Pfeffer
Strategic Thinking	Costas Markides
Managing Change	John Kotter
Managing Behaviour	Edgar Schein
Managing Complexity	Ron Leifetz
Motivation and Creativity	Daniel Pink

ENDNOTES

[1] Daniel Pink, *A Whole New Mind: Why Right-brainers will Rule the Future* (Penguin, 2005).

[2] JoAnne Brown, *The Definition of a Profession: the Authority of Metaphor in the History of Intelligence Testing, 1890–1930* (Princeton University Press, 1992).

[3] Everett Hughes, *Men and Their Work* (Free Press, 1958).

[4] Costas Markides and Paul A. Geroski, "Racing to be Second" (2004) December, Vol. 15 Issue 4 *Business Strategy Review* 25–31.

[5] Henry Mintzberg, *Managing* (Berrett-Koehler, 2009).

[6] Malcolm Gladwell, *Blink: The Power of Thinking without Thinking* (Little, Brown, 2007).

[7] Malcolm Gladwell, *Outliers: The Story of Success* (Little, Brown, 2008).

[8] Marina Fiori and John Antonakis, "Selective Attention to Emotional Stimuli: What IQ and Openness Do, and Emotional Intelligence Does Not" (2012) 40(3) *Intelligence* 245–254.

[9] K. Anders Ericsson, "The Role of Deliberate Practice in the Acquisition of Expert Performance" (1993) 100:3 *Psychological Review* 363–406.

[10] Howard Gardner, *Multiple Intelligences: The Theory in Practice* (Basic Books, 1993).

[11] Robert Sternberg, *Why Smart People Can Be So Stupid* (Yale Press, 2003).

[12] Daniel Goleman, *Social Intelligence: The New Science of Human Relationships* (Bantam Dell, 2006).

[13] Howard Gardner, *Multiple Intelligences: The Theory in Practice* (Basic Books, 1993).

[14] *Ibid.*

[15] Teresa M. Amabile and Steven J. Kramer, "The Power of Small Wins" (2011) Vol. 89 No. 5 *Harvard Business Review* 70–80.

[16] Frederick Herzberg, "One More Time – How do you Motivate Employees?" (1986) January–February *Harvard Business Review* 53–62.

[17] Gary Hamel, "Management 2.0" (2008) Vol. 7 February *Labnotes*.

[18] *Ibid.*

[19] Ruben Vardanian, in Robert Goffee and Gareth Jones, *Clever: Leading Your Smartest, Most Creative People* (Harvard Business Press, 2009).

[20] Justin Menkes, *Executive Intelligence* (HarperCollins, 2009).

[21] Donald A. Schön, *The Reflective Practitioner: How Professionals Think in Action* (Basic Books, 1983).

Chapter 2

Strategy and the Professional

Everything should be made as simple as possible, but no simpler.

Albert Einstein

Introduction

This chapter is intended to help any organisation, particularly those comprised of professionals, to generate a meaningful and effective strategy, one that recognises the different types of professional work, and to structure the organisation accordingly. The right structure provides the vehicle for the growth of the organisation and consequently the opportunity for motivational career paths. In this way, a suitable strategy and structure facilitates the management of professionals.

This chapter starts by summarising the current model of strategy formulation and then introduces a more powerful approach that leverages innovation, insight and foresight. This approach has been especially developed for professionals such as accountants, designers, architects, town planners, engineers, journalists, marketers, doctors and lawyers. It emphasises the power of knowledge and relationship-building in becoming a 'trusted advisor', or in simply moving up the professional value curve. The chapter also offers useful illustrations on how to craft such a strategy, as well as revealing many of the pitfalls that undermine strategic thinking and implementation.

Converging Strategies

Firms of professionals share business strategies that are almost identical: each aspires to be a leader in its chosen field; each promotes professional integrity; each asserts that customer service will be paramount. Typical statements can be bland, generic, uninspiring, clichéd and meaningless:

> "Our strategy is to target the following clients in the following designated industries and serve them with the following key services."[1]

> "Our mission is to be the best-managed company in the world in the [*fill in blank*] industry through our commitment to total customer satisfaction delivered by our totally empowered employees who work in the new team paradigm to continuously improve our position of unequalled quality and lowest costs, and in so doing, produce superior returns for our shareholders"[2] (mischievously quoted by futurist Eileen Shapiro).

If we took the mission statements of 100 large industrial companies, mixed them up while everyone was asleep, and reassigned them at random, would anyone wake up tomorrow and cry: 'My gosh, where has our mission statement gone?'

To compound matters, professional firms also know what to do in pursuit of their strategy; after all, they are comprised of clever, well-educated people. Their proposed actions invariably focus on building reputation, winning more higher-echelon business and achieving a more rewarding professional and personal life. The issue, however, is not what to do, but just doing it: translating the strategic aspirations (which are common to all) into concrete actions.

Key Factors for Firms of Professionals

The standard approach to strategy in professional firms typically fails to recognise the importance of a number of other significant factors:

1. Achieving the optimal skill balance
2. Scheduling for best results in both the short and long term
3. Increasing performance through appropriate career pathways and incentives
4. Increasing productivity and not simply increasing production
5. Recognising the dynamics of competing in the market for talent
6. Developing talent though challenge, coaching and collaboration
7. Creating a truly differentiated strategy.

Firms of professionals offer specialised skills, and often these markets are subject to extreme fluctuations in demand. As well as experiencing economic cycles and seasonal variations, they must cope with jumps and slumps in demand, making the management of such organisations particularly challenging. In the following sections, suggestions are made to help get the balance right to better cope with these fluctuations.

Getting the Balance and Structure Right

Success depends on matching skill sets to these variations in demand, and it is especially important to get the balance right between experience levels, so that profitability is managed and secured. On any significant project, the work will require a range of professional skills – but also the actual type of work will differ substantially. For example, part of the work may involve an analytical ability, another part may best be performed by those with experience, and a third part may best be performed by talented 'rainmakers' who will both win the business (based on their prior reputation) but also offer the client comfort in terms of quality assurance and star capability when needed.

These three types of work are typically performed by the professional, starting with newly-minted junior staff, to experienced heads ('grey hairs'), or by practiced leaders (with 'halos' rather than hair!), as explained below.

Grinders, Minders and Finders:
Three Levels of Professional Staff

Stereotypes persist because they resemble known types sufficiently well. Accordingly, and inspired by David Maister, three levels of professional service staff can be classified as follows:

1. Grinders: (hopefully) smart but inexperienced juniors who crank out the detailed work.
2. Minders: reliable, experienced ('grey') heads who have seen the problem before and can use their experience to formulate a solution.
3. Finders: 'rainmakers' whose 'star quality' opens business doors and closes winning deals.

Dilemmas arise when this talent mix does not match the contracts won; using 'stars' to do the detailed work is likely to be unprofitable, and using inexperienced heads instead of those with 'grey hair' can cause quality issues and downstream cost penalties.

Getting the Career Path Right

This talent mix problem is further exacerbated by the essentially fixed nature of employee contracts: in the short and medium term, staffing costs are largely fixed, irrespective of any revenue shortfalls, meaning that unwanted staff cannot be released economically by the organisation.

Furthermore, the 'shelf life' of employee time is zero, unless it is managed correctly: an unsold hour evaporates immediately and is lost forever. Time lost, unlike other losses, can never really be recovered.

To further complicate matters, professionals, by their very nature, tend to seek fresh challenges and variety in their assignments; few professionals want to stay in routine work for long. It can be difficult, therefore, to take advantage of the learning curve, meaning that the gains to be had through the repetition of work are frequently not captured. In other words, 'economies of experience' are hard to extract.

To counter these factors, professional firms need to:

(a) generate the right type of business that matches their skill profile and staff availability (difficult – depends on external factors);
(b) schedule strategically, combining clever use of non-billable time to develop staff capabilities;
(c) leverage experience ('grey hair') and star talent with junior staff;
(d) have a career progression path that produces the right talent and retains the *loyalty* of those who leave the organisation, whether voluntarily or not (the best firms have so well developed their people, that even when they leave the firm, they still regard their experience there as valuable, and continue to support the firm, if the opportunity arises);
(e) resolve the under-delegation syndrome, whereby senior staff maintain their indispensability by retaining work that should be passed to more junior staff;

(f)   develop systems that increase individual and group productivity and not just production capacity through the addition of more resources;

(g)   develop a closeness to existing and future clients to generate enough demand so that the firm can effectively choose its preferred projects;

(h)   realise that quality of service is more than just quality of work performed.

In summary, in executing these actions, perhaps the most crucial aspects are realising the importance of getting the best skills mix, scheduling strategically, delegating sensibly, designing career paths, courting clients ahead of actual need, and satisfying clients by delivering more than the required 'technical' solution.

Appreciating the Client's Perspective

These elements are largely inter-related, as satisfying clients will lead to a greater market share, which will, in turn, improve the scope for more strategic scheduling and enhance the firm's ability to attract the right talent.

The best starting-point to out-perform rivals is to have a particular emphasis on satisfying clients, and to learn from that particular perspective. Without innovation (achieved, for example, through this fresh client-focused perspective), professional services can become commodity-like. Professional competence in a given area becomes taken for granted, leaving buyers to select on the basis of price, or perhaps on simple preferences, such as ease of doing business.

When all products and services are alike, the deciding factor can be the client's perception of how well they were treated, which can rest on whether they feel they were truly 'understood' and appreciated. While much of this just makes common sense, it is not automatic that a professional, trained for a particular task, will have the requisite disposition or will have the necessary skills and aptitude to really 'listen' to a client. The ultimate goal, for most advice-givers, is to become a **trusted advisor**, intimately involved and highly rewarded. This is the ultimate in professional relationships, and an aspiration that only those high in *emotional* and *social*, as well as '*technical*', skills can fulfil.

Becoming a Trusted Advisor: Building Trust

While economists claim that Man is entirely rational, pursuing his own self-interest logically, good marketers know that a great many buying decisions are based on emotion, and justified afterwards with logic.

Becoming a trusted advisor means delivering excellent service, but transcending transactions so that the level of trust is so high that the client will reach for your advice, pay your bill without question and give you benefit of doubt. The client will forgive, protect and respect you. In return, the client gets a sense that the trusted advisor understands him or her well and will help the client think better.

The Evolution of Professional Service: the Path to Becoming a Trusted Advisor

The figure below shows the evolution from a standard service-based offering, with its focus on timeliness, price and efficiency, right through to the apex of becoming a 'trusted advisor', where quality, effectiveness and intimacy are the hallmarks, and price is not an issue.

The evolutionary pathway starts at the 'transactional' level, whereby a generic service is offered in the standard way, with little emphasis on anything but price. The client has questions answered, in a timely manner, but the relationship is tenuous, at best.

The next stage on the evolutionary path is to better understand the client's need and proactively solve his problem, not just provide a standard, one-size-fits-all service.

A still higher level of service occurs when the relationship deepens, and the client's needs are anticipated; the level of 'intimacy' is such that the professional can offer ideas and insights well beyond a standard service.

The final level shown, that of **trusted advisor**, has a still deeper level of intimacy. In such mutually committed relationships, deeper insights and strategic advice can be provided, to the benefit of both parties.

THE PATH TO BECOMING A TRUSTED ADVISOR

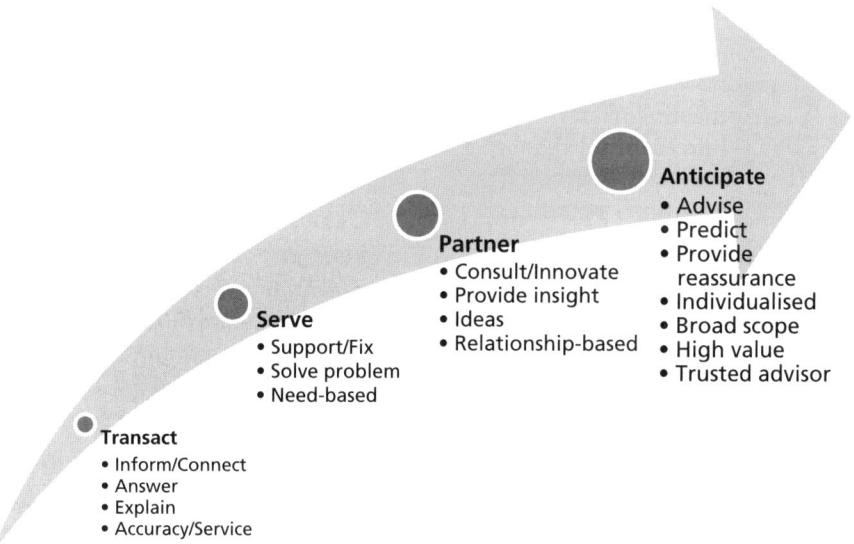

Realising the Information Value Cycle

To deliver better advice, consider also how the value of information passes through a cycle, as shown in the next figure, starting with valuable, fresh information before eventually becoming commoditised as 'common knowledge'.

For example, a large accounting firm might devise a new way to manage investment funds, based on early knowledge of legislative changes or new sources of funds. It could then use that knowledge for favoured clients, such as corporations or high net-worth individuals, earning a premium for such consulting. As the application of this new knowledge spreads, it could enhance its reputation by being seen as the eminent provider, lecturing on the subject. Ultimately, this knowledge becomes so widespread that it is 'common knowledge'. Professional firms should be keenly aware of this cycle, where innovation is primed by fresh information (R&D), then perhaps delivered as part of leading-edge consulting before becoming a commodity, widely available and, of course, much less valuable.

THE INFORMATION VALUE CYCLE

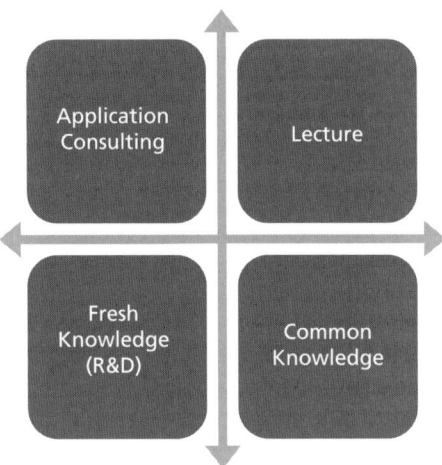

Developing Credibility and Trust

Providing valuable information, tailored very specifically to your client and to his ability to digest the advice, is ultimately essential for sustained success; while necessary, it is not, however, sufficient to earn clients' trust. Trust relies on *credibility*, and forging a better relationship, as shown below. To better develop trust, be aware of the components of trust:

1. Build credibility by using the right words and phrases, so that the client can trust what you say.
2. Consciously and ethically build the relationship through meaningful actions, not just words.
3. Recognise that the client has fears, uncertainties and doubts. Deal with the client on the emotional as well as the 'technical' level.
4. Realise that the client is a person in his or her own right: care for the client and show that care. Demonstrate that your heart is in the right place for him or her.

Component of trust	Area	What the client should think as a result
Credibility	Words	I can trust what he says about …
Relationship	Actions	I can trust him to do X, Y, Z
Intimacy	Emotions	I feel comfortable
Self-orientation	Motives	I can trust that s/he cares

In the final analysis, if people like you, they will listen to you; if people *trust* you, they will do business with you.

> *"No one cares how much you know until they know how much you care."*
> Ralph Waldo Emerson

The following illustration shows how trust gears up the power of the advice:

THE GEARS OF TRUST

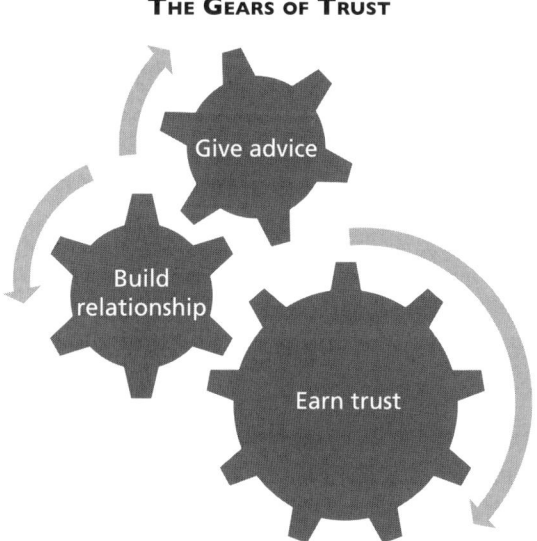

As the relationship is caused to deepen, the nature of the service moves from answers to more-or-less standard problems (however difficult), through problem-solving and question-raising, and into a safe place where the trusted advisor and client share similar goals and can discuss all matters intimately and openly, for mutual reward, as shown below. Where the service is basic, it provides answers, and the professional's energy goes into providing those answers. The client receives information, and the indicators of success are timeliness and reliability. At the trusted advisor level, the professional provides guidance, based on trust, with his or her energy directed at understanding the client's needs, providing a safe haven for the client's thoughts. At this level, price is no longer the issue, and the relationship becomes high value – for both the client and the professional.

	Focus	**Energy**	**Client receives**	**Success indicator**
Service	Answers	Explaining	Information	Timely, reliable
Needs	Problems	Problem-solving	Solutions	Resolution
Wants	Questions	Insights	Ideas	Repeat business
Guidance	Trust	Understanding	Safe haven	Value, not price

This involves a generous exchange of ideas, knowledge and accumulated experience, underpinned by shared values and principles. The client must really know that you will do what you say you will.

In these relationships, it's not what you say, it's what you ask that matters. As the proverb says: "You can tell a man is clever by his answers, but you can tell a man is wise by his questions."

> *"Believe those who are seeking the truth. Doubt those who find it."*
> André Gide

Improving the System

Even if individuals in an organisation are willing and able to deliver excellent service, the overall operational or business system can often be inadequate. While the component parts of the professional firm may well be optimised individually, as a whole they are not sufficiently coherent to provide seamless service. Systems are often designed to maximise efficiency, but the real challenge is to maximise effectiveness; for example, reducing photocopying costs at the expense of delaying service to a client is the ultimate inefficiency. In simpler terms, professional firms can often be isolated islands of excellence. 'Joining the dots' so that the whole business system performs well has to be a strategic goal for those who want to achieve high levels of performance.

Intensive, active listening to clients not only improves current satisfaction but provides a platform both for higher levels of business and more challenging assignments. This can transform the firm's ability to arrange the assignment schedule to mix 'Grinders', 'Minders' and 'Finders' economically, but also to provide delegation opportunities that provide appropriate challenges in order to develop careers. It also provides enough security to more senior staff that they can, indeed must, bring along more junior staff, while at the same time enhancing their own reputations, both as technical directors and leaders of people.

Marketing Professional Firms

Marketing features high on the list of under-developed aspirations in many professional firms. Frequently confused with simple advertising, genuine marketing involves finding the sweet spot between clients' needs (latent or explicit) and the firm's capability. It is the identification of particular values that enough clients will appreciate and reward with appropriate economic returns. Your firm will offer, consciously or otherwise, a value proposition to the customer, somewhere on the value spectrum from low to high value. 'Branding', then, is the representation of your value proposition in potential clients' minds. Iconic brands, such as BMW and Mercedes Benz, evoke distinctive images in the customer's mind: one being the ultimate driving machine; and the other a by-word for reliability and comfort.

In the hierarchy of effectiveness, the most effective techniques are those that promote intimacy with specific, desired client groupings. The least effective are mass advertising, as professional services cannot be promoted through self-assertion. Below are ranked, according to effectiveness, various marketing and promotion techniques for developing business:

HIERARCHY OF EFFECTIVENESS IN BUSINESS DEVELOPMENT FOR FIRMS OF PROFESSIONALS

1. Seminars to industry groupings
2. Requested articles in trade press
3. Research papers and peer-reviewed studies
4. Media endorsements
5. Selective networking
6. Newsletters and paid-for publicity
7. Brochures and direct mail
8. Cold calling
9. Mass advertising

These rankings reveal that the best marketing is predicated on the relevance of the targeted group, the intimacy of the setting (large seminars, for example, can be too broad and distant an audience) and the credibility generated; this credibility depends on endorsement by others, not on self-promotion or broadcasting.

Selling Professional Services

Selling is a rare art that takes particular drive to perform well. Selling yourself as a professional intensifies the pressures, as the stakes are high and very personal.

The selling effort, however, can be made easier by inverting the client relationship and stepping briefly into the buyer's shoes. Professional services are hard to specify, difficult to warrant and hard to assess; these factors increase buyer anxiety and the 'salesperson' who makes it easy and safe for the client to buy will enjoy more success. Adopt this attitude, drop cheesy sales techniques, and help the client to see how you add value. Use your portfolio to show how you match client requirements; let the work you have performed speak for itself.

How to Structure a Professional Services Organisation

The design of an effective organisation depends largely on the nature of the work, routine or custom, and the ease with which outputs can be valued, measured and subsequently compensated. For example, a factory producing wooden pallets has tangible outputs and well-defined, routine processes, and so it can readily measure the work performed.

By contrast, the work of most professionals is varied, hard to assess and dependent on high levels of motivation, and so it is difficult to decide how best to organise resources and structure compensation systems. The dominant model is the partnership one, where professionals pass through a series of escalating 'apprenticeships', culminating potentially in full partnership, possibly with equity participation. While this has the advantage of simplicity, it lacks nuance. Different models that allow degrees of partnership (e.g. with or without equity participant) can help resolve the skill-mix issue, particularly now with the de-structuring of the professional workforce to meet family and work–life balance demands. (Later chapters of this book show how to improve productivity and how to improve one's psychological balance and emotional well-being.)

How to Develop an Effective Strategy for Professional Organisations

This section is a guide for those with the ambition to grow a business, and particularly for those who want to develop a professional organisation. It starts with an orthodox or classic strategy model, then adds three elements:

1. suggestions on HOW to succeed in the various steps and activities, e.g. how to be creative and find winning ideas;
2. practical considerations for those risking their time or their money in the venture, e.g. how to decide whether to spend money on advertising when the bank manager is pressing you about your overdraft;
3. pointers on where to get more help or other references, e.g. where to find more detailed instructions on preparing a pitch to investors.

The emphasis here is on producing a strategy that results in profit and growth, and consequently the focus is on marketing and business development. There is no real intention here to be comprehensive: clarity, therefore, is prioritised at the expense of conventional textbook comprehensiveness.

The basic premise is that the many great uncertainties need to be recognised and managed. The classic linear approach is predicated on a simplistic belief that a strategy can (and should be) fully planned – even when new products, services or business models are involved. The fresher, newer approach described here adopts a more **agile** stance: instead of the 'big bet' inherent in the classic model, it seeks to hedge those bets. It shows how to develop, and respond to, a range of scenarios. Entrepreneurs make more money from 'Plan B' than they ever made from 'Plan A'; the original concept is rarely the finished article.

Extreme turbulence, deep recession and massive technological and social change demand a new approach to developing a business, especially emerging and early-stage businesses. The classic approach to strategy is too limited to adequately respond to today's crises – and opportunities. It presupposes that situations are analysable, whereas, in practice, situations are complex, dynamic and obscure. It also assumes that decision-making is actually rational, even under the stresses inevitable when decisions are being made against a background of tremendous uncertainty.

The classic approach is explained here before proceeding to an approach that is based more on insight, and foresight. This newer, more 'agile' approach was honed by Don Sull, a business leader who is a Professor at the London Business School. Specifically, Sull showed how to seize opportunities in an uncertain world in his ground-breaking book, *The Upside of Turbulence*.[3] The examples he used can help businesses of all sizes and ages. His insider view of how a small company in Brazil became the world's largest brewer showed how a business person – with the right attitudes and skills – could greatly enhance their success through strategic growth.

Professor Richard Rumelt of UCLA, an experienced strategy advisor to major corporations and governments, has said:

> "In suddenly volatile and different times, you must have a strategy. I don't mean most of the things people call strategy – mission statements, audacious goals, three- to five-year budget plans. I mean a *real* strategy.
>
> For many managers, the word has become a verbal tic. Business lingo has transformed marketing into marketing strategy, data processing into IT strategy, acquisitions into growth strategy. Cut prices and you have a low-price strategy. Equating strategy with success, audacity, or ambition creates still more confusion. A lot of people label anything that bears the CEO's signature as strategic — a definition based on the decider's pay grade, not the decision.
>
> By strategy, I mean a cohesive response to a challenge. A real strategy is neither a document nor a forecast but rather an overall approach based on a diagnosis of a challenge. The most important element of a strategy is a coherent viewpoint about the forces at work, not a plan."[4]

Strategy and Winning Value

Strategy, in the purest sense, is about securing a defensible position that gives superior financial returns over the longer term. More conventionally, it is about the search for winning value propositions. Invariably, it will be a search for either uniqueness (differentiation, and the premium it provides) or lower cost. The conventional, classic approach to business strategy focuses on maintaining and developing the organisation, while a separate approach is taken to developing innovations. However, a more holistic approach is needed to fuse these two seemingly distinct worlds.

> *"The real voyage of discovery consists not in seeking new lands but seeing with new eyes."*
>
> Marcel Proust

The Classic Approach to Strategy

The classic strategy model is illustrated below, with the first, simpler 'roadmap' representing four separate elements:

- visioning (goal setting);
- external analysis;
- internal analysis; and
- planning (especially financial planning).

THE CLASSIC STRATEGY MODEL

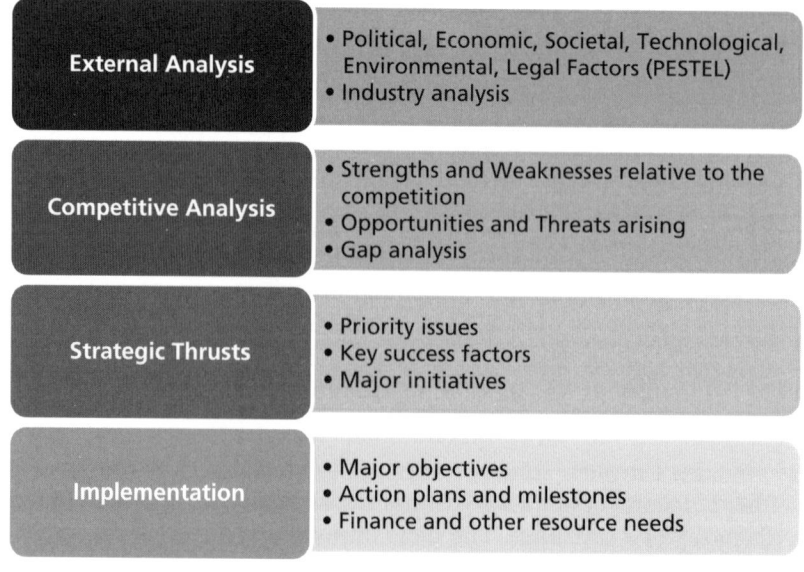

External Analysis	• Political, Economic, Societal, Technological, Environmental, Legal Factors (PESTEL) • Industry analysis
Competitive Analysis	• Strengths and Weaknesses relative to the competition • Opportunities and Threats arising • Gap analysis
Strategic Thrusts	• Priority issues • Key success factors • Major initiatives
Implementation	• Major objectives • Action plans and milestones • Finance and other resource needs

As the graphic suggests, many newcomers to strategy work regard strategy-making as an essentially linear, step-by-step approach, with activities separated into distinct blocks, perhaps starting with a clarification of the organisation's (or the founder's) vision and values, and ending with a simple, clear (but unrealistic) plan. In reality, such plans and decisions are difficult to achieve, clouded as they are with stressful emotions and blurred by the lack of practical tools to sharpen such visions or articulate the values intended. In the following sections, suggestions will be provided on how to improve such matters.

The Agile Approach to Strategy

A better approach is to regard strategising as an iterative learning process. This is the approach Professor Don Sull has seen used successfully by organisations, large and small, professional and otherwise.

AGILE STRATEGY: LEARNING FROM SUCCESS AND FAILURE

This model emphasises the idea of **(1)** making sense of a situation, trying to peer through the murkiness ahead and then correcting course as needed. The destination is kept firmly in mind, but there is a realisation that not every step of the journey can be pre-planned: allowance is made for the need to change tack occasionally. Consider a yacht: the crew have to 'make sense' of their situation, deciding which way the wind might blow, tacking to port and starboard, never actually pointing directly at their destination, always adjusting to the prevailing circumstances but never losing sight of their ultimate goal.

The more conventional strategy model assumes everything is knowable in advance, and everything can be pre-planned. Such belief in rational planning runs aground on the rocks of real-world uncertainty: a more 'agile' approach helps the crew adapt to unexpected obstacles and unforeseeable hazards.

Making choices **(2)** means generating some viable options in the first place, rather than being confined to a single path or simply extrapolating the present into the future. A good strategy is discriminating. It makes choices. It does not attempt to do everything, e.g. to become a low-cost and premium provider at the same time. Professional firms, given their high-achievement history, too often, in my experience, want to do both simultaneously.

Making it happen **(3)** – implementing the strategic plan – is predicated on people buying in, and becoming accountable for agreed actions. Much of this depends on the quality of the discourse about the strategy, their emotional connection with drawing up the plans and consequently their desire to reach an agreed destination ('vision'). A good strategic plan makes provision for setbacks and delays; in true project management style, it provides a 'Plan B'.[5] It explicitly assesses risk and develops counter-measures, ensuring that the plan is robust and viable.

The revision stage **(4)** reviews the learnings to date, revisits the initial assumptions and seeks to learn from mistakes: this is true learning (a concept explored again in later chapters). Learning in this manner allows for fresh information to navigate around rocks – and even to discover a better destination.

The cycle promotes the idea that learning is constant and that adjustment is necessary. It does not allow wholesale changing of plans or needless tinkering, but is dynamic and adaptable rather than rigid and blind.

While the idea of learning is central to good strategy, as Einstein noted: "Any intelligent fool can make things bigger, more complex, and more violent. It takes a touch of genius – and a lot of courage – to move in the opposite direction."

Strategic Drift, Escapism, Tinkering and Imperialism

Real strategy formation is emotionally and intellectually difficult. Without proper strategic planning, however, drift into irrelevance is almost inevitable. There are dangers, as shown in the figure below, in being too broad in scope and/ or too shallow in depth, chasing sales leads indiscriminately, leading to lack of focus and strategic drift. As David Allen notes: "You can do anything – but not everything."[6] Strategy involves making hard choices, not just about what you will do (e.g. what market segments to serve), but, what you will not do (e.g. which clients to drop). It is about having the courage to make things simple.

As Kevin Roberts has written: "We cannot allow the multiplicity of possibilities to drag us into complexity."[7] Equally, a strategic focus that is too narrow is likely to be insufficient for meaningful change: such a pragmatic 'craftsman' approach (so called because of its emphasis on practicality and a disdain for more intellectual approaches) leads merely to tinkering around the edges.

A 'pioneering' or cavalier approach taken to extremes similarly may morph into escapism, while those favouring power may be inclined to attempt too much or need 'imperial' force to succeed.

Each approach reflects the personality of the organisation or its leader, and predicts what will happen if that personality remains unchecked.

STRATEGY AND PERSONALITY: THE DANGERS OF EXCESS[8]

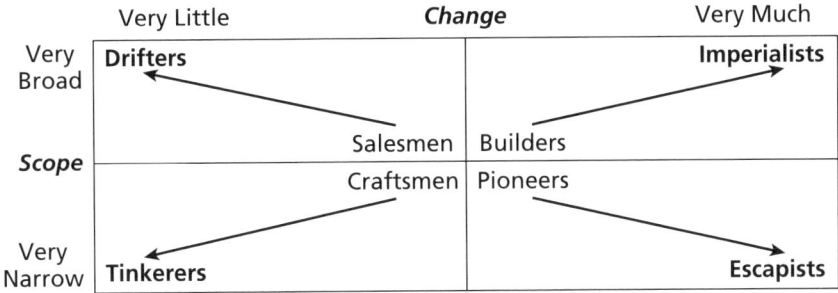

A more balanced approach can be formed by considering the 'strategic diamond' (see below) in order to determine the economic logic of your proposition and to address key questions, such as how the organisation will achieve its strategic goals.

The Strategic Diamond

The diamond graphic below shows the hard economic logic that must under-pin any good strategy and focuses on means (such as developing differentiated services) to achieve ends (such as premium fees and attractive financial returns).

HAMBRICK'S STRATEGIC DIAMOND[9]

The value of Donald Hambrick's 'Diamond' is its emphasis on 'staging' (the timing of strategic moves) and on 'vehicles' (such as alliances) to achieve the strategic vision. It also puts economic logic at the centre, focusing on achieving premium returns.

Testing your Strategy: Inimitability

Industry rivals will seek to imitate successful strategies: if these strategies are based on easily acquired assets (e.g. IT equipment, machinery), they can be easily replicated. On the other hand, if the strategy requires them to modify their culture or acquire intangible assets (such as tacit knowledge, see below) or reputational assets (positive brand identity or image), such imitation will scarcely be feasible. Professional firms would do well to pay considerable attention to developing these intangible assets (developing tacit knowledge, nurturing reputation).

Having affordable access to constrained supply (such as licences, qualifications or especially talented individuals) is similarly effective, and explains some of the war for talent among professionals. Talented individuals provide those crucial, inimitable resources, based on hard-to-define tacit knowledge and elusive qualities, such as business acumen or *nous*. The illustration below shows the categorisation of assets (tangible or intangible, imitable or otherwise). The most effective sector is that based on inimitable know-how (seen in the bottom-right sector of the figure):

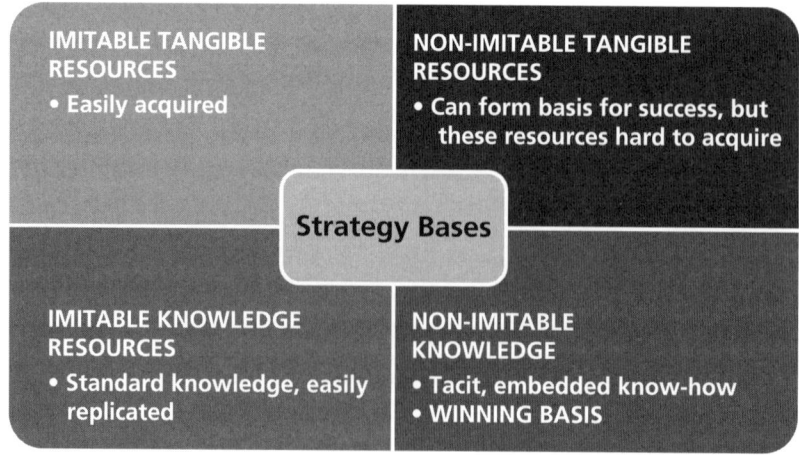

EMBEDDED TACIT KNOWLEDGE AS THE BASIS FOR SUCCESSFUL STRATEGY[10]

The test of a good strategy, therefore, is whether it is observable in the first place; if not, imitators will not be able to detect such strategic moves. Another test is sustainability: if the strategy requires imitators to invest energy or money over long periods, their imitation will not be sustainable.

These tests of a good strategy can be summarised by the OASIS acronym:

O Observable – is it/can it be made 'invisible' to rivals, i.e. hard to detect?
A Actionable – can you actually implement it/is it feasible?
S Sustainable – or just a quick, once-off win?
I Inimitable – or is it something that anyone can copy?
S Sufficient – i.e. will it generate sufficient returns at acceptable risk?

Strategy and Implementation

Strategy-making is not intended to be an academic exercise, undertaken in isolation, removed from reality or the preserve of the elite: implementation is crucial, and to achieve that, engaging people, but especially smart professionals and thought-leaders, is vital. Too often, the refrain is that 'the strategy was great, but implementation poor'. A good strategy with poor implementation is not just a wasted opportunity; the associated display of weak leadership will ferment disassociation and brew trouble. Powerful implementation and inappropriate strategy is like playing roulette with a loaded gun, as shown below:

STRATEGY AND IMPLEMENTATION

		Strategy	
		Appropriate	**Inappropriate**
Implementation	**Good**	Success	Roulette
	Poor	Trouble	Failure

Integrating Strategy and Implementation

The model below shows the links between the main elements in creating a strategy, including controls to check if the organisation is still on course; the guiding philosophy comes from the organisation's sense of what it is (mission, purpose, values) and where it wants to go (vision, expectations).

STRATEGY IMPLEMENTATION – VISION, VALUES, MISSION

Strategy Implementation and Alignment

The value of the McKinsey '7 S' model, shown in the next figure, lies in its emphasis on the wholeness of the strategy. Just as a fast car with no brakes has a fatal weakness, so too does an organisation's strategy that has a major deficiency in, for example, the skills or systems needed to succeed.

THE MCKINSEY '7 S' MODEL[11]

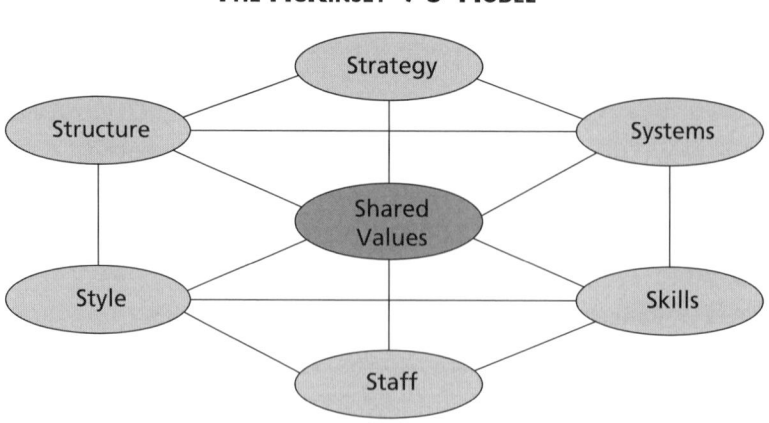

Strategy and Values

Pivotal to strategic alignment (see the '7 S' model, above) is the degree to which organisational values are held in common. Seemingly a soft, non-business issue, such as differences in fundamental values (beliefs about people, profits, ethics, social responsibility), can eventually cause 'seismic' eruptions, especially in professional firms.

McKinsey underscore their belief in the independence and autonomy of their 'members' with the following extract of their values statement:

> "Every member of the firm has a responsibility to question firm decisions that he or she disagrees with."

Merck Sharp & Dohme, for many years the most admired employer in the US, cherished this epic statement:

> "We believe that research work carried on with patience and persistence will bring industry and commerce new life; and we have faith that in this new laboratory, with the tools we have supplied, science will be advanced, knowledge increased, and human life win even a greater freedom from suffering and disease … We pledge our every aid that this enterprise shall merit the faith we have in it…".

Disney simply want "to make people happy", while myriad others want to capture market share.

Purpose, Values and Vision

Sloganism aside, well-crafted statements can clarify purpose, values and vision. A good purpose statement, for example, should be broad, fundamental, inspirational and enduring, guiding the organisation eternally and grabbing the 'soul' of the smart professional. My personal favourite is Michelangelo's declaration that "the greatest danger for most of us is not that our aim is too high and we miss it, but that it is too low and we reach it".

Peter Hawkins[12] uses the 'star' model illustrated below for professional organisations to capture the strategic links and to highlight the importance of intellectual assets, change and learning:

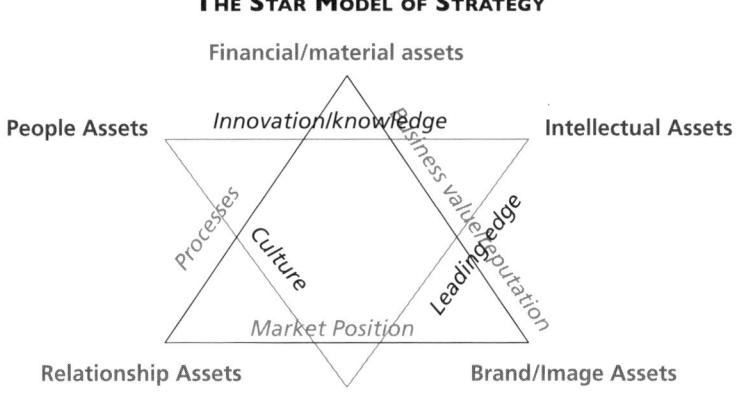

THE STAR MODEL OF STRATEGY

The model in a simple way integrates the essential elements, including the less tangible ones such as brand and other relationship 'assets'.

Analysing the Industry for Competitiveness

This introspective activity is then followed by an analysis of the subject industry, invariably using Michael Porter's model of the forces impacting on an incumbent in the industry to assess whether an industry is 'attractive' or not. While Porter's classic work has great validity, and no strategic analysis would be complete without considering it, the conclusion of almost every such analysis is that (at least for newcomers) the industry will be 'unattractive' because that industry is already commoditised (as most industries obviously are) and/or the barriers to entry are formidable. In other words, the model has limited use for professional firms, as their profession usually dictates which 'industry' they enter.

This 'Five Forces' analysis will customarily be taken in conjunction with an assessment of the wider world, along six dimensions, using the acronym 'PESTEL' – Political, Economic, Social, Technological, Environmental and Legal. This inevitably presents a daunting spectrum of topics. The key, however, is to realise that the goal is to scan the PESTEL horizon with a view to identifying threats and opportunities, rather than a futile attempt to map the entire PESTEL landscape.

Company versus Competitor Analysis: 'SWOT'

The next step involves an analysis, this time at the company or firm level (the earlier analyses concerned the world at large or the hard-to-define 'industry'). Again, the standard tool is little more than an acronym – SWOT: **S**trengths, **W**eaknesses, **O**pportunities, **T**hreats.

To make the analysis more pointed, it is useful at this stage to include a sharpening of the organisation's vision (where you are headed) and values (what you stand for). Particularly, in professional service firms, these are the soft, intangible, seemingly indefinable elements that make the essential difference between success and failure. The leading firms devote great effort to making sure that the stories, legends, values and vision are infused throughout the organisation: the resulting culture is the glue that holds the company together and gives it unity of purpose. It also provides a basis for marketing the company: the true goal of marketing is not just to have your logo (and tag line) widely recognised (brand awareness) but to have that stand for something important and valuable – **in the client's mind**.

Classically, internal 'strengths' are expected to lead to external market 'opportunities', while an organisation's 'weaknesses' indicate vulnerability to 'threats' from competitors and critical stakeholders.

ALIGNING STRATEGY, GOALS, VISION AND VALUES

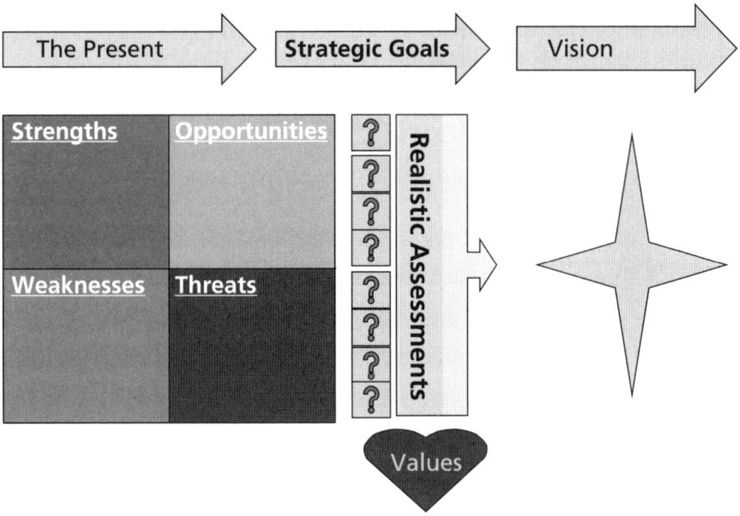

The Real Value of Intangible Assets

Traditionally, physical assets, such as building and equipment, were listed as strengths, but in today's information age the real strengths are the intangibles, those assets that are hard to observe, let alone replicate:

> ### STRENGTHS
>
> - Know-how and expertise
> - Brand awareness and value
> - Enabling cultures
> - Valuable relations, linkages, partnerships
> - Client bases, prospect lists
> - Intellectual property
> - Licences and regulatory approvals
> - Management, marketing, selling and other 'techniques'.

The **weaknesses**, classically, were trade union relations, dependency on key suppliers, poor marketing and so on. The difficulty is to achieve some measure of objectivity: how great (and relevant) are the relative strengths if assessed objectively? How even to decide the parameters to measure, and how to gather reliable, objective measurements?

The difficulty is compounded when, as frequently happens, a parameter is simultaneously considered a strength *and* a weakness. For example, ownership of a factory or office building confers potential financial strength, but can also serve to limit options. It is not unknown for a company to list their staff as both an asset and a liability, representing the twin-sided nature of most significant resources, human and otherwise. The SWOT analysis is a useful framework, even if it is barely more than a set of acronyms.

Strategic Objectives: Hard Choices

For professional services organisations, the strategy usually revolves around four key objectives:

1. Raising client satisfaction
2. Increasing skill-building and dissemination of skills
3. Improving productivity (not just production)
4. Getting better business (more suited to the organization, with higher net returns).

While most organisations aspire to do all four, simultaneously, effective strategies must make hard choices and select a specific course, if they are to navigate successfully.

Developing a good strategy is hard to do as it involves confronting some harsh facts, about you or your organisation. For example, your competitor may have outsmarted you or have had the luck or foresight to have cheaper resources (people, property, patents).

Strategy, Insight and Inventiveness

It is also difficult because a good strategy will invariably require insight, inventiveness and energy:

- insight, to discover the nuance of the problem;
- inventiveness, to come up with a fresh approach that overcomes (or, better still, circumvents) the problem; and
- a capacity to join the dots – it is the coherence of the plan that makes it viable. A good strategic plan will have considered the risks intensely, and will have a means of reducing or overcoming the risks that is commensurate with the reward. A good entrepreneur or a good strategist will take (considered) risks, not blind chances.

Exhortation, Hope and Effort are No Substitutes for Planning

A good strategist will realise that aspiration and ambition are all very well, but they do not provide a basis for strategic action. A strategy to 'grow the business by 50%' sounds lofty and energising, but unless it is accompanied by a real plan, it is merely an aspiration.

Similarly, exhortation is not a strategy: urging more effort is fine, but thinking that perseverance alone will work is mistaking cliché for planning.

Blind commitment to a plan ('quitters never win, and winners never quit') can ensure that plans can never be revisited, even when the need is clear (to others, at least).

Though optimism is a pre-condition for successful business, there is real danger when optimism becomes delusion: the nay-sayers are a nuisance, but constructive critique is essential.

It is vital to enshrine critique when planning to strategise and co-ordinate resources to accomplish an important end. Many organisations, most of the time, do not have this. Instead, they have multiple goals and initiatives that symbolise progress, but no coherent approach to accomplishing that progress other than 'spend more and try harder'.

In many respects, the real value of developing a strategy is not so much the actions finally proposed but the understanding and commitment that follows when all members of the organisation have been deeply engaged in the process. As Jeffrey Pfeffer says, "Culture eats strategy for breakfast",[13] therefore it is vital to get real commitment.

Conclusion

To emphasise the earlier points, strategy is about insight and innovation, creating distinctive value propositions, being differentiated in a meaningful way and generating superior returns. It starts with a focus on the customer/ client as a way of building a sense of accomplishment and pride in the staff who serve that customer/client. For most professional firms, the ultimate goal is to be so respected that they earn the status of trusted advisor and garner superior outcomes, financial and otherwise.

This chapter has provided a brief guide to developing strategy for those not familiar with the standard tools and techniques, and then goes further, drawing on leading edge theory and the author's extensive experience in helping firms develop distinctive winning strategies. The approaches advocated here are developed with knowledge-intensive professional firms in mind. In professional firms, the primary assets are people, and it is especially important that efforts are aligned, and that their potential is not undermined through discord and a lack of unifying values. The chapter introduced more fluid ('agile') approaches that better suit today's knowledge-intensive world before concluding with suggestions on how to secure professionals' commitment and to implement strategic plans, always remembering that 'plans are nothing, but planning is everything'.

ENDNOTES

[1] David H. Maister, *Managing the Professional Service Firm* (Harvard Business School Press, 1993).

[2] Eileen Shapiro, *Fad Surfing in the Boardroom: Reclaiming the Courage to Manage in the Age of Instant Answers* (HarperBusiness, 1995).

[3] Donald Sull, *The Upside of Turbulence: Seizing Opportunity in an Uncertain World* (HarperCollins, 2009).

[4] Richard Rumelt, *Good Strategy, Bad Strategy: The Perils of Bad Strategy* (Harvard Business Review Books, 2003).

[5] Dermot Duff, *Project Management: A Practical Guide* (Management Briefs, 2011).

[6] David Allen, *Getting Things Done: How to Achieve Stress-Free Productivity* (Hachette, 2001).

[7] Kevin Roberts, *Lovemarks: The Future Beyond Brands* (Murdoch Books Pty Limited, 2004).

[8] David Beck, "The Rise and Fall of Great Companies" (1991) 12:4 *Journal of Business Strategy* 62–64.

[9] Donald C. Hambrick and James W. Fredrickson, "Are You Sure You Have a Strategy?" (2001) Vol. 15 No. 4 *The Academy of Management Executives.*

[10] Keith Ward, Cliff Bowman and Andrew Kakabadse, *Designing World Class Corporate Strategies* (Elsevier, 2005).

[11] Robert Waterman, Thomas J. Peters and Julien R. Phillips, "Structure is not Organization" (1980) 23:3 *Business Horizons* 14–26.

[12] Peter Hawkins, *Leadership Team Coaching: Developing Collective Transformational Leaders* (Kogan Page, 2011).

[13] Jeffrey Pfeffer, "The Smart Talk Trap" (May–June 1999) 77(3) *Harvard Business Review* 134–142.

Chapter 3

Developing Leadership: In Yourself and Other Professionals

The most dangerous leadership myth is that leaders are born – that there is a genetic factor to leadership … That's nonsense; in fact, the opposite is true. Leaders are made rather than born.

Warren G. Bennis

This chapter shows how leadership can be systematically developed in almost any intelligent professional, through awareness, development and education, and despite the common perception that leadership ability is essentially fixed.

The chapter reveals recent discoveries in leadership development. Starting with situational leadership, the chapter then shows how one's leadership style can adjust to the person being 'managed', and how one can move from a basic 'transactional' style of management to 'transformational' leadership. A practical leadership development pathway is then suggested.

Finally, it suggests how to lead by proactively coaching people and how to shift from the present form of intermittent performance review to a more effective approach.

Leadership *Can* be Developed

It has long been hotly debated whether leaders are born or made. It is only recently (through the work of Bernard Bass, Bruce Avolio and John Antonakis[1]) that the verdict can be delivered: leadership capability can be developed in most people. This is especially true for those who have the requisite intelligence, if they know and follow the right steps. To develop leadership, the professional must grow in four dimensions, or go through four main stages of development:

1.   first, as a **whole person**, grounded and rounded;
2.   as a team member, capable of interacting with and influencing others;
3.   as a contributor to leadership tasks (such as strategy formation or planning); and
4.   as a leader in their own right.

While leadership is notoriously dependent on the individual situation and the particular context (this is explored in depth later in this chapter), the universal skills and attributes required to be an effective leader are shown in the following figure:

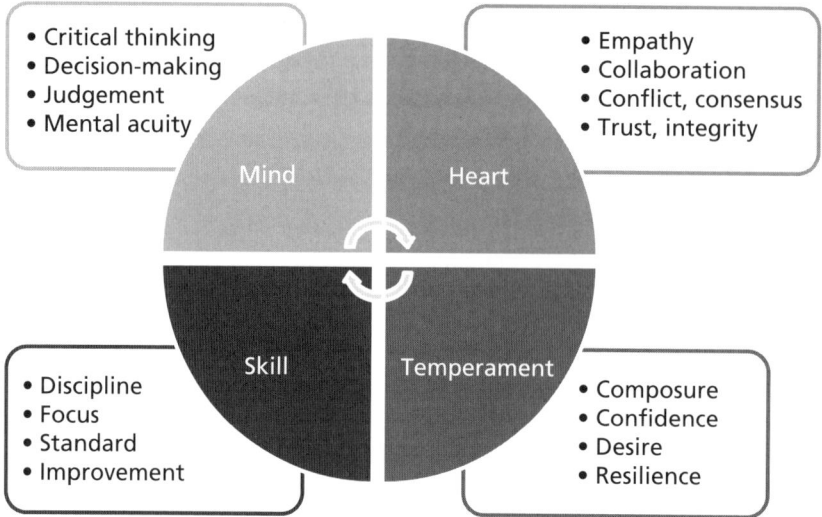

DEVELOPING LEADERSHIP: THE FOUR QUADRANTS

Leadership capacity evolves through developing particular 'learnable' skills, such as critical thinking, decision-making and problem-solving. Discipline and focus can similarly be enhanced through practice and training. Even elusive elements, such as empathy and the ability to collaborate, can be deepened though experience and self-awareness.

One's inherent level of self-confidence, however, tends to be quite firmly stuck, and it is a difficult quality to enhance. While it generally grows over time, there is little research-based advice available on how to grow in confidence. For this reason, **Chapter 11** investigates this area and suggests means to promote the growth of self-confidence. Increased self-confidence can greatly improve one's demeanour and spur desire to achieve one's potential. Tapping into one's source of inner motivation can promote this and increase resilience.

Intelligence is a necessary prerequisite to effective leadership but, while necessary, it is not sufficient: cognitive ability needs to be joined with 'emotional' intelligence, as explained in **Chapter 12**.

The model below captures the specific attributes and skills in a different form. More importantly, it places the person at the core in order to highlight that personal growth must be the starting point of effective leadership. Without a solid self at the core, there is no basis to manage others. The next layer is where interpersonal aspects play out. The outer layer is that of the job, where value is finally added.

DEVELOPING LEADERSHIP: START AT THE CORE

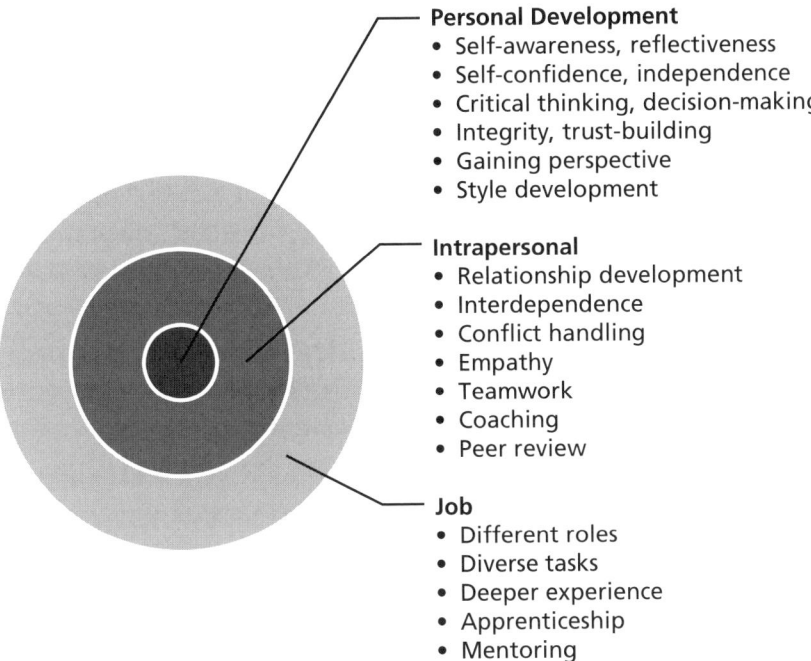

Personal Development
- Self-awareness, reflectiveness
- Self-confidence, independence
- Critical thinking, decision-making
- Integrity, trust-building
- Gaining perspective
- Style development

Intrapersonal
- Relationship development
- Interdependence
- Conflict handling
- Empathy
- Teamwork
- Coaching
- Peer review

Job
- Different roles
- Diverse tasks
- Deeper experience
- Apprenticeship
- Mentoring

The development of a leader starts with his or her development as a person, someone who is self-aware and self-assured. This can be achieved through an education that widens and shifts perspectives, promotes understanding, enhances critical ability and aids problem-solving and decision-making capability.

A good coach is invaluable in such personal development, and some bosses have helpful skills in this area, even if they are untutored formally (great sports coaches come to mind, from Yogi Berra to Bill Shankly).

In combination with this personal development, interpersonal development can be assisted by deeper understanding of different team roles, appreciation of different psychological types, nurturing of empathy, better management of conflict, enhanced emotional intelligence and, especially, a broadening of the palette of styles or leadership approaches to better deal with the variety of 'people issues' that may arise: different folks will require different strokes.

Increase the Range of Leadership Styles in Use

Research in the UK indicates that the average manager relies on just a single style of leadership. This 'one-size-fits-all' style seems to mainly arise from the well-intentioned but mistaken view that all employees should be treated the same; rather, they should be treated equally but not necessarily the same, as employees will have different personalities, different sources of motivation and different levels of development. It is very important to adapt one's management style to the individual and to the situation; for this reason, a section is included later in this chapter on 'situational' leadership.

Moving to more advanced leadership, additional skills may be needed, especially in communications and in developing authority (termed 'Presence' in the figure below):

ENHANCING LEADERSHIP: EXPANDING BEYOND THE CORE

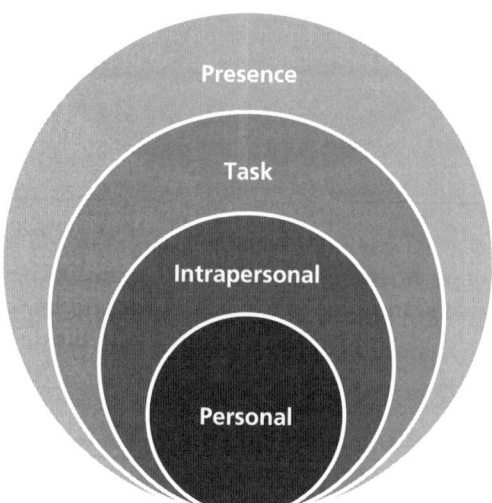

The third area, labelled 'Task' above, involves increasing one's ability in actual leadership tasks *per se*, such as developing a vision, formulating a strategy, presenting a plan, managing resources, setting structure, dealing with stakeholders or deciding tactics.

> *"Before you are a leader, success is all about growing yourself. When you become a leader, success is all about growing others."*
>
> Jack Welch

Developing a Leadership Pathway

While development as a leader will involve many cycles of experience, education and training, the figure below serves to illustrate a sequence of development activities over, say, a five-year period.

DEVELOPING LEADERSHIP SKILLS: A TIMELINE

Personal Development
Self-awareness, new experiences, challenges, role variety, coaching, reflection, resilience

Education: leadership course, team-building, influencing, communication and negotiating skills

Self-confidence and assertion, strategic thinking and innovation capabilities, motivational skills

The foundation of a leadership pathway is personal development: self-awareness, emotional intelligence, developing resilience, perhaps being coached by a suitable mentor. Accepting challenges, such as new roles, will help accumulate real experience and deepen awareness of oneself and others. Reflecting and learning from these experiences will deepen leadership capabilities.

The path to leadership can be accelerated by learning from others, not just one's own successes and failures. Experience is a dear school, but a fool will learn in no other. Education can play a pivotal role by opening new perspectives and by providing fresh approaches to leadership; this is the purpose of executive education and military leadership schools. For example, learning the tactics of negotiation and understanding the principles of influence greatly increase one's leadership capacity. Communication and team-building are subtle arts, but the right educational environment can help the novice immeasurably.

Self-confidence is crucial to leadership, and an entire chapter of this book (see **Chapter 11**) focuses on how to nurture this elusive quality. Strategic thinking and even innovation capacity can be enhanced through exposure to informative or inspiring examples. Business schools use the 'case' method to simulate a realistic environment in which to experiment with strategic decisions. Motivation, of course, lies at the heart of leadership and, for this reason, complete chapters (see **Chapters 6** and **7**) are dedicated to the theory and practice of motivation. Furthermore, **Chapter 5** examines personality types, to allow a fuller understanding of different motivational 'drivers'. **Chapter 13** covers coaching and mentoring professional staff, and **Chapter 8** discusses 'action-learning', through which one plans, acts and reflects purposefully in search of deeper learning.

GROWING AS A LEADER: SOME PRACTICAL MEANS

- Develop a good reading habit.
- Belong to useful networks.
- Use your peers wisely.
- Set yourself challenges.
- Change roles, change perspective.
- Take a global view.
- Debate with other informed people.
- Learn how you seem to others.
- Know 'the man in the mirror', i.e. yourself.
- Undertake charity work.
- Listen to what your detractors say.
- Consciously seek feedback.
- Pursue your emotional development.
- Sharpen your values by articulating them.
- Gain experience in high-stakes activities.
- Teach a familiar and unfamiliar topic.
- Adopt a mentor, and coach someone yourself.
- Enhance your mental capability through simulations, games, quizzes.
- Undertake a peer review.
- Develop your technical or task skills.
- Reflect constructively on successes as well as failures.

While leaders are sometimes *born*, they are always *made*: in other words, leadership invariably requires some nurturing and development, a process which can be accelerated, as described above. Leadership ability is no longer considered the unique preserve of royal 'blue bloods'. Neither is it regarded as being based on certain personality types or character traits. Even briefly examining the list of notable desirable 'traits' (distinguishing personal characteristics, such as patience, drive, dynamism, forbearance and empathy), it quickly becomes evident that the list is long, unreliable and even dichotomous (e.g. how to be simultaneously energetic and patient, driven and empathetic?).

In the final analysis, knowing if someone is leading or not is simply a question of whether people are following their leadership! As circular as that definition seems, it remains a good test of one's leadership abilities, and it has the virtue of shifting attention from oneself outwards towards others.

Epic leaders, such as US Presidents Obama or Clinton, have that ability to engage followers. Clinton had an amazing ability to make each individual feel that they alone were the focus of his attention.

Obama, similarly, tapped into people's hope. He told them there was a "change that we can believe in" and "yes, we can" achieve it.

Both leaders developed themselves over the years. Obama, a lawyer and a dedicated student of Martin Luther King Jr., modelled his inauguration speech on King's landmark address in Washington in 1963, and his phrase "Yes, we can" echoes King's inspirational, "I have a dream".

Obama also learned from how Abraham Lincoln, in the aftermath of the American Civil War, had embraced his political foes and included even dissenting voices in his Cabinet. Such profound acts of forgiveness, as with Nelson Mandela, make huge differences and raise the leader out of the ordinary. Even in the workplace or the environment of the professional firm, there is frequent opportunity for leadership to rise above the petty squabbles and demonstrate such qualities of forgiveness and integrity. Ultimately, what most organisations, and certainly smart organisations, want is leadership at all levels, not just by the very top executive, and in a variety of ways, not just in the core tasks.

It will be noted that even the greatest leaders have flaws (sometimes significant ones), and that a leader who is great in one era (for example, Churchill during the Second World War) may not fit another era (Churchill and his party were defeated in the 1945 general election). A prime example would be Mayor Rudy Giuliani, who did the seemingly impossible by cleaning up the 'Rotten Apple' that was New York, only to lose favour with the city's voters a few years later when he divorced his wife – by fax! He then regained popularity in the aftermath of the 9/11 tragedy, but lost it again through another unfortunate divorce message – this time by text!

Earlier researchers had focused on 'traits' in their search for the elusive qualities thought to compose a leader's personality. However, the research ultimately revealed too many contradictions. No set of traits was sufficient in describing or predicting leadership ability, although certain traits – notably intelligence – were essential. Similarly, a selective list of notable leaders reveals the extreme variety in disposition and personality:

- Mahatma Gandhi, master of passive protest and civil disobedience in the cause of India;
- Margaret Thatcher, mistress of industrial reform in the UK;
- Bill Clinton, charismatic leader; and
- Winston Churchill, resilient 'Bulldog' leader.

Levels of Leadership

What leaders seem to have in common is not similarities in personality but in character: they have drive, energy, empathy, integrity, resilience, insight, foresight and – yes – intelligence. This combination of social and conventional intelligence is powerful, particularly if it can be channelled by having the right perspective, i.e. one that seeks to serve rather than dominate or domineer.

Jim Collins (author of *Good to Great: Why Some Companies Make the Leap…and Others Don't*[2]) shows how one can progress from individual contributor ('Level 1') through competent manager to effective executive and, ultimately, to being a 'Level 5' leader who develops enduring institutions. Such a leader has both belief in the cause and humility in its service, such that others follow. Whereas Level 4 is high-order administration, Level 5 is more visionary and strategic in its thinking. Such a leader seeks to serve, not be served. They tend to have a great humility; they are not the egotistical demigods so heavily featured in the popular press. Rather, they set out to build enduring organisations, and pursue this mission with resolve. They have a deep-seated belief in the purpose of the organisation and its vision for the future.

LEVELS OF LEADERSHIP

Level 5 – The Level 5 Leader
Builds an enduring, great organisation through a combination of personal humility and resolve.

Level 4 – The Effective Executive
Builds widespread commitment to a clear and compelling vision; stimulates people to high performance.

Level 3 – Competent Manager
Sets plans and organises people for effective pursuit of objectives.

Level 2 – Contributing Team Member
Contributes to the achievement of team goals; works effectively with others in the group.

Level 1 – Highly Capable Individual
Productive contributor; has talent, knowledge skills, and good work habits as an individual employee.

The key point is to note that leadership is about what one actually *says and does*, and less about inherent traits or personality types. In other words, leadership capability can be advanced in most people (through education, experience and training), and it can certainly be developed in smart professionals. The potential inhibitor in developing smart people is often their excessive belief in conventional intelligence and their disregard for the harder-to-measure social and emotional intelligences.

For example, it is notoriously difficult for even the best trainers to stimulate interest in engineers, scientists, accountants and IT people in the psychology of managing people, due to its intangible nature and scarcity of logical 'proof'. Trainers report, however, that if this hurdle of disbelief is overcome, these are the very professionals who benefit most from their new awareness. Sometimes, the transformation can be dramatic, for example when a scientist expands his range of intelligences to think more strategically, when an accountant learns how to have enough empathy to manage a team, or when an engineer develops enough *nous* to engage clients effectively.

DIMENSIONS OF LEADERSHIP

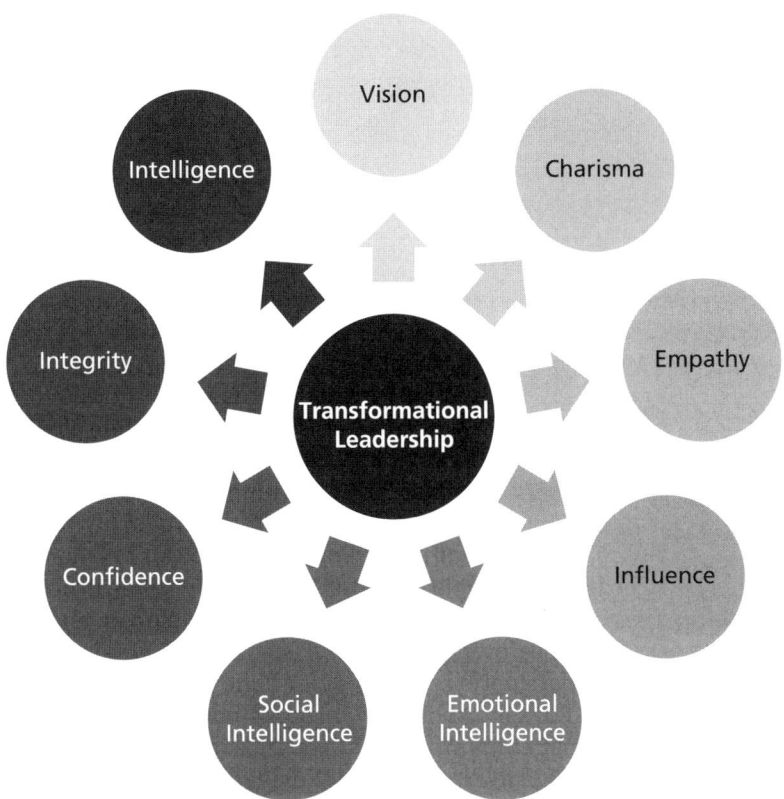

Transformational Leadership:
A Breakthrough in Leadership Development

> *"People buy into the leader before they buy into the vision."*
>
> John C. Maxwell

A 'transformational leader', as defined by Bernard Bass,[3] has similar qualities to Level 5 leaders: the special additional skills required to transform an organisation revolve around visioning, influencing and change management. Transformation, of course, is not an everyday but an occasional occurrence, whereas Level 5 leadership is more continuous and less sporadic.

A transformational leader is one who can turn followers into leaders themselves. It is an approach that, according to Bernard Bass and Bruce Avolio,[4] engenders positive change in followers. It achieves this by enhancing the motivation, morale and performance of his follower group. Transformational leaders inspire others to achieve extraordinary outcomes and, in that process, develop their own leadership capability. Transformational leadership can be contrasted with the more common 'transactional' management where, fundamentally, a manager exchanges rewards (money and other extrinsic motivators) for employees' efforts. A transformational leader, in this sense, helps followers grow by responding to individual followers' specific needs, by acting as an inspirational role model, by stimulating their thought processes and, ultimately, by instilling them with the confidence and ambition to become transformational leaders themselves. In many types of professional work, this is exactly what is needed for superior performance: the ability to add to much vaunted technical skills these transformational abilities, whether in the management of staff or in the service of clients.

Transactional management, on the other hand, operates on the basis of contingent reward (exchange of reward for effort). This is valid, of course, but not as valuable as transformational leadership in effecting meaningful change. *Laissez-faire management* (see illustration below) avoids making necessary decisions and abdicates responsibility. An intermediate state is *management by exception*, where a manager is alert for errors and deviations, and moves to correct them. Similar – but worse again – is its passive form, where a manager waits until intervention is unavoidable.

**FROM AVOIDANCE AND TRANSACTION MANAGEMENT
TO TRANSFORMATIONAL MANAGEMENT**

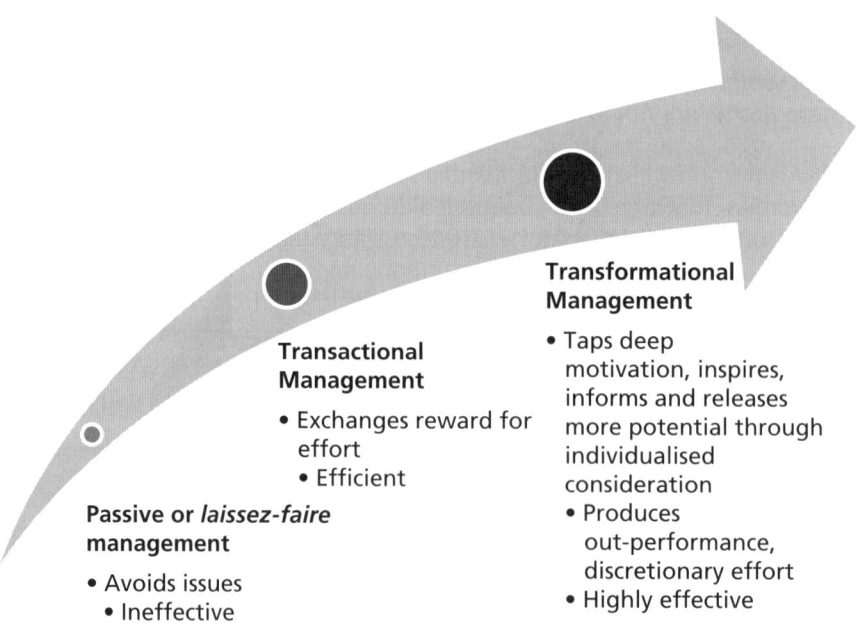

Transformational Management

- Taps deep motivation, inspires, informs and releases more potential through individualised consideration
- Produces out-performance, discretionary effort
- Highly effective

Transactional Management

- Exchanges reward for effort
- Efficient

Passive or *laissez-faire* management

- Avoids issues
- Ineffective

Transactional leadership is akin to standard, conventional management, where one value (e.g. monetary reward or bonuses for the employee) is exchanged for another (the organisation's value, e.g. reaching a sales target or an employee giving discretionary effort and going that extra mile). While these 'transactions' can be very satisfactory and useful, they do not 'transform' an organisation or lift employees onto a higher plane.

Transformational leadership adds meaning, common purpose and collective effort. Importantly, John Antonakis's extensive research indicates that such leadership can actually be learned.[5] Moreover, this research convincingly shows that the best leaders seem to have emerged by overcoming a trauma or setback in their lives and, consequently, learning about themselves and developing their depth of resolve. The old adage seems to apply: "What doesn't kill you makes you stronger."

Transformational leadership enhances the motivation, morale and performance of followers by:

- engaging the followers' sense of identity with the over-arching goal and the collective identity of the organisation;
- providing followers with an inspiring role model;
- challenging followers to achieve goals they previously felt were out of their reach; and
- giving followers the necessary confidence to attempt new endeavours and to become leaders themselves.

The transforming approach creates significant change in the life of people and organisations. It redesigns perceptions and values, and changes the expectations and aspirations of employees. Unlike the transactional approach, it is not based on a 'give and take' relationship, but on the leader's personality, character traits and ability to make a change through example, articulation of an energising vision and challenging goals. Transforming leaders are 'idealised' in the sense that they are a moral exemplar of working towards the benefit of the team, organisation and/or community.

The concept of transformational leadership can be traced to Aristotle's writing in the *Rhetoric* on three kinds of persuasion: ethos, pathos and logos, based on leader character, follower emotions and objective proof, respectively. Bernard Bass and Bruce Avolio agree with Aristotle's assertion; leadership can be developed consciously through three main routes. First, seek to develop discipline and other aspects of character ('ethos'). Secondly, develop 'pathos', the ability to relate to others. Thirdly, work on one's 'logos' – the ability to reason logically and to express ideas, debate and communicate. Rhetoric emerges from these areas and, indeed, this ability is perhaps needed now more than in less information-rich times.

The extent to which a leader is 'transformational' can be gauged in terms of his or her influence on followers. The followers of such a leader feel trust, admiration, loyalty and respect for the leader. Because of these qualities in the transformational leader, followers are willing to work harder than might have been expected. The transformational leader provides staff with an inspiring vision and gives them a valued identity. The leader transforms followers through his or her idealised influence ('charisma'), intellectual stimulation ('challenge') and individual consideration ('personal attention'). A true leader in an organisation of professionals will simultaneously display both transformational and transactional leadership – leading and managing.

THE FOUR ELEMENTS OF TRANSFORMATIONAL LEADERSHIP

1.   **Individualised consideration (personal attention)** is the extent to which a leader gives particular emotional and social support to a follower. He or she does this by understanding the follower's expressed and latent needs, and coaches the follower. The empathic leader gives empathy and support, keeps communication open, places challenges before the follower, and respects and celebrates the individual contribution that each follower makes to the team. (Subsequent chapters in this book are dedicated to coaching staff, building confidence and developing emotional intelligence.)

2.   **Intellectual stimulation (think, learn)** is the degree to which the leader validly challenges outdated or incorrect assumptions, takes worthwhile risks, elicits followers' ideas and encourages creativity. Transformational leaders nurture and develop people who think independently. For such leaders, learning is valued, and unexpected situations are seen as opportunities to learn.

3.   **Inspirational motivation (set the bar high and coach people to jump the bar)** is the degree to which the leader articulates a vision that is motivating and appealing. Such leaders inspire followers to achieve high standards. They radiate optimism about future goals, and provide meaning for even the more mundane tasks.

4.   **Idealised influence (similar to charisma)** is the emotional component of leadership. By virtue of the leader's character and self-sacrifice, this offers a role model for high ethical behaviour, instils pride, gains trust and, consequently, promotes extraordinary achievement in followers. The leader arouses – and satisfies – followers' needs for achievement, affiliation and power. In stark contrast to those who rely on memos and e-mails, such leaders communicate through symbols, resonate emotionally, use imagery extensively and are compelling storytellers.

Applying Transformational Leadership

Transformational leadership is a transcending type of leadership that embraces both the rational and emotional elements of individuals. It promotes learning-in-action, and encourages people to set, and achieve, high standards, often leading to organisational change. It infuses tasks with a higher order of meaning, and provides opportunities for self-fulfilment, affiliation (a sense of team or community) and pride. The figure below shows how the various aspects of transformational leadership promote such noble behaviours as:

1.   a willingness to change fundamentally;
2.   a willingness to really think;

3. a willingness to give back to the community; and
4. a role model for higher performance and ethical behaviour.

COMPONENTS OF TRANSFORMATIONAL LEADERSHIP

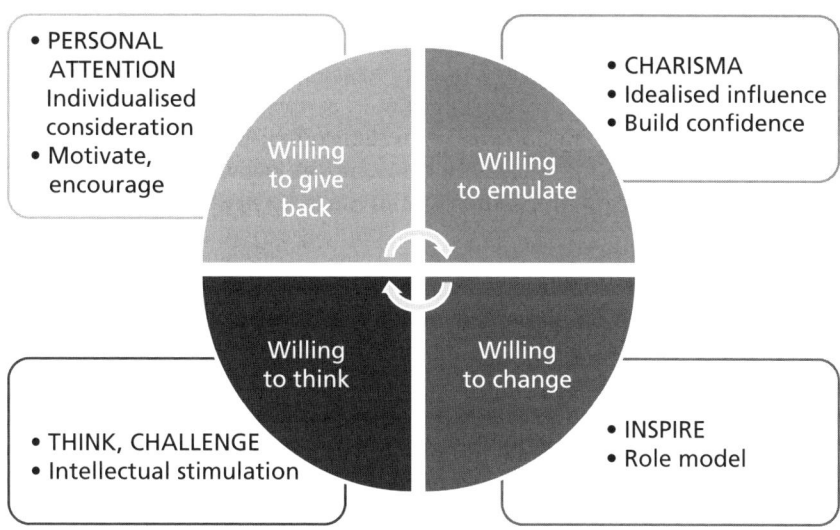

- PERSONAL ATTENTION Individualised consideration
- Motivate, encourage

- CHARISMA
- Idealised influence
- Build confidence

Willing to give back

Willing to emulate

Willing to think

Willing to change

- THINK, CHALLENGE
- Intellectual stimulation

- INSPIRE
- Role model

APPLICATIONS FOR MANAGERS: TACTICS AND TIPS IN USING TRANSFORMATIONAL LEADERSHIP

1. Develop a challenging and attractive vision, in commune with staff.
2. Tie the vision to a strategy for its achievement.
3. Develop the vision, specify and translate it into actions.
4. Express confidence (even where it is not fully felt), decisiveness and optimism about the vision and its implementation.
5. Realise the vision through small, planned steps and small successes in the path towards its full implementation.
6. Understand your followers and individualise the vision and the associated tasks.
7. Use stories and metaphor to illustrate your ideas: learn from Martin Luther King Jr. (and Barack Obama) how to use contrast, alliteration and repetition to express ideas and relate emotionally to people.
8. Use events, especially surprising events and setbacks, as learning opportunities.

9. Do not rely on emotion alone: let rational and objective thinking prevail.
10. Set high standards and stretch goals – and help individuals have the confidence (and desire) to reach them.

Perhaps most startling is the now proven idea that such transformational leadership can really be learned by almost any professional or smart person. The specific behaviours can be imitated. The philosophy can be adopted. For most people, the underlying principles can be absorbed. The tactics can be copied. Most of all, Aristotle's teachings on persuasion (ethos, pathos, logos) remain valid today – even if they are widely neglected. The astute manager would do well to 'sit' at Aristotle's feet and transcend into a transformational manager.

Situational Leadership:
Managing all Equally – but Not all the Same

The style of management and leadership, as we have seen, must vary with the context and the situation. This also applies to people as they progress through their development as employees and professionals, a point often overlooked. Many professions, such as medicine, have rigorous and defined progression levels but, in my experience, a widespread approach is to (inappropriately) treat everyone as if they were all the same. While the mantra is to treat all employees equally, it is a mistake to treat all employees the same: the new hire may be enthusiastic, but will still lack experience of the organisation and will, therefore, need – and expect – some direction.

The experienced employee, well-versed in the ways of the company and professionally developed, can be expected to resent close direction, and will anticipate being given opportunities to run their own activities. This delegation contrasts with the direct supervision of the new recruit. In between, the unit leader should make decisions through dialogue with staff.

The 'situational leadership' model illustrated in the figure below is based on the model developed by Hersey and Blanchard.[6] The style of management needed depends on the situation: how experienced or confident is the person being 'managed'? A high-performing, experienced and confident professional should be managed differently from a novice. The inexperienced person can (and usually should) be told what to do and how to do it, whereas with the experienced professional that would be destructive micro-management. In this sense, the inexperienced person is being managed (directed) in a 'task' manner, with a low focus on relationship. The proven performer should be ready to take responsibility for delegated tasks. As the work relationship is now mature, involvement, in that sense, can be low. Clearly, different situations demand different styles of management of the task and of the relationship. As ability and confidence develop, the style can change from the initial 'tell' style through 'sell' to 'participate' and finally to 'delegate'.

SITUATIONAL LEADERSHIP: TELL, SELL, PARTICIPATE OR DELEGATE?

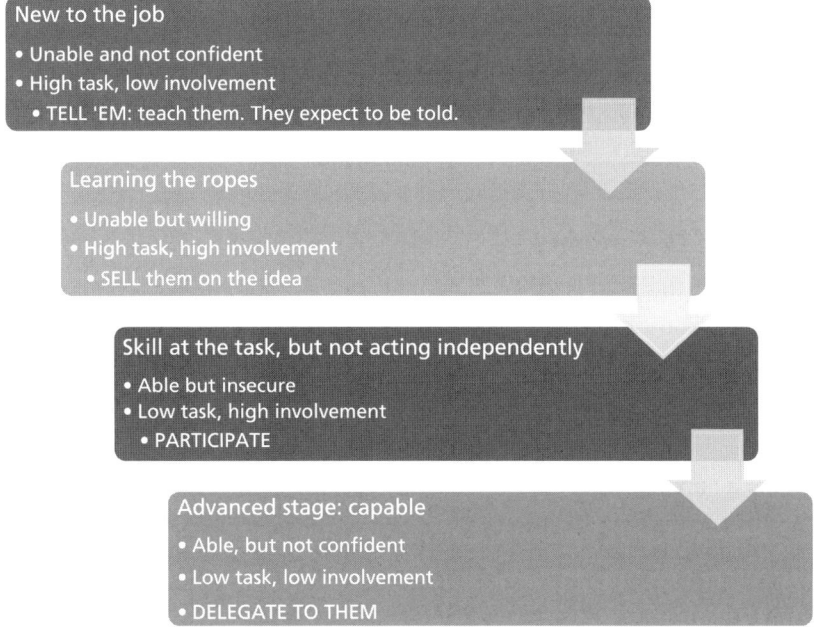

New to the job
- Unable and not confident
- High task, low involvement
  - TELL 'EM: teach them. They expect to be told.

Learning the ropes
- Unable but willing
- High task, high involvement
  - SELL them on the idea

Skill at the task, but not acting independently
- Able but insecure
- Low task, high involvement
  - PARTICIPATE

Advanced stage: capable
- Able, but not confident
- Low task, low involvement
- DELEGATE TO THEM

Note that the evolution may not be seamless, and particular difficulties arise when performance declines, and the relationship might need to revert from a consensual participative style (for example) to a directive 'tell' style. In such situations the relationship can become awkward, and even bitter, leading to a toxic atmosphere or separation. Instead, it is important to focus on the previous high performance and good relationship, emphasising that recovery is possible. Point out that it is not the person who is being criticised, just current behaviour or performance. Focus on achieving small wins and rebuilding confidence. In other words, believe in the person, and use the coaching techniques described later in this book (see **Chapter 13**). If, despite these efforts, performance does not eventually improve, separation may be necessary, but you will know you have been a good manager: fair, constructive and authentic.

Authentic Leadership

While intelligence is an indispensable ingredient in leadership, it is character that ultimately provides the basis for leadership. Although character is difficult to change, the requirement is simply to be authentic (not a fraud), as almost any style can be effective, as has been discussed above. There is no need to be perfect or saintly (recall the many flaws even in the best leaders), just to avoid hypocrisy, duplicity and disloyalty. Gareth Jones puts it succinctly when he says (somewhat ungrammatically): "Be yourself, more, but with skill."[7] This is a licence to use your native or natural style. Jones urges aspiring leaders to be themselves, "more", with the proviso that this is done with skill and respect in dealing with people.

The killer question, as Gareth Jones puts it, becomes: "Why should any-one be led by you?" Hierarchical or 'position' power only grants leadership in name or title. Professionals have such autonomy and intelligence that they expect to be led, but not micro-managed; in other words, *influence* must be the means of achievement.

Furthermore, the ultimate goal is not to have one leader, but to have staff show the qualities of leadership by displaying initiative, drive, commitment and foresight.

Developing Community

A curious feature of organisations full of professionals is the extent to which the professional essentially works alone – even in the midst of others. This is often true of accountants, as well as more obvious examples, such as den-tists or doctors (GPs). In addition, many professional organisations do not consciously develop the organisation as a whole, perhaps regarding this as a peripheral activity or superfluous 'fluff'. Organisations, however, that can combine a concern for people as well as tasks will have a more optimal cul-ture, one that leads to high performance. These organisations can be regard-ed as effective communities, high on *association* (the degree to which they hold each other in high regard and, hence, will be more likely to collaborate effectively) and high on *achievement* (see figure below).

In contrast, organisations that lack a sense of friendship and have a weak focus on achieving the task will splinter, lacking social ties or single-goal commitment.

Organisations that are merely social but do not focus on the main task can euphemistically be said to be 'networked', while the opposite is the 'merce-nary' organisation, commercial and unbounded, focused on the end itself, irrespective of the means, with little regard for niceties such as sociability.

FOUR TYPES OF PROFESSIONAL COMMUNITY

(*Note:* 'assoc.' in the above figure is an abbreviation of 'association'.)

The goal, of course, is to maximise 'heart' and 'head': to have people so bonded to the right cause that success becomes nearly inevitable.

Professional organisations, with their assumption of the pre-eminent superiority of rational intelligence, tend more to the head side than the heart. They may need more persuasion than conventional organisations of the importance of emotional and social intelligence. For these reasons, a chapter of this book is devoted to the psychological aspects of managing smart people – see **Chapter 5**.

In the final analysis, leading and managing smart organisations means getting out of people's way, creating the right conditions that will let talent flourish, and consciously designing the organisation to promote achievement and kinship. The temptation is to believe that having the title 'manager' (or its equivalent) means you should 'manage' when actually you must lead – lead not from the front, but from behind, creating leaders of them rather than creating a demigod of yourself.

LESS IS MORE: THE CASE OF AN EDUCATIONAL TRUST

A long-established trust was dismayed to find that its most successful periods were when there was no chief executive in position. Actually, having an official 'leader' suppressed the leadership initiative of senior staff. Ironically, having a chief executive seemed to destroy value significantly. Whenever a CEO was absent for long periods or there was a gap between appointments, the senior staff (who had real experience and who could act autonomously) filled the void by using their own initiative.

While it is unconventional not to have a designated leader, the 'smart people' in this situation simply did not need someone to 'manage' them, at least not in the short term. When the syndrome was first observed, it was felt by staff that the negative correlation between leadership and results was an anomaly, but a string of successive leadership absences provided evidence that was hard to refute. Finally, one CEO decided to act on the principle, and he let it be known that he was standing back to allow others move forward. The results were clear: in the ensuing six months, the senior staff orchestrated a complete recovery in the organisation's finances, launching new initiatives, actively marketing related services and generally acting more coherently with one another. Needless to say, the lesson was promptly 'unlearned': the CEO 'took charge' again and the organisation returned to its old, conventional ways, with catastrophic results for both the organisation and the CEO, who eventually lost his position.

Extended leadership vacuums, where no CEO is in charge, would presumably lead to the eventual disintegration of such an organisation, but it is useful to note that while staff are capable of independent operation and already have sufficient motivation, the wisest course is simply to retreat to the sideline and cheer them on. This is especially appropriate if the outcomes (such as revenues earned) can be made visible and therefore used to stimulate peer pressure. In the case of this organisation, this was certainly the case: the top earners were known and quietly fêted. Pressure came on the lower earners to up their game, with allowances made for traditionally difficult areas and for seasonal or cyclical factors. Effectively, the 'market' decided who were the winners and losers, not the chief executive. Thus, it becomes clear that the role of the CEO is not to manage experienced staff directly, but to set up the conditions for successful operation.

Leadership and Communication

Effective leaders are masters of the classical elements of rhetoric. They can reach people through logic, by presenting rational arguments in favour of their proposals. In addition, a leader can use pathos, appealing to emotions, or base their case on people's sense of values or ethos. Successful leaders almost over-communicate, expressing their views regularly through different channels to be heard by the different types of individuals. They have the gift, like Presidents Obama and Clinton, of being able to convey complex ideas simply.

The better you know staff (and other stakeholders), the better the chance of constructing and transmitting the type of communication that will resonate with them. Of course, to know your target audience means actively listening and receiving, as well as 'transmitting'. Bear in mind that most communication is not through words but through tone and body language; most of all, the message rises or falls depending on the example the leader sets. Hypocrisy will easily be detected, and credibility, once lost, is almost impossible to recover.

Telling the Hard Truths

Max De Pree, legendary leader of progressive office furniture design and manufacturing company Herman Miller, says, "The first test of a leader is to confront reality."[8] A leader must discover what is really going on and be able to diagnose what is happening and why. This could be in analysing the market or assessing the top management team. How much of any bad news to share, and how, is the point: if the boss reveals all his or her doubts about, for example, the market, staff might be petrified or the banks fazed if the portrayal were excessively pessimistic. The message must be real, but delivered in conjunction with measured amounts of optimism. For example, Winston Churchill's Allied forces took devastating blows at the Battle of Gallipoli during the First World War, with 100,000 casualties. Churchill faced the dreadful reality and took personal responsibility, with the result that he was able to recover and lead his side successfully in the Second World War, with stirring words about "never, ever" giving in and fighting "on the beaches, in the trenches" to the bitter end. The true leader not only knows the reality of a situation but can show the way out of the morass.

Leadership and Organisation Design

Thomas Jefferson believed deeply in the twin virtues of education and democracy, and designed the famous University of Virginia campus, near his home, to be an "academical village"; this was a pleasant, open, self-governing community designed in accordance with clear core values and purpose. It shows the importance of purposeful design in creating the context for the exchange of ideas. In recent times, companies have deliberately created circulation spaces to encourage interaction and promote chance encounters between staff, many of whom would not otherwise share ideas.

DREAMING THE GUGGENHEIM

Frank Gehry, architect of the Guggenheim Museum in Bilbao, a magnet for the elite and the ordinary citizen alike, similarly showed how design flows from values and intention, starting with his initial rough visualisations based on key principles. Gehry lets himself dream to conjure up the possibilities, before dealing with the limitations and constraints. The initial concepts, and the tension between the possibilities and the constraints, are then teased out through conversations; an iterative process requiring patience and debate. This 'story-telling' process is a way of conjuring the right vision. Whether in architecture or business, strategies and visions are not tablets of stone discovered by an heroic leader, but must be fashioned and shaped through real conversations.

Mirror, Mirror – Reflections on Leading Smart People

Can leading people really depend, in the first instance, on *smiling* enough? Is it really true that we reap what we sow; that smiling lights up the atmosphere? That good humour warms the heart?

Neuroscience has finally proven that the old adage is true: "Smile, and the whole world smiles with you." Italian scientists have discovered that the brain has a widespread network of mirror neurons dedicated to mimicking and, therefore, detecting emotions.[9] Curiously, these neurons simply reflect what is happening emotionally; when you smile or laugh, the equivalent response is stimulated in the other person. This is a pattern we develop from early infancy. These mirror neurons provide a mechanism that allows us to share emotions and, potentially, develop bonds. The intuitive or socially intelligent leader radiates enough warmth to attract enthusiastic followers.

Research by Fabio Sala[10] has shown that better leaders prompted laughter three times as often as average leaders; a good mood helps people both to process information and be creative.

Humour alone, of course, is not enough; it is generally necessary but not sufficient. Consider, for example, the contrasting leadership careers of two leading professionals, both experts in their fields but one more socially adept than the other. Where one was terse and impersonal, a relentless perfectionist and stingy with praise, the other was more approachable, playful and smiling. Both were equally demanding, with high standards, but the latter brought out the best in others, both socially and professionally, and promotion followed readily.

To learn more on leadership and emotional intelligence, read Daniel Goleman in the September 2008 issue of the *Harvard Business Review*.[11] For more about changing your behaviour, read Annie McKee's 2001 article in the same journal, "Primal Leadership – The Hidden Driver of Great Performance".[12]

Social Intelligence

At one end of the leadership spectrum are the charismatics, who can hold followers in thrall. At the other end are the socially inept, usually as a result of their upbringing or personal disposition. (In extreme cases, certain conditions, such as Asperger's Syndrome, can limit social capability, even when those affected have genius levels of ability. There are many savants who cannot interpret social signals sufficiently well to engage with others in a meaningful way.) A useful short exercise is to rate yourself as a leader. It can add precision to your self-rating to use benchmarks or examples, such as Nelson Mandela at one end of the charisma spectrum and perhaps Margaret Thatcher at the other.

Social skill can, of course, be used mischievously, but the intent here is to deploy means of increasing social intelligence, not for any Machiavellian reason.

SHORTCUTS TO SOCIAL INTELLIGENCE – PRACTICE THE VOWEL SOUNDS: A E I O U

- **A**wareness: simply being aware of others' reactions is the essential first step. People find it hard to disguise their feelings, which will be manifested in their facial expressions and in their body language.
- **E**mpathy: walk a mile in the other person's shoes to understand their perspective.
- **I**nterest: show interest in others through sympathetic enquiry.
- **O**penness and optimism: let the light in, and remember the glass is half full, always.
- **U**nderstanding: what people *feel* is as important as what people think.

Make Stress Work: the Cortisol Connection

Occasional stress, as often associated with deadlines, can be very useful in focusing the mind and in achieving goals. Beyond an individual's threshold, however, stress inhibits clarity of thought: the focus shifts away from the actual issue to the threat itself (often focusing on the 'carrier' boss). Levels of cortisol, the lubricant of the brain, and associated adrenaline rise to detrimental levels. When those under stress feel the contempt or disgust of others, such as a boss, further emotional distress is added to the cognitive stress, resulting in serious disorder. The explosion of these stress hormones can drive people to seek vengeance, or lead to mental paralysis. Ironically, the principle of social contagion still applies: the stress generated can rebound on the boss and can even spread to the entire group or department, as others become embroiled in the discord.

TEN THINGS GREAT LEADERS DO AT WORK

1. **Maintain your sense of humour – especially during a crisis**. Great leaders stop a crisis turning into a drama by staying cool, keeping perspective and plotting a solution. It is then they show their true capabilities of fortitude, flexibility and forgiveness by rising above the drama.

2. **Tell people – nicely – when they're shooting themselves in the foot**. The best leaders can deliver a hard message in such a way that the receiver can accept it without losing face or without losing hope. This ability to be perfectly frank (honest without being too honest, clear without being blunt) separates good leaders from the merely functional ones.

3. **Be the boss, but don't act like a bully**. Bad leaders let their egos in the way of being human. They pretend to know more than everyone else, and they then become detached from reality. Flaunting power diminishes leaders, and keeps them from engaging authentically with people. The most admired leaders are humble (Level 5 leaders – see above).

4. **Have confidence to be themselves**. It should be easy, but being yourself takes such honesty and courage, it is actually difficult. Erecting facades only works if you are really, really good at it – and few are. People can smell BS from vast distances. True confidence is being a regular human being, all the time.

5. **Hire and support people who are better than themselves**. The best leaders don't just get the best out of themselves, they get the best out of their whole team. Increasing your own performance 10% is minuscule in comparison to raising the performance of a dozen staff the same amount. Weak leaders surround themselves with dross, hoping to look good by comparison. The best leaders bask in the reflected glow of a dozen stars shining brightly. An organisation can never have too much talent, so grow your people.

6. **Listen to subordinates**. That's it: just listen – and learn!
7. **Compliment employees**. One of the worst bosses I knew could never bring himself to give a compliment even where it was richly deserved. Even if you wrote the compliment for him and all he had to do was send it, the begrudger in him saw it as a sign of weakness.
8. **Great leaders teach the toughest lessons**. An organisation can buy talent, or grow it – or simply hope to get lucky. Over time, the best companies learn how to impart the toughest lessons, finding how to give frank feedback in such a way that it is accepted, and even welcomed, by the professional. Often, the leader is the best teacher, as her lessons, delivered straight from the heart, have the biggest and most meaningful impact.
9. **Do the right thing**. Smart people generally have enough cognitive ability to select which is the better choice. Having the moral courage to stay the correct course is altogether another story, and few have the courage of their convictions. Those few are the extraordinary leaders that most professionals revere and want to follow.
10. **Do what has to be done**. Real leaders avoid the smart-talk trap and do what has to be done, no matter what. It might involve great personal sacrifice or simply the inconvenience of jumping on a plane to meet a client, but when the going gets tough, the tough get going.

"Smartest Employees Most Difficult to Manage"

International HR firm BlessingWhite report[13] that smart employees, so essential to your organisation, are also demanding, sometimes rebellious, intellectually agile and often insular and uncommunicative. In other words, the brightest minds can also be your organisation's biggest headache. They tend to over-value intellect and under-value aspects such as emotions. As they have achieved so much because of their intellect, correspondingly they have a lot to lose should their cognitive powers be undermined or seen as inferior. Professionals sometimes, therefore, develop a protective shell to avoid this, and consequently may resist change or direction from others.

Bosses of these difficult-to-manage employees are often technical professionals themselves, rising through the ranks because of their specific expertise and not necessarily their people skills. They tend to err toward two extremes: telling their people exactly how to do things, or spending so much time on their own projects that they do not 'get around to' their leadership duties until there's a crisis.

Being Nice is Not Enough

In the Blessing White report referred to above, the highest-ranked leaders rated themselves as most competent in soft skills such as "building trust with my team" and "building collaborative relationships throughout my organisation". At the same time, the greatest shortcoming these leaders share appears to be coaching and developing their teams. Although 83% rated this leadership action as critical, only 46% think they do it well.

The implication is that while they are good at being nice, they are not so good at helping their people acquire skills or apply their expertise in challenging and innovative assignments. This finding is particularly disturbing because technical professionals place high value on personal development and crave exciting work.

Advanced Manoeuvres Required

The individuals who design bridges, discover vaccines and create tomorrow's leading IT applications might not speak the same technical language, but they do share a combination and intensity of similar characteristics. It takes deft leadership, not supervision, to unleash and align their energy and talents to deliver what your organisation requires. Effective means of leading talented employees include:

- Setting goals without impinging on team members' desire for autonomy.
- Delegating responsibility in a way that involves team members in the decision-making process and connects the work with a larger organisational goal (see the earlier section on situational leadership in this regard).
- Creating a work environment that fosters creativity, camaraderie and individual achievements while focusing efforts on team goals and organisational priorities.
- Remembering that while their cognitive intelligence is well developed, their emotional and social intelligence may not be so advanced.

Understand what makes technical professionals tick. This workforce exhibits a high need for achievement, autonomy, collegiality, staying ahead, professional identification and participation in the mission and goals.

Performance Reviews – The Real Test

Performance reviews, usually conducted annually, are seen as essential in modern organisations. The reality, though, is that they are a mixed blessing, causing as much strife as benefit and often leaving a bitter aftertaste. To overcome the 'damned-if-you-do, damned-if-you-don't' nature of these reviews, re-frame the overall purpose. Realise that these reviews should be less about retrospective judgement and more about encouraging and helping people to perform better. The real test of a good performance discussion is whether the person emerges motivated, keen to progress, eager to achieve more than he or she thought possible. It is surely a sign of a failed opportunity when the session ends in rancour or despondency.

To get the professional excited at the prospect of change, focus on personal and professional growth, setting targets that are worthwhile and just-about-achievable if he or she approaches them the right way. Be explicit about what that right way is: have a mental roadmap of the journey and the refuelling points: training programmes, coaching sessions, CPD, projects, further help. Adopt a coaching perspective, helping the professional get the most out of their potential. Hold the 'judgement' aspects for another day. Hold separate reviews for any salary negotiations. Have coaching/mentoring sessions to actually improve performance, and only use the 'rear-view mirror' as a guide.

When coaching, remember the observation made elsewhere in this book, that "everybody wants to learn, but nobody wants to be taught", meaning that professionals avoid being put into 'student' roles but will gladly learn under the right conditions. Coaching is different from teaching, and there is a danger of over-helping, as the parable of the butterfly, below, relates.

The whole basis of managing (through coaching) is to move from simply interfering to positively enabling people. The key is to get past one's immediate (and ever-present) 'anxiety self-defence'. For example, if your own personality tends to seek control, this anxiety will manifest itself. Such shadows of anxiety hang over everything, often leading to recurring failure. There is a massive paradox in that the very element that you fear, not being ever-present, is what comes back to haunt you, and to invade the coaching relationship.

COACHING – THE PARABLE OF THE BUTTERFLY

A man found a cocoon for a butterfly. One day a small opening appeared. He sat and watched the butterfly for several hours as it struggled to force its body through the little hole. Then it seemed to stop making any progress. It appeared stuck.

The man decided to help the butterfly and with a pair of scissors he cut open the cocoon. The butterfly then emerged easily. Something was strange, however. The butterfly had a swollen body and shrivelled wings. The man watched the butterfly, expecting it to take on its correct proportions.

But nothing changed. The butterfly stayed the same. It was never able to fly.

In his kindness and haste the man did not realise that the butterfly's struggle to get through the small opening of the cocoon is nature's way of forcing fluid from the body of the butterfly into its wings, so that it would be ready for flight.

Like the sapling which grows strong from being buffeted by the wind, in life we all need to struggle sometimes to make us strong.

When we coach and teach others, it is helpful to recognise when people need to do things for themselves.

For a practical example of these principles in action, see the next chapter, **Chapter 4**, by the eminent surgeon Dr James Sheehan, founder of the renowned Galway Clinic, a pioneer in designing artificial hips and also a dedicated advocate of principled leadership.

Summary

This chapter has shown how leadership can be systematically developed and how professionals can progress from traditional management to transformational ('Level 5') leadership. Ideas on emotional and social intelligence have been introduced (and will be expanded upon in later chapters) to help leaders find their authentic self, and to engage people with skill. Situational leadership shows how to use different strokes with different folks, and that one leadership size does not actually fit all. The divisive aspect of performance management can be altered by having more positive conversations designed to help, not judge, people or their performance. A coaching approach can have wondrous benefits, if properly handled; a full chapter is devoted to coaching (see **Chapter 13**).

ENDNOTES

[1] John Antonakis and David Day, *The Nature of Leadership* (Sage, 2012). See references to the work of Bass and also Avolio, below.

[2] Jim Collins, *Good to Great: Why Some Companies Make the Leap... and Others Don't* (Random House, 2001).

[3] Bernard Bass, "Personal Selling and Transactional/Transformational Leadership" (1997) Vol. XVII No. 3 *Journal of Personal Selling & Sales Management* 19–28.

[4] Bruce Avolio, *Full Range Leadership Development* (Sage, 2011).

[5] John Antonakis and David Day, *The Nature of Leadership* (Sage, 2012).

[6] Paul Hersey and Ken Blanchard, *Management of Organisational Behaviour: Utilising Human Resources* (Prentice Hall, 1977).

[7] Robert Goffee and Gareth Jones, *Clever: Leading Your Smartest, Most Creative People* (Harvard Business Press, 2009).

[8] Max De Pree, *Leadership is an Art* (Crown Publishing Group, 2004).

[9] Jennifer A. Mangels, Brady Butterfield, *et al.*, "Why Do Beliefs about Intelligence Influence Learning Success? A Social Cognitive Neuroscience Model" (2006) Vol. 1 No. 2 *Social Cognitive and Affective Neuroscience* 75–86.

[10] Fabio Sala, "Laughing All the Way to the Bank" (2003) Vol. 81 No. 9 *Harvard Business Review* 16–17.

[11] Daniel Goleman and Richard Boyatzis, "Social Intelligence and the Biology of Leadership" (2008) September *Harvard Business Review* 74–81.

[12] Daniel Goleman, Richard Boyatzis and Annie McKee, "Primal Leadership: The Hidden Driver of Great Performance" (2001) December *Harvard Business Review* 42–51.

[13] Mary Ann Masarech, *Developing Smart Doers into Smart Leaders* (BlessingWhite, 2009). http://www.blessingwhite.com/developingsmartdoers.asp

Chapter 4

Leadership in Practice: Managing Professional Peers – Case Study

Dr James M. Sheehan

We make a living by what we get, but we make a life by what we give.

(attributed to) Winston Churchill

Introduction

The Galway Clinic (www.galwayclinic.com) emerges like a cathedral from the rugged fields of the West of Ireland. Here, world-renowned orthopaedic surgeon Dr James M. Sheehan ("just call me Jimmy") and his colleagues have pursued their vision of top-class surgical intervention and unsurpassed care. They have built a hospital that is especially noteworthy for its twin philosophy of high (ethical) values and high value (surgeries not commonly available elsewhere, performed at reasonable cost).

Previously, Jimmy Sheehan founded Ireland's first major private clinic, in Blackrock, County Dublin, and has worldwide patents for artificial hips and knees. He is also prominent in Irish society for his many crusades to reform key aspects of the political and economic system.

In this chapter, Jimmy shares some of his experiences and insights in managing the diverse elements of a complex, high-tech operation, with particular emphasis on the people aspects.

His value system (high care, high standards and high challenge) is evident throughout. He quietly sets out his management philosophy, which was developed over many years of research and application in practice. Modest to a fault, Jimmy has not claimed any credit for this philosophy, and I have taken the liberty (at the end of the chapter) of suggesting a framework that might help others to manage in a similar way.

MANAGING PROFESSIONAL PEERS
BY DR JAMES M. SHEEHAN

After 40 years as an active orthopaedic surgeon my career path changed to that of a medical administrator/CEO. It was very much a case of poacher turned gamekeeper. As a surgeon I can openly criticise my own profession. We are a highly trained and educated group. Training for most surgeons spans a period of 15 to 20 years combined with the rigours of endless hours on duty, occasionally 24 hours or more at a stretch, and in some instances testing one's limits of ability. We are an arrogant bunch of humans with a rapid decision-making process. For example, when you're watching a spurting vessel rapidly exsanguinating a patient, you do not have too much time on your hands, and do not weigh up the pros and cons of different forms of stopping the bleeding.

We see most things in black and white, and tend to eliminate the grey areas as much as possible. We command respect from juniors, are pretty well intolerant of all other human beings, tend to be bad communicators and have a short fuse most of the time. I hope that our good qualities include: being totally focused on patients' well-being and recovery; seeing safety as paramount; being prepared to work day and night to achieve a satisfactory outcome; and being motivated by our humanity and sense of responsibility for the sick and less well-off members of our community.

Can anyone think of a more challenging group of professionals to attempt to manage than one's own peer group? Such is the role of a hospital administrator. Traditionally, hospital administrators were appointed because they understood the needs of patients and the complexity of disease. Due to the increased workload of medical administrators, additional secretarial resources were devoted to them, and thus the origin of the entire hospital administration system. In most instances, the assistants included an accountant, as financial affairs became more and more critical as health expenditure gradually increased. Having worked in my formative years in the early 1960s with a medical hospital administrator in Glasgow, where such positions were commonplace, I found that the system under their leadership worked very well.

Being involved in hospital development for the last three decades, I decided that a new hospital venture, as a green-field site where it was laden with debt, including personal guarantees on my part, for more than I wish to think, sharpened my mind and stimulated me to take on the challenge of hospital administrator. What greater challenge than to try to manage and advise one's peers? Many lessons have been learned over the last five years and I can share these lessons under a number of headings or groups of experience.

Working Alongside your Peers

Having served on hospital boards for many years, it was apparent to me that one can exert very little influence at board level. Boards lay down strategy, and instruct the Executive on roles that they would like to see them play. However, to have direct influence on staff it is necessary to work alongside them. There is no substitute for presence on the 'shop floor'. I would strongly advocate, as a CEO, that you do not have an office, and that any administrative work can be done offsite and out of core hours. How better to spend your time at work than walking around from one department to another? Meetings in doctors' own offices are much more effective and the very concept of going to see them, rather than asking them to come and see you, sets a significant tone for a meeting. Doctors are very busy people, scheduled from morning to evening. It is easy to slip into their offices for brief meetings that are pertinent. The alternative of trying to arrange a mutually convenient time where a doctor designates 30 to 60 minutes for a formal meeting can be very difficult to achieve. Brevity at these meetings is important. If people realise after the first one or two meetings that you do not settle into their office for long periods, they are much more welcoming. One-to-one meetings are much more effective than group meetings. First, it is very difficult to get people to synchronise their time, other than very early morning meetings, and secondly, group meetings rarely achieve consensus. Physicians view meetings generally as a waste of time and diverting them from seeing patients.

Rules Apply to Everyone but Doctors

As a profession, we are great for introducing care pathways and protocols. Strict enforcement of discipline and hospital rules is also within our remit. However, physicians and surgeons themselves have no understanding of the rules that govern hospitals. They wish to use their time effectively and efficiently. Their own schedule is their focus and the use of everyone else's time is secondary. This is manifest in many ways, such as punctuality. Occasionally six or seven people may be waiting in an operating theatre for the surgeon (or 'prima donna') to arrive. Through carelessness, they may frequently forget to tell you that they are going to be late. There is absolutely no use confronting them because undoubtedly they will have been "saving lives", even if this only meant dealing with the children and dropping them to school. There is no point in tackling them head-on about late attendances. However, if these are habitual, getting another surgeon to insert a short case before their list leads to their bewilderment and amazement when they arrive late and find that staff are already occupied. It is surprising how territorially we all behave and how we like to defend our own burrow. Time-keeping tends to improve enormously when such changes are made.

Reluctance to Change

Physicians and surgeons tend to be somewhat different. Some years ago, an elderly professor of surgery and his brother, an equally eminent professor of medicine, were overheard in discussion. The surgeon stated that his life was extraordinarily difficult compared to that of a physician: "How would you like to operate on a patient for hours on end, standing motionless, to achieve the end result?" The physician replied: "How would you like to be treating patients for years on end without knowing what's wrong with them?!"

Physicians, generally, tend to be very traditional in their method of treatment and exhibit great reluctance to change. Surgeons, on the other hand, are much more technically minded and a number of them are keen to play with the latest 'Meccano set'. Thus, as an administrator or manager, different approaches to these mentalities are required. We are all creatures of habit –"why change it if it ain't broken?". For physicians to implement change, a campaign must be embarked upon to stress how change is not only necessary, but how it will differentiate their actions from the past and how beneficial it will be for patients in the future.

With surgeons, the opposite may be the case, in that one is hesitant to introduce change for the sake of change and, frequently, having attended a recent conference and learned of a new technique, surgeons may be all too willing to embark on introducing new techniques. Peer review by selected members of the staff is very helpful under these circumstances, to ensure that a balanced view of new technology is undertaken.

Them Versus Us

Doctors value their autonomy. Any interference with their management of patient care is strongly resisted. Administrators are seen as uncaring in relation to the patient, being much more interested in the finance, and as a result a conflict of interest frequently arises. The great advantage of an administrator also being a medic is their understanding of patient care and the true delivery of healthcare. It makes for a much easier relationship with colleagues.

Doctors' Apparent Loss of Power

Just as doctors value their independence, they also feel that they should be in control of medical institutions at all times. While this may have been true in the past, corporate governance measures now ensure strict surveillance of outcomes and doctors' management of patients, and as a result doctors feel that they are somewhat under scrutiny and losing their absolute power. While full control of the patient remains vested with the doctor, the needs of the institution are much greater, and doctors must remain answerable to the medical director. Requirements, such as availability by mobile phone, holiday cover in their absence, on call rotas, etc., need to be monitored. It is difficult to strike a balance with such monitoring without causing offence. Ideally, peer review groups, such as audit review groups and medical advisory groups, formed with their peers is a very satisfactory and direct method of monitoring their behaviour and outcomes and transfers this responsibility from the administrator.

A Patient's Journey

As William Mayo of the Mayo Clinic once said: "It is not just that we are concerned about the patient's journey, it is the only thing that matters." Emphasis on the patient's journey harmonises both the administrative and medical views. The emphasis of an institution should be centred around the patient and how they can have the best possible experience when hospitalised. Thus, working towards improvements in the patient's journey should bring the administrators and medical members of the organisation closer together.

Improvements in the patient's journey are unending, as every aspect of their journey can have defects which require rectification. A good motto for an institution to have is that "everything that we currently do can be done better". By emphasising the care of the patient, discussions become far less emotional and less doctor-centred. No business employs such a pool of talent as healthcare, ranging from the medical staff to nurses, radiographers, physicists, to mention only a few. The challenge of administration is to channel this extraordinary group of professionals and to focus them on considering every activity in their daily work which is undertaken for patient care. They must ask themselves how every aspect of this journey can be improved and thus bring about a better outcome and experience for the patient.

The practice of medicine frequently discourages innovation and change as there is a constant anxiety about inferior results. Change must then be focused on positive outcomes and utilisation of small incremental steps to achieve the end point. Affirmation of innovative thinking among medical personnel should become part of their lives, not just in the workplace but embedded in their minds throughout their waking hours. Administrators are frequently seen to be discouraging of new innovations and a culture where innovation becomes a predominant part of the organisation will unify administrators and medics with a common bond. All doctors are obsessed with quality outcomes. Innovation should become inextricably linked to quality. Thus, concern by administrators and doctors for both innovation and quality strike a common note.

People involved in campaigns of one type or another will tell you that a campaign mentality is developed over a period of time. It is not easy to win the hearts and minds of any group and indeed it is a long term-battle. Thus, disappointment should not be expressed too readily, particularly if early attempts at collaboration are seen to be unsatisfactory.

Think of the bamboo plant. For some extraordinary reason, when it is planted it remains below ground for up to five years while it develops its root structure. When finally it does sprout, it grows at a rapid pace and may reach up to 90 feet in height.

Appear to Take a Back Seat

Highly motivated people, such as doctors, frequently feel the need to be seen to be leading their organisations. They should be allowed to take on this role. It is the foolish CEO who tries to challenge their leadership role, and far more can be achieved by working quietly, very often behind the scenes, and sometimes having to gulp for a deep breath. Remember the old saying: "The Lord gave us two ears, but only one tongue." We should develop our ability to listen.

Avoid Conflict

Conflict over simple and trivial matters is very unproductive, and it may damage relationships necessary for much more significant decisions. Remember: the true measure of a leader is not the number of people who serve him or her, but the number of people he or she serves. Portray at all times that you are there to help, rather than hinder. Be proactive in suggestions and be mindful of the demands made of your peers in order to make their lives more tolerable.

Once active collaboration is seen, it will encourage a positive relationship between doctors and administrators, and the outcomes can be most rewarding. Working on the shop floor, alongside colleagues, rather than appearing to have placed oneself at a different level can excite others to exceptional performance. If an administrator/manager shows enthusiasm about all aspects of activity under his domain, it cannot but excite others as it is hard to be lethargic in the presence of enthusiasm. Indeed, the great defect in our health service is the lack of inspirational leaders who can help others to work collaboratively. How much more productive is a co-operative event rather than individuals working in isolation.

Modern medical delivery requires considerable team work and we have a great deal to learn from the airline industry where, mainly for safety reasons, cockpit resource management was introduced. This means that all members on the flight deck can question the decisions of others, including the captain. The key principle here is the breaking down of hierarchical barriers. The surgeon is no longer the only person who matters in the operating theatre; consideration should be given to all members of the team, including the cleaner (turnaround times between cases will be greatly assisted if there is enthusiasm about the cleaning process). Nobody in the team should be afraid to question what is happening and, indeed, it is the obligation of all team members to ensure that the safest outcome is as a result of them all contributing as much as possible.

Study Leadership

Those of us who have graduated into administrative roles, managing peers, have frequently had no formal training. No subject has more written about it than the role of leadership, and delving into this literature is extremely helpful. We should be mindful, however, that leadership applies equally to everyone in the organisation and, as an overall leader, you have an obligation to improve the leadership roles of all staff. It is a useful exercise to record pertinent leadership quotes and to refresh your memory frequently by looking at a typed page of your favourite guidelines. The following quotes are some of my favourites and a regular reference to them is refreshing:

- "If you think you are leading and no one is following, then you are only taking a walk."
- "Fear not that your life will come to an end, but that it will never have a beginning."(Cardinal Newman)
- "No person was ever honoured for what he received. Honour has been the reward of what he gave."
- "Even the right decision is the wrong decision, if it is made too late."
- "The first rule of holes: if you are in one, stop digging."
- "The measure of a leader is not the number of people who serve him, but the number of people he serves."
- "Leaders do not lead by exercising the power inherent in their office, they lead by example."
- "Character is doing the right thing when no one is looking."
- "Growth only happens outside of your comfort zone."
- "If you are part of a rat race and you win, you are still only a rat."
- "The person who does not smile should not run a shop." (Chinese proverb)

Urgency

Nothing achieves results better than a sense of urgency. Healthcare is an ideal field to impart such a sense and to engender a shared purpose. If we notice a problem or require a solution, in most instances there is already a sense of urgency to achieve this outcome as it may dictate an individual patient's management. Nominating time frames for solutions is equally helpful; otherwise, human nature being what it is, we tend to place things on the long finger. It is quite extraordinary the goodwill that exists in a healthcare organisation, like no other organisation, and what better group of people to inspire to rapid action than healthcare workers?

Helping Peers Develop

All medical personnel secretly wish to be Nobel Prize recipients. Encouragement of their research ambitions and a positive attitude towards any suggestions is helpful in nurturing close working relationships. Cynicism and negativity destroy relationships. Giving colleagues the opportunity to speak about their projects, and exposing them to some potential praise and adulation, goes a very long way. No matter how humble we may appear, who does not like to receive praise?

Some go through life with virtually no praise or recognition. A good friend of mine, a priest, when he was 86 years of age, received a bunch of flowers. It was the first time in his life that anyone had sent him flowers, and it left an indelible impression. It is very often the smallest acts of kindness, many of which we would dismiss without any thought, that can have significant effects. A friend of mine keeps a list of all his associates' birthdays in his diary, and a simple text or phone call to them on the day is always appreciated. A few short handwritten lines, when appropriate, are so much more effective than your secretary typing voluminous letters. With the advent of e-mail and text messaging, we seem to have forgotten the art of writing notes or letters. One particularly famous CEO is reputed to have written 30,000 letters or notes in the course of his tenure.

Involvement in Strategy

Deep down, we all feel paranoid at times that others are planning something behind our backs. Usually this is only a hunch, and has no validity. Inviting staff, particularly colleagues, to become actively involved in strategy and future strategic decisions removes suspicion and taps a source of goodwill. Apart from the creativity that is often unexpressed, active involvement allows people to have some say in shaping their future. Nothing irritates doctors more than new regulations being imposed upon them, whereas if they feel they were party to formulating those decisions, they are then accepted gracefully.

Become Long-term Partners

For the same reason as involving colleagues in strategy, let them feel that you are working with them as a long-term partner rather than as their superior. Partners should have equal opportunities, and thus share in the outcomes. Nothing is more satisfying than a successful outcome where multiple collaborators have been involved. True partnership is mutually beneficial and as we strive to satisfy colleagues' needs and demands to the best of our ability, a similar type relationship and outcome can be achieved in business partnerships.

The Development of Virtues

The concept of virtuous leadership as proposed by Alexandre Havard is an excellent starting point. His book, *Virtuous Leadership: An Agenda for Personal Excellence*[1] should not only be read but *studied* by all in a leadership role. The 'Virtues' date back to pre-Christian times, and we should ponder and reflect on these virtues on a regular basis. There are four major virtues: courage, justice, prudence and self-control. How often will the virtue of self-control be necessary in any leader, i.e. holding one's tongue, remembering that a few harsh words may never be forgotten or forgiven? And in some ways the 'minor' virtues such as magnanimity (thinking big), and humility, may be even more important.

Timing

Those of us who are parents know the importance of timing. Equally important when dealing with children is 'silent action'. They do not want a repetition, yet again, of what they know is expected of them, but have not heeded. Consider similar actions when dealing with peers. The last thing they desire is a confrontation when they are tired and stressed. Mayfly fishermen in the West of Ireland, when a fish bites, count up to three slowly before striking and they then hook the best fish! At times, deferring discussion on problems for even a few days or weeks can be very beneficial.

A relaxed discussion over a cup of coffee can solve many of the apparent problems of the world when the heat of the moment has subsided. By the same account, a lecture or diatribe by way of correction can be interpreted as offensive. Sometimes an oblique approach to the topic under discussion, as Jesus did with his Apostles when he spoke to them in parables, rather than bluntly, can get a message across very effectively.

Money Matters!

It would be remiss to conclude my remarks without a vulgar and basic discussion about money.

Some doctors, particularly the older generation, have little interest in financial affairs. Doctors were notorious for being hopeless managers of their own finances. Most of us, through hard work, have made very good livelihoods, but it was the effect of, rather than the reason for, being in medicine.

We are living in very different financial times and monetary affairs are now more pertinent, as doctors, like everyone else, are paying large mortgages, school fees, etc., as well as hefty medical practice expenses, such as medical indemnity. They expect to be well rewarded for their efforts, and do not underestimate their interest in worldly affairs. A late colleague once said that if you require a good attendance of doctors at any meeting, tell them that the first item on the agenda is redistribution of incomes!

In conclusion, working with one's peers in medicine can pose significant challenges. However, positive actions can greatly outweigh any negativity associated with such challenges. The importance of working closely with colleagues, in a collaborative fashion, cannot be underestimated, and anything that eases their administrative burden and allows them to concentrate on patient care is greatly welcomed.

Their strategic involvement in the future of the hospital gives them the confidence that the administrators are working closely with them, and at the end of the day the common pathway of the patient's journey will win through at all times.

Leadership and the Organisation Design of Hospitals

Hospitals are complex systems, with four main groups of workers having different priorities and tending to pull in different directions, as shown in the figure below (adapted from Glouberman and Mintzberg).[2] Reconciling these different worlds, with their divergent mindsets, make the job of the hospital administrator (manager) particularly onerous, with a high reliance on diplomacy and political skill to avoid the inherent potential for conflict. In fact, even the different medical professions (doctors and nurses, for example) have different perspectives and priorities.

THE FOUR WORLDS OF THE ACUTE HOSPITAL

Community — Trustees — Managing Up & Out

Control — Managers — Managing Up & In

Cure — Doctors — Managing Out & Down

Care — Nurses — Managing Down & In

A key message of this book is that effective leadership employs a variety of styles to suit the work performed and the personalities involved. Other important dimensions are the degree of standardisation of the work involved and the degree of direct 'client' (patient) interfacing. The graphic below shows the different types of work associated with the world of healthcare. These distinctions can often apply to other professional services organisations or firms.

Note the variances in type of work (standardised or customised), even though all require high skills (but of differing types). Some work, such as nursing, is performed at the 'client' (patient) interface ('front of house'); other work, such as pharmacology, is performed away from patients ('back-room'). Some work is diagnostic in nature, while other work is based on execution. The four types are exemplified here by nurses, psychiatrists, doctors and hospital pharmacists.

FOUR FUNDAMENTAL TYPES OF PROFESSIONAL WORK

• Nurse

Standardised process, Emphasis on execution, High client contact, Front of house

Customised process, Emphasis on diagnosis, High client contact, Front of house

• Psychiatrist

Standardised process, Emphasis on execution, Low client contact, Back-room

Customised process, Emphasis on diagnosis, Low client contact, Back-room

• Pharmacist

• Surgeon

Managing and leading in these intricate worlds is clearly complex and unending. As well as balancing the various forces, there is a real need for a manager to use different styles depending on the four fundamental kinds of work involved and (as we will see later) the different personalities of the people performing that work.

Adopting a Management and Leadership Philosophy

Most of the work in hospitals is complex (that is, hard to analyse) and complicated (hard to co-ordinate). Dr Jimmy Sheehan has recognised this, and has introduced an over-arching **philosophy** and a nuanced **management system** to try and adapt to these diverse elements. A management philosophy is not a 'nice-to-have' but a necessity, as there are simply too many situations to manage prescriptively. Having a management philosophy provides a moral compass ("First, do no harm", as the Hippocratic Oath requires). Such direction helps keep the organisation aligned and clear about the underlying organisational values. Having such a management system is necessary to make the interconnections between the four worlds and types of work, and especially to include those who rarely or never see the patient (e.g. administrators) but who are instrumental to the service.

Simplify and Unify

As the management system is necessarily complicated to adapt to the different worlds and different types of work, the key mantras repeatedly articulated by Dr Sheehan provide the vital urgency without which the system might atrophy into a heartless bureaucracy. Concentrating on "the patient's journey" is a way of unifying the links in the system at different stages.

Indeed, the realisation that some patients' journeys may be final ones raises awareness of the need for spiritual and emotional care, as well as physical treatment. In Jimmy Sheehan's hospital, the journey is tended by a nurse who knows the patient, not by orderlies. To make that possible, the Galway Clinic has installed special bed-moving robots so that the nurse can accompany and 'shepherd' the patient with finger-tip ease.

Use Simple Touch-points to Manage Complex Work

As well as providing a connection between the worlds of care, cure, control and community, the concept of the patient's journey provides discreet, manageable 'touch-points' and these have become the points of progress; the Galway Clinic, at last count, had 180 live projects to improve the patient journey. Such relentless, continuous improvement benefits both staff and patients, as it raises morale and creates an achievement culture.

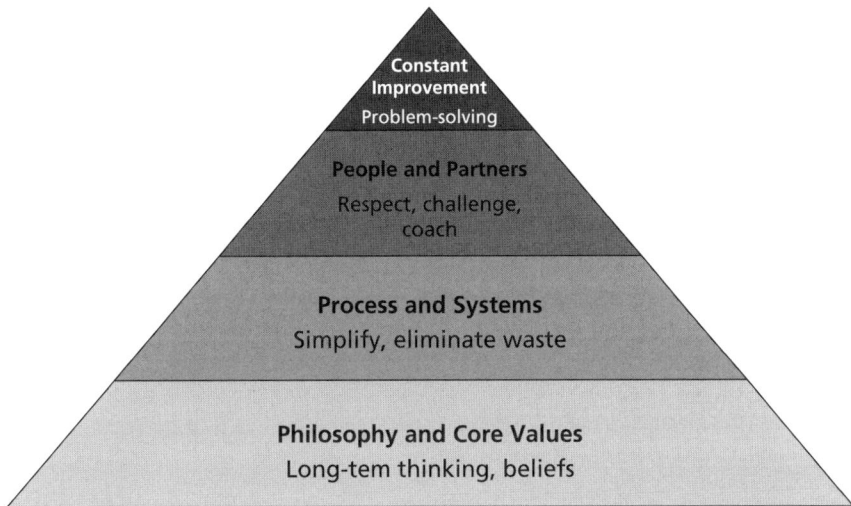

Dr Sheehan's approach reflects a deep understanding of 'World-class Operations' – a set of interconnected principles that have propelled companies (such as Toyota) to decades of continuous, profitable growth. These principles are summarised in the figure above; for more detail, see Part III of *Strategic Cost Reduction* by Tim McCormick and Dermot Duff.[3] Operational excellence starts with philosophy and core values as the foundations. If these foundations are solid, processes can be designed for purpose, simplified and made lean, with unnecessary elements (waste) eliminated. This in turn leads to the opportunity to release people's potential and, ultimately, to have the staff take the lead for themselves in continuous improvement.

It should be noted that leadership such as Jimmy's, as well as requiring an intellectual leap to a systematic approach to management, requires a leader to take a leap of faith in moving from conventional management to world-class leadership. Making a quantum leap in the management of innovation and of professional work (mental work as distinct to traditional physical work) is developed in **Chapter 9**, which uses a real example of such a system in practice.

Conclusion

Chapter 3 set out a framework and philosophy for the leadership of professionals. In this chapter, thanks to the contribution of Dr James Sheehan, that approach to leadership has been illustrated in practice. Dr Sheehan, consciously or otherwise, has absorbed proven principles from world-leading organisations and adopted them to a complex hospital environment. Key features of such a sophisticated system are:

1. The conscious espousing and promotion of a unifying system of management, with a core philosophy and an integrated approach.
2. The systematic and widespread development of transformational ('Level 5') leadership.
3. The use of tools and technology to improve quality, lower stress, remove error, streamline operations, reduce waste and make life easier and better for staff and patients.

Dr Sheehan has kindly provided a list of useful tips on leadership for those managing peers, and these are summarised below as a conclusion to the chapter:

---

1. Avoid unnecessary conflict: choose a suitable time and place.
2. Use parables and metaphors rather than blunt repetition to convey messages.
3. Appear to take a back-seat: use 'pull', not 'push', in managing people.
4. Study the art of leadership.
5. Adopt a conscious philosophy.
6. Develop character, in yourself and others.
7. Involve the whole team in strategy and leadership.
8. Manage for the long haul.
9. Urgency is vital: life may depend on it.
10. Do the right thing – even when no one is looking.

ENDNOTES

[1] Alexandre Havard, *Virtuous Leadership: An Agenda for Personal Excellence* (Scepter, 2007).
[2] Steven Glouberman and Henry Mintzberg, "Managing the Care of Health and the Cure of Disease – Part II: Integration". (2001) Winter Vol. 26 No. 1 *Healthcare Management Review* 70–84.
[3] Tim McCormick and Dermot Duff, *Strategic Cost Reduction* (2nd Edition, Chartered Accountants Ireland, 2011).

Chapter 5

Personality and Professionals: Releasing Potential

The greatest danger for most of us is not that our aim is too high and we miss it, but that it is too low, and we reach it.

Michelangelo

Introduction

The intelligent professional is not limited by any lack of mental horse-power; issues most often arise because of attitudinal problems and personality differences. Those who manage more 'awkward' professionals cite such factors as their narrow perspective (even a lack of common sense), prima donna behaviour, arrogance and a certain childishness. The best professionals, of course, are well-developed mentally, but many fail to realise their true potential because of a lack of maturity. Those who have the responsibility – and privilege – of managing intelligent professionals face challenges that this chapter addresses by providing an understanding of the different personality types. It also includes a significant section on managing 'difficult' people.

Also in this chapter, the relationship between personality and intelligence is explored, with an emphasis on what makes people 'tick'. Every person has strengths and weaknesses, and success is usually based on maximising those strengths, rather than eradicating the weaknesses. However, if a professional is to progress, he or she will invariably need to develop their understanding of human nature and particularly of personality 'types'. In this sense, professionals need to develop both sides of their brain: left and right, emotional and cognitive. The professional can develop such an 'opposable mind' by neutralising their weaknesses and extending his or her range of styles so that they can deal with different situations and different personalities. The welcome news is that people can change their behaviour to become more effective. You can adopt behaviours that improve, for example, your leadership capability, your interaction with other staff or your influence with clients. (The area of emotional intelligence is treated in **Chapter 12**.)

Personality Types

Since ancient times, people have been fascinated by personality types, seeking to understand fundamental human differences. Aristotle classified contributions to society under four headings:

1. Iconic – artistic and art-making
2. Pistic – common-sensical and care-taking

3.   Noetic – intuitive sensibility
4.   Diagnostic – reasoning and logical investigation.

Aristotle similarly categorised four basic temperaments:

• Melancholic
• Phlegmatic
• Sanguine
• Choleric.

Echoes of these four types permeated the work of Carl Jung, which in turn formed the basis of the extensive research performed by mother and daughter pair, Katherine Briggs and Isabel Briggs Myers in New York in the 1940s. This 'Myers–Briggs' model and its associated 'Type Indicator' (MBTI)[1] is a cornerstone of much contemporary personal and leadership development, as it provides a framework for analysing stereo-'types'.

The **Myers–Briggs model** uses four dimensions, similar to Aristotle's four headings, in its analysis:

Dimension 1.   the degree to which a person is oriented towards the internal or external world;
Dimension 2.   the weight given by a person to concrete facts versus abstract ideas;
Dimension 3.   the degree to which emotional aspects feature in an individual's decisions; and
Dimension 4.   the propensity to form a conclusion and act, versus leaving one's options open.

There is no 'value judgement' associated with these dimensions: in the same way that, naturally, a left-handed person, for example, is not 'worse' than a right-handed one. Similarly, an extrovert is neither better nor worse as a person than an introvert, or vice versa. This model looks purely at '*preferences*', all of which can be developed to some degree. For example, in a large accountancy practice, staff with a deep creative tendency (as opposed to an analytical preference) may well have developed, through necessity, their analytical skills, often to a high level. This often comes at a high price in mid-life, as that person may then question the purpose of their life, asking, 'what's it all about?'. They find themselves competent in their roles by dint of their conscientiousness in developing those analytical skills – but find they are still not 'naturals' for the role. Indeed, it can take deep introspection for them to understand their 'true selves'. Ironically, such situations can be turned to advantage, if the person (or their manager) recognises the underlying personality dynamics and uses the latent creativity productively, perhaps by adding a marketing role to that person's accounting skills.

For professionals such as accountants, architects, lawyers, engineers and many others, career progression often depends on adding people skills (the ability to interface with clients, staff, stakeholders and the like) to their technical knowledge. It is this elusive combination of both sides of the work of the brain that is especially valuable. The leading recruiters from firms such as Deloitte seek these rare, almost 'unnatural' combinations of, for example, numeracy and artistry in identifying the leaders and business winners of tomorrow. On the other hand, it can be important to appreciate from the outset that an extrovert might be better suited to a business development role, while the introverted professional might be a more natural fit for a more analytical or technical role. The idea is not to put square pegs into round holes, but to develop skills and personality-based behaviours so that the professional performs well on a broader spectrum.

Personality and Interpersonal Conflict at Work

Each of the personality dimensions outlined above potentially gives rise to natural tensions between people: for example, the introvert may dislike the extrovert's animation (Dimension 1).

In Dimension 2, the 'hard facts' person may come to abhor the incessant idea-generation of the intuitive, abstract-thinking person.

Similarly, frustration may arise when a 'strictly business' attitude in Dimension 3 grates on the sensibility of those who prefer to give more consideration to the human aspects of decisions. The discord between those who prefer people orientation and those who rely more on unemotional decision-making is particularly severe, as two sets of values collide, one person-orientated, the other more business orientated.

Finally, in Dimension 4, those who tend to leave tasks open-ended may shred the nerves of those who want to draw matters to a definite conclusion. Conversely, the urge to close off tasks may well bemuse the more flexible types who delay closure in the expectation of important, 'last-minute' information.

While the above personality differences may cause tensions in an organisation, groups without sufficiently distinctive personality types will lack the psychological variety required for good decision-making: their focus will be too narrow, dull, rigid or cold.

Carl Jung believed that a person always operated on both the conscious and unconscious levels, and that the two levels counterbalance one another. In other words, if the conscious level had psychological excesses this would lead to "imbalances" in the unconscious, often in the form of dreams. Similarly, the subconscious level could, for example, produce illnesses at the physical level. In other words, mind and matter (body) are intrinsically related.

More importantly, in a point well worth noting, Jung believed that as these were simply "behaviours", not inherent "traits", people could come to have a more extended range; for example, the introvert could adapt the behaviours of the extrovert, at least temporarily. Such shifts can be deep and prolonged enough to allow, for example, the introverted analytical chemist to make an engaging business pitch, or to allow the hard-headed accountant to take 'account' of human factors in decision-making.

These dimensions are continuums or spectrums along which a person's preferences can lie: a person could be just slightly extrovert (towards the middle of the spectrum or scale), or alternatively could be clearly introverted (towards the extremities of the scale). Note again that Jung did not see these preferences as absolutely fixed in any personality: he regarded them as behaviours that could be modified. The vital first step, of course, is to become aware of these unconscious, taken-for-granted preferences, so that one can begin to understand and purposefully address them. Just as a child becomes aware, at around three years of age, that he is a separate being to his mother, maturity increases when one realises the nuances of one's personality and the attendant proclivities, with their possibilities and inhibitions.

The Personality Spectrum

Myers and Briggs devoted many years to developing the classifications originated by Carl Jung. While these Myers–Briggs type indicators are extremely valuable in understanding oneself and others, an unfortunate result of categorising personality types as being introverted or extroverted, for example, is that it suggests that people are very definitely either one type or the other. In reality, as Myers–Briggs and their associates emphasise, a person falls somewhere along the spectrum, having tendencies towards one end or the other. In practice, however, people note that they are either extrovert or introvert, and often carry this designation as a kind of fixed cross to bear.

PERSONALITY TYPES: A SPECTRUM OF BEHAVIOUR

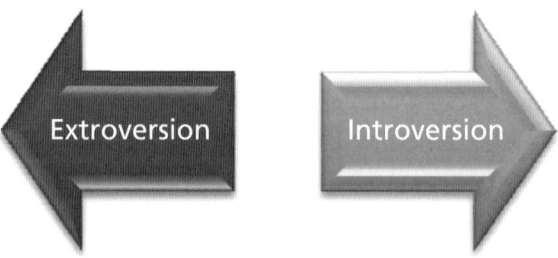

Such bi-polar, black-or-white thinking (i.e. a person is 'typed' as introvert or extrovert) is unfortunate and misleading. It can lead to a fixity of thinking, that modification is impossible, when in fact the limitations of either type can be overcome, at least for periods, even if the basic personality itself hardly shifts.

In developing his theories (later extended by Myers–Briggs), Jung considered Aristotle's 'Four Temperaments', as mentioned at the start of this chapter, but also noted two other 'functions' in addition to the introversion/ extroversion preference:

1.   how people gather information, i.e. whether they place higher regard on evidence they can physically detect ("Sense" in his words) or on abstract ideas ("Intuition");
2.   how people assess or judge, i.e. whether they base their decision-making on pure fact ("Thinking", in his terminology) or on the human effects ("Feeling").

The potentially misleading terminology Jung chose needs to be understood in context. He said that 'thinking' *and* 'feeling' are 'rational' because both are functions which evaluate experience; they reason, decide and judge.

Similarly, Jung said that 'intuition' and 'sensation' are 'irrational' since they are concerned with perception and do not evaluate matters "rationally": they simply gather information and perceive the nature of something – they do not reason or decide or judge.

Jung observed that improving our awareness and acceptance of the four functions within ourselves – whether as conscious or unconscious elements – is important for developing a healthy existence and 'life-balance'. For example, the extrovert can access his or her introverted side, at least for periods, by consciously reflecting and turning his or her attention inwards.

Conversely, extended repression of any of the functions, by oneself or by another person or pressure, is unhelpful and unhealthy and often leads to problems surfacing sooner or later, as described in the case of the accountant, above. To give another example, Karl was a senior accountant when he came on one of my business development courses. Unable to repress his artistic side any longer, he had embarked on a career in marketing custom textiles to high-end businesses and wealthy individuals who appreciated the finer things in life. Harry, similarly, had become frustrated with what he now saw as repetitive detail in his accountancy practice. He was on the point of walking away from accountancy entirely when it was pointed out to him the possibilities of being a business advisor, thereby putting his relationship skills and preference for task variety to good use. He now considers himself far happier, and much better rewarded in all senses in his new role.

Jung's Four Functional Types

The table below summarises Jung's Four Functional types of personality. It can be seen, for example, that someone 'sensible' (i.e. in the "Sensing" category below) prefers to deal with tangible facts, while those in the "Intuition" category are at the other end of the spectrum, preferring to dream, deal in the abstract and live somewhat in the future. Such differences can lead to the stereotypical fact-based accountant and the dreamy architect talking past each other on different wavelengths, or coming into conflict, each regarding the other as limited or even deranged!

JUNG'S FUNCTIONAL TYPES EXPLAINED

Primary Basis for Decision	Prime Value	Personality Indicators	Types of Function	
Thinking	what something is	meaning and understanding	analytic, objective, principles, standards, criteria	Both are opposite **reasoning** and **judging** functions – people consciously 'prefer' one or the other. Jung called these functions **'rational'**.
Feeling	whether it's good or not	weight and value	subjective, personal, valuing intimacy, humane	
Sensation	something exists	sensual perception	realistic, down-to-earth, practical, sensible	Both are opposite **perceiving** functions – people consciously 'prefer' one or the other. Jung called these functions **'irrational'**.
Intuition	where it's from and where it's going	possibilities and atmosphere	hunches, future, speculative, fantasy, imaginative	

Professionals tend to be exaggerated in their type: their natural tendencies, reinforced through academic success and technical excellence, coupled with the demands of the task at hand (e.g. accuracy, numeracy and rationality for accountancy professionals) foster a drift towards entrenched stereotypical behaviour. The choice of profession often reflects personality preferences; people-oriented folk tend to favour the caring professions, for example.

Exploring Personality Type

While there are indeed an infinite variety of personalities, defined types can help in understanding people and their psychological preferences. While it is potentially harmful to be categorical about types of personality (and especially to use them prescriptively in 'managing' people), it is useful to understand the four psychological layers that comprise an individual's personality. These layers approximate to the classic four temperaments as described above, but they provide a more fine-grained view of personality. In this section, the language and concepts of Carl Jung and Myers–Briggs have been adapted for more commonplace, less contentious terms.

The four layers of personality according to Myers–Briggs are:

1. How people face each other – whether they look externally or internally to process ideas (extrovert or introvert).
2. How people face information – whether they look upwards (abstract) or downwards (concrete).
3. How individuals face decisions – objectively (impersonal) or subjectively (human).
4. How they face conclusions (open-ended or closed).

> As mentioned, the Myers–Briggs model is similarly based on the above Jungian distinctions, but the terminology can be confounding. For example, the flexible type is termed "Perceiving" and the closed-ended type "Judging". The abstract thinker is deemed as "Intuitive", while the detailed thinker is deemed "Sensing". The third layer is termed "Thinking" or "Feeling", when, of course, most people do both. Nonetheless, the Myers–Briggs model has been well-researched over many decades, and any serious student of management is encouraged to delve further into that research. (See also the section about Myers–Briggs type indicators and the professions towards the end of **Chapter 15**.)

1. Extrovert or Introvert (E v L)

The **first** layer of personality concerns the degree to which people look externally (to the outside world) or internally (to the inside world) for ideas and stimulation. It is one of the most observable traits, manifesting itself as a preference for, e.g. active networking in the search for ideas and excitement (extroversion) or for contemplative reflection and solitary activity in the search for ideas (introversion). 'Extroversion' can be a confusing term, until one realises that it is a dual term, comprising both a social aspect (gregariousness) and a very productive action-oriented driven ('go-getting') behaviour. It is not merely socialising or giddiness but a preference for action, especially with the stimulation of interacting with people. This social action tendency is to be distinguished from caring for people, which is another dimension; it is an enjoyment of working with and through people.

As with each layer, neither behavioural *preference* (Jung was keen to say that these are people's preferred modes of operating, not fixed characteristics that were immutable) is inherently better than the other, but naturally some suit different situations. The extrovert will rarely relish the role of librarian and the introvert will not typically appreciate a role involving a lot of small-talk and social interaction. Both, of course, can do either role, but for a limited time, until frustration causes them to revert to a role more natural to them.

While no signs are infallible, an active orientation and animated conversation hints at an extrovert, while soft-spoken, quieter speech and calm demeanour points to an introverted type.

Put simplistically, the extrovert acts, thinks and acts again – in that order. On the other hand, the introvert thinks – acts – thinks. This can be extremely frustrating to both types: the introvert may regard the extrovert as an empty-headed chatterbox, while the extrovert may be confounded by the seemingly inert introvert.

2. Abstract or Grounded (A v G)

The **second** layer of personality concerns how people seek information, whether they prefer a big-picture, 'helicopter' view or prefer to look at firmer, more detailed information. One looks 'skyward', seeking general trends, the other drills down, placing a higher value on tangible facts in the here-and-now. Again, neither trait is preferable to the other, but abstract orientation is more closely connected with innovation though breakthrough or 'light-bulb' moments, while the more detailed types focus their innovation lens on examining concrete facts. One dreams and speculates; the other builds platforms. For example, the inventor of Velcro noticed how burrs stuck to his dog's coat, and developed this detail into a major product. On the other hand, Tim Berners-Lee, 'inventor' of the World Wide Web, noticed how technology was evolving and embarked on his grand scheme to link computers together, declaring in his first message: "This is for everyone".

3. Rationality or People Orientation (R v P)

The **third** personality layer concerns how people base their decisions, either on a 'strictly business' basis or one that prioritises the human aspects. Again, both have merit: an accountant, for example, might be expected to decide based on the numbers, whereas an artist might prioritise the human costs or benefits. Those attempting change on a purely 'rational' business basis will most likely fail unless they address 'irrational' human feelings, working with a true people person who can see the perspectives of others.

4. Flexible or Organised (F v O)

The **fourth** (and final) layer of personality concerns the individual's approach to tasks, with some 'flexible' types preferring to leave tasks open until the final moment, often in the hope of acquiring additional information or useful inputs. More 'organised' types prefer to have the task completed and the box ticked, even if that precludes the elusive, potentially valuable 'last-minute' intervention anticipated by their 'flexible' counterparts.

These two types frequently clash, often bitterly, as they interfere with each other's valued work practices, one favouring order and closure, the other espousing quantity and open-endedness.

The extrovert's exuberance and lack of reserve, too, will cause the introvert embarrassment, while the introvert's tendency to think before talking will slow the debate to levels that bewilder and frustrate the extrovert. Curiously, in another setting, such as social encounters, the extrovert and the introvert will suit each other, with one talking and one listening. In this sense, opposites attract, initially. The problem arises later on, when differences in fundamental values become more marked. For example, the 'strictly business' approach will chafe against some people's values, or incessant blue-sky thinking will appear as half-baked nonsense to the practical person. To avoid these clashes, one might be tempted to have only identical types work together, but this will lack the requisite variety needed for optimum results, or encourage group-think.

It should be noted that there are, of course, degrees along the spectrum for each trait, and a person could be, for example, a very moderate extrovert. Therefore, it is important not to see this as a bi-polar (either–or) categorisation but as relative preferences along the spectrum.

Compiling the Personality Profile: a Practical Approach

Forming a picture of a person's personality involves knitting together the four personality layers, as outlined above, to produce a composite representation. Consider the contrast between David and Mary in the following example

TYPES: THE ACCOUNTANT AND THE MARKETER

David works in the Finance Department. He is an accountant, clever and highly trained, and prides himself on his considered, careful approach. He likes to deal only in observable facts, and has little tolerance for conjecture or speculation or indeed unproven ideas. For him, the numbers are real, not just representations of reality. He holds a deep conviction that any capable business person should be able to interpret these numbers. He believes, unsurprisingly, that decisions should be made strictly on the basis of their impact on the numbers: things that cannot be counted should not count.

David likes his accounts to be timely and, above all, accurate. He is not inclined, by training or disposition, to seek novelty in their preparation or presentation. In speech, he is measured, and certainly not effusive or 'prattling'.

He is also a dedicated guardian of 'proper behaviour' and becomes animated if others transgress the accepted code of behaviour.

Mary, by contrast, is in Marketing, and revels in novelty and diversity. New possibilities have her in thrall. Charming her clients is an expected part of her repertoire. She habitually talks to people when she is thinking, and runs ideas past a few colleagues, checking their reaction. She knows that decisions only succeed and get implemented if people are consulted and considered. As a typical extrovert, Mary doesn't know what she thinks until she hears herself talk!

David and Mary are as different as chalk and cheese. They regard each other with fascination and horror, simultaneously admiring each other's capabilities in areas that they cannot countenance, yet appalled at the other's insensitivity or, alternatively, softness. David abhors Mary's giddiness, while she feels only his sullen reticence. One seems daft, the other dull.

These differences matter and can lead to conflict if not managed. For instance, on one occasion Mary received a call from a customer, went into a flap and dashed into David, pouring out the problems to him while he sat there, digesting the torrent of disjointed information and trying to compose a measured response. The pause nonplussed Mary, who took it as indifference, and stormed off to relate the issue to someone else who might care more.

David couldn't understand why Mary stormed off but nonetheless continued to work on the customer's problem, eventually getting at the facts. With a solution in mind, he e-mailed Mary, who received the mail with incredulity, bewildered that he hadn't the sense – or manners – to talk to her but instead sent a dry, factual e-mail.

Each person operated correctly, according to their nature, but they might as well have been on different planets with incompatible languages and beliefs. This is the tragedy of human interaction: we need the skills and perspectives of both Mary and David, but they seem divided by a common language.

Mapping their respective personalities, David was introverted, practical, objective and closed, whereas Mary was more extroverted, abstract, subjective and flexible, as shown below:

Personality Dimension	David	Mary
Source of Ideas	Introvert	Extrovert
Information	Grounded, practical	Abstract
Decision-making	Business, objective	People
Task flexibility	Closed	Flexible

For the organisation to benefit from having both sets of preferences, the potential of each must be cultivated. Each has strengths and weaknesses. One is outgoing and forward-looking, the other more reflective and careful. Each of them sees the world through different lenses, seeming to look through opposite ends of the telescope, David noticing the detail first, Mary seeing the generality. David wants to come to a timely conclusion, while Mary hopes that keeping matters open allows fresh information to be brought to bear.

Dealing with Different Personalities

Each personality type has its merits and, as demonstrated by the world-renowned researcher Dr Meredith Belbin,[2] a team or organisation comprised exclusively of one type or the other would be massively under-equipped to deal with complex questions or tasks. How, then, can one actually learn to manage or reconcile such contrasting personality types?

First, recognise – and appreciate – the differences. Opposites attract, they say. This may well be true, at least initially, because of the fascination they have for their diametric opposite, and this provides a basis for the understanding of each other at the cognitive (thinking) level.

However, opposite types eventually run into conflict when they have to combine their talents, and their natural tendencies then swamp their ability to recognise each other's native strengths; strong emotions can easily submerge cognitive ability. Avoiding this reversion to 'type' is the secret to recognising the sources of conflict before a vicious spiral erupts. The extrovert needs to remember the introvert's need to reflect and contemplate; the introvert needs to recognise the extrovert's search for stimulation and propensity for action.

Secondly, play to team members' characteristics, putting each of them in the right role, setting appropriate expectations about how they might interact, previewing the likely pitfalls and highlighting the value of each type.

Thirdly, provide clear, early communication – it is vital to understanding and collaboration. Different personality types need to express their individual needs to ensure a successful working relationship. If a well-organised, structured manager is working with a more spontaneous, open-ended decision-maker, he should, for example, clarify from the outset his requirement for regular updates on key milestones.

Clashes happen at the interfaces of personality. They can lead to severe irritation and misunderstanding, even though the differences are easily understood.

Dealing with Difficulties Arising from Differences in the Second Layer of Personality: A Basis for Gathering Information

The second layer in which people think top-down (abstractly) or bottom-up (concretely) are internal thinking styles. These lend themselves less to conflict but they can still prove frustrating, as one type can seem a chronic idea-killer and the other a perpetual 'idea-monger'. However, both are useful when paired, as one critiques the other's ideas for practicality. Note that the realist can, of course, innovate and imagine possibilities, but in a different way from the big-picture thinking of the more intuitive, abstract thinker.

As an example of unintended conflict between two well-intentioned types that were operating out of different sides of this information-processing divide, take the case of George and Michelle. George had lit upon a wonderful blue-sky opportunity, 'far out there', but exhilarating, if somewhat vague and possibly impractical. He was savouring the moment; he could sense the possibilities, and he was thrilled. He 'knew' that this blue-sky conjecture was impractical, but he also knew that it would kick-start more pragmatic spin-offs. Michelle, by contrast, was worried. All this conjecture, she feared, could only end in disappointment: the ideas lay far in the future, and today's problems were more pressing. She felt she simply had to drag George off his cloud and bring him back down to earth. How can we embark on a bright new future, she thought, when we don't even have a good filing system? How, she felt, could she explain this grand new plan to her staff, when they couldn't even get the stationery cupboard sorted?

Dealing with Difficulties Arising from the Third Layer of Personality: the Basis for Drawing Conclusions

The third layer's tensions centre on differing values in the basis on which a person comes to conclusions. One gives precedence to feelings (e.g. the effect of decisions on people) and the other to rational 'business-like' decisions. The 'business-focused' person has a task focus, while the other has more of a people focus. The latter has a greater ability, by virtue of their empathy, to influence people and lead a change campaign, while the task-focused, rational, business type's directness can alienate people undergoing the stress of change, even if that change is positive. (British theologian Richard Hooker declared that "change is not made without inconvenience, even from worse to better".)

This third layer of personality is potentially deeply contentious, as it strikes at core values: the 'rational' type will offend the more humanist person's preference for consideration of people, while the rational type will be bemused by their 'soft' subjectivity, which, they fear, will lead to even greater problems downstream. For example, the stereotypical accountant might decide that it was in the best interests of the company (staff included) to reduce the payroll by 20% on a strictly-business basis; the 'people-oriented' types would have greater concern for personal circumstances and individual considerations. Each could potentially be inflamed by the other's perspectives, whereas a judicious blend of both approaches would be optimal.

Again, raising awareness and signposting differences and respective value contributions can avert descent into cycles of conflict.

The Fourth Layer of Personality: Differences in Coming to Conclusions

Conflict involving the fourth layer of personality can be very destructive, as differences here will interfere with people's working style, their preferred pace of working and their need for conclusiveness and order (versus flexibility). The 'flexible' type believes that the longer spent in teasing out possibilities and developing solutions, right up to the last minute, provides maximum quality, even at the expense of orderliness. The other type believes that if the job is worth doing, it is worth doing early and getting it boxed off – better a good answer today than a great answer tomorrow. The 'flexible' one is seen as chaotic, while the 'organised' one is characterised as a rigid 'box-ticker'.

As each acts against the other's instincts and values, the resulting conflict can be bitter and prolonged, especially as it interferes with the orderliness or otherwise of daily working life. The organised person, for instance, who has a defined schedule for work and family life, might take a dim view of the creative type who arrives late and works into the evening.

Both types have merits, with the 'organised' type regarded as more conscientious and commendable. The 'flexible' types can appear to be last-minute charlatans, but are often 'productive procrastinators' as they hold off closure in the expectation that the extra time will yield a better result. The stand-off is essentially between quantity and quality, and while orthodox management will generally reward the organised versus those less so, a more insightful approach, especially in managing professionals, is to appreciate the underlying dynamics and the perpetual striving of the 'disorganised'. In other words, the more driven but less organised types sacrifice order for a greater stream of potentially valuable ideas. Generally, the client would prefer this, while the internal organisation would prefer the more orderly approach.

The example below helps illustrate these points in practice.

SALLY FORTH: THE CASE OF 'THE WOMAN WHO COULD'

Sally was a marketing specialist for a niche business school that had started as a not-for-profit government institute. The business school specialised in upmarket executive education for mid-scale businesses and State agencies.

Popular and dynamic, Sally worked well with clients, understanding their needs and pressure points, and always willing to adapt offerings to suit different industries and diverse organisations. As such, she needed an equally adaptable administrative support and a client-centred culture. Sadly, the organisation was very rigid in its approach and in its inflexible bureaucracy that resented any disruption to its orderly (but ruinous) ritual. New business was welcomed, of course, for the revenues it brought, but resented for its disruption. The old quip, "This would be a great business if it wasn't for the clients", seemed to be actual policy. Sally, as the provider of lucrative but 'disruptive' new business, was derided for working long into the night to meet client deadlines and chastised for not allowing 'enough time' and 'pressuring' staff to compile tender documentation.

While the organisation bled to death financially, the demise was blamed on 'the market'. The bureaucratic box-tickers continued to corral the business-generating 'rain-maker', while they remained unaware of their own part in 'managing' the organisation to near-extinction.

Tell-tale Signs that Reveal a Person's 'Type'

A person cannot deny their nature, and each individual eventually reveals his or her dispositions, usually unknowingly. Some manage to suppress their natural instincts, but these eventually emerge, often in a mid-life crisis, where they seek to be the person they 'truly' are (often with disastrous consequences for those who knew the original presenting personality).

The extrovert will gravitate towards more social activities in their free time and will opt for a more hectic series of interactions. The introvert might opt instead for hill-walking, painting and quiet contemplation, often including philosophy and history.

The big-picture thinker will invariably seek possibilities, linking different scenarios, anticipating future possibilities, whereas the more grounded will seek out facts and test the practicality of suggestions. An example of a 'practical' man placed in a scenario demanding a person of imagination is Karl Pilkington in the TV show *An Idiot Abroad*, where a reluctant Karl is plunged into exotic locations, and can only see the practical details, such as the discomfort, but not the romance of the Taj Mahal or the Pyramids.

The big-picture person can hardly stem the flow of connecting ideas, while the little-picture type cannot resist grounding possibilities in 'here-and-now' reality. The former is inclined to say, "wouldn't it be great if ...", while the latter say, "yes, but ... the plain facts are ...".

The third level of personality – business or feeling – reflects an orientation that is hard to disguise or suppress. The feeling person surrounds themselves with personal artefacts, mementoes, intimate bric-a-brac, while the 'business'-minded one eschews what they see as affectation and frippery.

The fourth and final level – flexible or organised – is characterised by the productive chaos born of pursuing multiple objectives versus the neat singularity of maintaining orderliness. One has an office drowned in happy haphazardness; the other has carefully annotated box-folders impeccably arranged. One has the ducks aligned in a row, while the other just might conjure a moment of genius out of the chaos. The virtue of orderliness meets the siren of serendipity, quite visibly.

'Big 5' Personality Factors

A disadvantage of the classic personality profilers, such as the Myers–Briggs Type Indicator, is their complexity: the number of factors used can serve to confuse, the terms require explanation and the 'types' are hard to remember. Starting with US Air Force researchers in the 1960s, later researchers such as Paul Costa and Robert McCrae in 1985[3] deduced that just five 'big' factors (clusters of traits) were sufficient to profile most personalities.

Additionally, certain IT communities in the US began to favour this 'five-factor' model as being sounder and more understandable. The 'Big 5 Factors' are consistent across cultures and contexts, and use more commonplace terms.

The Big 5 research also indicated that while much of one's personality is inherited ('nature'), as much as half is determined by one's life experiences ('nurture'). Naturally, early childhood experiences have a marked effect, but it has been shown that one can develop personality aspects later in life. Richard Branson, head of Virgin, and seemingly a natural-born extrovert, was continually obliged by his mother to seek out new experiences and to project himself. As a businessman, he still "gets a knot in his stomach" when he is performing some of his more outrageous publicity stunts in promoting his Virgin companies. The message, therefore, is that not only can a person self-develop, but managers can help professionals to add extrovert and other dimensions to their personalities.

The **personality traits** used in the five factor model are:

- Extroversion
- Agreeableness
- Conscientiousness
- Neuroticism, and
- Openness to experience.

While the descriptors used in the Big 5 model are intended to be more understandable than the Myers–Briggs Type Indicator terms, they still need some explanation: neuroticism may better be understood as a 'confidence' dimension, with confidence on one end and sensitivity on the other end of the spectrum.

Similarly, conscientiousness is intended to convey an attention to detail: the opposite is not sloppiness, but creativity (see the table below).

The positive or negative associations that these words have in everyday language are not intended to be pejorative. For instance, 'agreeableness' is usually an advantage in achieving popularity (and few would opt to be socially 'disagreeable'). Agreeableness, however, may not be helpful in situations that require tough or objective decisions.

Furthermore, the terms are not meant to be bipolar: 'disagreeableness' in this sense is not the polar opposite of agreeableness – they are just relative places on a scale. 'Disagreeable' people can make excellent technologists, judges or critics. The five traits in themselves are not positive or negative, but merely characteristics that people have to a greater or lesser extent. Noted psychologist Paul Sinclair[4] suggests the following dimensions to reflect the spectrums involved:

INTERPRETING THE BIG 5 DIMENSIONS – COMMON TERMS

Big 5 Dimension	Equivalent common term – one end of the spectrum	Equivalent common term – other end of the spectrum
Openness to experience	Creative	Conforming
Conscientiousness	Detail-conscious	Unstructured
Extroversion	Extroversion	Introversion
Agreeableness	Agreeable	Tough-minded
Neuroticism	Confidence	Sensitive

Each of these Big 5 personality traits are 'relative' terms, i.e. relative in degree, as compared to other people: everyone has all five of these traits to a greater or lesser degree. For example, two individuals could be described as 'agreeable' but could differ substantially in the relative degree of their 'agreeableness'.

Extroversion

Extroversion is characterised by pronounced engagement with the external world: gregariousness, energy and positive disposition. Extroverts tend to be enthusiastic, action-oriented, seeking excitement. They like to talk and to assert themselves.

Introverts show less obvious enthusiasm and action-orientation, are inward-focused, less impulsive and socially withdrawn. This is neither shyness nor depression, but reflects their relatively low need for stimulation. While their reserve is often mistaken for unfriendliness, an introvert who scores high on 'agreeableness' will be inclined to be pleasant when approached (even though they usually won't initiate such an engagement).

Agreeableness

Agreeable individuals value social harmony and are consequently more considerate, friendly, generous, helpful and willing to compromise. They also have a positive view of human nature, believing people to be honest, decent and trustworthy by nature.

Disagreeable individuals are more sceptical and suspicious, less concerned with others' well-being, and more inclined to be unco-operative.

Conscientiousness

Conscientiousness concerns both a regard for detail and an ability to regulate destructive impulses. Impulsive behaviour, even when not seriously destructive, diminishes a person's effectiveness in significant ways. Acting impulsively disallows contemplating alternative courses of action, some of which would have been wiser than the impulsive choice. Impulsivity also sidetracks people during projects that require organised sequences of steps or stages. The accomplishments of an impulsive person therefore tend to be small, scattered and inconsistent.

A hallmark of intelligence is the capacity to think through future consequences before acting. Intelligence involves consideration of long-range goals, and planning means to achieve them, declining the pleasure of short-term impulses. The term 'prudence' captures the twin elements of being both wise and cautious. Conscientious types can also be perfectionists and workaholics – 'stuffy' and stultifying. Less conscientious types, though, are often regarded as unreliable and erratic.

Neuroticism

Neuroticism, as understood here, is the tendency to experience negative feelings, such as anxiety, anger or depression. Neurotic behaviour involves relatively intense emotional reaction, regarding ordinary situations as threatening, and minor frustrations as hopelessly difficult. The reactions of such people tend to persist, meaning that they are in bad moods for longer. This reduces their ability to make decisions well, think clearly and manage stress.

Individuals who are lower in neuroticism tend to be more even, calm, stable, with less persistent negative feelings. This does not necessarily mean that they experience a lot of positive feelings, which is an element of extroversion.

Openness to Experience

Openness to experience is a dimension of thinking that distinguishes those open to new experiences from those more pragmatic, down-to-earth people. These 'open' people are intellectually curious, appreciative of art and sensitive to beauty; they tend to be more aware of their feelings and to act in individualistic and nonconforming ways. Intellectuals score high on this factor, being more open to experience new ideas. Incidentally, this is only moderately related to years of education and IQ scores.

A characteristic of the open cognitive style is a capability for abstract thinking and conceptualisation. This manifests itself as logical or mathematical thinking, facility with metaphor, music composition or the visual arts. Those scoring low on openness to experience prefer the plain and obvious over the complex and subtle, regarding the arts and sciences as abstruse or of no practical value. Closed people prefer familiarity over novelty. They favour the status quo and are disinclined to initiate changes in, for instance, work practices.

The intellectual style of the open person may serve well in strategy formation or in academic pursuits, but 'closed' thinking produces superior job performance in dealing with more practical occupations.

The table below provides more descriptors associated with each of the Big 5 dimensions of personality. For example, the term 'neuroticism' is expanded to show its sub-facets, such as anxiety, anger or self-consciousness.

BIG 5 DIMENSIONS – EXPANDED

Personality Trait	Facets
Extroversion	Friendliness Gregariousness Assertiveness Activity Level Excitement-seeking Cheerfulness

(Continued)

Personality Trait	Facets
Agreeableness	Trust Morality Altruism Co-operation Modesty Sympathy
Conscientiousness	Self-efficacy Orderliness Dutifulness Achievement-striving Self-discipline Cautiousness
Neuroticism	Anxiety Anger Depression Self-consciousness Immoderation Vulnerability
Openness to Experience	Imagination Artistic Interests Emotionality Adventurousness Intellect Liberalism

These personality traits are like two sides of the same coin: any dimension taken to excess, in either direction, is usually problematic. Agreeableness, for example, in excess can become submissiveness, while the contending opposite to such agreeableness can be argumentativeness. Conscientiousness can become excessive micro-managing on the one hand, and sloppiness on the other. Openness can become unfocused, while at the other end of the spectrum is closed-mindedness. The need for stability can become uninspired, overly calm behaviour, or alternatively can be excitability. The extrovert can be overwhelming, while the introvert may seem self-absorbed.

The poles of the Big 5 dimensions are captured in the table below, along with some counter-measures to avoid excessive use of these behaviours.

DEALING WITH EXCESSES IN BEHAVIOURAL STYLE

Big 5 Dimension	Behaviour in excess	Effect	Counter-measures
Openness+	Too innovative	Unsettling	Ration your creativity; stick with key points
	Too orthodox	Risk averse	Try something new daily
Conscientiousness+	Too thorough	Micro-managing	Ask, don't tell. Delegate. Relax.
	Too decided	Hasty	Check facts. Consult others.
Extroversion+	Too assertive	Domineering	Listen. Slow down. Respect others
	Too inward	Stony, mute	Engage with people in bursts
Agreeableness+	Too considerate	Naïve, weak	Don't seek to be liked but respected
	Too competitive	Argumentative	Compete well – without conflict
Neuroticism+	Too explosive	Short-tempered	Pre-empt anger, express feelings
	Too calm	Unrealistic	Recognise risks, downsides

The value of the 'Big 5' personality trait approach is that it simplifies the profiling of an individual. While the terms used still need interpretation, the terms have the advantage of being in common use. Finally, the reduction of factors to just five clusters makes it easier to remember and to apply in practice, and for these reasons use of the Big 5 approach is becoming more prevalent.

Introduction to Types in Professionals

Even when condensed into the Big 5 dimensions, it is still difficult to form a composite 'picture' of a professional's personality. David Keirsey, an originator of modern personality assessment methods, uses a simple matrix to help appreciate the differences between work 'types', as shown below, where he uses evocative terms such as 'artisan' or 'idealist' to denote the distinctive types:

KEIRSEY'S OCCUPATIONAL TYPES[5]

Artisan says what is, does what works	Rationalist says what's possible, does what works
Guardian says what is, does what's right	**Idealist** says what's possible, does what's right

On this grid, one could say that the stereotypical accountant might fit the 'Guardian' box, for example, saying what the actual situation is and doing what's correct and proper.

The 'Idealist' is inclined to explore possibilities to a greater degree, while the 'Artisan' works like a craftsman, shaping the material at hand. Relating this to the personality models we have introduced and discussed above, the 'Guardian' favours sensing facts and 'judging' ('organising', 'bringing to a conclusion' are more meaningful and accurate terms than the misleading term 'judging'). The stereotype of the accountant, with the ability to be immersed in rule-based systems and set procedures, matches this 'Sensing-Judging' (SJ)/ 'Guardian' type.

PSYCHOLOGICAL TYPES AND OCCUPATIONS

ARTISAN	Grounded, Flexible and	RATIONAL	Abstract thinker, Rational and ....
Promoter	Extroverted, rational	Field-marshal	Extroverted, organised
Crafter	Introverted, rational	Mastermind	Introverted, organised
Performer	Extroverted, people	Inventor	Extroverted, flexible
Composer	Introverted, people	Architect	Introverted, flexible
GUARDIAN	**Grounded,** **Organised and ...**	**IDEALIST**	**Abstract thinker,** **People-oriented** **and ...**
Supervisor	Extroverted, Rational	Teacher	Extroverted, organised
Inspector	Introverted, Rational	Counsellor/Guide	Introverted, organised
Provider	Extroverted, People	Champion	Extroverted, flexible
Protector	Introverted, People	Healer	Introverted, flexible

Nobody is exclusively just one temperament or type. Every individual, however, will have a preference for one type and will have a principal style, augmented by a mixture of some of the other types. Different people possess differing combinations of these 'preferences'. The challenge is to be aware and appreciative of the differences between people; just as there is no justification for a bias against left- or right-handed people, there is no reason to infer that 'sensing' (concrete) thinkers are better or worse than their abstract 'intuitive' counterparts. It is clear, however, that different types suit different occupations, and a misalignment will eventually make the person weary and out-of-sorts. For such reasons, many misaligned professionals seek a change from their original occupation. This is particularly true if their calling is towards the artistic or caring occupations, and this can prompt a mid-life crisis as the person seeks to become the person they were 'really' meant to be.

Developing a Range of Styles

Carl Jung believed strongly that individuals had psychological preferences, not fixed inherent traits. He believed, for example, that an extrovert could access introversion through awareness and practice. He believed that a person with a preference for 'perceiving' (leaving matters open-ended) could adopt a 'judging' (organising, concluding) orientation by being more systematic, by breaking tasks into chunks and by creating artificially early deadlines to promote closure. Similarly, the 'judging' type could avoid premature closure by appreciating the extra quality to be gained by leaving a window open to new ideas or additional information.

The tendency to introversion can be offset by repeated practice at social engagement, networking, public speaking, exposure to events, spontaneous brainstorming or a focus on go-getting. Conversely, the extrovert can limit the tendency to spontaneity and excitement by listening more, respecting silences and observing social protocols more closely.

The empathy characteristic of 'feeling' types can be appreciated by exposure to others perhaps less fortunate, by role-sharing and by realising that life is by, for and about people. While for the 'feeler', facts are subjective, the feeler is better at anticipating and dealing with people's reactions. This makes them more adroit at influencing people, developing commitment and personal loyalty and ultimately better at managing transformation.

The 'thinking' preference can be developed by training (e.g. in problem-solving, determining cause and effect, decision-making, investment appraisal) and immersion in logic and systems thinking.

MEETING(S) OF MINDS?

Meetings are a microcosm of organisational life and can reveal tensions in even this most mundane of settings.

Eddie, a 'thinking' type, came into the meeting, sat down and immediately got on with the task at hand. Fabian, a 'feeler', was miffed, perturbed that his presence was not even acknowledged; after all, he figured, it would only take a minute – if only Eddie cared at all.

A few minutes into the meeting, Sam the 'senser' was becoming fraught at Ina's constant stream of abstract ('unworkable!') ideas. Ina, for her part, couldn't tolerate Sam's slowness, his pedantic need to have a step-by-step approach.

Jill, the 'judging' type, had her files meticulously arranged, colour-coded and cross-referenced: she detested the sloppiness of Peter, with papers scattered over the table, intruding into her space. How, she wondered, could anybody work in such a mess? Peter could only wonder at Jill's ability to keep matters in order, but he despaired at her rigorous attitude to time. Surely, he wondered, she could keep proposals open to the last minute in case he managed to get some game-changing information?

Beneath the veneer of their business attire, each had simmering resentments and festering psychological sores that they would pick over incessantly: Eddie's lack of feeling, Sam's pedantry, Peter's procrastination, Jill's need for order.

Eddie, if he noticed people at all, had scant regard for Fabian's 'soppiness'. Each had difficulty with the other, which limited their regard for each other and reduced their capacity to work together. It was as if they lived in different worlds, or transmitted on incompatible channels. The sources of conflict was deep, as their core values were transgressed, and none of them were aware of these transgressions.

Despite this, the remedies were actually simple, practical and immediate and here are some suggestions for Eddie, Fabian and the others:

- Eddie: practice meeting and greeting people with grace and style – simply say hello, be sure to make eye contact to acknowledge a person's presence. Shake hands with people! Pass out some compliments: it costs almost nothing, just a moment, yet lasts a long while.
- Fabian: use your 'feeling' preference to put yourself in Eddie's place. Realise why Eddie behaves in a particular way. Put your empathy to use to facilitate the meeting and its emotional under-currents.
- Ina: keep generating ideas, but keep them to yourself until you have screened them for impracticality.
- Sam: remember there is nothing as practical as a good theory, and there is more to a situation than just bare facts. Go with the flow for a while, take a step off the beaten path, and enjoy the view of this new landscape.
- Jill: realise that you can't make an omelette without breaking eggs. Peter's tolerance for messiness allows him to come up with wonderful concoctions.

- Peter: just get a folder and put your papers there; keep your coffee mug to one side. Pretend the deadline is earlier than it really is, and get those proposals to Jill way ahead of time. Don't worry if they might get better, given time. Break the work into bite-sized chunks, and have those ready for delivery in advance.

WHAT'S THE PROBLEM HERE? THE EXTROVERT MEETS THE INTROVERT

Extroverted Len found a problem with the new prototype, and rushed to introverted Ida with it, animatedly wondering what had happened, speculating on the likely dire consequences, wondering who he should tell and crying out for attention. Ida pondered the situation impassively, contemplating the facts and inwardly processing the information. With no solution forthcoming, and apparently no response from Ida, Len dashed out. He quickly embroiled half a dozen others in the unfolding drama.

Going back to his office, Len just had to chat with a few close associates, and almost forgot the problem. When he finally got to his desk, he noticed that Ida had e-mailed him, looking for more information. Len was infuriated: he felt that she could at least have come to talk to him, rather than sending just an e-mail, calmly – coldly! – requesting further information. Didn't Ida care at all? Why didn't he get up and go solve the problem? For her part, Ida was bemused at all the drama, and resented Len's intrusion on her personal space: why didn't Len just think before reacting, she wondered to herself?

In this example, the extrovert and introvert have different *modus operandi*, and each annoys the other, unwittingly. To improve matters, Len should take a moment, breathe deeply, think, and stop the crisis becoming a drama. Ida needs to wake up to Len's need to talk things through and to see some action. Ida should take the analytical role in solving the problem, and Len should take the action role. Each to their own, and two heads are better than one – but only if they are managed right.

Becoming More Effective by Extending your Range of Styles

Most people can adapt their styles according to different situations. The ability to adapt or bring into play different personal styles in response to different situations is arguably the most powerful capability that anyone, especially a manager of people, can possess. Understanding personality models such as the Four Temperaments is therefore of direct help in achieving such personal awareness and adaptability. Understanding personality helps you recognise behaviour and type in others – and in yourself. Recognising behaviour is an obvious prerequisite for adapting behaviour – in you, and in helping others to adapt too.

Matching the Four Temperaments to Modern Personality Types

Hans Eysenck, the eminent and controversial psychologist, used the ancient temperaments, with their colourful terms, as a basis for understanding personality types.[6] He regarded the **choleric** and **melancholic** temperaments as being **unstable** ('**emotional**'), and the **sanguine** and **phlegmatic** temperaments as being **stable** ('**unemotional**').

Eysenck's theory sees the **phlegmatic** and **melancholic** temperaments as being **introverted**, and the **choleric** and **sanguine** temperaments as being extroverted. The Eysenck theory therefore produces four main types of personality, resembling the Four Temperaments:

1. **Melancholic**: unstable-introverted (emotional–introverted)
2. **Choleric**: unstable-extroverted (emotional–extroverted)
3. **Phlegmatic**: stable-introverted (unemotional–introverted)
4. **Sanguine**: stable-extroverted (unemotional-extroverted).

Expanding Eysenck's types provides everyday descriptors of people's personalities:

EYSENCK'S PERSONALITY TYPES

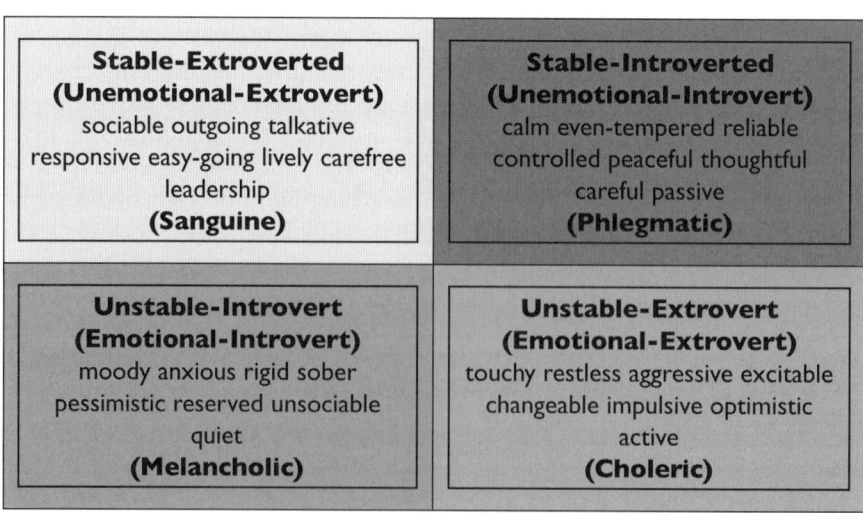

Stable-Extroverted **(Unemotional-Extrovert)** sociable outgoing talkative responsive easy-going lively carefree leadership **(Sanguine)**	**Stable-Introverted** **(Unemotional-Introvert)** calm even-tempered reliable controlled peaceful thoughtful careful passive **(Phlegmatic)**
Unstable-Introvert **(Emotional-Introvert)** moody anxious rigid sober pessimistic reserved unsociable quiet **(Melancholic)**	**Unstable-Extrovert** **(Emotional-Extrovert)** touchy restless aggressive excitable changeable impulsive optimistic active **(Choleric)**

While the fit between this model and the Four Temperaments is not precise, these classic types help develop insight into the behaviours of different individuals.

Eysenck's terms are evident in the DISC personality testing system (a simpler but less fundamental model than Myers–Briggs Types, as explained below) and relate back to the Four Temperaments.

The DISC Personality Model

The DISC model of personality assessment was developed by Dr W.M. Marston around the same time as Myers–Briggs were developing Jung's ideas into their assessment model.[7] The DISC model is relatively simple, with fewer questions needed to produce a profile.

The advantage of DISC is its relative simplicity, especially in understanding how different types of people will typically respond when under stress, as often happens in conflict situations. Indeed, the DISC model predicts emotional responses when the 'difficult' person is put under more extreme stress, i.e. is put under duress.

The DISC model presents four main 'type' descriptions (Dominance, Influence, Steadiness and Compliance). DISC attempts to identify people's dominant or preferred type, plus one or more supporting types. The main motivating force in each of the four types differ as follows:

- the **D**ominant type is motivated by achievement and responsibility, and seeks to lead;
- the **I**nfluencer is driven by recognition and personal approval, and seeks to motivate others;
- the **S**teady type seeks time and space to do things properly, according to a process;
- the **C**ompliant type is motivated by the search for detailed perfection.

DISC BASIC PERSONALITY TYPES MODEL

Dominant	Influencer	Steady	Compliant
Motivated by responsibility and achievement	Motivated by recognition and personal approval	Motivated by time and space to do things properly	Motivated by attention to detail, perfection and truth

The four different types deliver best results when the emotional environment matches their motivational drive, e.g. the Dominant works best when leading, and abhors being told what to do. Interestingly, this includes setting challenges for the Dominant – and allowing the Dominant set the pace. The Dominant can also be a powerful agent of change, pushing tasks through: the significant downside is that the push for achievement can overspill into bullying behaviour through insufficient regard for others, with likely push-back from those affected.

The Fear Factors: Negative Aspects of Each of the Four Types

Each of the four types has an inescapable 'shadow side', a stereotypical fear factor that influences their responses:

- the Dominant fears failure and loss of power;
- the Influencer fears rejection and loss of reputation;
- the Steady type fears insecurity and change;
- the Compliance-oriented type fears inaccuracy and unpredictability.

UNDERLYING FEAR FACTORS OF THE FOUR DISC TYPES

D	I	S	C
Fears failure and loss of power	Fears rejection and loss of reputation	Fears insecurity and change	Fears inaccuracy and unpredictability

The DISC model is therefore very useful in understanding – and anticipating – the typical reactions of each of the four types. For example, the Dominant type will classically sulk if he does not get his own way. If pushed further (from this 'stress' into 'distress'), it is likely that the Dominant will seek to restore himself to prominence, even to the extent of sabotaging the 'offender's' efforts. The Dominant type perceives the world as unfavourable and potentially hostile. He or she seeks to overcome his or her environment and, when pushed, will retreat into a passive-aggressive sulk. When pushed further, this sulk will give way to sabotage, such as the undermining of the task or project at hand.

Managing Smart People and Other Professionals using the DISC Model

Your leadership style, communication style and even parenting style are heavily influenced by your personality type and, of course, the same is true for all others. How you communicate with people, form relationships or even network at meetings depends on the interaction between your style and the style of others. These differences can get in the way of communication and understanding. By having a lens to understand these differences, you can work with people much more effectively. This is what the 'DISC' human behaviour model does: it provides a simple but effective framework for understanding people better.

For example, imagine you have spent the last seven years honing your accounting or technical skills, and now you have finally made it – you got the promotion to manager, with some perks, a better job title and higher pay grade.

With it, however, come bigger, less malleable problems – people! Modesty aside, you're the best in the department; you know your stuff and you have attended some management courses. People problems should be easy for you ... but the business development manager frustrates you because she "never gets the details". The administrative assistants irritate you by talking about personal issues. The service people cost your firm money because they simply won't say "no" to customers. These represent some of the contending opposites in mindset; the 'conflicting paradigms' or lenses through which different types see the world. Each of us interprets the world differently because of our lens, our different perspective or our different starting-points. Because these are taken-for-granted assumptions, each acts on their own paradigm, essentially unaware of their paradigm. Conflict arises when the contending world views collide, or where the planets simply pass each other by.

The people problems 'technical' people face as managers tend to be somewhat predictable. Professionals in highly specialised fields, like engineering, medicine or accounting, often see the world through a common filter. Crucially, they often expect other people to show the same precision their profession demands. The potential *tragedy* (i.e. when a small flaw produces a huge effect) is that what made them good accountants or engineers may well be the hidden barriers to further success: their blindness to other paradigms, and unthinking adherence to their own paradigm may cause them to fall into the rift between the two.

As a *manager*, people skills – and especially the inclination and ability to see the other person's point of view – are more significant than specialist technical skills.

The Unconscious Nature of Behaviour

People go about their business trying to fulfil their own needs (social, physical, psychological) with, understandably, scarcely any conscious consideration of your needs. That does not mean people are perpetually heedless or inconsiderate, just that their focus is naturally on themselves and their own needs: they simply do not have any real consciousness about your needs.

This unconsciousness (like paradigm blindness) often leads to your own needs as a person being unmet. These unmet needs are often behind serious frustration, evident in such common complaints as:

- "They just dawdle along/they talk far too fast!"
- "They jump straight to conclusions/they never get to the point!"
- "They worry and fret too much about the petty details."
- "They spend too much/little time talking with other people."

The DISC model captures these contentions, showing fast-paced people on opposite sides to slower types, and people-oriented types opposite to task-focused types:

THE **DISC** MODEL OF PERSONALITY

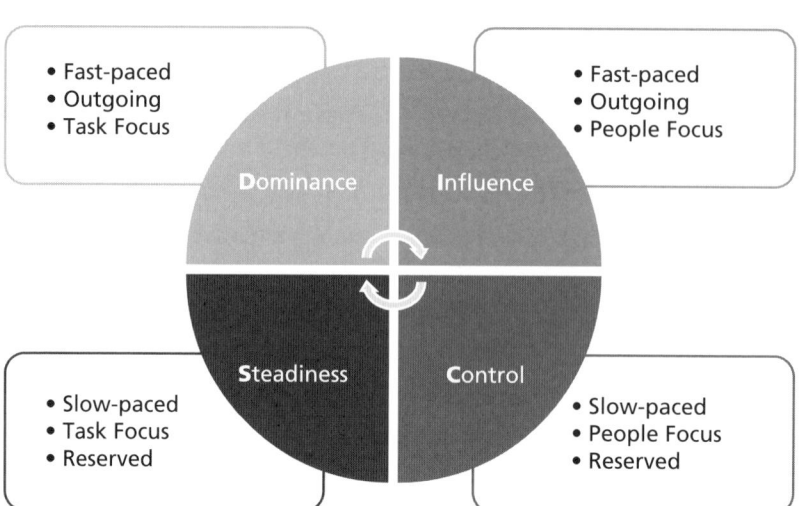

- Fast-paced
- Outgoing
- Task Focus

Dominance

- Fast-paced
- Outgoing
- People Focus

Influence

Steadiness

- Slow-paced
- Task Focus
- Reserved

Control

- Slow-paced
- People Focus
- Reserved

(**Note***: the complaints listed above all originate from the complainer's side, showing the speaker's perspective. Importantly, they all indicate an unmet need or violated expectation.*)

By taking the trouble to see the world through the other person's eyes, you will be able to see – and avoid – sources of conflict and to develop empathy by 'standing in their shoes' for a moment. Consider this expenditure of time as an investment: just as one has to make a bank deposit before one can withdraw funds, good relationships depend on someone making the initial commitment.

While everybody has their own natural style, the best people managers have more than one single style. They have a broad enough range of styles to allow them adopt the most suitable style for the situation and the personalities involved. In other words, good managers understand where the other person (such as a disgruntled employee) is coming from. They understand the style of the other person in, for example, approaching a task; whether it will be 'strictly business' or 'fun'. They flex their style to achieve better rapport and more common ground as a starting-point. They can predict what will be the irritators for the different types: a fast pace will upset the more analytical types (but please the dominant types). A very people-orientated approach will suit the steady types (but irritate the task-focused dominant types).

It is important to recognise that we cannot really change other people; we can only modify our own behaviour. While we might influence others' overt behaviours, we cannot change their fundamental needs. This means that we can only influence others by adapting our own behaviours to best fit the situation. This has the very important benefit of reducing conflict and encouraging collaboration, while producing satisfactory results through people (the true job of the manager).

Understanding the DISC Model

People have deeply ingrained beliefs and patterns that shape what they do, from how they approach problems at work, to how they drive a car. So much is based on behavioural style; the dominant person will drive differently from a more compliant person.

For example, people who choose a technical profession tend to have a very analytical, task-oriented approach to life. The choice of vocation is often an expression of personality as much as anything else. They often see life as a collection of problems that need to be solved – a disorder that needs to be organised. (It is probably one of the reasons that my management institute is populated with former engineers, who feel they can crack the insoluble, situational problems of management!) Other equally intelligent and capable people, on the other hand, see life as a series of potentially stimulating inter-actions with other people.

The Four Worlds in the DISC Model

As an initial representation, people can be divided into two worlds or 'halves', as depicted below. The upper half represents outgoing or fast-paced people. The lower half represents reserved or slower-paced people. Outgoing people tend to move fast, talk fast and decide fast. Reserved people tend to speak more slowly and softer than outgoing people and they generally prefer to consider things thoroughly before making a decision.

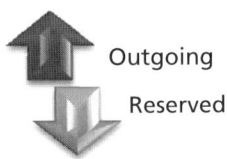

Outgoing

Reserved

This 'world' can also be divided in another way: the left half represents task-oriented people. The right half represents people-oriented people. Task-oriented people tend to focus on logic, data, results and projects. People-oriented people tend to focus on experiences, feelings, relationships and interactions with other people.

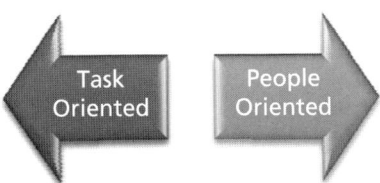

Task Oriented   People Oriented

Summarised below are the main features of each of the four DISC types, present-ing a brief pen picture of each. In understanding people's different orientations, the manager can better understand (and deal with) the latent sources of person-ality-based conflict. There can be many ironies in these personality clashes; active types (such as the dominant) can bring great energy to a situation, but are also likely to irritate their less active colleagues and thereby require the involvement of the manager in resolving personnel issues.

SUMMARY OF DISC TYPES AND UNDERLYING BELIEFS

D individuals are outgoing and task-oriented. They tend to be *Dominant* and *Decisive*. They usually focus on results and the bottom-line. Their underlying belief is that the environment is unfavourable and that they must strive to overcome it.

I individuals are outgoing and people-oriented. They tend to be *Inspiring* and *Influencing*. They usually focus on talking and having fun. Their underlying belief is that the environment is bountiful, offering opportunities for excitement.

S individuals are reserved and people-oriented. They tend to be *Supportive* and *Steady*. They usually focus on peace and harmony. Their underlying belief is that the environment is bountiful, and must not be put at risk.

C individuals are reserved and task-oriented. They tend to be *Cautious* and *Conscientious*. They usually focus on analysis, facts and rules. Their underlying belief is that the environment is unfavourable and must be controlled.

The DISC model below now adds some short names to each of the four quadrants to help capture the most salient characteristics. For example, the 'I' (for 'Influence') type can be inspiring. This type is inclined to interact with people, influencing and being influenced.

THE FOUR QUADRANTS OF DISC

- Driver
- Doer

Dominant

- Inspiring
- Interactive

Influence

Control

Steady

- Careful
- Cautious

- Supportive
- Stable

Origins of Personality-based Conflict at Work

Conflict often comes from a clash between such different styles. For example, the fast speech, lack of attention to detail and tendency of an I-type person to speak about feelings rather than facts might frustrate a C-type person, who is cautious and conscientious.

Likewise, the C-type person's slower pace, constant questioning and apparent lack of concern for people could frustrate the I-type person, who is inspiring and influencing.

The table below captures the key preferences, fears, reactions and counter-measures associated with the four DISC types; it can be used to make an initial, provisional analysis of a person and to indicate how best to manage them and, specifically, to find a direction by which to motivate and manage the different types.

KEY ELEMENTS OF DISC TYPES

Type	Dominant	Influencing	Steadiness	Compliant
Name	DIRECTOR	INSPIRER	SUPPORTER	CRITIC
They seek:	Results	Flexibility	Friendliness	Standards
They value:	Action	Options	Harmony	Details
They desire:	Achievement	Recognition	Approval	Consistency
Typically say:	"Here's what should be done"	"How can I help?"	"Reassure me"	"What, when, where, how, who?"
Motivation:	To be challenged	To be recognised	To be stable	To be accurate
They need:	Control, power	Flexibility, options	Time to adjust	Time to analyse
Considered:	Overpowering	Impulsive	Soft	Very quiet
Perceived as:	Intimidating, Alienating	Selfish, Egomaniacal	Vague, Powerless	Indifferent, Passive
They fear:	Being taken advantage of	Low social recognition	Being challenged, Changes	Imperfection, Careless acts
They detest:	Personal criticism	Criticism	Personal rejection	Anger
Traits:	Create results, Take charge, Creates change	Talkative, Enthusiastic, Likes change	Passive, Slow to change, Can help change	Well organised, Detail oriented, Justifies change

(Continued)

Type	Dominant	Influencing	Steadiness	Compliant
Under stress they become:	Openly hostile, Bossy, Aggressive, Loud, Impatient	Gets emotional, Sells too hard, Sees opportunity	Slows more, Sulky, Opts out	Critical, Strict, Wants space
To recover the situation with them	Be specific, Talk about action, Talk about results	Talk about ideas, Use enthusiasm, Listen to them	Talk with them, Pace them, Be empathetic	Be accurate, Show logic, Link steps

Relating DISC to the Four Temperaments

The representation of the DISC model below uses shading and pattern to show the correlations to two of the Four Temperaments and two of Keirsey's occupational main types (D = Phlegmatic/Rational; I = Choleric/Idealist) and the Jungian Extrovert-Introvert 'attitudes'.

D	I	S	C
Dominance	**Influence**	**Steadiness**	**Compliance**
generally proactive and extrovert		generally reactive and introvert	
decisive, dominant, self-assured, forceful, task-oriented, instigates, leads and directs	motivates others via influence and persuasion, good communication skills, presents well, friendly, affable, inspires others, intuitive, gregarious, friendly	dependable, systematic, good listener, friendly, trustworthy, solid, ethical, finishes tasks others leave, methodical	painstaking, investigative, curious, decides using facts and figures, correct, checker, detailed,
Things	People	People	Things
motivated by responsibility and achievement	motivated by recognition and personal approval	motivated by time, space and context to do things properly	motivated by attention to detail, perfection and truth

(Continued)

D	**I**	**S**	**C**
Dominance	**Influence**	**Steadiness**	**Compliance**
strong focus on task and forceful style can upset people	emphasis on image can neglect substance	dependence on process can become resistance	need for perfection can delay or obstruct
fears failure and loss of power	fears rejection and loss of reputation	fears insecurity and change	fears inaccuracy and unpredictability
Intuitive–Thinking	Intuitive–Feeling	Sensing–Feeling	Sensing–Thinking

Dealing with Personality Dysfunction: Managing Difficult People

The above sections are concerned with managing the naturally occurring 'normal' types of people. Many, if not most, people have the added complexity of personality deficiencies (and outright dysfunctions, such as aggression). Managing these 'difficult' people is the focus of the discussion in this section.

People may be born with certain dispositions, as described above, and these are naturally occurring, inevitable and are not to be regarded as being good or bad, *per se*. Some people, however, become difficult because of experiences in childhood or simply because their needs are not being met. Usually, the difficult person is someone who is working from the negative side of their personality, rather than a conscious desire to be difficult. The person is often unaware of themselves and how they affect others. They also do not realise how harmful their actions are to their own success and career prospects.

Some people are quick to anger and take their frustrations out on the nearest person to them. Often, this simply produces a backlash: we then react negatively by taking their anger personally, and become 'difficult' ourselves. In other words, even though we are meant to manage and rise above all this, we have actually become part of the problem.

This stressful type of conflict is rooted in personality and relationships. As well as the natural variations in personality discussed throughout this chapter, the more 'difficult' types have a dysfunctional element, often caused by an over-use of a particular style (e.g. moving from a naturally active dominant style to outright bullying) or by excessive behaviour (such as moving from a detail orientation to obsessive micromanagement). Such dysfunction is often caused by the individual's fear of discovery, e.g. the truculent, irrational objector is perhaps disguising his or her lack of factual objectivity. Similarly, the over-nice person who automatically agrees to every suggestion may be hiding a fear of conflict or an inability to reach decisions. These types can be understood, and managed, by first recognising their type when exaggerated as a caricature, as explained below.

Recognising the Cast of Characters

Sylvia Lafair[8] names the most common dysfunctional 'characters' (familiar to anyone who has ever worked in an office) – these are exaggerations of the basic types discussed throughout this chapter:

1. Super Achiever
2. Rebel
3. Persecutor
4. Victim
5. Rescuer
6. Clown
7. Martyr
8. Splitter
9. Procrastinator
10. Drama Queen/King,
11. Pleaser
12. Denier
13. Avoider.

The 'Super Achiever', for example, is a caricature of the dominant type. The 'Rebel' is another dominant type, but one that exaggerates the independent streak.

Strategies for Dealing with Difficult People

While these 'difficult' people can be maddening, a strategy for dealing with them involves buying time (even just a moment) to analyse their deficiency and to take the right steps in achieving the optimum outcome – one that satisfies your needs with the lowest cost in time and emotional energy. The situation becomes explosive when the irritating behaviour (and/or your response to that) leads to assumptions about deeper values, i.e. when one side or the other infers that the lazy behaviour is characteristic of that person's inherent indolence or sheer fecklessness.

Take the situation where a talented but sullen employee is refusing to talk. To deal with the situation, follow the 'ABCDE' sequence:

A.   Analyse the situation
B.   Behaviour – decide what 'dysfunction' is present.
C.   Consider what it is that he or she is trying to achieve.
D.   Decide your reaction (rather than submit to your impulse).
E.   Execute the corrective steps with deliberation and care.

The 'ABCDE' technique is demonstrated in the following examples:

EXAMPLE 1: THE 'KNOW-IT-ALL' PROFESSIONAL

Symptom: this person knows it all – they don't want you to dare question them.

This symptom will be familiar to anyone managing or dealing with engineers, but many other professionals can share the symptom, such as lawyers, computer programmers, software developers, doctors and accountants.

For instance, we can easily imagine a situation in which an IT professional is asked straightforward questions about the possibility of changing, say, a database report, triggering a reaction like: "How dare you question my professional judgement? How dare you question a person of my experience!"

To deal with the situation, use the **ABCDE** method introduced above:

A. Analyse the situation. This symptom is a sign of insecurity and arrogance, a defence against vulnerability, often learned in childhood when parents criticise a child for not being good enough (see **Chapter 11** on building confidence).

B. Behaviour. This person is anxious, fearful of being seen as incompetent, and instinctively mounts a defensive shield against attack. This artificial defence protects them for a while, but it is obvious to everyone else that it is false.

C. Consider what they are trying to achieve. Such arrogant, defensive people are seeking to preserve credibility and respect. The thing they fear most is loss of respect. Ironically, given their behaviour, people will refuse to deal with them, or won't believe what they say.

D. Decide your reaction. By taking a moment to analyse the situation and the underlying psychology, you are making time to consider your reaction, and to see through the behaviour to the person beneath. It would be easy to shout back, but this would just escalate the situation. Simply withdrawing causes the situation to fester, and makes the next encounter more volatile. Instead, be assertive, not aggressive, and offer initially some words of respect ("I realise you are vastly experienced in this area"), then give them the opportunity to gather their thoughts, as they too will be upset by the encounter ("Perhaps if we could meet tomorrow to explore this further ...?").

E. Execute. Bearing in mind that this was a straightforward request you have made, hold a meeting with the 'difficult' person, keeping it brief and based on facts. When the atmosphere becomes calm enough, do not demand an apology (unless the explosion could be heard all over the office!), but state your need to have such requests dealt with simply, without drama.

EXAMPLE 2: THE OSTRICH – DEALING WITH THE PROFESSIONAL WHO WILL NOT ENGAGE

Symptom: the 'ostrich' who buries his head in the sand, and won't communicate.

In this situation, the professional has buried his head in the sand and can't (or, more likely, won't) communicate. The dilemma for the manager is whether to respect their silence and allow this behaviour or to confront it somehow. Again, analyse the situation and the person: realise that while this reticent, silent behaviour is passive, it is also aggressive. It is not mere bashfulness, in this case, but is actually an active ploy by the 'ostrich' to avoid confrontation. The answer is to calmly request an answer, and wait. Then be prepared to wait some more! (Consider how long a short journey in an elevator seems to take, given that uncomfortable silence.) If this pressure is not sufficient to force a response, then try to talk about the silence itself (not just the original issue at hand). If these 'talks-about-talks' do not produce a result, escalate the matter to disciplinary levels.

Applying the **ABCDE** technique in this situation, the sequence then is:

- **A**nalyse. This person is withholding communication.
- **B**ehaviour. The behaviour appears passive, but is actually aggressive.
- **C**onsider. The person wants you (or the issue) to walk away and leave him be.
- **D**ecide. The person is relatively calm, and is orchestrating a tactical silence. This is not an acceptable manoeuvre, so confront it. Plan to wait, patiently, possibly for a seemingly long while (two minutes of social silence is more than enough).
- **E**xecute. Stay with the plan. If there is no response, move away from the triggering issue, and discuss instead the question of the silence itself. Agree a suitable time and place then to discuss this silence. Be prepared to escalate the matter.

Potential Downsides of Normally Positive Characteristics

Every personality type has its shadow side: for example, a dominant type (using the DISC types outlined above) will be energetic and thrusting, and often will be keen to lead an initiative. The positive side of such dominance is **leadership**. When such a person is working from the positive side of their personality, they can be effective and even charming, but when threatened or even when their advice is not heeded, their instinctual reaction can be to sulk and withdraw their effort. They move from being active contributors to being passive resistors, blocking tasks or resisting changes. If the dominant's sulking does not achieve its intended result (i.e. the restoration to the dominant of his or her power), the next, deeper phase is often sabotage: the dominant will spin out of control, and actively undermine the task or initiative. The dominant will often eventually 'explode'. This may seem to come without warning but one may be able to see the stress building up, if you look for the signs. In the end, that person loses their ability to control events – which, ironically, is what they fear most.

Many dominants are driven to control their environment by becoming prominent business leaders, only to eventually fail if the shadow side of their personality becomes evident through such outbursts. Leaders who allow this shadow side to emerge are often fired publicly, causing them great humiliation and complete loss of control over events. Needless to say, those employees who have been subjected to their tyranny are joyous in celebrating their leader's misfortune.

The effects of and results for domineering people are:

- People will avoid them or refuse to deal with them.
- People will not tell them the truth or provide them with vital information that might help them make better decisions.
- People learn to ignore or discount their opinions or decisions.
- People will avoid implementing their ideas and subvert their authority (consciously or unconsciously).
- Organisations will punish their bad decisions and poor leadership.

TIPS FOR DEALING WITH 'DIFFICULT PEOPLE'

1. When you see someone go into 'attack' mode or excessive defensiveness, recognise that it is useless to argue with them.
2. Realise that the person is feeling very insecure at that time.
3. Don't continue to push them – they will only get worse.
4. If the symptoms only seem to occur when the person is under stress, wait until another time to pursue the discussion.
5. If they are always overly defensive or always attacking others, you may need to find another person to work with who does not have the same problem.
6. Keep your own sense of self-confidence.

TIPS FOR SUPERVISING 'DIFFICULT PEOPLE'

1. Help the person see how badly their negative behaviour is damaging their career potential; they may not realise how detrimental their behaviour actually is.
2. Project-manage the improvement: agree milestones for them to learn how to work better with others and coach them to modify their behaviour.

3. Monitor their behaviour until it is seen to improve.
4. If it does not improve within the agreed time, carry out the sanction, which might include transferring them to other work (if you believe they will benefit from that second chance), otherwise severance may be the final option.

TIPS FOR OVERCOMING NEGATIVE ASPECTS IN YOURSELF WHEN MANAGING OTHERS

1. Learn to recognise when your defensive mechanisms start to come into play.
2. Realise that you are probably not really being personally attacked at all.
3. When you catch yourself feeling defensive, pause before reacting.
4. Learn how to actively listen when someone asks a question or makes a suggestion.
5. If necessary, ask people to re-state their question/comment/suggestion.
6. Confirm if you have understood what others are saying by synopsising what you think you heard.
7. Find someone who can help you work on these aspects of your behaviour.
8. Recognise that changing learned patterns of insecurity may take time and effort.
9. Learn to understand your own personality and your unique strengths and weaknesses.
10. The effort to improve your ability to get along with others will be rewarded as you find more career opportunities open up for you.

The Holland Hexagon: Professions and Personality

> *"The choice of a vocation is an expression of personality."*
>
> John Holland

Psychologist John Holland[9] classified vocational choices according to personality types, arguing that six principal factors could describe essential elements in both persons and work environments. Holland's theory does not assume that a person is just one type or that there are 'only six types of people in the world', but rather that any person could be described as having interests associated with each of the six types in a descending order of preference. While this theoretically leads to a large number (720) of combinations of types, in practice only a person's most dominant codes are used to guide career choices.

GRAPHICAL REPRESENTATION OF HOLLAND'S DOMINANT CODES

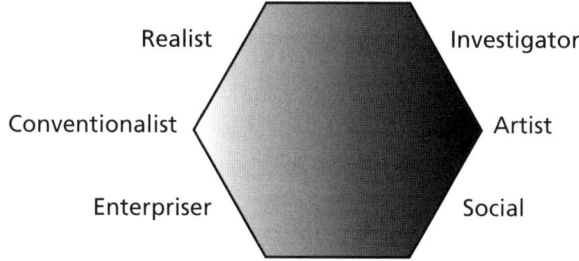

As shown above, Holland graphically represented the six types in a hexagon to describe the relations between the types; the shorter the distance between their corners on the hexagon, the more closely the types are related. The six personality and work environment types described by Holland are as follows:

- Realistic – practical, physical, hands-on, tool-oriented.
- Investigative – analytical, intellectual, scientific, explorative.
- Artistic – creative, original, independent, chaotic.
- Social – co-operative, supporting, helping, healing/nurturing.
- Enterprising – competitive, dynamic, opportunistic, persuasive.
- Conventional – detail-oriented, organising, clerical.

Explaining these types, Holland emphasises that these are degrees of preference: the realist ('doer'), for example, is not prevented by definition from performing a helping or social role, merely that their inclination and preference is for a pragmatic, hands-on approach.

Holland developed a profile of each type, abbreviated here to show only principal professions and careers:

HOLLAND CODES: VOCATIONAL CHOICES AND PERSONALITY

Doer (Realistic)

- Working with one's hands, with tools, machines and things; practical, mechanically inclined and physical: archaeologist, architect, chemical/civil/electrical/mechanical engineer, information technologist, pharmacist, physical therapist, pilot, veterinarian.
- Manage the realist by referring to the grounded, practical nature of the issue under consideration; emphasise fact, not opinion. Focus on what works, now in the present – not what might work in the future. Use plain language and present a sensible profile.

Thinker (Investigative)

- Working with theory and information: analytical, intellectual, scientific: actuary, economist, engineer, financier, lawyer, pharmacist, physician, professor, psychologist, psychiatrist, scientist, statistician, surgeon.

- Manage the thinker by drawing in information and placing it in context. Refer to the trends and possible future directions. Try to integrate information into a pattern, exploring possibilities, to gain credibility with this 'thinking' type.

Creator (Artistic)

- Non-conforming, original, independent, chaotic, creative: actor, writer, graphic designer, musician.
- Manage the creator by establishing your belief in a better way and by expressing your regard for individuality and experimentation. Bring some order to the tasks by agreeing deadlines that invoke subtle peer pressure; this will encourage the creative type to come to a conclusion, and limit procrastination.

Helper (Social)

- Co-operativeenvironments,supporting,helping,healing/nurturing: therapist, counsellor, educationalist, nurse, nutritionist, physician, professor, psychologist, social worker, teacher, theologian.
- Manage this caring type by placing people centre-stage in your approach. Reassure the helper type that businesses and other organisations are fundamentally about people. Allow flexibility in approach, recognising that individuals differ markedly, and try not to impose prescriptive standardised processes on them.

Persuader (Enterprising)

- Competitive environments, leading, persuading, selling, dominating, promoting, status: administration, communications, investment banker, journalist, lawyer, marketing/advertising, management, management consultant, publisher, public relations specialist, policymaker, stockbroker, salesperson.
- Manage the enterprising persuader by getting out of their way! Give them challenges, and let their competitive instincts drive them on. Channel that energy by letting them know when they have crossed the line, but do so without hectoring them or nit-picking; instead, present boundaries as part of the challenge, and manage the expectations of the less competitive types by making them aware of the value of the enterprising type, despite their unfortunate propensity to offend or irritate colleagues, often unknowingly.

Organiser (Conventional)

- Precise, perfect attention to detail, orderly, organising, status: accountant, actuary, administrator, banker, clerk, librarian, secretary, technical writer.
- Manage the conventional, organised type, such as the classical accountant, by presenting your arguments in a rational, logical and comprehensive sequence, sticking to the facts and avoiding conjecture or speculation. Do not rush into establishing personal relationships, but instead observe protocol, precedents and traditional practices. Do not embroider your case with elaboration or attempts at humour, but rely on factual accounts and tested solutions. Do not be surprised if your attempts to establish a warm relationship are not immediately reciprocated: realise that the precise, organised types place facts to the forefront of any work relationship.

In the above categorisations, note the fundamental importance of aspects of the individual's basic personality (such as introversion, thinking style, or decision-making style). For example, the 'typical' accountant may indeed be inward-focused, prefer to deal in facts, objective in decision-making and well-organised, but his or her individuality is also paramount; treat each as a unique case.

The polar opposite type to the accountant's classic 'type' is the extroverted type who is intellectually abstract (inclined to deal in theory, not in practical application, probably valuing intuition highly), with a high concern for the impact of people (empathy) and a tendency to be open-ended and inconclusive in their actions (which they perceive as flexibility). While this is classed, somewhat flatteringly, as an heroic type, risk-taking, with a feel for people and their ambitions, such a type will invariably run counter to the more grounded nature of someone drawn to the practical professions, such as accountancy.

All types mentioned throughout this chapter are, naturally, generalised stereotypes, presented as a means of understanding the bewildering array of personalities in the real world. All these stereotypes are common and absolutely 'normal', but some types are naturally more suited to particular professions. Some individuals, of course, can suffer from dysfunction (narcissism, paranoia, aggression), but these too should be understood in context, often being unfortunate exaggerations of their basic type, or formed by ill-judged attempts to compensate for other personality deficiencies.

Conclusion

Intelligent people are wonderful assets, deserving careful consideration and expert attention. Frequently misunderstood, and even dismissed as 'geeks' or 'eggheads', smart professionals deserve respect and an educated approach to their development. By understanding personality types, and the associated drivers of behaviour, professionals can be guided to high achievement, for the benefit of their organisations but also for themselves as people.

It is not useful to assume that highly intelligent people are emotionally and socially intelligent as well. The wise manager will come to know what levers and brakes to apply, and this chapter has attempted to reveal what is 'under the bonnet' in people. Certainly, understanding the mechanical aspects of personality type can be demanding, but it is certainly preferable to letting people career out of control, or dealing with the messiness of unnecessary conflict.

Professionals, because of their intense training and inherent drive, have very defined personalities, sometimes tending towards extremes of behaviour. Understanding different 'types' not only helps manage them but also can provide insight into our own personality.

This chapter has explained how conflict arises from the differences between personality types (although it is these very differences that make opposing types useful to us). Fracture occurs at the interface between types: recognising the different 'languages' each type speaks (verbally and otherwise) can help overcome the communications deficiencies.

We have also looked at different models to help understand the main stereotypes and then progress to a more nuanced understanding of complex individuals and their dysfunctions, suggesting how to avoid or reduce conflict and how to release the latent human potential of smart people. Use of the Holland Codes, for example, shows the link between personality and vocational choices (such as accountant or artist).

ENDNOTES

[1] Isabel Briggs Myers with Peter B. Myers, *Gifts Differing: Understanding Personality Type* (Davies-Black Publishing, 1995).

[2] Meredith Belbin, *Management Teams: Why They Succeed or Fail* (Butterworth-Heinemann, 1993).

[3] Paul Costa Jnr. and Robert McCrae, *The NEO Personality Inventory Manual* (Psychological Assessment Resources 1985).

[4] Paul Sinclair, *Personality and Performance* (British Psychological Society – Selection and Development, 1990).

[5] David Keirsey, *Please Understand Me II: Temperament, Character, Intelligence* (Prometheus Nemesis Book Company, 1998).

[6] Hans Eysenck, *Genius: The Natural History of Creativity* (Cambridge University Press, 1995).

[7] William Moulton Marston, *Emotions of Normal People* (Kegan Paul, Trench, Trubner & Co., 1928).

[8] Sylvia Lafair, *Don't Bring it to Work* (Jossey-Bass, 2009).

[9] John Holland, *Making Vocational Choices: A Theory of Careers* (Prentice-Hall, 1973).

Chapter 6

Engaging and Motivating Professionals: A New HR Framework

Dr Mary Collins

In this chapter, Dr Mary Collins, Head of Talent Development and Learning at Deloitte, Dublin, reveals how to get the best from professional employees by understanding the 'psychological contract' that exists in all organisations, large and small. Mary offers deep insight into the nature of this relationship based on her doctoral studies, and complements this with pragmatic advice from her experience as a HR manager in a leading professional firm. She suggests innovative ways to attract, develop and retain those key employees who make the difference between success and failure. Mary's research involved a sample of 500 professionals in the fields of law, accountancy and engineering. The comprehensive field research was comprised of an online survey, focus groups and in-depth interviews. Her findings apply across the professional spectrum, and even smaller firms will find that her suggestions make excellent sense, yielding great rewards, both human and financial. As well as showing how to use performance appraisals to engage professionals, she introduces her comprehensive, yet simple, 'MOTIVATE' framework to guide managers in effectively managing people to high performance and job satisfaction.

Introduction

This chapter looks at the challenge of how to motivate and engage 'smart people' to reach and maintain high performance levels in the organisation. These 'smart' professionals are typically self-motivated and driven. However, the challenge for organisations is to sustain high engagement levels in order to avoid losing top talent. These people characteristically enjoy variety, challenge and stretch in their roles, and get bored easily.

We will begin by looking at the implicit or explicit psychological contract that underpins the relationship between professionals and their organisation, before addressing performance management and employee engagement. Based on my doctoral research in the professional services sector,[1] the 'MOTIVATE' framework is then applied as a practical toolkit to manage 'smart' professionals. This section will conclude with some 'typical situations' based on real-life examples of issues that have emerged around the management of 'smart' people. Suggestions of how to deal with these typical situations are offered so that managers can develop and retain these talented individuals and maximise their performance. This chapter commences with an exploration of the 'psychological contract', an important concept in the area of workplace motivation.

The Psychological Contract

While the term 'psychological contract' was first used by Chris Argyris in the 1960s, it became more popular following the economic downturn in the early 1990s. It is gaining new importance now as employers aim to work their way out of the current recession. Wage freezes and cuts are the norm in the present environment. Also, there is a greater focus on regulation and accountability in the professional services sector.

Denise Rousseau defined the psychological contract as "the individual beliefs, shaped by the organisation, regarding the terms of an implicit exchange agreement between employees and their organisation".[2] These obligations will often be informal and imprecise: they may be inferred from actions or from what has happened in the past, as well as from statements made by the employer, for example during the recruitment process or in performance appraisals. Some obligations may be seen as 'promises' and others as 'expectations'. The important thing is that they are believed by the employee to be part of the relationship with the employer.

The psychological contract can be distinguished from the legal contract of employment, which will, in many cases, offer only a limited and uncertain representation of the reality of the employment relationship. The employee may have contributed little to its terms beyond accepting them.

The psychological contract, on the other hand, looks at the reality of the situation as perceived by the parties, and may be more influential than the formal contract in affecting how employees behave from day to day. It is the psychological contract that effectively tells employees what they are required to do in order to meet their side of the bargain, and what they can expect from their job.

A useful model of the psychological contract is offered by Professor David Guest of Kings College London (see the figure below). In outline, the model suggests that:

- The extent to which employers adopt people management practices will influence the state of the psychological contract.
- The contract is based on employees' sense of fairness and trust, and their belief that the employer is honouring the 'deal' between them.
- Where the psychological contract is positive, increased employee commitment and satisfaction will have a positive impact on business performance.

A Model of the Psychological Contract (Guest)[3]

Inputs	Content	Outputs
Employee characteristics	• Fairness	• Employee behaviour
Organisational characteristics	• Trust	• Performance
HR practices	• Delivery	

The psychological contract has increased in importance during the current economic downturn, as it relates to the following workplace changes:

- **The nature of jobs** More employees are on part-time and temporary contracts; more jobs are being outsourced; tight job definitions are out, functional flexibility is in.
- **Organisations have downsized and de-layered** 'Leanness' means doing more with less, so individual employees have to carry more weight.
- **Markets, technology and products are constantly changing** Customers and clients are becoming ever more demanding; quality and service standards are constantly going up.
- **Technology and finance are less important as sources of competitive advantage** 'Human capital' is becoming more critical to business performance in the knowledge-based economy.
- **Traditional organisational structures are becoming more fluid** Teams are often the basic building-block; new methods of managing are required.

The effect of these changes is that employees are increasingly recognised as the key business drivers. The ability of a business or professional firm to add value rests on its 'human capital'. Organisations that wish to succeed have to get the most out of this resource. In order to do this, employers have to know what employees expect from their work. The psychological contract offers a framework for monitoring employee attitudes and priorities on those dimensions that can be shown to influence performance.

The kinds of commitments employers and employees might make to one another, and which are reflected in employment propositions, are as follows.

Employer/Employee Commitments (CIPD)[4]

Employees promise to:	Employers promise to provide:
Work hard	Pay commensurate with performance
Uphold company reputation	Opportunities for training and development

Maintain high levels of attendance and punctuality	Opportunities for promotion
Show loyalty to the organisation	Recognition for innovation or new ideas
Work extra hours when required	Feedback on performance
Develop new skills and update old ones	Interesting tasks
Be flexible, for example by taking on a colleague's work	An attractive benefits package
Be courteous to clients and colleagues	Respectful treatment
Be honest	Reasonable job security
Come up with new ideas	A pleasant and safe working environment

Implications for Organisation Strategy

The psychological contract may have implications for organisational strategy in a number of areas, for example:

- **Process fairness** People want to know that their interests will be taken into account when important decisions are taken. They would like to be treated with respect, and they are more likely to be satisfied with their job if they are consulted about change. Managers cannot guarantee that employees will accept that outcomes on, for example, pay and promotion are fair, but they can put in place procedures that will make acceptance of the results more likely.
- **Communications** Although collective bargaining is still widely practised in the public sector, in large areas of the private sector trade unions now have no visible presence. It is no longer possible for managers in these areas to rely on 'joint regulation' in order to communicate with employees or secure their co-operation. An effective two-way dialogue between employer and employees is a necessary means of giving expression to employee 'voice'.
- **Management style** In many organisations, managers can no longer control the business from the 'top down'; they have to adopt a more 'bottom up' style. Crucial feedback about business performance flows in from customers and suppliers, and front line employees will often be best

able to interpret it. Managers have to draw on the strategic knowledge in employees' heads.

- **Managing expectations** Employers need to make clear to new recruits what they can expect from the job. Managers may have a tendency to emphasise positive messages and play down more negative ones. But employees can usually distinguish rhetoric from reality, and management failure to do so will undermine employees' trust. Managing expectations, particularly when bad news is anticipated, will increase the chances of establishing a realistic psychological contract.
- **Measuring employee attitudes** Employers should monitor employee attitudes on a regular basis as a means of identifying where action may be needed to improve performance. Some employers use indicators of employee satisfaction with management as part of the process for determining the pay of line managers. Other employers, particularly in the service sector, recognise strong links between employee and customer satisfaction.

Reciprocal Obligations

Denise Rousseau found that psychological contracts are comprised of two types of reciprocal obligation[5]:

(a) transactional obligations of pay and career advancement in exchange for hard work; and
(b) relational obligations of job security in exchange for loyalty and a minimum length of stay.

Psychological contracts are embodied in employees' unwritten expectations that the organisation will fulfil its promises of job security, high pay, merit pay, training and development. In return, the organisation expects its employees to be loyal, work overtime, stay a minimum length of time and give sufficient notice if they resign.[6]

The psychological contract covers the unwritten understandings, values, expectations and assumptions held by the retrospective parties. Professor David Guest has stated that "the extent to which employers adopt people management practices will influence the state of the psychological contract; the contract is based on employees' sense of fairness and trust, and their belief that the employer is honouring the 'deal' between them", continuing that "where the psychological contract is positive, increased employee commitment and satisfaction will have a positive impact on business performance".[7]

The psychological contract looks at the reality of the situation as perceived by the two parties, and may be more influential than the formal contract in affecting how employees behave from day to day.[8] Guest also sees the psychological contract as "a key element of affecting the high production levels of all workers, connecting motivation, motivators and effort".[9]

Failure to understand what motivates employees can prove costly to an organisation, will bring lower levels of engagement, trust and commitment from employees, and ultimately lead to high turnover rates.[10] Further research shows that where employees believe that management has broken promises or failed to deliver on commitments, this will have a negative effect on job satisfaction and commitment, and on the psychological contract as a whole. This is particularly important, as job satisfaction is expected to increase as people progress through career life stages.

Trust and the Psychological Contract

Trust between management and staff, company and customer and key stakeholders is essential to the success of organisations in the current business environment. While there are many definitions of trust, it can be described as the willingness of one party to be vulnerable to the actions of another party based on the expectation that the other will carry out a specific task important to the trustor, irrespective of the ability to monitor or control the other party.[11] Trust is a psychological state,[12] composed of the psychological experiences of individuals and organisations.

Trust should matter to organisations because it is an essential success factor of most business, professional and employment relationships, especially during an industry downturn or in times of crisis.[13] Trust in leadership affects a broad spectrum of employee work behaviours and outcomes.

Specifically, in their analysis of trust, Kurt Dirks and Donald Ferrin found that employee trust in organisations is positively related to organisational commitment, turnover intentions, job satisfaction, job performance, belief in information provided by management, commitment to decisions, satisfaction with leadership and leader–team member exchange.[14] Organisations with high levels of trust will be more successful, adaptive and innovative than organisations with low levels of trust.

Trust is easier to destroy than to create,[15] and it can be destroyed instantly. Accordingly, wherever trust exists, so does the possibility of violating that trust. In the modern marketplace, there is growing concern about distrust and the violation of trust in organisations.

Performance Management

In the current business climate, you cannot have a successful organisation if the smart people employed are not performing to their full potential. Professional staff members are being asked to 'go the extra mile' against the backdrop of wage freezes, pay cuts and reduced benefits. In this section, we explore how managers can be more innovative about how they recognise and reward high performers, and how they can be tougher when dealing with underperformance.

The use of, and satisfaction with, performance-management systems remains problematic. There is a considerable gap between theory and practice!

John Bernardin and Lawrence Klatt found that small firms tended to rely heavily on trait-based approaches, while larger firms relied on a combination of trait, behavioural and results-based techniques.[16] They note that one in five organisations do not give employees the opportunity to review their performance appraisal results.

Sylvia Hewlett stresses the importance of "keeping performance up when business is down",[17] suggesting some strategies to enhance performance levels during difficult economic times:

1. **Create a 'no spin' zone**   Use frequent and frank communication to quell anxiety and build trust.
2. **Think locally and focus on team leaders**   Encourage team leaders to strengthen camaraderie among their teams, and focus on active mentoring for this key group.
3. **Give employees meaningful non-monetary rewards**   Develop new ways to show recognition, from saying a simple 'thank you' to employees for a job well done to corporate social responsibility initiatives.
4. **Develop a fair restructuring process**   Ensure transparency in all processes related to redundancy; ask staff for creative ways to cut costs.
5. **Hold on to your women**   Establish a range of flexible working options to ensure that women, who typically are the principal care-givers, have opportunities to continue their careers despite 'off ramping' at specific life stages.
6. **Show that senior management cares**   In difficult economic times, it is important that there are more 'touch points' with leaders, even in small firms, for example communication briefings with small groups of staff.
7. **Recreate pride, purpose and direction**   Give employees reasons to feel good about the company; highlight success stories and recommit to social responsibility.

High-performance Work Culture

A high-performance work culture is essential to realise the potential of employees. Culture is more important than strategy, as it is all encompassing in an organisation. Peter Drucker famously said in one of his lectures: "culture eats strategy for breakfast". If the culture is wrong, no amount of strategising will make a difference.

> *"High performance is a by-product of a culture based not on any sense of entitlement or perfectionism, but squarely on the principle of value added."*
> Stephen R. Covey

Key Features of a High-performance Work Culture:

Jean-François Manzoni suggests that the high-performance culture is present in an organisation where employees set challenging goals for themselves and are emotionally committed to their organisation, while striving to exceed their work targets.[18] People discuss issues intensively before they take any action. They talk solutions, not problems. It's an organisation where there is no such thing as 'satisfactory underperformance'.

A high-performance work culture involves every system in the organisation working towards a single goal of superior performance and a distinctive customer proposition. It involves the organisation's beliefs and values, its strategy and vision, its management practices and HR practices. In 1968, Frederick Herzberg suggested that intrinsic factors, such as challenge and interesting work, answer people's needs to grow and achieve.[19] People's motivations differ, and what motivates one person will not necessarily motivate another. The high-performance work culture derives its strength from its flexibility; it incorporates different practices to meet different needs, such as:

- appropriate recruitment and selection processes;
- comprehensive induction and training;
- coherent performance management;
- flexible workforce skills;
- job variety and team working;
- communication and quality improvement teams;
- competitive pay and rewards linked to performance; and
- work–life balance.

A planned and systematic approach is required in order to create a high-performance work culture. It requires action in four areas:

1. customer, stakeholder and employee satisfaction;
2. superlative work processes;
3. improving people, facilities, information, technology and suppliers; and
4. understanding your organisation's unique cultural and organisational characteristics, and a dedication to ever-improving levels of performance.

Good leadership breeds confidence and brings out the best in people. This, coupled with a strong vision that is embraced by everyone, leads to high performance. Leaders in high-performing organisations identify and develop the best people and provide 'fanatical' training and development. There is a thirst for results, information, speed and quality, above everything else. Relationships are sought and nourished with customers. Employees are trusted and feel obliged to meet expectations, and they have an assumptive winning attitude. There is no single set of changes or practices that will give an organisation a high-performance work culture. A high-performance work culture must enable people to produce and deliver products and services that meet customer requirements in the context of environments that change rapidly.

Matthew Juechter's more straightforward view of the high-performance culture suggests that high-performance organisations have the following characteristics[20]:

1. strategic focus;
2. clear view of reality;
3. commitment rather than compliance; and
4. aligned behaviour.

Underpinning these characteristics are five essentials: a relevant focus; driven from the top; leader's commitment; comprehensive involvement; and external coaches.

Juechter suggests that an organisation can be viewed as a system with three sub-systems:

Juechter's Organisation Systems Model[21]

Most organisations focus their change efforts on the first two sub-systems. They are often imposed and done in isolation. There is no real engagement for the change in the organisation.

Richard Osborne suggests that the one defining characteristic of a high-performing organisation is "wide open, highly defined communication about expectations".[22] Every employee knows what is expected of them, how they will be measured and how they are doing. Triumphs are celebrated daily – failure is unthinkable. High-performing organisations are obsessed with beating the competition.

The key characteristics of a high-performing work culture can be categorised under four main headings:

1. **Employees**

   - Set challenging goals for themselves.
   - Are emotionally committed to the organisation and strive to exceed their objectives.
   - Talk solutions, not problems.
   - Participate in the organisation's direction and strategic goals.
   - Are provided with regular training and development.
   - Are trusted by their leaders.

2. **Performance management**

   - There is no such thing as satisfactory underperformance.
   - Employees receive formal performance appraisals and regular feedback.

3. **Organisational factors/cultural issues**

   - The organisation has the right attitudes, beliefs and behaviours.
   - It supports work–life balance.
   - Customer satisfaction is a priority.
   - There are superior work processes in place.
   - There are improved facilities, information and technology resources.
   - A dedication to improvement permeates the organisation.
   - Everyone in the organisation embraces a strong vision.
   - There is a thirst for results and quality in everything.
   - There is a positive 'can do' attitude at all levels.

4. **Leadership**

   - There is strong leadership that brings out the best in everyone.
   - Leaders identify and develop the best talent.
   - They provide the resources to achieve high performance.

Leadership Effectiveness in Professional Services Firms

The leadership provided in an organisation is critical in shaping its management style and culture. DeLong *et al.* in their study, "When Professionals Have to Lead: a New Model of High Performance", have developed an integrated leadership model based on extensive research on leaders in professional services.[23] Their research found that excellent professional services firm leaders create a sense of purpose and a clear focus on execution, while supporting and gaining the commitment of their people. As a result, they develop teams and work cultures that attract top people who want to grow and do an outstanding job.

The leadership framework developed from the research is activity-based in that it deals with actual, observable behaviours that leaders may learn so as to become more effective. The model consists of four distinct but highly interrelated sets of leadership activities:

The Leader's Role in Professional Service Firms[24]

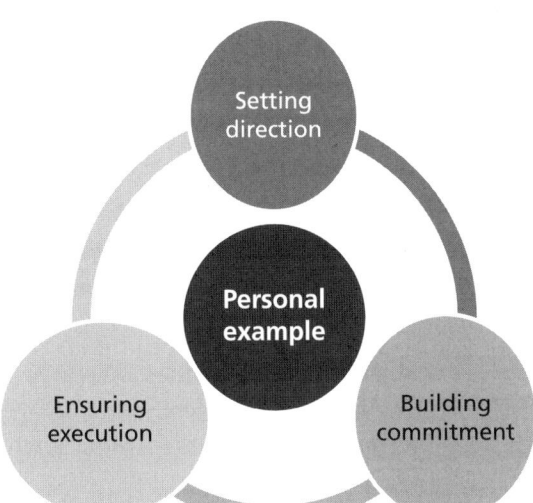

Setting Direction

Leaders of professionals often focus on the short term and spend little time providing direction on where the firm or practice is going and why. Since professionals are often solely focused on specific goals and tasks, they need leaders to articulate the organisation's objectives and how their work relates to those objectives.

Gaining Commitment to the Strategic Direction

DeLong *et al.* describe how professionals have an innate need to be involved and included: they want to be heard. Many strong contributors who are not the star players at a firm often feel as if their contributions are being undervalued. When professionals feel excluded, they can feel alienated and fail to focus on the task at hand. Gaining commitment increases the odds that people will work harder and more creatively to move a firm, practice or project in the desired direction.

Execution

Execution is defined in the DeLong *et al.* study as "the process of meeting the financial goals that have been set and holding professionals at all levels accountable." Execution is a key activity for leaders who are intimately involved in business development, selling, client service and delivery.

Setting a Personal Example

Providing a positive personal example is crucial when leading professionals. In the often stressful environments of professional services firms, it matters what leaders actually do through word and deed. Leaders must be role models in relation to the firm's stated values and goals, or those values and goals become meaningless for professionals. Gaining commitment requires that leaders display personal integrity, support their professionals and take responsibility for their own actions – including mistakes.

Transformational Leadership

Recently, the concept of transformational leadership has gained popularity because of its qualitatively different approach to motivating followers. Specifically, Bernard Bass argued that transformational leaders motivate followers by raising awareness of the importance and value of the organisation's mission and goals, getting followers to transcend their own self-interests, and shifting followers' needs from lower- to higher-level needs.[25]

John W. Gardner explains that a major differentiator of this approach from other leadership styles is the transformational leader's efforts to actively improve followers' concepts of themselves, including self-esteem, self-efficacy and self-confidence.[26] As a result, the nature of the relationships that transformational leaders establish with their followers is based on a higher level of emotional engagement with, and personal liking for, the leader.[27]

For more on this theme, see **Chapter 4**, which is devoted to leadership.

Emotionally Intelligent Leadership

Daniel Goleman entitled his book on emotional intelligence and leadership *Primal Leadership*[28] because, as he explains, "great leaders move us; they ignite our passion and inspire the best in us. When we try to explain why they are so effective, we speak of strategy, vision or powerful ideas. The reality is much more primal; great leadership works through the emotions."

Goleman's ground-breaking work in this field is based on the four central dimensions of emotional intelligence theory:

1. Emotional Self-awareness

This refers to understanding one's own emotions, knowing one's strengths and limits and having self-confidence. In a large-scale study Goleman conducted of CEOs globally, emotional self-awareness was the top trait of the most successful leaders. This success was not just financial but also related to success in the areas of health, emotional well-being and relationships.

2. Self-management

This essential dimension relates to the managing of one's emotions; keeping disruptive emotions and impulses under control. Leaders who practice self-management tend to be optimistic in nature.

3. Social Awareness

This dimension of emotional intelligence centres on showing empathy to others and servicing follower, client or customer needs.

4. Relationship Management

The final dimension of emotionally intelligent leadership refers to the leader's ability to inspire, guide and motivate with a compelling vision. It also refers to developing others through feedback and guidance.

Emotional intelligence is discussed further in **Chapter 12**. Interested readers will also find separate chapters on mentoring professionals (**Chapter 13**) and on building self-confidence (**Chapter 11**).

Authentic Leadership

'Authentic' leadership echoes the 'self-awareness' aspect of the transformational leadership concept. One of the foremost writers and speakers in this field is Dr Gareth Jones, now of the London Business School and formerly the HR advisor to the charismatic Greg Dyke when he was head of the BBC. His article in the *Harvard Business Review*, "Why should anyone be led by you?"[29] is the basis for leadership development programmes across the globe. The basic premise to this concept is that the traditional leadership qualities of vision, energy, authority and strategic direction are a given. Jones identifies four consistent qualities of inspirational leaders:

1. They selectively show their weaknesses – this exposes their humanity.
2. They rely heavily on intuition to gauge how and when to act.
3. They manage employees with a quality referred to as 'tough empathy'. Authentic leaders care passionately about people and also about the work they do. They can flex between empathy and constructive feedback when required.
4. They reveal their differences: true leaders revel in diversity and capitalise on what is unique and different to them.

Mentoring

Mentoring is based on the belief that two people can work together as colleagues and form a learning partnership, with one person taking a guiding role as the mentor, while the other – the mentee – is the one being guided.

Mentoring is very widely used in the business world where experienced mentors provide support to protégés in order to further the protégé's career prospects. Mentoring can be a formal or informal arrangement, and there are positive and negative aspects to both. David Clutterbuck believes that informal mentoring is often a very positive experience, and this is possible when both parties have benefited from positive formal mentoring experiences.[30] However, he does recommend a formal mentoring programme as the preferred initial mentoring experience for several reasons, among them the fact that formal mentors will have received some training and will have contact with other mentors, which provides opportunities to support and learn from one another.

The analogy used by Laurent Daloz to illustrate the concept of mentoring is thought-provoking when he describes learning or education as a "transformational journey".[31] This promotes growth and personal development.

Angi Malderez and Caroline Bodoczky state the mentor's desired outcome of the mentoring process is "my trainee mustn't become a second 'me', but an enriched 'herself'."[32]

Lev Vygotsky maintains that the mentor is a "support structure or scaffold in the learning process stimulating the mentee to reach her 'zone of proximal' development."[33]

Mentoring has the capacity to encourage reflective practice. This is made possible by the mentor using discussion, questioning and feedback to encourage reflection. Through this process, the mentee is encouraged to reflect and, thus, begins to use reflection to enhance teaching and learning. Donald Schön describes reflection as having three steps: returning to the experience; attending to feelings; and evaluating the experience. Whereas David Kolb mentions four stages in the process[34]:

1. **experience**;
2. **observe**: standing back from the situation and observing;
3. **reflect**: think about it, form an opinion and make a plan; and
4. **practice**: put the plan into practice.

Reflection can enhance learning, as it ensures that a learner actively engages with the learning process rather than going through it automatically.

Note that the mentor is called upon to play different roles according to the mentee's needs. The needs will vary throughout the life of the mentoring relationship and as the mentee gains more experience and confidence in their own ability to perform their professional role.

Mentoring: Advantages and Disadvantages

From an organisational perspective, mentoring can be described as a low-cost, high-impact intervention and actively demonstrates how the collective expertise and experience of staff can be used as a resource within an organisation. The challenge for management is to support and value the mentoring system by ensuring that mentors are given appropriate training and support to be effective in their role. The view expressed by Wayne Turk that mentors need to be mentored illustrates the need to provide continuous support to those who take on a mentoring role in an organisation.[35]

Mentees have the opportunity to access one-to-one, personalised, confidential support through their mentor. This will encourage and develop the confidence and competence of the mentee and increase effectiveness.

Mentors need to have the skills to encourage and support the learner to discover their own wisdom and, in so doing, develop competence and build confidence. It is essential that mentors demonstrate best practice in their own application to their work if they are to promote best practice through the mentoring process.

For more on mentoring, see **Chapter 13**.

Motivating 'Smart Professionals' through Employee Engagement

Traditional theories regarding employee motivation, such as Herzberg's Motivators and Hygiene Factors[36] and Adams' Equity Theory,[37] as presented below, while still having a certain validity, have been surpassed by more progressive studies based on motivating workers in a knowledge economy:

Herzberg's Motivators and Hygiene Factors

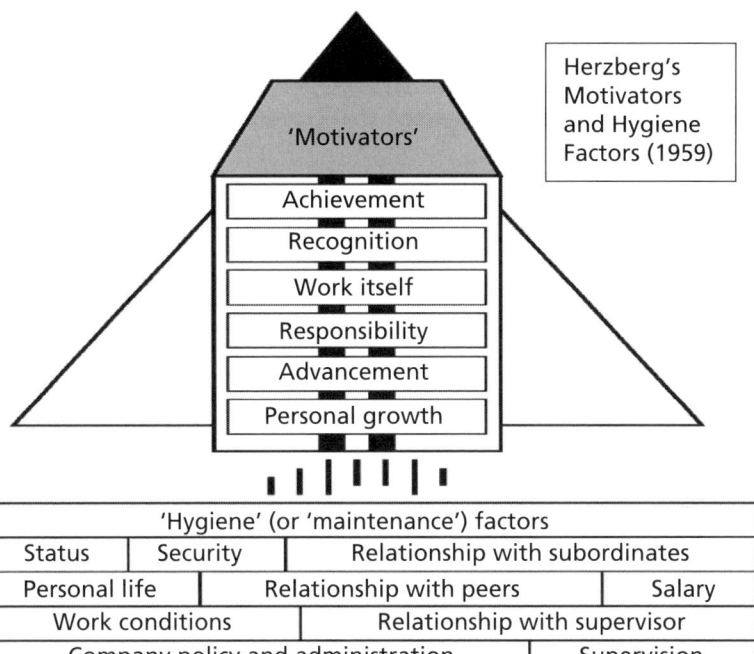

Hygiene factors are merely a launch pad – when damaged or undermined we have no platform, but in themselves they do not motivate.

Adams' Equity Theory (1963)

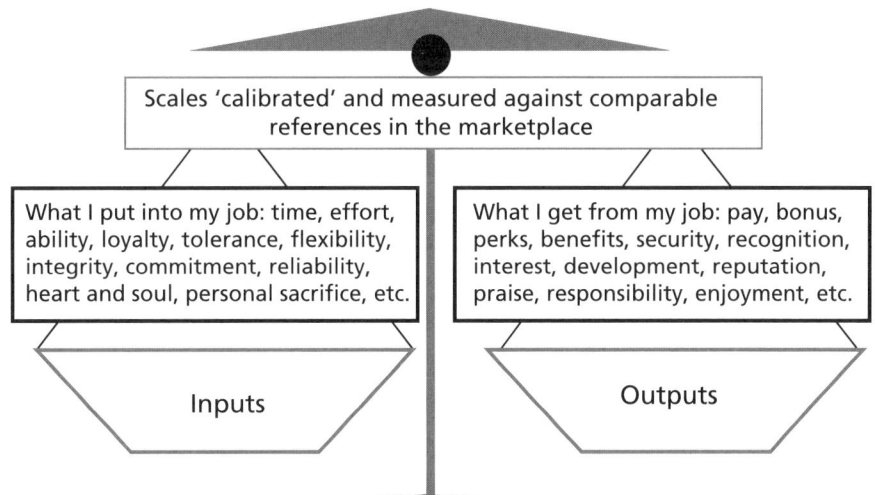

People become demotivated, reduce input and/or seek change/improvement whenever they feel their inputs are not being fairly rewarded. Fairness is based on perceived market norms.

New Thinking on Motivation

Nitin Nohria *et al.* describe some exciting progress in the area of human motivation through the marriage of different fields of study, among them neuroscience and evolutionary psychology.[38] In their groundbreaking study, they identify four basic drivers of motivation, which are the drives to:

1. **acquire**: obtain scarce goods, including intangibles such as social status;
2. **bond**: form connections with individuals and groups;
3. **comprehend**: satisfy our curiosity and master the world around us; and
4. **defend**: protect against external threats and promote justice.

These drives underlie everything we do

Nitin Nohria *et al.*'s research showed that an organisation's ability to meet the four fundamental drives explains, on average, about 60% of employees' variance on motivational indicators (previous models have explained about 30%). They also found that certain drives influence some motivational indicators more than others. Fulfilling the drive to bond, for example, has the greatest effect on employee commitment, whereas meeting the drive to comprehend is most closely linked with employee engagement. A company can best improve overall motivational scores by satisfying all four drives in concert. The whole is more than the sum of its parts: a poor showing on one drive substantially diminishes the impact of high scores on the other three.

Four Basic Drives of Motivation: a New Model

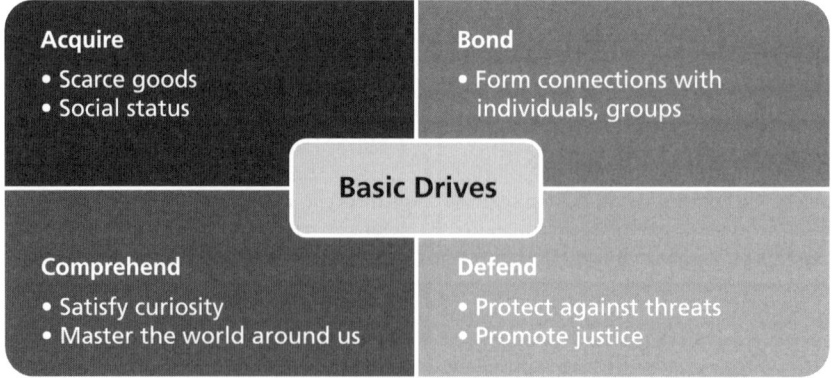

Employee Engagement

Engagement is a beneficial, two-way relationship where employees and employers go the extra mile for one another. Wilmar Schaufell sees engagement "as a positive, fulfilling, work related state of mind that is characterised by vigour, dedication and absorption".[39] Employee engagement can be considered to be: cognitive – employees' beliefs about the organisation, their leaders and culture; emotional – how the employees feel about the organisation, leaders and colleagues; and behavioural – the amount of effort employees put into work.[40] It is a mutual contact between the employee and the employer.

Engagement ultimately comes down to people's desire and willingness to give **discretionary effort** to their jobs.

The Gallup Management Group showed that improving employee engagement is important because engaged employees have[41]:

- 51% lower turnover;
- 27% less absenteeism;
- 18% more productivity; and
- 12% higher profitability.

As the economy changes and employee demands become more specific, employee engagement provides an opportunity to increase productivity and, in turn, profitability, while satisfying employee needs. The Gallup Research outlines the following measurable benefits to employee engagement:

- Engaged employees perform 20% better than non-engaged employees.
- Offices with engaged employees are 43% more productive.[42]
- Employers with the highest percentage of engaged employees, on average, increase operating margins by 3.64% and net profit margins by 2.06%.[43]
- Organisations with the lowest percentage of engaged employees showed declines of 2% in operating margins and 1.38% in profit margins.[44]

The *Best Companies Guide UK 2008*[45] highlights seven possible organisational factors that can improve employee engagement:

1. **Leadership:** good leadership leads to a happy team.
2. **My company:** how much people value their company, and are proud to work there.
3. **Personal growth:** whether employees feel challenged by their job.
4. **My manager:** the employee–manager relationship.
5. **Giving something back:** community service and volunteering opportunities.
6. **Fair deal:** how well pay and benefits compare to similar organisations.
7. **Well-being:** balance between work and home life.

Employee Retention

Retention can be defined as the "effort by an employer to keep desirable workers in order to meet business objectives", while turnover is often used to describe the unplanned loss of workers who voluntarily leave and whom the employer would prefer to keep.

A retention strategy is a long-term commitment to attract, develop, retain and motivate talented people. Organisations cannot hope to either attract or retain the right people if they take a reactive rather than strategic approach to talent management. To grow and maintain a competitive edge, organisations should have a strategy in place to retain their top performers. Retention is implicit in a business strategy based around people as a winning resource.

Effective strategy development is about analysis as well as creativity, since in order to implement a retention strategy an organisation needs to understand itself, the people within it and the world in which it operates before it can make effective strategic choices. A retention strategy takes into account the particular retention issues that an organisation is facing and sets out ways in which these issues can be dealt with.

Peter Cappelli states that an organisation will ultimately determine the movement of its employees, believing that people cannot be shielded from attractive opportunities and aggressive recruiters, and suggests "the old goal of human resource management – to minimise overall employee turnover – needs to be replaced by a new goal: to influence who leaves and when".[46]

Creating a retention strategy means placing the employee's needs and expectations at the centre of the firm's long-term agenda in order to ensure the professional satisfaction of the employee and to create a trusted relationship between management and staff. In this stable relationship, the employee stays in the firm by personal choice, based on free will and considered decision.

As well as keeping costs under control, cleverly thought-out retention objectives that support resourcing and business goals will also strengthen the internal brand and contribute to the organisation's ability to attract new talent at the right price.

Retaining talented, productive employees and eliminating poor-performing employees is essential to the long-term success of an organisation.

Maintaining Trust in Difficult Times

Amy Lyman describes "trustworthy behaviour" as "the glue that holds a group of people together, keeps people contributing for the betterment of all, allows creative ideas to flow, and keeps people's spirits up when facing challenges."[47] She describes five specific actions that leaders and managers can take to ensure that trust is maintained during difficult times, as follows:

1. Involve People

It is important to remember that everyone is aware of what is going on. To mitigate the impact of job changes, involve employees in developing the strategies you seek to implement. Employees may come up with creative ideas for staffing changes – rotating unpaid days off, taking unpaid leave, reducing hours – or may be open to early retirement packages that could prevent lay-offs. When people are involved in addressing difficult situations, not only are you able to gain from their creative ideas but you also give them a portion of control over what is happening to them. A sense of loss of control is one of the most harmful aspects of difficult situations – harmful to people's health and harmful to the camaraderie and commitment of the group.

2. Share Information Broadly and Consistently

In times of uncertainty, the grapevine and rumour mill are in high gear. People will create their own answers to questions if they do not receive enough information or if they receive inconsistent information from leaders. Therefore, it is of great importance to let people know what is happening in the business on a regular basis. For leaders or managers it is important to be seen as a source of information about what steps are being taken to address the current situation, even when full answers to questions cannot be given.

3. Show up, Be Available, Say "Thank You"

Leaders and managers can help to convey a sense of confidence that the difficult times facing the organisation are being addressed, simply by making themselves available and being visible. This is definitely a time to visit people individually.

Listen to what people are saying, and answer with the information that you have. Let people know what you are doing, how you are keeping yourself informed. And let people know that you appreciate their contributions and hard work. Saying "thank you" is one of the most powerful ways of showing appreciation.

4. Start with Yourself

If cuts need to be made, leaders and managers need to be the first ones to make changes in their own pay. Generally, hours do not get reduced for leaders during difficult times, yet reduced salaries can have a tremendous impact on the perception among employees that "we are all in this together."

5. Lay-offs as a Last Resort

Decisions about layoffs are some of the most difficult ones for leaders to make. Yet, after everything else has been tried, sometimes lay-offs are necessary. Remember as well to pay attention to the employees who stay. Much has been written about 'survivor guilt' for those who make it through a lay-off.

In the Irish context, in my doctoral research study of 500 professionals in the legal, accounting and engineering sectors, I developed a framework to provide practical strategies to enhance engagement levels of professional staff.

The MOTIVATE Framework©

The MOTIVATE Framework[48] provides strategies that will strengthen the psychological contract with 'smart' employees. This framework identifies tangible ways to increase engagement and performance levels of professional staff – a key priority for employers in the current marketplace.

Senior management in organisations need their professional staff to be committed, performing at a high level and fully engaged in order for their organisations to be successful. The successful implementation of this framework in organisations is a 'win–win' for management and staff.

The MOTIVATE Framework

| Meaning and Purpose | Opportunity and Challenge | Timely, Honest Communication |

Key Imperatives in the Management of Professional Employees

| Interest in Personal Career Path | | Values and Vision |

| Attentive Management | Terms & Conditions | Energy Management |

© Mary E Collins 2010

Meaning and Purpose

Providing meaning and purpose to employees in their work is essential for them to be engaged to perform at a high level. The work needs to be interesting and challenging, and they need to see how it fits with 'the bigger picture'. 'Interesting work' is described by one smart professional as follows:

> "Work needs to be challenging and interesting. I know a number of classmates who are working in a multinational that is extremely good at retaining employees with very low turnover. The reason being is that they are engineers doing engineers' work, and they are involved in very high-tech R&D development of particular products, but it comes down to the fact that the work is interesting, and I think that's the key thing to retain people."

Expectations should be clearly explained from the outset, including the strategic 'big picture' and how employees fit into it, in other words employees should be given a sense of belonging.

Gurnek Bains *et al.* in their study, "Meaning Inc.", describe how successful organisations will create meaning for employees through "an invigorating sense of purpose, unequivocal values, and a sense of belonging and day-to-day leadership".[49] A critical issue is how to provide meaning authentically as opposed to 'going through the motions'.

One striking aspect of the doctoral research was a phrase that came up numerous times: "I do not want to be treated as just another number." This represented to me the importance of employees feeling valued by leaders in the organisation and doing meaningful work.

Employees should be included in regular strategy briefings in their respective organisations, even in the smallest firms. Their work should be a mix of operational and more strategic tasks. Every employee should be aware of his or her role in the organisation's strategy.

Opportunity and Challenge

My research has clearly indicated that providing opportunity and challenge are key factors in maximising the performance of 'smart' professionals. Opportunity has many facets: the opportunity to learn and develop; the opportunity for regular feedback; the opportunity for advancement. This is one of the most significant themes I encountered in conducting my research.

One of the engineering employees interviewed in the research study explained the following:

> "On the job training is very important and providing opportunities for growth. I think it's the manager recognising that there are opportunities for this person to develop in a certain area."[50]

This is linked to the area of 'attentive management' with the manager playing a key role as mentor in understanding and recommending specific areas for development for the employee in question. A simple and effective recommendation would be to allow the employee to accompany a senior person to a meeting and 'shadow' them, or to recommend them to attend a particular conference or training course of relevance.

Petra Wilton describes how opportunity for progression does not necessarily have to be linear.[51] Organisations should consider options like project work, cross-functional activities and secondments to industry to develop transferable skills. While this will require some short-term investment of time and resources, the benefits in terms of retention could be significant. This is particularly relevant in the context of a professional services firm. Frequently, I hear at employee exit interviews that one of the main reasons ambitious professionals leave is to get 'industry experience'.

The opportunity to learn and develop is critical to talented people. This came through from my research. Chris Argyris describes the need to move from 'single-loop' to 'double-loop' learning.[52] He explains double-loop learning as not simply a function of how people feel but "a reflection of how they think, the cognitive roles or reasoning they use to design and implement their actions". He uses the example of Enron and Anderson having award-winning leadership development programmes yet, ultimately, it was the lack of leadership that caused the downfall of these two organisations.

Argyris explains that the key to teaching employees to reason productively is to "connect the program to real business problems". They are not just solving problems; they are developing "a far deeper and more textured" understanding of their role as members of the organisation. (For more on this, see also the chapter on knowledge and innovation, **Chapter 8**.)

I see this working in practice through the 'action learning' part of the Management Development Programme at Deloitte. Young managers are asked to work together in project teams to solve real-life challenges the firm faces, e.g. employee engagement in a downturn, competitiveness and business development. The teams work on solutions to the challenges and present these to the firm's executive partners. This is one aspect of the project that consistently gets the best feedback. It is a real example of 'double-loop' learning in action.

This is particularly relevant in the contemporary organisation where individuals bring more of themselves (their ideas, their feelings) to their work. I also found from my research that today's employees are more articulate than previous generations and are very vocal in voicing dissatisfaction. Organisations should harness this openness and regularly get feedback from employees to involve them in changes in the business environment.

Timely, Honest Communication

A key area of focus when we talk about employee engagement and motivation is communication, and this came through as a clear theme in my work.

One interviewee in the research study spoke of the importance of honest communication, particularly through the difficult economic times. She stressed how much better it would have been if management had said: "'We really could do with your help to get the company through to the other side so we all survive.' If it's explained to you, it does make you feel a lot more secure and a lot more loyal to the company."

Organisations should involve their bright workforce in devising solutions to difficult restructuring decisions. This was trialled in Deloitte in one department where redundancies were looming. A number of staff focus groups were held, and some of the employees came up with excellent suggestions around reduced hours for the department in order to save jobs.

Another interviewee stated the importance of having good structures in place in this regard: "having an honest, effective communication structure in place will be the organisation that'll be perceived to be better employers, even if they announce tough decisions, honest communication is critical."

It is clear from my research that employees like to feel involved. Holding regular meetings and briefings can assist with this.

James O'Toole and Warren Bennis describe how we will not be able to rebuild trust in institutions "until leaders learn to communicate honestly – and create organisations where that is the norm".[53] They explain how leaders need to "make a conscious decision to support transparency and create a culture of candour". The traditional yardstick of success – to create wealth for investors – has shifted to a new metric of corporate leadership that requires executives to create organisations that are "economically, ethically and socially sustainable".

The theme of communication was strong throughout the focus groups, interviews and the online survey of my research. It is important to ensure that staff are briefed regularly on the organisation's strategy, particularly through the performance-appraisal process, and that communication skills are built into manager training on performance appraisal. A psychometric tool like the Myers–Briggs Type Indicator (MBTI) is a useful profile in understanding different communication styles and the need to flex one's style based on the audience to hand. (This tool is described in **Chapter 5**.)

Professionals should be consistently provided with constructive feedback, on a daily basis. Likewise, they should be informed when they have done a good job, be given immediate praise, recognition and rewards for good performance. This workforce has grown up getting constant feedback and recognition, so they expect to be told how they are doing.

Karl Hulett suggests providing professionals with as much choice as possible, for example with regard to work scheduling or a choice of job duties, as more choices offer higher perceived individual control, leading to greater satisfaction.[54]

Barbro Anell and Timothy Wilson suggest the following qualities might be required in employees:

> "…a desire to seek feedback on performance, a desire to improve, an ability to see multiple perspectives, a broad vision, an ability to visualize relationships, a readiness to accept responsibility for decisions, self-confidence, pro-activity, a liking for change and a desire for cooperative independence."[55]

Interest in Personal Career Path

Out of all the recommendations of my study, this one is key to enhancing the psychological contract and, hence, retention levels of smart employees. Taking an interest in the employee's personal career path is vitally important to maintain their motivation and performance levels. It is about creating an environment where they feel "someone is looking out for me". Professionals are clearly a highly confident, ambitious group, despite the current economic challenges, and career progression remains critically important to them. In fact, it somewhat surprised me in the survey findings to see that lack of career progression is the key reason why they predict they will leave their current organisation.

One interviewee described the importance of a clear career path:

> "You have to have scope for a clear career path so that you can progress in the organisation and go different places, and also the fact that you're getting a diverse experience that, if needs be, you have transferable skills to take your career to another company."

Career development was defined by another interviewee as follows:

> "It means that you're being given more responsibility, you can see your career progressing, you can see where it is going, you can see there is not a glass ceiling, you can keep moving forward..."

Charles Mills discussed the importance of taking an individual approach to career development, as each person will have a different perspective.[56] He states how for different people work may be a "mere source of livelihood, or the most significant part of one's inner life".

Smart professionals want a clear path for advancement, and they are driven to make an immediate impact in their positions. They are more likely to be aware of the need for constant skill development and updating and should therefore be given as many opportunities as possible for skill-building.[57]

Employees should be given training and support when they join an organisation because inductions help ensure that people joining an organisation are able to integrate effectively into the workplace early on. A recent report found that there are still a high proportion of new starters leaving organisations within the first six months.[58]

Professionals want to know where they are going in an organisation, and organisations are stepping up their career training and detailing to employees what they need to do to get to the next level.

Deloitte has implemented learning pathways across each department, so each department has a programme of learning at each level to ensure development of technical and behavioural skills.

As Jim Westerman and Jeanne Yamamura found, younger employees are now likelier to take a more active role in their career planning and execution.[59] Michael Armstrong states that "dissatisfaction with career prospects is a major cause of turnover".[60]

The organisation that aims to retain good professionals has to have a planned promotion strategy. Succession planning, vital to continued productivity when a valued employee leaves, depends on 'growing your own' to a large extent. Promotion retains talent, knowledge and skills, and boosts employee morale.

Values and Vision

A further recommendation is that organisations review their core values. Are these values really lived in the organisation or merely words on the back of a business card? The better employees want to work for managers with strong values and a vision for the future.

The Great Places to Work Institute describes trust as the essential ingredient in the relationship between employees and management, and states that it is driven by three key factors[61]:

- credibility;
- respect;
- fairness.

Credibility means that managers regularly communicate with employees about the company's direction and plans – and solicit their ideas. It involves co-ordinating people and resources efficiently and effectively, so that employees know how their work relates to the company's goals. It is the integrity management brings to the business. To be credible, words must be followed by action. This goes back to the idea of Authentic Leadership discussed earlier.

Respect involves providing employees with the equipment, resources and training they need to do their job. It means appreciating good work and extra effort. It includes reaching out to employees and making them partners in the company's activities, fostering a spirit of collaboration across departments and creating a work environment that is safe and healthy. Respect means that work–life balance is a practice, not a slogan.

Fairness means that economic success is shared equitably through compensation and benefit programmes. Everybody receives equitable opportunity for recognition. Decisions on hiring and promotions are made impartially, and the workplace seeks to free itself of discrimination, with clear processes for appealing and adjudicating disputes. To be fair, you must be just.

Jim Collins and Jerry Porras claim that: "Companies that enjoy enduring success have core values and a core purpose that remain fixed while their business strategies and practices endlessly adapt to a changing world."[62] Given the recent economic scandals in the financial sector, never has this statement held more resonance.

In their article, Collins and Porras go on to describe how 'vision' has become one of the most overused and least understood words. Their framework on "articulating a vision" (see figure below) consists of two major components:

1. **Core ideology** defines what we stand for and why we exist, and is unchanging.
2. **Envisioned future** is what we aspire to become, to achieve or to create – something that will require significant change and progress to attain.

Articulating a Vision

According to William Taylor and Polly LaBarre in their book *Mavericks at Work*, companies should use values to help define a corporate purpose because "high minded values can drive cutting edge corporate performance".[63] They go on to say that:

> "Great companies are built on genuine passion, plus a day to day commitment to great execution. Employees won't feel the passion, and can't maintain the operating discipline, unless they feel good about what the company sells and the values that it stands for."

Cultural values are thus key to a high-performing organisation.

Attentive Management

Another key recommendation for organisations based on my study is well described by Cara Spiro as "personalised motivation".[64] She describes this as a "method of profiling employees to determine how each individual prefers to be managed". This approach can enable employees to give managers information on the best ways to motivate them and, therefore, maximise their potential.

This idea came through with almost every employee I interviewed: they really appreciate the 'personal touch'. For example, a manager taking a genuine interest in them in terms of their ambitions, values and, in essence, tapping into their value systems and understanding what is most important to them in life generally and in the workplace. Managers who are successful at this will generate high loyalty and trust with their staff.

Peter McDonald describes how the new generation of professionals are "sociable and eager to engage with their supervisors. They have been raised on instant communication and frequent parental input and seek a similar relationship with bosses, looking to them for 'almost constant feedback'".[65] Performance reviews every three months instead of annual reviews may prove to be a good motivational force. Frequent communication and interaction between employee and manager will ensure candid communication and, in turn, generate feelings of security and appreciation.

Recognition appears to have a significant impact on performance. As one interviewee said:

> "I love to be recognised … if a manager says you've done a good job, it mightn't mean much but subconsciously you find yourself willing to work harder for that manager … that two line recognition … really spurs you on."

This same interviewee described the importance of meaningful feedback and recognition:

> "You don't want somebody to turn around to you every single day and go 'thanks a million guys, that was great today' … but if you feel like you've done something well, you do want to be recognised, even if just so you can differentiate between what you're doing that is fine and what you're doing that's that little bit better … just so you know someone is keeping an eye on you … you don't want to be a little number walking around the place."

Carolyn Martin states that the modern employee "wants clear direction and managerial support, but they also demand freedom and flexibility".[66] She states that if organisations know "how to energise and focus" the talents of their employees and "how to turn high maintenance into high productivity", they will ultimately have a "strategic advantage over their competitors".

Jennifer Deal believes that all generations expect the same things from leaders: to be credible and trustworthy, to listen, be farsighted and to be encouraging.[67]

It is known that employees with different work characteristics will be more effective and productive with different leadership styles.[68] Bruce Tulgan describes the need to transform the workforce: "Managers will have to discard traditional authority, rules and red tape and become highly engaged in one–one negotiation and coaching with employees to drive productivity, quality and innovation."[69]

Cara Spiro describes how coaching is one of the most successful methods for retaining this population, as it allows them to "thrive in an environment designed to enable their success".[70] Coaching and mentoring "challenges new employees to take on more challenging work; it takes advantage of employee potential by playing to their strengths".

Carolyn Martin claims that leaders who know how to energise and focus the talents of this workforce, who know how to turn high maintenance into high productivity, will have a strategic advantage over their competitors.[71]

Richard Scase describes how people now are looking for a kind of 'self-management' as opposed to the traditional command and control approach to management.[72] He explains the conflict between the traditional approach and this generation who instead want to collaborate and work in teams. He suggests that large organisations have to break up into small operating units to create an entrepreneurial culture that will allow employees to exercise their creativity and that such business units can be highly innovative and dynamic.

Terms and Conditions – Job Security and Fair Pay

A key theme running through all aspects of my research was the area of job security and fair pay. Employees who, for the most part, have never experienced 'difficult times' are living through one of the worst ever economic recessions. A junior manager I interviewed stated that job security was the number one factor in the workplace, adding, "whereas this time last year it probably wouldn't have ranked at all, it would have been taken for granted, now it has to be number one. I'd say things have turned very much in favour of the employer versus the employee."

Research shows that even though compensation is important, to retain top talent employers need to pay more attention to issues such as job quality, flexibility and individual differences. Money remains a hygiene factor, but learning opportunities, personal growth, work variation, autonomy at work and intellectual stimulation must feature highly in the strategy to retain this workforce.

Michael Armstrong believes that dealing with uncompetitive, inequitable or unfair pay systems is one of the first actions that an organisation can take to improve retention.[73] Karin Lanigan also notes that organisations need to be creative and offer not just the traditional inducements to retain quality employees.[74]

At a focus group I ran in Deloitte with some employees (consultants), they made the point that they understood it would be difficult to implement pay increases in the current environment, but asked that the firm consider more creative ways of increasing workplace compensation and benefits, e.g. increasing the annual leave entitlement.

Energy Management – Balancing Work and Life

Despite the economic context, the area of work–life balance is still important. I notice that when speaking of work–life balance as a concept with regard to employees, people often make the wrong assumption that the younger generation are not willing to work hard and can be perceived as 'lazier' than other generations. From conducting my research, I would disagree with this view. The key point is that they want more flexibility around work. Some employees I spoke with would prefer to log on and work at night and come to work later in the day. I believe that elements such as this will be part of the workplace of the future.

The employees in my study were very aware of the need for work–life balance, and both males and females spoke of the particular need for flexibility when they reach the family stage in life:

> "You want something that sits in with your life ... conscious of the fact that you have a life outside [work] ... and even in terms of further down the line if I was to have children ... I would be very aware that I can't be working all the hours that God sends ... flexibility in that sense would certainly be most important."

Richard Scase states the importance of breaking down the barriers between work and non-work.[75] In a world where people want remote working, where people want flexible working, the agile organisation will be successful if it gives people the opportunity to work as they want, where they want and how they want, as long as they deliver the results.

Flexibility is a key requirement for this generation both now for life balance but, more importantly, for the future, as both males and females that I surveyed alluded to the fact that they want to spend time with their children and partners. Organisations will need to be much more flexible in their work practices and encourage remote working, flexible working hours and other innovative practices.

Flexibility has been frequently identified as a key human resource policy goal or outcome, along with strategic intention, quality and employee commitment, "ensuring an adaptable organisation structure".[76] Michael Armstrong recommends that organisations should take steps to improve work–life balance by developing policies that include flexible working to recognise the needs of employees outside of work.[77] Karin Lanigan agrees that employers that offer flexible working arrangements and that encourage the promotion of a work–life balance ethic can be very attractive to employees and potential employees.[78]

The employee workforce wants their managers to understand that they have a life outside of work and to help them balance obligations to both.

For this workforce, it is important that the workplace is social and fun. Companies should have occasional parties and get-togethers to make their employees feel valued and make the workplace fun and happy.[79] Interestingly, my research showed that employees are keener to socialise with colleagues during the working day rather than at evening events. One example of this working well was the simple introduction of birthday cakes in one department in Deloitte. This small gesture of providing tea and cake for someone's birthday has proved very successful, creating a more social atmosphere in the office.

The following case studies are based on real challenges faced managing the development of 'smart professionals'. The response in each scenario is based on aspects of the MOTIVATE framework.

Cameo Case: Situation I

Declan was an A-grade student all his academic life and an exceptional auditor. He progressed quickly and successfully from graduate trainee to middle management in the firm. It was at this point in his career, however, that the limitations in his leadership style began to emerge. Declan's name started to come up in exit interview conversations with the HR department; junior staff found his style demanding at best and bullying in the extreme. He had exceptionally high standards in everything he did and little tolerance for those who operated to a different standard. Although the senior management found his high performance commendable, as did clients, the department was now haemorrhaging talented junior staff. The issue had to be addressed.

Declan was asked to work with a HR coach to focus on developing his 'people management' skills. This intervention proved to be transformational for Declan. The coach started the development process by going through an anonymous, confidential, 360° feedback tool to ensure a range of perspectives. Declan, having a preference for facts and data, could no longer ignore the trends that were presented to him from the range of feedback gathered. In his own words, "the penny dropped." With this new awareness of his impact, he was keen to understand how he could change. Declan's coach suggested he participate in a leadership programme that was running in-house and that he read a text on the area of emotional intelligence, as the core development areas were around self-awareness and empathy. Declan changed his behaviour in many small ways; for example, he made time for coaching meetings each week with junior staff to give them the time and space to address any work issues they were having.

After six months, there was a distinct change in the feedback regarding Declan, and his name was now being discussed in a more positive light. He was recently promoted to director, and acknowledges that he needs to continue to be mindful of his management style and not revert to type, particularly when under pressure.

CAMEO CASE: SITUATION 2

Helen is a director in the forensics department of a successful SME firm employing 30 people. She joined the firm five years ago from a large firm. She had a meteoric career rise in her previous organisation and enjoyed all the 'status' benefits of working as part of a large leadership group. Helen is qualified at the highest levels, with a PhD in her chosen field. One of her values is around personal growth and development, and it is important for her to feel she is continuing to progress and develop. The MD of the company relies on Helen to manage the business to a large degree while he focuses on strategic client relationships. Helen is performing at a high level; and staff really enjoy working with her. The company was placed in the 'Great Places to Work' listing this year for the first time, and this was widely acknowledged to be thanks to Helen's leadership. Helen sees the MD only if there is an operational issue and has limited involvement in the strategic direction of the company.

Recently, Helen scheduled a meeting with the MD to discuss her career development. She was quite candid with him and shared the fact that she was "bored with the job". She felt she had no challenge anymore. Although she enjoyed working with the staff, she felt she had hit a ceiling and there was nothing more for her to learn.

The MD was quite troubled by this and also concerned about retaining the 'cornerstone' of his business. He reflected on the meeting and sought the advice of a former retired boss and mentor. From these discussions, he came to the conclusion that he had been taking Helen for granted and had made the assumption that she would be happy to continue in the same role indefinitely. He realised that in order to keep her engaged and motivated, he needed to look at her role and make some changes to provide her with the challenge she was craving. He suggested they have monthly meetings to review her career development and the scope of her role. Helen expressed an interest in getting involved in strategic business development and moving away from operations management. She is now getting gradually more involved in this area and is thriving from the opportunity and, more importantly, from the 'attentive management' of the MD. She is also due to start a management development programme with one of the business schools supported by the company.

CAMEO CASE: SITUATION 3

Geoff is MD of a small, specialist engineering firm. Because of their technical expertise and agility, they have survived the economic downturn relatively unscathed. International opportunities, particularly in the Middle East, are keeping the practice very busy.

Geoff is extremely frustrated, however, as, yet again, he has received notice of resignation from one of his young graduate engineers. The emerging trend is that these bright, first-class honours engineering students are availing of the excellent training experience of working in this small, specialist practice, but after about two years, when they are really starting to add value, they decide to resign. The interesting trend is that they are not leaving to go to other engineering firms but to travel and 'see the world'.

In discussions with Geoff around potential solutions to this graduate retention issue, a number of possibilities were discussed. One option, favoured by the large financial houses during the boom years, is to support the graduates' travel plans for six months by offering to pay for a return flight and keeping the position open for the young engineer. This may not be feasible in a small practice, and there are no guarantees that the individual will decide to return, but it certainly would encourage this to happen. Another option may be to consider a secondment to an international firm. Geoff has a wide range of contacts from his doctoral studies in the US and could arrange for a reciprocal agreement with similarly qualified graduate engineers. A more local solution would be to make sure he is connected and in-tune with his young engineers and to ensure that they feel their development is being supported and they are being challenged in the work they are doing. It is also important that they see a clear career progression. At present, Geoff has limited HR structures in place, but it is important to put a proper career and performance management system in place as his firm grows.

Conclusion

Professional services firms' main asset is the talent and commitment of their people and, in this chapter, Dr Mary Collins has shared her MOTIVATE framework as a guide both to enhance performance and increase employee satisfaction. Starting with the unseen power of the psychological contract, she has shown how performance management, when done in the manner described, can materially help managers and employees to achieve those twin goals. By articulating the inherent forces that drive people, she has shown how those drives can be made mutually productive. In these ways, she has gone beyond the conventional approach to 'Human Resources Management' to show how both parties to the psychological contract can win. She concludes her contribution with three cases where these 'win–win' principles are demonstrated in action.

This is a pivotal chapter in the book, and her references to emotional intelligence, coaching, leadership and motivation are continued in separate, dedicated chapters.

Mary's contribution and the support of her company are gratefully acknowledged.

Mary's doctorate focused on how best to engage and motivate professionals, and she personifies the spirit of her findings: even a cursory meeting with Mary will allow her firm belief in the potential of people to shine through. This inspiring faith in the potential of people, coupled with her practical approach to enhancing confidence and performance, puts the pathway to more productive and rewarding engagement with staff on firmer ground. Managers are likely to find Mary's advice helpful in dealing with staff in a newer and more positive way.

ENDNOTES

[1] Collins, M. "How Best to Manage Graduate Employees in Professional Services to Enhance their Performance" (Ed. Doc thesis, Dublin City University, 2010).

[2] Rousseau, D. "Psychological and Implied Contracts in Organisations" (1989) 2 *The Employee Rights and Responsibilities Journal* 121–139.

[3] Guest, D. and Conway, N., *Pressure at Work and the Psychological Contract* (CIPD, 2002).

[4] CIPD Figure http://www.cipd.co.uk/hr-resources/factsheets/psychological-contract.aspx

[5] Rousseau, D.M., "New Hire Perceptions of their Own and their Employer's Obligations: A Study of Psychological Contracts", (1990) 11 *Journal of Organizational Behaviour* 389–400.

[6] Rousseau, D.M., *Psychological Contracts in Organizations: Understanding Written and Unwritten Agreements* (SAGE Publications, 1995).

[7] Guest, D.E. and Conway, N., "Communicating the Psychological Contract: An Employer Perspective", (2002) 12 (2) *Human Resource Management Journal* 22–38.

[8] CIPD 2006 http://www.cipd.co.uk/hr-resources/factsheets/psychological-contract.aspx

[9] Guest, D.E., "Is the Psychological Contract Worth Taking Seriously? (1998) 19 *Journal of Organizational Behaviour* 649–664.

[10] Buchanan, D. and Badham, R., "Politics and Organizational Change: the Lived Experience", (1999) Vol. 52 No. 5 *Human Relations* 609–629.

[11] Mayer, C. *et al.*, "An Integrative Model of Organizational Trust" (July 1995) Vol. 20 No. 3 *The Academy of Management Review* 709–734.

[12] Kramer, R.M., "Trust and Distrust in Organizations: Emerging Perspectives, Enduring Questions" (1999) Vol. 50 *Annual Review of Psychology* 569–598.

[13] Lewickil, R. *et al.*, "Models of Interpersonal Trust Development: Theoretical Approaches, Empirical Evidence, and Future Directions" (December 2006) Vol. 32 No. 6 *Journal of Management* 991–1022.

14 Dirks, K.T. and Ferrin, D.L., "Trust in leadership: Meta-analytic Findings and Implications for Organizational Research" (2002) 87 *Journal of Applied Psychology* 611–628.

15 Kramer, R.M., "Trust and Distrust in Organizations: Emerging Perspectives, Enduring Questions" (1999) Vol. 50 *Annual Review of Psychology* 569–598.

16 Bernardin, J.H. and Klatt, L.A., "Managerial Appraisal Systems: has Practice Caught up to the State of the Art?" (1985) November *Personnel Administrator* 79–82, 84–86.

17 Hewlett, S., Top Talent: Keeping Performance Up When Business Is Down (Harvard Business Press, 2009).

18 Manzoni, J-F, *Management Control: Toward a New Paradigm* (JAI Press, 2002).

19 Herzberg, F., *Work and the Nature of Man* (Crosby, 1968).

20 Juechter, W.M., Fisher, C., and Alford, R.J., "Five Conditions for High Performance Cultures" (May 1998) 52 (5) *Training & Development* 63–68.

21 *Ibid.*

22 Osborne, R. *et al.*, "High-performance Companies: the Distinguishing Profile" (2002) Vol. 40 No. 3 *Management Decision* 227–231.

23 DeLong, Thomas J., John J. Gabarro and Robert Lees, "Juggling Isn't the Same as Leading" (December 2007) *American Lawyer* 124–130 (excerpt from the book *When Professionals Have to Lead.*)

24 *Ibid.*

25 Bass, B., *Handbook of Leadership* (Free Press, 1990).

26 Gardner, W., "The Charismatic Relationship" (1998) Vol. 23 No. 1 *Academy of Management Review* 32–58.

27 Kouzes, J. and Posner, B., *The Leadership Challenge,* (Jossey-Bass, 1987).

28 Goleman, D., *Primal Leadership* (Harvard Business School Press, 2002).

29 Goffee, R. and Jones, G., "Why Should Anyone be Led by You?" (Sept–Oct 2000) *Harvard Business Review* 63–70.

30 Megginson, D. and Clutterbuck, D., *Techniques for Coaching and Mentoring* (Elsevier Butterworth Heinemann, 2005).

31 Daloz, L.A., *Effective Teaching and Mentoring* (Jossey-Bass, 1986).

32 Malderez, A., and Bodoczky, C., *Mentor Courses: A Resource Book for Trainer-Trainers* (Cambridge University Press, 1999).

33 Vygotsky, L.S., "Consciousness as a Problem in the Psychology of Behavior" (1979) Vol. 17 No. 4 *Journal of Russian and East European Psychology* 3–35.

34 Kolb, D.A., *Experiential Learning* (Prentice Hall, 1984).

35 Turk, W., "Be a Mentor" (September–October 2011) *Defense AT&L: Better Buying Power* 64–66.

36 Herzberg, F., *Work and the Nature of Man* (Crosby, 1968).

37 Adams, J.S., Towards An Understanding of Inequality" (1963) 67 *Journal of Abnormal and Normal Social Psychology* 422–436.

38 Nohria, N., Groysberg, B. and Lee, L. "Employee Motivation: A Powerful New Model" (July–August 2008) *Harvard Business Review* 78.

[39] Schaufeli, W. *et al.*, "The Measurement of Burnout and Engagement: A Confirmative Analytic Approach" (2002) 3 *Journal of Happiness Studies* 71–92.

[40] Ansari, A. and Lockwood, D., "Recruiting and Retaining Scare Information Technology Talent" (1999) 99/6 *Journal of Industrial Management and Data Systems* 251–256.

[41] www.gallop.com

[42] www.haygroup.com

[43] Towers Perrin, *Global Workforce Study* (2007). Towers Perrin website.

[44] http://www.towersperrin.com/tp/getwebcachedoc?webc=HRS/USA/2008/200802/GWS_handout_web.pdf Truss C., Soane

[45] http://bestcompaniesguide.co.uk

[46] Cappelli, P., *Talent on Demand: Managing Talent in an Age of Uncertainty* (Harvard Business Press, 2008).

[47] Lynman, A., "Creating Trust is Worth the Effort", (Great Place to Work Institute Whitepaper, 2008).

[48] Collins, M, "How Best to Manage Graduate Employees in Professional Services to Enhance their Performance (Ed. Doc thesis, Dublin City University, 2010).

[49] Bains, G. et al., *Meaning Inc.* (Profile Books, 2007).

[50] Collins, M, "How Best to Manage Graduate Employees in Professional Services to Enhance their Performance (Ed. Doc thesis, Dublin City University, 2010).

[51] Wilton, P., "Unlocking the Talent of Generation Y" (2008) 3(14) *Engineering & Technology* 80–83.

[52] Argyris, C., "Teaching Smart People To Learn", (May–June 1991) Vol. 69 No. 3 *Harvard Business Review* 99–109.

[53] O'Toole, J. and Bennis, W., "What's Needed Next: A Culture of Candor" (June 2009) *Harvard Business Review* 54–61.

[54] Hulett, K., "They are Here to Replace Us: Recruiting and Retaining Millennials" (2006) 17 *Journal of Financial Planning* (available from http://www.fpanet.org).

[55] Anell B. and Wilson T.L., "Flexible Working" (2001) *Journal of Workplace Learning*.

[56] Mills C.W., *White Collar: The American Middle Classes* (OUP, 1956).

[57] Hulett, K., "They are Here to Replace Us: Recruiting and Retaining Millennials" (2006) 17 *Journal of Financial Planning* (available from http://www.fpanet.org).

[58] CIPD factsheet at www.cipd.co.uk

[59] Westerman, J.W. and Yamamura, J.H., "Generational Preferences for Work Environment Fit: Effects on Employee Outcomes" (2007) 12: 2 *Career Development International* 150–161.

[60] Armstrong, M., *A Handbook Of Human Resource Management Practice* (10th ed., Kogan Page, 2006).

[61] www.greatplacetowork.ie

[62] Collins, J.C. and Porras, J., "Building Your Company's Vision" (September–October 1996) *Harvard Business Review* 65–77.

[63] Taylor W. and Labarre P., *Mavericks at Work: Why the Most Original Minds in Business Win* (HarperCollins 2006).

[64] Spiro C., "Generation Y In The Workplace" (Nov–Dec 2006) *Defense AT&L* 16–19.

[65] McDonald, P. and Hovland G., "The Multigenerational Workforce" (2008) Vol. 65 Issue 5 *Internal Auditor* 60–67.

[66] Martin, C., "From High Maintenance to High Productivity: What Managers Need to Know About Generation Y" (2005) Vol. 37 Issue 1 *Industrial and Commercial Training* 39–44.

[67] Deal, J., "Generational Differences" (2007) Vol. 24 Issue 6 *Leadership Excellence* 11.

[68] Martin, C. and Tulgan, B., *Managing Generation Y: Global Citizens Born in the Late Seventies and Early Eighties* (HRD Press, 2001).

[69] *Ibid.*

[70] Spiro C., "Generation Y In The Workplace" (Nov–Dec 2006) *Defense AT&L* 16–19.

[71] Martin, C., "From High Maintenance to High Productivity: What Managers Need to Know About Generation Y" (2005) Vol. 37 Issue 1 *Industrial and Commercial Training* 39–44.

[72] Scase, R., *Global Remix: The Fight for Competitive Advantage* (Kogan Page, 2007).

[73] Armstrong, M., *A Handbook of Human Resource Management Practice* (10th ed., Kogan Page, 2006).

[74] Lanigan, K., "Retaining People: Practical Strategies To Reduce Staff Turnover", (2008) Vol. 40 Number 1 *Accountancy Ireland* 48–50.

[75] Scase, R., *Global Remix: The Fight for Competitive Advantage* (Kogan Page, 2007).

[76] Guest, D.E., "Is the Psychological Contract Worth Taking Seriously?" (1998) 19 *Journal of Organizational Behaviour* 649–664.

[77] Armstrong, M., *A Handbook of Human Resource Management Practice* (10th ed., Kogan Page, 2006).

[78] Lanigan, K., "Retaining People: Practical Strategies To Reduce Staff Turnover", (2008) Vol. 40 Number 1 *Accountancy Ireland* 48–50.

[79] Strong, M., "Give Gen Y-Ers A Reason To Stay at your Agency" (2008) 79:14 *Advertising Age* 24.

Chapter 7

Motivating Professionals: New Discoveries

The only way to do great work is to love what you do.

Steve Jobs

This chapter highlights surprising new discoveries in how to motivate professionals and other people for higher performance. It debunks four of the most common myths about motivation, explains why too much incentivisation is counter-productive, and shows how even small wins drive success. The text then explains how unexpected rewards and acts of recognition can have a tremendous effect on performance. Significantly, it makes the case that achievement at work, in itself, can lead to heightened job satisfaction, which (with a degree of happiness) comes from meeting appropriate challenges, not from enjoying comfortable mediocrity.

Also discussed is how ability can be increased, even in high-performing professionals, by adopting the right attitudes ('mindset'). The chapter then demonstrates how professionals can increase even their high potential and "become their best self". Finally, core approaches to motivation are summarised and integrated into a single framework.

Highlights of this chapter on motivating professionals:

- Too much incentivisation is counter-productive.
- The carrot becomes an expensive stick.
- Fear is not the best motivator.
- The Tom Sawyer Effect.
- Common myths of motivation.
- The Achievement Principle.
- Mastery is a mindset: escaping self-imposed limiting thoughts.
- Progress itself is a motivator.
- Prize and pride go together.
- Competitiveness can sharpen motivation.
- Rapture: the joy of achievement.
- Avoiding 'country club' or 'work camp' management styles.
- Turn your people on by turning off the de-motivating factors.
- Bringing the component elements of motivation together.

In the preceding chapter, Dr Mary Collins laid out a compelling and effective HR framework for managing people. In this chapter, the theme is continued, with a particular emphasis on motivating very smart people, starting with a short anecdote about rocket science involving chemists, physicists and technicians.

IT IS ROCKET SCIENCE

On a recent trip to Colorado, I had the unusual pleasure of joining a local 'Rocket Club' for a day. This was a group of amateurs (mainly chemists and physicists) who delighted in sending missiles (of all sizes, up to 2 metres in length, at considerable expense) high into the desert air. Later, another group of friends devised a home-made launcher (hewn from an oxygen tank) that blasted a normal bowling ball 1,500 feet into the evening gloom (the explosive moment is popular on YouTube!). Why? Simply because they could, and because they got huge enjoyment from playing with fire and from competing with each other. Similarly, the Ansari X Prize, a $10 million award for the first privately funded manned spacecraft to break through the Earth's atmosphere, was won by designers who had spent many times that amount to produce the spaceship: it was worth it, they said, for the bragging rights.

The motivation for all these smart people centres on achievement, intellectual stimulation, a sense of pride in making a unique contribution, and simple fun. The lesson is that these same motivations can still prevail at professional work of all kinds.

Encouraging Achievement: Pride and Prizes

Professor Josh Lerner has answered the question of whether rewards such as the Ansari X Prize actually motivate inventors to produce new ideas and create things they would not otherwise have. Using data that went back a century and included some very prosaic prizes, the results were indisputable: "The prizes had a real impact", says Lerner. "They seem to not only have stimulated activity but also to have actually led to more innovation."[1] In those years that recognitions were offered in particular areas of science, the number of prize submissions shot up – as did the number of patents and renewals.

Moreover, it did not seem to matter how much money was made available for the prizes – or even if any money was offered at all. In areas where a gold medal replaced a cash prize, competition was just as fierce and the innovations just as plentiful.

Lerner concludes that prestige alone was enough to spur the innovation, offering inventors a 'seal of approval' they could then use to show that their idea had merit.

This is the same phenomenon as the amateur programmer who designs open-source software as a calling card, or the blogger who wants to establish herself as an expert in a field. While Lerner says more work must be done to determine the best ways to maximise participation, the evidence shows that such prizes can be a valuable approach to spurring innovation.

Motivation: The Carrot Becomes A Stick

Daniel Pink, author of *Drive*[2] and *A Whole New Mind*,[3] shows that using financial incentives as a 'carrot' can turn fun into work, and that greater reward does not usually spur greater achievement, as might be widely believed. For creative work, **the pressure of additional incentives actually seems to cause outcomes to deteriorate**.

Pink's account begins with the findings of the Nobel prize-winning psychologist Daniel Kahneman, who debunked the prevailing orthodoxy that man is a rational, economic animal, responding predictably to incentives and sanctions. Pink describes Kahneman's experiments, in which participants would forego even large sums of money for such human reasons as a sense of fair play or a desire for revenge, even where such revenge is self-defeating. In other words, "rational wealth maximization" is sacrificed for emotional *human* reasons. People therefore are not automatically wealth maximisers, but are often willing to exchange money for more fulfilling 'human' reasons. Money is indeed a real motivator for most people, including high-earning professionals, but its power as a motivating factor declines as one's earnings increase. Above certain thresholds, people tend to turn their focus towards self-fulfilment, as will be explored more towards the end of this chapter.

Similarly, people will pursue arduous tasks, such as mountain-climbing or learning the oboe or completing Sudoku puzzles, in the name of leisure. Paying people to do such tasks, however, would turn the fun into work! Club players love their weekend golf, but for those who turn professional, it becomes a livelihood, not so much a pleasure.

There are still a great many tasks (cleaning hotel rooms, mining coal, assembling widgets, etc.) that require incentivisation and that are difficult to infuse with fun or meaning. For professionals, however, and indeed most occupations, this is not the case, as the work involves some element of intellectual challenge, creativity, variety and autonomy.

Curiosity: a Perpetual Wellspring of Motivation

It emerges that there is another powerful inherent drive in humans that goes deeper than extrinsic (financial) rewards. Curiosity is present from birth, and children explore and play, just for the fun of it. Gradually, curiosity and creativity appear to fade away, perhaps through societal norms to 'grow up'. In truth, the urge to self-determine, to travel further, to push boundaries does not actually disappear, even if it goes dormant. A good manager will be able to wake up this sleeping inner drive, especially in professionals and other smart people, as these will have been propelled to succeed in the first place.

Mark Twain pointed out that "work consists of whatever a body is obliged to do". He noted how 'gentlemen' would pay heavily for the privilege of driving horse-coaches 100 miles – but would never oblige if they were offered a wage for this 'work'! Amateur cyclists push themselves for 100 km over mountains for 'fun', but would baulk at a job that paid them for that journey. In other words, incorrect (and expensive) incentivisation can turn interesting activities into drudgery.

> Tom Sawyer inverted this principle and showed how work can be transformed into fun. In Mark Twain's *The Adventures of Tom Sawyer*, Tom convinced his friends that painting a fence was so much fun that they paid him for the privilege. Tom, of course, had been given the chore as a punishment.

KILLING THE JOY: DRAWING CONCLUSIONS

Daniel Pink recounts[4] an experiment in which school kids who enjoyed drawing were placed into three groups. The first group were offered a reward (a certificate of achievement) and asked if they wanted to draw.

The second group were asked just if they wanted to draw, and were later given an unexpected award (the same certificate) as a prize.

The third group were again just asked if they wanted to draw, but were neither promised nor received any reward.

The researchers returned two weeks later to secretly observe the children when they again had the chance to draw: their observations surprised them. The second and third groups took the opportunity to draw with relish, but the first group, who had received the expected reward, showed little enthusiasm. The 'Tom Sawyer Effect' had kicked in.

Note that it was not the rewards *per se* that had made the difference to the young students: it was where the reward was contingent ('if you do this, you will get that') that interest waned. The fun of drawing had been turned into work.

To see if the 'Sawyer Effect' worked universally, economist Dan Ariely ran a series of experiments in India.[5] He devised games in which small, medium- and super-sized financial rewards were offered. These rewards were equivalent to a worker's pay for a day, month and five months. Astonishingly, the results for the small and medium rewards were about the same – but the super-sized rewards had a strong negative effect, because the players simply choked under the 'pressure'. Perhaps the fun was taken away, but in any case, the incentives backfired. The over-incentivisation was both expensive and counter-productive. This may have huge implications for how people, generally, are rewarded, especially those in professions with a creative aspect, such as engineering, design, marketing or architecture, where innovation is a central activity. Simply put, people can have too much of a good thing.

This is not a licence to under-pay or exploit people: the whole premise of these theories of motivation is that they are founded on genuine, authentic engagement with people, not in manipulating them. It is important to design people's work so that it has meaning, and superior results can then emerge. The research outlined above indicates that if you treat people with respect, they will generally reciprocate that respect. The message is to pay people well enough, but to also design the work so that it is challenging. Create meaningful rewards to satisfy intrinsic motivation **and** to harness the drive for curiosity. This is not just an appeal to be 'nice' for its own sake: set the bar high and coach people to achieve challenging goals. The achievement principle says that happiness emerges from achievement. Achievement, not employee satisfaction, is the starting point in the cycle.

Extrinsic rewards, such as financial payments, should be somewhat unexpected, a pleasant surprise, not simply 'contingent' on a certain effort. The work of Dr John Antonakis of IMD Lausanne explains that managing people through such 'contingent' rewards creates an overly mercantile mindset that limits discretionary effort (where people go the 'extra mile' because they want to, not because of a financial inducement). A system of contingent reward introduces a negative side-effect: it tends to make all effort the subject of a financial negotiation, i.e. people adopt a posture that says that unless the reward is high enough, they won't agree to do certain tasks. In her research, Dr Teresa Amabile of Harvard University has confirmed this principle of unexpectedness: "that the highest levels of creativity were produced by subjects who received an award as a kind of bonus".[6] This is discussed also in **Chapter 1** and **Chapter 8**.

FOUR COMMON MYTHS ABOUT MOTIVATION

Myth 1: Fear is a good motivator Not usually – a certain unease that overcomes complacency and perhaps a tinge of fear of the boss might not be bad, but generally fear (including the fear of not getting that large reward) inhibits all but the most routine work. Incentivisation, as explained above, has its limits.

Myth 2: I can motivate people Not really – ultimately, people can only motivate themselves. What a good manager does is help her people discover their own inner motivation and release their inherent drive.

Myth 3: Increased job satisfaction means increased job performance Perhaps, but this is best understood in the sense that achievement drives satisfaction, not the other way around.

Myth 4: I know what motivates me, so I know what motivates my people Not true – people have varying values, value different rewards and are motivated differently depending on their situation. The best – and simplest – way of finding what this is, is to ask them.

Mastery is a Mindset: Escaping the Psychic Prison by Avoiding Self-limiting Thoughts

Professor Carol Dweck uses the phrase "mastery is a mindset" to express the contrast between those who believe that intelligence is a fixed 'entity', and those who believe intelligence can be 'incremented' with effort and application.[7] She explains that those who set out to learn, as distinct from demonstrating their smartness, actually perform better at applying their newly acquired knowledge, and are more resolute in attempting new applications. The difference, she says, is that those people with a learning bias are less inhibited or fearful of failure. Those who set out to prove they are smart fear failure, perceiving it as 'proof' of a limit to their intelligence.

That intelligent people can become anxious and defensive is discussed further in **Chapter 11**, but it is important to mention at this point that success, and intelligence, can foster a serious, 'shadow' side that can breed arrogance and fear of failure.

To encapsulate the above ideas, remember '**PAM**' – Purpose, Autonomy, Mastery:

- Start by infusing work with some element of meaning, attaching it to higher **purposes**.
- Develop the person, design the work and delegate so that eventually **autonomy** is earned.
- Encourage oneself and others to believe that learning and improvement is possible and obligatory – strive for excellence in one's work and pursue **mastery**.

Finally, as a manager, don't use money as your only bargaining chip. Strive instead to get people to want to make that discretionary effort. Be sure to recognise achievement in genuine ways, with a generosity of spirit. Don't believe you know what motivates others: it is not a case of 'do unto others as you would have them do unto you'. Rather, it's '**do unto others as they would have done unto them**'. Give them personalised attention. As Elton Mayo proved decades ago,[8] the psychological stimulus of being treated this way, even for mundane work, dramatically increases productivity.

Small Wins, Big Ideas: The Progress Principle

Harvard's Teresa Amabile has found that while the fruits of innovation are often in plain view, the seeds of creativity are much harder to spot – occurring deep inside what she calls the "inner work life" of employees.[9] "Creativity requires very high levels of intrinsic motivation", she says – that is, it has much more to do with an employee's inner passion for doing great work than any outside motivators, like incentives.

In an effort to better understand where that motivation comes from, Amabile managed a study of more than 200 knowledge workers over a three-year period, asking them to keep journal entries of their successes and frustrations at work. What she found was unexpected: it was not recognition or awards that most ignited employees and freed up their creative juices. Rather, employees tended to be most engaged by regular, incremental progress toward the accomplishment of a meaningful goal – a phenomenon Amabile calls the 'Progress Principle'.

Analysing some 12,000 cases, Amabile consistently found that these so-called 'small wins' were closely associated with the positive emotions and intrinsic motivation that, in turn, generated the creativity needed to develop innovative approaches to problems. This means that managers do have some control over the internal processes of the minds of the people they manage. "As a manager of people, you should regard this as very good news", Amabile concludes. "The key to motivation turns out to be largely within your control."

By setting clear, achievable goals, allowing autonomy in achieving those goals and removing distractions or unnecessary time pressures, managers can help free up creative impulses and guide people down the path of real innovations that can help the firm. Amabile makes a distinction between creativity (the origination of new ideas) and innovation (the exploitation or commercialisation of these new ideas):

> "In contrast to the creative process, the innovation process can happen when people are in a more extrinsically motivated state, focusing on the deadline, the profitability goals. Ideally, they will still be passionate about the work, but it's important at that point to focus in and to make sure the details of implementation are right."[10]

The Right Fit

Creative work does not fit neatly with office routine; the 'muse' cannot be commanded to appear at a set time. People in creative fields tend to be more free-spirited thinkers than the norm. Their lack of standardisation can cause difficulties for their more orthodox managers. Bosses who have relied on financial incentives may find this can backfire, as creative types often despise such approaches, regarding them as crass manipulation.

Because creativity cannot be produced to order, goal-setting can be sporadic and somewhat random. Finally, such incentivisation is expensive and may even be demeaning. Certainly, rewards will be accepted, but using money alone may be counter-productive.

In their research London Business School professors, Karim Lakhani and Kevin Boudreau have found a dramatic difference between those who like to compete and those who do not.[11] Those participants who enjoyed competition performed twice as well as the rest. They clocked up more hours and produced better results than the less competitive groups. Interestingly, increasing the financial incentive (to a maximum of $1,000) had no effect on the best. It did, however, increase the hours worked by the average performers, but not those of the lower skilled workers.

Lakhani advises that it is important for managers to discover who works best autonomously, as distinct from those who work best in a team situation. Putting workers in the right environment may be a more effective way to motivate people, whether they are paid more or not.

Accomplishment and Happiness – in that order

It emerges that one of the best ways to motivate employees is to help them move forward every day. Reversing the conventional belief that staff satisfaction increases productivity, the opposite seems more correct – achievement produces satisfaction. This is especially true if those doing the work consider it to be meaningful. Obvious once discovered, this is a powerful principle for those who manage professionals. Achievement, success and satisfaction are self-reinforcing, it emerges.

Naturally, just increasing the level of burden, or otherwise exploiting the principle, will not lead to sustained performance, but if used authentically this principle is a true win–win for all concerned. If a person is happy at the end of the work day, it is likely that he or she has achieved something, whereas their unhappiness could well be due to frustration. This 'achievement principle' further implies that it behoves managers to arrange work so that employees' overall well-being is enhanced. To do this, managers should work on developing meaningful goals, consistent with the time and resources available, and creating the possibility of getting recognition – and pride – for a job well done.

Conversely, managers should work to offset the debilitating effects of setbacks or other frustrations, offering encouragement, finding silver linings and generally cheerleading.

Even regular work can be invested with meaning. The janitors at NASA believe they are helping put men on Mars. The work simply must be made to matter to the person doing it.

THE POWER OF PROGRESS

Research by Harvard's Teresa Amabile[12] confirms that what motivates people is progress itself. While it is one thing to suspect this, it is entirely another to have it proven by a researcher of such eminence. The current beliefs about what satisfies and motivates people are generally seen in this order, with recognition foremost:

1. Recognition.
2. Incentives.
3. Interpersonal support.
4. Organisational support for the task.
5. Clear goals to guide tasks.

It emerges that it is really **progress itself** that builds motivation. This important finding makes sense: progress provides reward, recognition, encouragement, positive feedback and can even contribute to life happiness, as well as satisfaction at work.

Climbing the Ladder of Happiness

Martin Seligman,[13] a leading figure in psychology, declares that people seem happiest when they have, in ascending order:

1. *Pleasure* (physical comfort, decent food, good and safe surroundings).
2. *Engagement* (absorption in a challenging but somehow enjoyable activity).
3. *Relationships* (friendship and good family ties often preface happiness).
4. *Meaning* (a feeling of belonging to something worthy or bigger than oneself).
5. *Accomplishments* (achieving significant, demonstrable goals).

SELIGMAN'S LADDER OF ACHIEVEMENT AND HAPPINESS

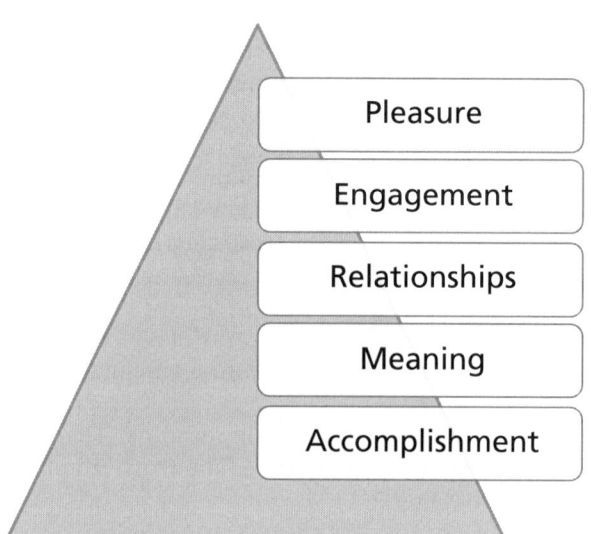

These findings support Abraham Maslow's[14] seminal 'hierarchy of needs', a pyramid depicting the levels of human need, from its foundation in physical security (shelter, clothing, food) through relationships and right up to self-actualisation, as illustrated below. The highest level is self-actualisation, in which maturity and self-acceptance combine with creativity. At such times, a person might be said to be 'in the zone'. The high points are sometimes described as moments of rapture, where things click and come together. These rare moments are based on a deeper understanding, and a sense of achievement, a kind of wholeness. Ironically, achieving challenging goals and doing the right kind of work in a conducive environment is one of the ways to access these rare states. The euphoria that comes from such moments is evident not just in sporting achievement but also in the launch of new products: Apple's product launches are an obvious example; and Tracy Kidder captures the joys and tribulations of creating new products in his classic book *The Soul of a New Machine*.[15]

MASLOW'S HIERARCHY OF NEEDS

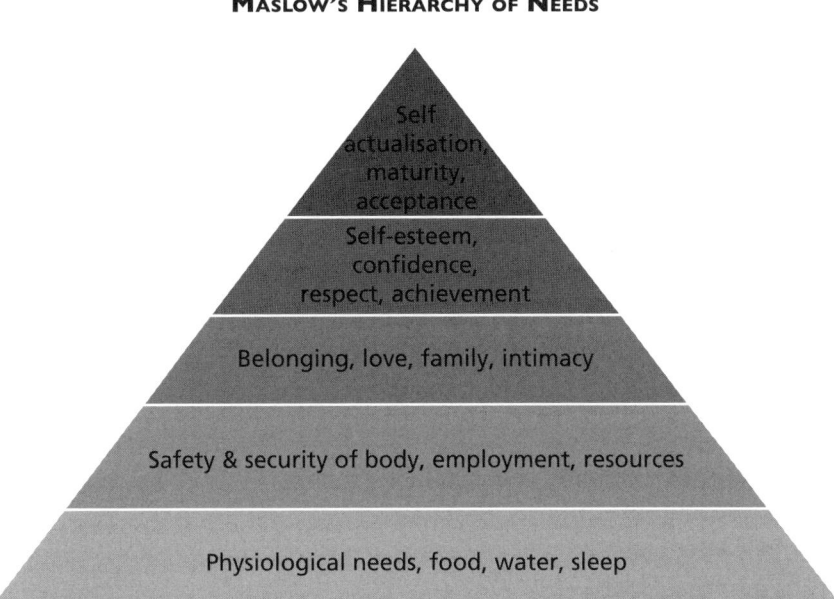

The implication of the Maslow model is that setting agreed, challenging goals is a powerful motivational factor in itself, producing both achievement and indeed happiness for employees. This also explains why moribund organisations (as may be found in both the private and public sectors) may provide comfort to employees but do not provide any serious degree of fulfilment.

A word of caution: do not misinterpret these findings. It is not enough for a mischievous boss to simply set high goals! This is exploitation, and it will not work for any length of time as it does not provide a supportive environment, lacks the correct work context and fails to really access people's true source of motivation. People, especially smart people, quickly recognise manipulation and hypocrisy, will quickly withdraw their support, and will be slow in allowing trust to be re-established.

A conclusion from the above discussion might be simply stated: 'success breeds success'. This contradicts the more conventional belief that people must be 'happy' to produce good work, when in fact happiness more often comes from achievement.

More on Motivation

Maslow's hierarchy of needs can be understood by expressing the levels as:

- existence,
- relatedness, and
- growth

as illustrated below, not in pyramid form but as an escalation of needs.

MOTIVATION: MASLOW RE-INTERPRETED

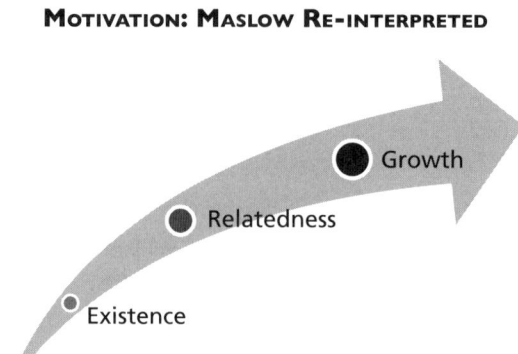

The key point for managers of people to take from Maslow is the relentlessly upward drive: people truly are almost never satisfied. The fulfilment of one level of need will naturally and inevitably lead to a higher level desire. Once basic physical needs are met, the search moves progressively upward, to security needs, then belonging (affiliation needs), then on to self-actualisation (creativity and maturity). Fulfilment of a basic human need (such as provided by an adequate salary) fades as a work motivator once it is satisfied. For managers of most professionals this will be the case, meaning that the next frontier of motivation shifts to 'relatedness' (i.e. a sense of belonging) and then to growth (self-actualisation – reaching one's human potential, being one's 'best self').

The noteworthy aspect of this is that with money diminishing as a motivator, other cost-free opportunities arise through generating that sense of belonging, giving due recognition and creating opportunities for the person to be their 'best self'. These 'soft' motivators provide hard benefits, and do so in a more wholesome and productive environment. While many managers and practice leaders may cling to 'old school' management, Maslow's theory provides an unmistakable opportunity for enlightened self-interest.

Dissatisfaction is *not* the Opposite of Satisfaction: Herzberg's Two Factor Theory

Frederick Herzberg, interviewing 272 accountants and engineers in 1959, made another valuable discovery: there are two very different kinds of factors that affect motivation, and they act in completely different ways.[16] The positive motivators (see illustration below) include factors such as recognition, advancement, growth, job challenge, increased responsibility and achievement itself. The negative motivators include "dissatisfiers" such as poor working conditions, restrictive policies and bureaucratic administration.

HERZBERG'S TWO DISTINCT FACTORS WORK INDEPENDENTLY

Motivators
Achievement
Recognition
Career advancement
Job challenge
Responsibility
Recognition

Dissatisfiers
Poor working conditions
Chafing policies
Unwarranted bureaucracy
Perceived unfairness
Status concerns
Relationship with supervisor

1. **Hygiene factors can only demotivate** While so-called 'hygiene factors' create dissatisfaction if staff perceive them as inadequate or inequitable, individuals will not be significantly motivated if these elements are brought up to standard. Hygiene factors are 'extrinsic' (beyond the person) and include factors such as irritating policies, bureaucracy and poor working conditions. Pay has elements of intrinsic and extrinsic motivation: the amount itself is not as important as its perceived relativity to others doing similar work.
2. **Only intrinsic factors are motivators** Motivators are intrinsic factors, such as a sense of achievement, recognition, responsibility and personal growth.

Hygiene factors determine dissatisfaction, and motivators determine satisfaction. Removing the hygiene factors decreases dissatisfaction, but it does not actually lead to heightened motivation: that stems from more intrinsic factors, such as achievement accompanied by recognition and appreciation. The sequence is illustrated below:

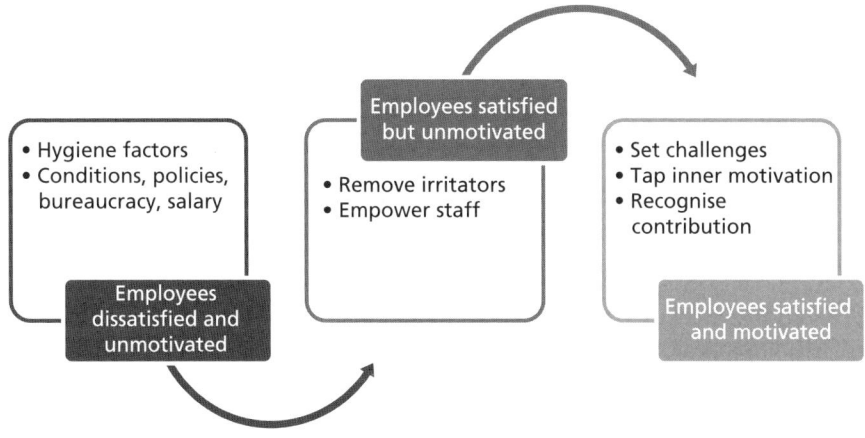

As shown in the following figure, poor policy and administration can have an extremely negative effect on motivation. Some irritating factors (e.g. unnecessary bureaucracy, poor lighting, broken equipment) can be sorted out quickly, generating a disproportionately large effect on motivation. This is closely followed by recognition ('well done'), whereas the effect of pay is much more moderate.

FACTORS AFFECTING JOB ATTRIBUTES: HERZBERG'S TWO FACTORS IN DETAIL[17]

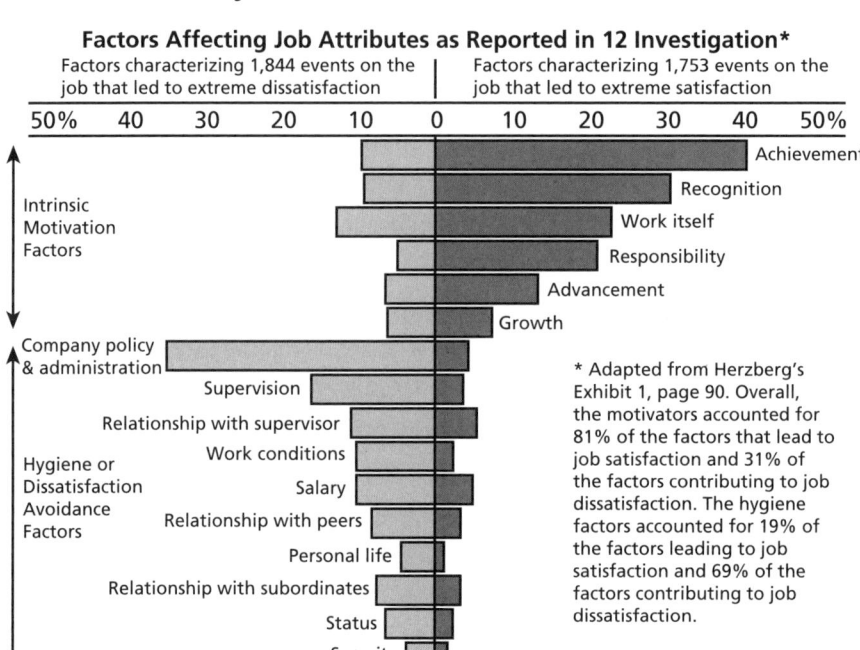

Herzberg's 'two factors' help explain why employees continue to be unmotivated, even when salary, terms and conditions are adequate; true motivation lies deeper in the human psyche, which is why a pure task orientation is not as effective as more intrinsically inspiring approaches. Conversely, trying to motivate staff who are distracted by irritators like hard-to-comprehend policies and inferior conditions is unlikely to produce satisfactory results.

Motivational Drive: Using Inherent Achievement Needs for Best Results

For more effective motivation, it is useful to recognise a person's basic motivational drive. David McClelland has distinguished three basic drives and explains how the needs for achievement, power or affiliation affect the actions of people, from a managerial viewpoint[18]:

McClelland's Three Basic Drives

Need for Achievement	Need for Affiliation	Need for Power
• Task Mastery • Independence	• Belonging • Harmony	• Dominance • Control

Need for Achievement A person with a high need for achievement will inevitably seek achievement and challenging goals. He or she will have a strong need for positive feedback on achievement and progress, and will look for a sense of accomplishment, often taking personal responsibility for tasks – and this is usually a welcome gift for his or her manager, with the proviso that this drive does not result in such a focus on task that the driven professional disregards protocols, disdains social niceties or disrespects less-driven people. Denying this basic need means that the person with a need for achievement (and most professionals have at least some of this drive) just means that the person will look elsewhere to satisfy that need, seeking challenges that allow him or her demonstrate mastery of a subject (e.g. in leading an association, pioneering a social initiative, immersion in a hobby).

Need for Affiliation This person will seek harmony and consensus, and will consequently be much more social than other types. They will seek acceptance by other people, and will have a 'people' orientation rather than the task one, above. As a result, if their workplace doesn't provide them with a sense of affiliation they will gravitate to settings that do satisfy that need to belong, such as choirs, groups, drama societies and social clubs. Again, this is a lost opportunity if a professional or other worker has to look outside the work organisation to satisfy their needs.

Need for Power This person wants to direct and command other people, and often seeks positions of dominance. While this potentially provides the organisation with leaders who are prepared to take on responsibility, it can also lead to interpersonal conflict and petty political difficulties.

These categories of needs are not exclusive, as individuals have all three needs to some degree, but over time a bias towards one main need may emerge. By identifying a person's main driver, a manager can try to place that person in a suitable position. For example, a person with a strong need for achievement will more readily accept a task that offers a chance to demonstrate mastery, even if that demands unusual degrees of perseverance. On the other hand, a person with a strong need for affiliation will not thrive in such a situation but will perform better in roles that provide more human contact. A person with a strong drive for power will not easily fit in a subservient role, and will deploy their energies in situations where they can be dominant. The savvy manager recognises the different drives, and harnesses them for the organisation's benefit, capturing energy and commitment that would otherwise be channelled elsewhere.

Managers Have Needs: Origins of Different Management Styles

Managers themselves, of course, have such needs, and these will usually shape their management style. For example, people-oriented managers have a subconscious tendency to prefer a soft, harmonious style, with benefits as noted above, but with the risk that an absence of task focus will create an overly relaxed 'country club' style. Conversely, task-driven types will tend towards a 'work camp' style, and may be regarded by other types as heartless 'slave-drivers'. These contrasting styles are represented in the Mouton–Blake grid, shown below. Managers with a strong orientation towards social harmony will tend to favour the 'country club' approach, high in regard to people, but low on task commitment. On the other hand, the driven task master may assume people will adopt his productivity-first approach and focus on the task in hand, to the exclusion of concern for human factors. Note that a compromise style (a bit of both styles) is neither 'fish nor fowl', and that the optimum style is one that is high in both dimensions (people *and* task).

The illustration below shows these styles, including the extremities, the 'produce-or-perish' task orientation and the 'country club' style of management. The ideal is not the middle-of-the-road position, because this misses the opportunity to have **both** a concern for people as well as for tasks. It is not a question of people OR task, but people AND task, represented as 'Team' in the depiction below.

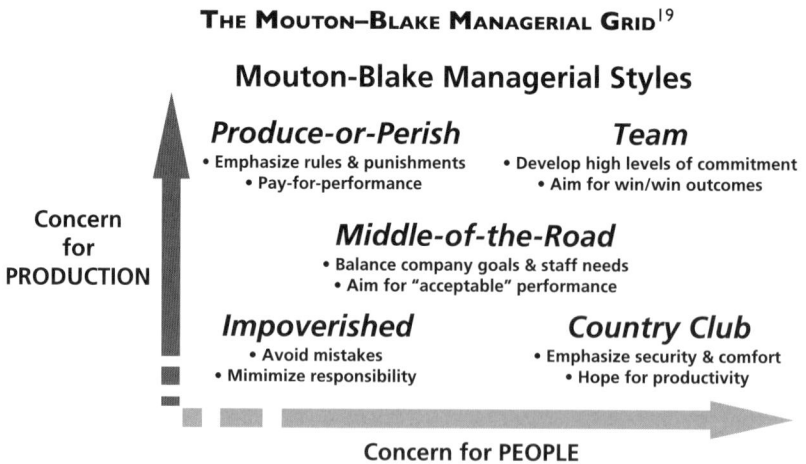

THE MOUTON–BLAKE MANAGERIAL GRID[19]

Shaping Perception for Increased Employee Motivation

Victor Vroom developed his 'expectancy theory' as a systematic explanation of workplace motivation.[20] His analysis indicates there are three main components, and the absence of any one component seriously reduces a person's motivational force.

Vroom says that a person's motivation to behave in a particular way is determined by his or her '**expectation**' that the effort will lead to the desired result, multiplied by the belief that the chosen method will be '**instrumental**' and multiplied in turn by the value ('**valence**') he or she attributes to that outcome.

This model implies that if any one of the components is low, then overall motivational force will consequently be low. For example, say a professional has to make a presentation to secure a new client. If she believes that success is unlikely, or that making the effort is doomed, or that the new client is not valuable, she is suffering from low expectancy, low instrumentality and low valence. Failure then becomes almost inevitable.

Motivational Force – A Product of Expectancy × Instrumentality × Valance

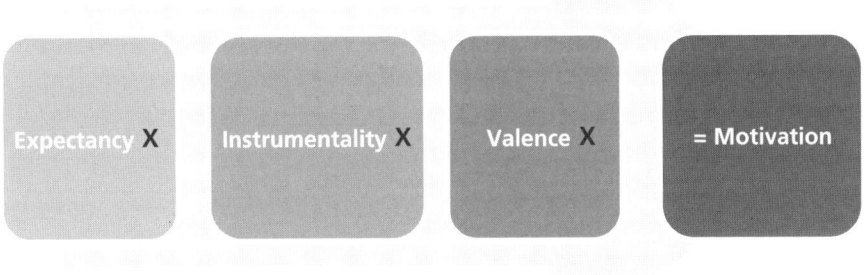

Both expectancy and instrumentality are cognitions, and can therefore be changed through a person's experience, or by the persuasiveness of the manager. These are perceptions held by the individual, and they can be changed by an effective manager who realises and counteracts the underlying beliefs. A professional might start out highly motivated because she believes that her effort will lead to a high performance rating (*Expectancy*), and that a high performance rating will lead to increased pay or a promotion (*Instrumentality*), and she really values pay or promotion (*Valence*). However, if after working hard, she gets a low performance rating, her expectancy will likely drop. Similarly, if despite getting excellent performance ratings, she gets the same pay as those with merely acceptable ratings, her belief in instrumentality is likely to decline and her motivational force will tend to weaken.

Note here the effect of *perception* in motivating people towards goals. Astute managers will influence people's perception of the effort needed to achieve particular goals and will similarly shape expectations of the value or desirability of these goals. For example, a professional might be reluctant to adopt new methods or technologies, even where these are well proven. The well-informed manager can assess the source of the reluctance (such as an exaggerated but unstated fear of failure or a lack of regard for the reward on offer) and respond appropriately. Such a manager could help the professional put that fear into proper perspective and could highlight the value of the proposed reward, or simply substitute a reward that the professional actually values.

It is worth noting that 'equity theory', as discussed below, states that the *perceived fairness* of rewards and recognition is as important as their actual value to the person.

Lyman Porter and Edward Lawler expanded expectancy theory and showed the linkage between *perceived effort*, *equity* (perceived fairness of the resultant rewards and the assessment process), *intrinsic reward* (mainly recognition, sense of achievement) and *extrinsic reward* (money and other compensation for effort):[21]

LINKING EFFORT, FAIRNESS AND REWARD: THE PORTER–LAWLER MODEL

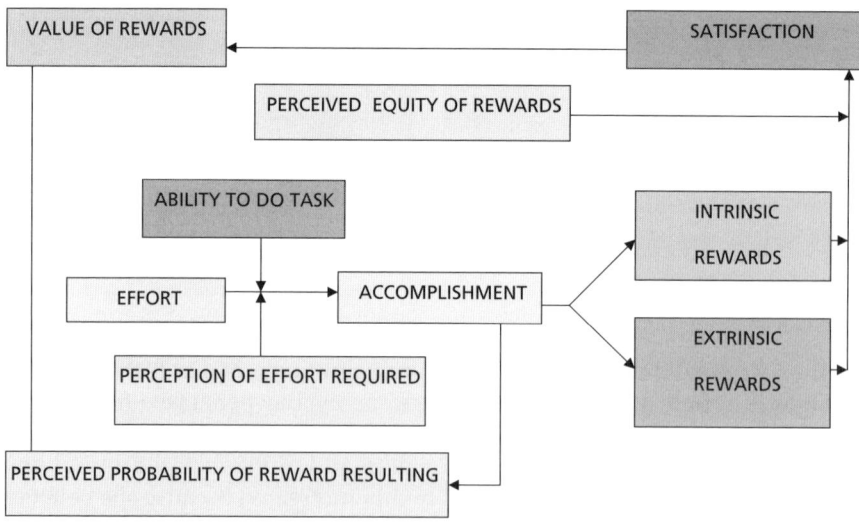

Good managers, even those with a high concern for costs, utilise these perceptual factors in raising output. Great managers use these factors because it is the right thing to do in helping people towards maximum achievement and satisfaction and, of course, the achievement of organisational goals.

As a final caution, note that motivation lives within the individual. Nobody can actually 'motivate' another person, but effective managers can spark the fires of motivation by creating the right conditions to mobilise a person's innate inner drives.

Motivation, Leadership and Personality: Integration

To deepen understanding of motivation, see also the earlier chapters on leadership and personality. These chapters explore ways in which motivation can be individualised for different personalities. Later chapters suggest practical ways to coach professionals towards higher performance and also to build self-confidence.

The figure below shows the inter-relationship of various elements of motivation to help map the terrain for managers who want to deepen their knowledge.

INTEGRATING THE ELEMENTS OF MOTIVATION

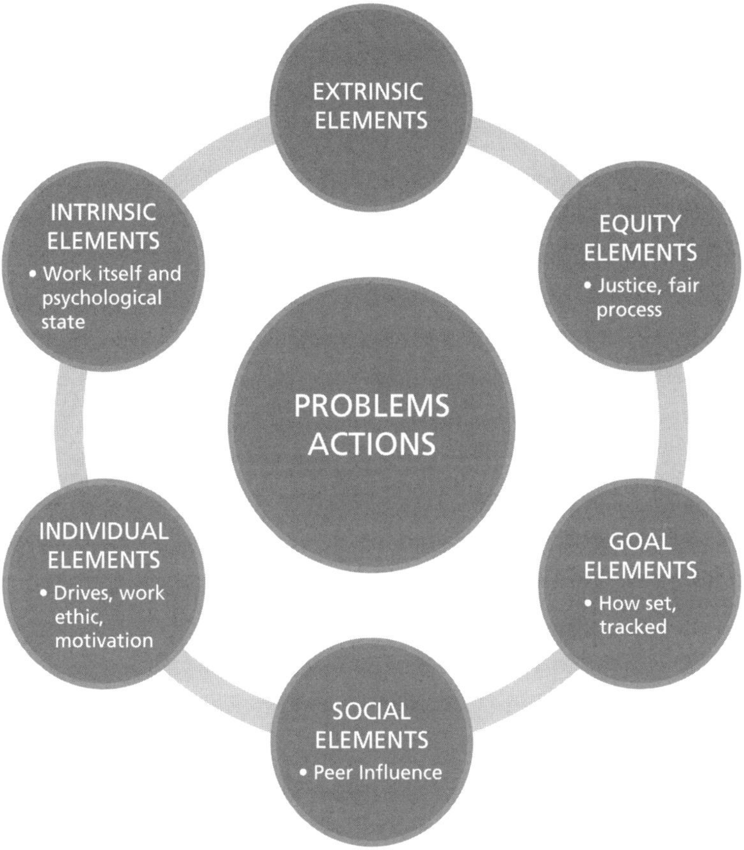

Conclusion

The models of motivation popularised over the last century need serious adjustment to the modern world of high-intellect work. Smart professionals seek careers, not just jobs, and their achievement orientation means that they respond well to meaningful challenge, especially in an environment that has strong values and a vibrant culture. In such settings, smart professionals work best when allowed to self-select when teamwork is required. As bright people will usually have quickly ascended Maslow's hierarchy, self-fulfilment becomes the new priority. Taken together, this means that supervisory management is less effective with smart people: the new order demands that managers actually lead by creating the right environment, designing an achievement culture and steering from behind, as a navigator rather than a commander.

> *"Change your thoughts, and you change your world."*
>
> Norman Vincent Peale

ENDNOTES

[1] Josh Lerner *et al.*, "Inducement Prizes and Innovation" (2012) Vol. 60 No. 4 *Journal of Industrial Economics*.

[2] Daniel Pink, *Drive: The Surprising Truth about What Motivates Us* (Canongate Books, 2010).

[3] Daniel Pink, *A Whole New Mind: Why Right-brainers will Rule the Future* (Penguin, 2005).

[4] *Ibid.*

[5] Dan Ariely, *Predictably Irrational: The Hidden Forces That Shape Our Decisions* (HarperCollins, 2009).

[6] Teresa M. Amabile and Steven J. Kramer, "The Power of Small Wins" (2011) Vol. 89 No. 5 *Harvard Business Review* 70–80.

[7] Carol Dweck, *Mindset: The New Psychology of Success* (Random House, 2006).

[8] Elton Mayo, *Hawthorne and the Western Electric Company: The Social Problems of an Industrial Civilisation* (Routledge, 1949).

[9] Teresa M. Amabile and Steven J. Kramer, "The Power of Small Wins" (2011) Vol. 89 No. 5 *Harvard Business Review* 70–80.

[10] *Ibid.*

[11] Kevin Boudreau and Karim R. Lakhani, "'FIT': Field Experimental Evidence On Sorting, Incentives and Creative Worker Performance" (Harvard Business School Working Paper, 2011).

[12] Teresa M. Amabile and Steven J. Kramer, "The Power of Small Wins" (2011) Vol. 89 No. 5 *Harvard Business Review* 70–80.

[13] Martin Seligman, *Authentic Happiness: Using the New Positive Psychology to Realize your Potential for Lasting Fulfillment* (Simon & Schuster, 2002).

[14] Abraham Maslow, *Towards a Psychology of Being* (3rd ed., John Wiley & Sons, 1999).

[15] Tracy Kidder, *The Soul of A New Machine* (Back Bay Books, 2000).

[16] Frederick Herzberg, "One More Time – How do you Motivate Employees?" January–February (1968) *Harvard Business Review* 53–62.

[17] *Ibid.*

[18] David McClelland *et al.*, *The Achievement Motive* (Appleton-Century-Crofts, 1953).

[19] Jane Mouton and Robert Blake, *The Managerial Grid III: The Key To Leadership Excellence* (Gulf Publishing Co., 1985).

[20] Victor H. Vroom, *Work and Motivation* (John Wiley & Sons, 1994).

[21] Lyman W. Porter and Edward E. Lawler, *Managerial Attitudes and Performance* (Irwin-Dorsey Press, 1968).

Chapter 8

Developing Know-how: Managing Knowledge and Innovation

To make knowledge workers productive will be the great management task of this century, just as to make manual workers productive was the great management task of the last century.

Peter Drucker

Introduction

Organisations are incessantly bombarded with the exhortation to innovate: this is a simple imperative, but difficult to execute. What is missing is guidance on how to actually achieve such abstract tasks as innovating and creating new knowledge. Organisations clearly depend on knowledge, but the most vital knowledge is often unarticulated, tacit knowledge, perhaps barely understood at the conscious level.

Similarly, while organisations need acumen in making business decisions and wisdom in dealing with people, the tacit nature of knowledge means there is as yet little practical advice available to help them develop these critical, but abstract, functions.

In this chapter we investigate the nature of innovation, intuition and knowledge. We then indicate how these can be 'managed' using a simple framework, followed in the next chapter by an example of how a professional organisation within a major multinational company has successfully deployed the principles.

Managing knowledge and fostering creativity depends not so much on high intellect (which professionals already have in abundance) but on the character of the organisation and its people. High challenge and high achievement depend, in turn, on trust and collegiality. For groups to coalesce into high-performing communities (not just teams in the conventional sense), there must be mutual respect, security (emotional and job-related), appropriate challenge levels and a meaningful sense of mission.

Such trust has to be earned. Integrity cannot simply be asserted – by an individual or an organisation – it, too, must be demonstrated in deed as well as word. Without sufficient challenge, the 'community' (in the collaborative sense mentioned above) languishes, losing its momentum. Without emotional and job security, risks that should be countenanced will too often be avoided. In this chapter we will examine how to nurture such a 'community of common purpose' and how to blend autonomy with discipline in appropriate measure.

While building a culture of excellence fosters high achievement, it also has the happy consequence of making the management of creative professionals and other smart people less fraught. The techniques suggested here rely only on character and human qualities; they do not require expenditure of significant time or money.

Earlier efforts to 'manage' knowledge have largely failed, but the approach presented here, in first recognising the subtle human factors that undermined those attempts, has been demonstrated to work. Recent research has revealed the little-known ingredients for success (and failure), and explained phenomena such as why underdogs triumph so often, and why excellent physical facilities fail to deliver on their promise (Spartan boot-camps produce the champions in sport and business).

The Lessons from Past Failures in Knowledge Management

Corporate giants such as Shell and IBM have made well-resourced efforts to manage knowledge, yet their expectations of collaborative knowledge working and 'shared learning' have not been met. This is largely because of the very human tendency to seek recognition for developing valuable information, and the understandable desire to retain the power associated with special knowledge ('turf protection').

While talent can arise naturally, powerful new evidence (from Malcolm Gladwell, Daniel Coyle and others) shows that talent can also result from systematic, deliberate practice – and so can be emulated in business. The core skill here is the ability to engage not just in conventional practice, but to systematically learn from that practice by critiquing one's own performance, i.e. to 'practice, better'. This requires overcoming the instinctual tendency to be defensive, so that practice is meaningful and progressive. This ability to 'practice, better' applies to the development of expertise in a number of fields, of course, not just sports.

Knowledge-management failures can also be understood by realising that information itself needs to be understood: knowledge is inferred from information, and it depends on the context and the situation. The figure below (regarding 'whole-brain thinking') represents this hierarchy, starting with raw 'facts'. The raw **data**, if endowed with meaning, can sometimes be converted into **information**, usually by answering questions (such as who, when, where, how many) that lead to a quantification of the facts. The next level in the hierarchy requires a further interpretation of this new information, an **understanding** of 'why' – for example, why something causes a particular effect. **Wisdom**, the highest level, may interpret the past, but its orientation is on the future, judging what seems best going forward into the unknown. **Intuition** in this sense is a kind of wisdom, based on valid experience, yet so nuanced and complex as to be beyond normal powers of expression. **Tacit knowledge** shares a similar property of being beyond description – it is unconscious knowledge that cannot be articulated.

The serious attempts by Shell and others at knowledge management were based on breakthroughs in computer technology and involved populating databases, but administering such repositories made knowledge management an unwelcome chore. This was compounded by the added frustration that such information quickly becomes outdated and loses value. As a trivial example, very few people want to read yesterday's newspaper, but having tomorrow's edition today would be invaluable!

The challenge is particularly acute in managing professionals because of their innate or inculcated scepticism, their desire not to be 'wrong', their desire for autonomy, their typically individualistic roles and, occasionally, their resistance to changes not of their own making. Furthermore, managers in professional organisations lack the kind of power common in conventional organisations: they manage only with the consent of their peers, making transformation more difficult. Without such 'position' power, they must rely on their 'personal' power, their ability to influence and their motivational abilities.

This chapter aims to address these issues by changing the focus from managing knowledge to developing professionals (and other smart people) in a supportive 'ecosystem' that has high achievement, collegiality and a sense of mission at its very core.

The individual professional will also benefit, professionally and personally, from this conscious development of hard-to-access skills and capabilities.

> "The secret of Toyota's success is that the company encourages every worker, no matter how far down the production line, to consider himself a knowledge worker and to think creatively about improving."
>
> Stephen Spears

Developing Expertise

In this section we will investigate how to grow intellectual and emotional capacity in otherwise smart professionals, taking a 'whole brain' approach to enhancing both the right- and left-brain elements – analysis and creativity. Intelligence, *per se*, can be improved only slightly, but the application of that intelligence can certainly be boosted. Intellectual quotient (IQ) multiplied by emotional quotient (EQ) then becomes a powerful product.

The whole-brain thinking model, adapted in the figure below from the original by Ned Herrmann,[1] divides the brain into four functioning segments, with the **left** brain housing the fact-based, analytical, problem-solving capacities and associated planning abilities. The **right** brain is depicted as housing abstract visioning, artistic and intuitive capacities, along with the visceral reactions and emotional feelings.

Whole-brain Thinking

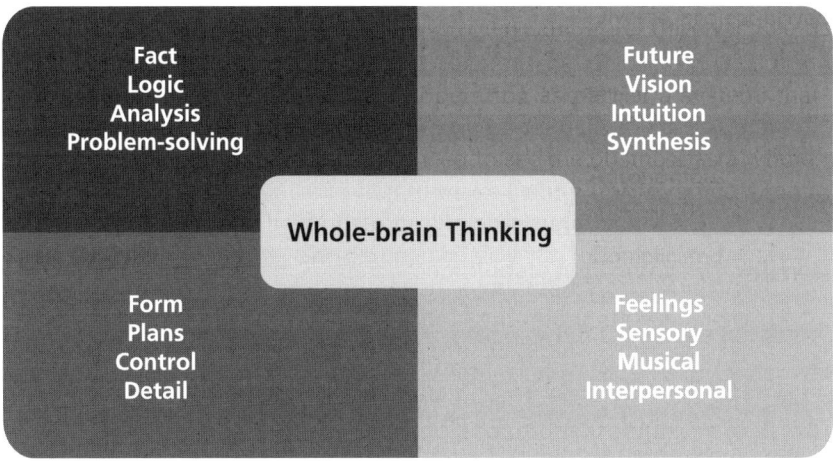

Fact Logic Analysis Problem-solving	Future Vision Intuition Synthesis
Whole-brain Thinking	
Form Plans Control Detail	Feelings Sensory Musical Interpersonal

It should be noted that the brain system simplistically represented here can be hijacked by more primitive forces (the instincts to either fight or flight) located in the lower stem of the brain, the *amygdala*. Containing these 'amygdala hijacks' is vital in avoiding the escalating of conflict through 'blind fury' and other rages. Daniel Goleman and Reuven Bar-On have devised tests of 'emotional intelligence' to profile the level of development of related abilities, including a person's 'impulse control'.[2] (Emotional intelligence is discussed in detail in **Chapter 12**.)

Teaching Smart People How to Learn

In a landmark *Harvard Business Review* article, "Teaching Smart People How to Learn",[3] which is summarised here (with emphasis added), Chris Argyris has noted that:

"Every company faces a learning dilemma: **the smartest people find it the hardest to learn**."

Success in the marketplace increasingly depends on learning, yet most people do not know how to learn. Furthermore, those members of the organisation who many assume to be the best at learning are, in fact, not very good at it. In this, Argyris is referring to the well-educated, high-powered, high-commitment professionals who occupy key leadership positions in the modern corporation.

Most companies not only have tremendous difficulty addressing this learning dilemma, they are not even aware that it exists. Why? They misunderstand what learning is and how to bring it about. As a result, they tend to make two mistakes in their efforts to become learning organisations:

1. **Most people define learning too narrowly** as mere 'problem-solving', so they focus on identifying and correcting errors in the

external environment. While solving problems is important, if learning is to persist, managers and employees must also look inward. They need to reflect critically on their own behaviour, identify the ways they often inadvertently contribute to the organisation's problems, and then change how they act. In particular, they must learn how the very way they go about defining and solving problems can be a source of problems in its own right.

In order to capture this crucial distinction in approaches to and types of learning, Argyris has coined the terms **'single loop'** and **'double loop'**. He illustrates this with a simple analogy: a thermostat that automatically turns on the heat whenever the temperature in a room drops below 68 degrees is a good example of *single-loop learning*. A thermostat that could ask, 'Why am I set at 68 degrees?' and then explore whether or not some other temperature might more economically achieve the goal of heating the room would be engaging in *double-loop learning*. Highly skilled professionals are frequently very good at single-loop learning. After all, they have spent much of their lives acquiring academic credentials, mastering one or a number of intellectual disciplines, and applying those disciplines to solve real-world problems. But, ironically, this very fact helps explain why professionals are often weak at double-loop learning.

Put simply, **because many professionals are almost always successful at what they do, they rarely experience failure**. And because they have rarely failed, they have never learned how to learn from failure. So, whenever their single-loop learning strategies go wrong, they become defensive, screen out criticism and put the 'blame' on anyone and everyone but themselves. In short, their ability to learn shuts down precisely at the moment they need it the most.

2. The propensity among professionals to behave defensively helps shed light on the **second mistake** that companies make about learning. **It is commonly assumed that getting people to learn is largely a matter of motivation**. When people have the right attitude and commitment, learning automatically follows. So, companies focus on creating new organisational structures – compensation programmes, performance reviews, corporate cultures and so on – that are designed to create motivated and committed employees.

However, effective double-loop learning is not simply a function of how people **feel**. It is a reflection of how they **think** – that is, the cognitive rules or reasoning they use to design and implement their actions. Think of these rules as a kind of 'master programme' stored in the brain, governing all behaviour. Defensive reasoning can block learning even when the individual commitment to it is high, just as a computer program with hidden bugs can produce results exactly the opposite of what its designers had planned.

Companies can learn how to resolve the learning dilemma. What it takes is to make the ways managers and employees reason about their behaviour a focus of organisational learning and continuous improvement programmes. Teaching people how to reason about their behaviour in new and more effective ways breaks down the defences that block learning.

More and more jobs involve 'knowledge work'. People at all levels of the organisation must combine highly specialised technical expertise with the ability to work effectively in teams, form productive relationships with clients and customers, and critically reflect on and then change their own organisational practices. And the nuts and bolts of management – whether it is of high-powered consultants or service representatives, senior managers or factory technicians – increasingly consists of integrating the autonomous work of highly skilled people.

Teaching Professionals How to Learn

Learning to learn, as Chris Argyris has wryly noted, does not involve expense, just a change of mind, resetting the mental mind map that unconsciously shapes our decisions, and re-examining entrenched beliefs. This shift in attitude can be difficult, because of deep, hidden assumptions. Bertrand Russell pithily claimed that "many men would rather die than think. Most of them do". Moses Maimonides, an Egyptian physician (1135–1204 AD), similarly asserted that "Men like the opinions to which they have become accustomed from youth; this prevents them from finding the truth, for they cling to the opinions of habit." In some cases, however, just a small shift can make a major impact.

Little changes can make a big difference: take, for example, evidence from a Harvard study in the US that 30 seconds of additional attention, such as expressing concern for patients and being particularly courteous, reduces the probability of the doctor being sued by the patient significantly – as much as 80%.[4]

Biases that Distort Decision-making and Judgement in Intelligent People

Chris Argyris has observed the challenge in "teaching smart people to learn", and attributes this to the resistances that set in when a professional comes to believe they already know enough or have seen certain situations sufficiently often. Such mental short-cuts are understandable, as they lead to quicker decisions, but they are ultimately limiting and can even be dangerous in certain critical situations. The 'Abilene Paradox' relates how collections of individuals can agree on a sub-optimal course of action that none of them actually wants. Professor Jerry Harvey of George Washington University, who first articulated this breakdown of communication, tells the story of how a group of intelligent people travelled hundreds of miles by car on a steaming hot day all the way to a restaurant in Abilene, Texas – even though individually none thought it a good idea.

The Bay of Pigs fiasco for the US military in Cuba in 1962 is another example of groupthink, one which had potentially disastrous consequences. A deliberately assembled group of bright minds blundered drastically in deciding US policy on Castro's Cuba. The reason, apparently, was the assumption that intelligence alone would suffice, and an over-regard for each other's intellect.

The exhibit below lists, names and defines some of the more surprising or pernicious psychological syndromes that affect thinking, even in bright people.

SYNDROMES THAT AFFECT THINKING, EVEN IN SMART PEOPLE

- Bandwagon effect — another kind of groupthink, an un-thinking, herd-like behaviour.
- Confirmation bias — the tendency to search for or interpret information in a way that confirms one's preconceptions.
- Professional 'deformation' — the tendency to look at things according to the narrow conventions of one's own profession, ignoring other views.
- Endowment effect — people often demand much more to give up an object than they would be willing to pay to acquire it. This is a loss aversion, whereby people value what they already have disproportionately.
- Focusing effect — this is a prediction bias occurring when people place too much importance on one single aspect of an event, rather than considering the whole thing.
- Framing — using a narrow approach to the issue by 'framing' the question in a false or restricted way. This leads the person to pose – and answer – the wrong question.
- Illusion of control — the tendency for people (and especially professionals, if they happen to be arrogant) to believe they can control an outcome that they actually cannot.
- Information bias — the tendency to seek information even when it cannot affect action. This is a paralysis by analysis.
- Irrational escalation — the tendency to make irrational decisions based upon rational decisions in the past — 'throwing good money after bad'.
- Loss aversion — "the disutility of giving up an object is greater than the utility associated with acquiring it". An irrational, emotional overestimation of the loss of an asset versus the identical cost of acquiring that same thing.

- Exposure effect — the tendency for people to express undue liking for things merely because they are familiar with them. Familiarity in this sense does breed contempt.
- Need for closure — the need to reach a verdict in important matters; to have an answer and to escape the feeling of doubt and uncertainty. It seems odd, but, as psychologist Virginia Satir has noted, many people "prefer the certainty of misery to the misery of uncertainty". (This issue is addressed at length in the chapter on personality types, **Chapter 5**).
- Neglect of probability — the tendency to disregard probability when making a decision under uncertainty. Bi-polar, all-or-nothing, black-and-white thinking.
- Outcome bias — the tendency to judge a decision by its eventual outcome instead of based on the quality of the decision at the time it was made. Mixing cause and effect.
- Planning fallacy — the tendency to assume that the plan itself is enough and to underestimate task completion times.
- Rationalisation — the tendency to invent a rationale after-the-event. The syndrome is often evident just after someone has placed a bet with a bookmaker: it is then they are most certain of a good outcome!
- Reactance — the urge to do the opposite of what someone wants you to do out of a need to resist a perceived attempt to constrain your freedom of choice (my personal favourite).
- Selective perception — the tendency for expectations to affect perception: whether you believe you will or believe you won't, you'll be right (to borrow Norman Vincent Peale's phrase).

As distinct from the above psychological syndromes, certain biases can similarly afflict judgement, even in intelligent people:

COMMON THINKING BIASES — ERRONEOUS BELIEFS

- Ease of recall — overestimating what is more likely by accessing convenient, recent or vivid memories, such as reacting to the most recent or remarkable news.
- Repetition — a process in which a belief gains more and more plausibility through its repetition in public (or: 'repeat something often enough and it will become true').
- Gambler's fallacy — the tendency to assume that individual random events are influenced by previous random events. For example: tossing a coin, getting three heads in a row, and assuming the next toss will more likely be tails. Each loss is random and independent.

- Hindsight bias — 'I-knew-it-all-along' effect: the inclination to see past events as conforming to our expectations.
- Positive outcome bias — a tendency in prediction to overestimate the probability of good things happening to them (wishful thinking).

Examining these biases, it can be seen that many of them have psychological origins or can be traced to narcissistic or paranoid behaviours. Many arise simply from the surfeit of intelligence and over-concentration in a narrow area, reinforced by lengthy professional training. For smart professionals to be truly effective, they need to remain grounded, have social ties and maintain a balance between their intellectual, physical and personal selves. Such measures will extend the useful life of the expert, as well as increasing productivity along that journey.

Expertise consists of those characteristics, skills and knowledge that distinguish experts from novices and the less experienced. In some areas, there are objective measures of performance capable of distinguishing experts from novices: expert tax accountants will achieve more for their clients; expert chess players will usually win games against recreational chess players; expert medical specialists are more likely to diagnose a disease correctly.

Dr Jimmy Sheehan, in his discussion of leadership and managing peers (see **Chapter 4**), develops these points about experts, such as surgeons, needing to develop further as people and to have a balance between narrow areas of expertise and social development. **Chapter 9** shows how these concepts around developing 'whole people' are applied in practice in an organisation comprised mainly of professional engineers.

THE HAMMERSTEIN MODEL: ELEVATE THE INTELLIGENT, LAZY PEOPLE

Kurt Von Hammerstein had a whimsical view of intelligence and laziness.[5] He was a German army commander between the First and Second World Wars, but staunchly opposed the Nazi regime. He held some surprising views about intelligence and diligence, including the following impolitic observation, quoted in a military handbook in 1933:

"I divide my officers into four classes; the clever, the lazy, the industrious, and the stupid. Most often two of these qualities come together. The officers who are clever and industrious are fitted for the highest staff appointments. Those who are stupid and lazy make up around 90% of every army in the world, and they can be used for routine work. The man who is clever and lazy, however, is for the very highest command; he has the temperament and nerves to deal with

all situations. But whoever is stupid and industrious is a menace and must be removed immediately!"

Developing Talent: Malcolm Gladwell and the '10,000 hour' Rule

Malcolm Gladwell has effectively answered (with a resounding 'Yes') the question of whether it is possible for individuals to acquire outstanding talent. In his book *Outliers: The Story of Success*,[6] Gladwell provides strong evidence that, except in very rare cases, success is achieved through hard work early in life, intelligent practice and deliberate learning. He cites a litany of cases where the achieved level of attainment is not due to an accident of birth or some inherent quality, but to the results of sustained practice, achieved at an early age, before others have clocked up the same time: 10 years or 10,000 hours of clever practice and openness to feedback.

Gladwell's observation, supported by Andres Ericsson's research,[7] was that "the biggest misconception about success is that we do it solely on our smarts, ambition, hustle and hard work". He claims there is much more to success than conventional intelligence. He uses the term 'outlier' to indicate people with exceptional achievement who are at the fringes of the statistically possible, such as nuclear physicist J. Robert Oppenheimer (part of the Manhattan Project to develop the first atomic bomb), Bill Gates and The Beatles.

While the careers of these people illustrate how chance can shape success, they also reveal the power of deliberate practice: Gladwell's '10,000-Hour Rule' confirms that greatness is the product of intelligent endeavour (not just natural genius) and, importantly, can be *learned*. He points out how The Beatles performed live in Hamburg nearly a thousand times between 1960 and 1964. This intense apprenticeship, difficult at the time, meant that "they sounded like no one else. It was the making of them". Similarly, Bill Gates accumulated 10,000 hours at an early stage: at the age of 13, in 1968, he had access to one of the first computers.

Gladwell concludes that success "is not exceptional or mysterious. It is grounded in a web of advantages and inheritances, some deserved, some not, some earned, some just plain lucky". The proof that success can be achieved though deliberate practice will surely encourage the conscious pursuit of excellence in professionals.

Is Star Talent Overrated?

The march of innovation would seem to have increased the power of the individual over the lumbering herd, but is the talented individual overrated? Going back to the earliest days of computing, Fred Brooks (IBM mainframe designer and author of the classic project management text *The Mythical Man-Month: Essays on Software Engineering*[8]) asserted that a single star engineer is worth more than a score of good ones. This is a claim echoed today by Facebook CEO Mark Zuckerberg, and by legendary Netscape founder Marc Andreessen, who both assert that the bright star is worth 'hundreds' of lesser lights. While this may be an exaggeration, nevertheless a Shakespeare may indeed be worth more than 100 ordinary writers.

To help retain star talent, IBM set up an incubating unit for free-wheeling talent, and produced a guide called *Staying Extreme*, which describes the way talented young people do their best work and warns against arrogance and self-centredness. "To be clear," it warns, "when you leave Extreme Blue and join another group at IBM (or any other company for that matter), we will be watching. And if we find out that you are making the program look like we are producing a bunch of arrogant wannabes, we will forget we ever knew you. Be ambitious. Be a leader. But do not belittle others in pursuit of your ambition."[9]

Malcolm Gladwell in "The Talent Myth" assessed the current obsession with hiring the best and the brightest, and warned that the problem with this star-studded approach is the "assumption that an organization's intelligence is simply a function of the intelligence of its employees". Some companies believe in stars, because they don't believe in systems. In a way, that's understandable, because our lives are so obviously enriched by individual brilliance. Groups don't write great novels, and a committee didn't come up with the theory of relativity. But companies work by different rules. They don't just create; they execute and compete and coordinate the efforts of many different people, and the organizations that are most successful at that task are the ones where the system is the star."[10]

In other words, the star needs the system, as much as the system needs the star. This mutual interdependency, often unrecognised, is crucial, and making this interdependency clear can help bridge the divide between star and system.

Gladwell instances Enron, famously populated with the brightest people from elite institutions, before its collapse. "The reasons for [Enron's] collapse are complex, needless to say. But what if Enron failed not in spite of its talent mind-set but because of it? What if smart people are overrated?"

Deliberate Learning – from Mistakes

"Learning without thought is labour lost: thought without learning is perilous."
Confucius

A breakthrough study, documented in *The Talent Code* by Daniel Coyle,[11] also presents evidence that "greatness isn't born, it's grown". Coyle spent two years visiting talent hotbeds like Brazil's 'soccer factory', Moscow's Spartan tennis training campground, and various arts and music talent clusters. After studying "deliberate practising", he concludes that, far from being an abstract quality (essentially pre-determined at birth), **ability really can be created**.

He reveals how seemingly unremarkable people suddenly make a quantum leap in ability, because of their willingness and capacity to learn from their mistakes, and apply the learnings consciously. He suggests that early enjoyment under a nurturing teacher, later supported by a more challenging teacher, is very effective. The inference is that people can achieve their potential if they train the right way, and get the right support at the right time.

To follow his own advice, he decided to experiment with his two daughters, and successfully trained them to become international chess grandmasters at a very early age.

LEADERS: BORN OR MADE?

A study into 2,000 sets of identical twins found that around 30% of leadership characteristics are inherent, i.e. just 30% "are born", but 70% "are made".[12] Leaders are sometimes born, but are always made: interestingly, a consistent requirement across many studies is that a prerequisite for true leadership capability is a certain level or threshold of intelligence. Being smart, therefore, really matters in leadership, but ultimately it is training, experience and early achievement that makes the difference and helps turn the person into a genuine leader.

Learning is essentially a human disposition: every living person has innate curiosity, and it could be said that 'if you aren't learning, you aren't living'. The question then becomes whether one is learning well enough? Leadership is essentially about learning. Great leaders translate their experiences into heightened self-awareness and improved performance to create organisational cultures in which talent thrives. Great leaders who demonstrate 'learning agility' are more inclined to seek out new challenges, to encourage feedback from others, to self-reflect and to plan what they will do as a result.

Learning to Lead; Leading to Learn

"In the end, it is important to remember that we cannot become what we need to be by remaining what we are."

Max De Pree

Many factors shape the extent to which an individual becomes a leader, including genetic predisposition, family, school, hardships and challenges, job experiences, authority figures, organisational incentives and training. Leaders are born *and* made. The 'wheel' of leadership development (see also **Chapters 3 and 4** about leadership, and **Chapter 7** about motivation) is portrayed below.

FOUR ELEMENTS IN LEARNING TO BECOME A LEADER

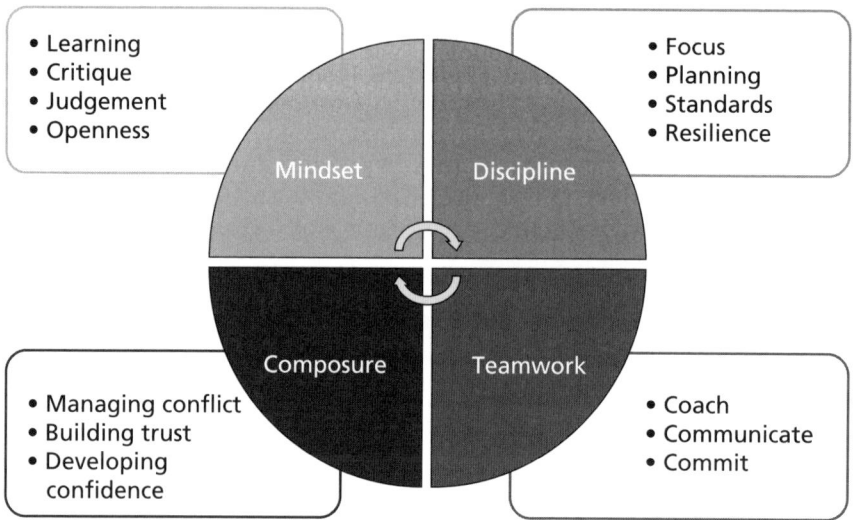

• Learning
• Critique
• Judgement
• Openness

Mindset

• Focus
• Planning
• Standards
• Resilience

Discipline

Composure

Teamwork

• Managing conflict
• Building trust
• Developing
  confidence

• Coach
• Communicate
• Commit

The figure summarises the key activities that help a person learn to lead. The prerequisites, as mentioned above, are a certain minimum level of cognitive intelligence and an open mind-set (not a defensive one). With these in place, willpower and discipline are needed to achieve the deliberate practice needed to hone leadership skills: the individual must stay the course and be 'resilient', not ceding to debilitating mental syndromes such as 'all or nothing' thinking, 'awful' thoughts ("isn't it awful that … ?") or self-perpetuating negative outlooks ("I can never learn … I am useless"). Composure – emotional intelligence – is needed to avoid interpersonal conflict becoming bitter and fruitless, to build trust and to develop confidence in oneself and in others. Finally, communication and coaching, and a commitment to a specific goal or cause, foster the necessary elements of teamwork.

Applying this view of learning to organisations, not just individuals, MIT Professor Peter Senge claims that:

> "the rate at which organizations learn may become the only sustainable source of competitive advantage. The only sustainable advantage for a corporation is the ability to learn".[13]

Whole-brain Capability, *Acumen* and *Nous*

The professional who has 'whole-brain capability' (see above) invariably has high potential value. Steve Jobs, after being pushed out of the company he co-founded with Steve Wozniak, was brought back and revitalised Apple with stunning results over a decade, introducing a slew of innovative products. His value was not just that of a senior engineer but of an innovator and a marketing superstar. Interestingly, his awesome talent could have been even more productive with better people management, as he could have carried more talented people with him on his odyssey.

Such scarce, valuable levels of expertise can be defined with elusive terms such as *nous* or *acumen*.

> 'Nous' is a philosophical term for the faculty of the human mind, described in classical philosophy as necessary for understanding what is real or true. Close in meaning to intuition, it is often regarded as a type of perception within the mind rather than only through the physical senses. Aristotle distinguished the subtle intelligence of *nous* from *logos* (logic or rational reason).

This abstract, '*tacit*', intuitive capability completes the journey from apprentice to master, from novice to expert. It is analogous to moving up the hierarchy of knowledge, from data to information to understanding and on to wisdom, as described earlier in this chapter. Similarly, intuition can be regarded as latent or unconscious knowledge, lying dormant and waiting to be discovered. *Nous* or intuition is not unfounded instinct or irrational bias but a real, if unarticulated, sense of emerging knowledge.

Explicit Knowledge

'Know-how' is practical knowledge of how to get an activity done, as distinct from 'know-what' (facts), 'know-why' (science), or 'know-who' (networking). Know-how is often tacit knowledge, meaning that its ephemeral quality makes it difficult to transfer to another person verbally or through the written word. The obverse of tacit knowledge is 'explicit' knowledge, which can be codified and hence catalogued and disseminated.

Tacit Knowledge

The tacit aspects of knowledge are those that cannot be codified, but can only be transmitted via training or through personal experience. One example of tacit knowledge comes from the learning of a language – it is not possible to learn a language simply by being taught the rules of grammar – a native speaker picks it up through assimilation at a young age, almost entirely unaware of the formal grammar. Riding a bike cannot be learned solely from a book.

SCIENCE: OBJECTIVE AND SUBJECTIVE KNOWLEDGE

> Eminent economist and scientist Michael Polanyi is vocal in his opposition to the prevailing rational view of science, arguing that it has failed to recognise the part which personal commitment and tacit knowledge play in science.[14]

Polanyi saw absolute objectivity as a delusion and false ideal, and he criticised the prevailing notion that the scientific method yields truth mechanically to the scientist. Instead, he argued that all knowing is personal, and as such relies upon fallible commitments. People are never separate from the universe they observe, but instead participate personally in it and thus cannot develop purely 'objective' (e.g. unbiased) knowledge. Human skills, biases and passions are not flaws but play an important and necessary role in guiding discovery and validation.

He observes that the mark of a great scientist is the ability to identify for investigation those scientific questions which are likely to lead to successful resolution. This ability derives not only from the scientist's ability to perceive patterns and connections, but also from personal interests and biases. In turn, these biases fuel the scientist's willingness to risk his or her reputation by committing to a hypothesis and advocating it. He gives the example of Copernicus, who rejected the reigning interpretation of the evidence of the sun, the moon and the stars rising daily in the east and setting in the west to posit that the heavens did not revolve around the Earth. Polanyi claimed that Copernicus arrived at the objective truth of the Earth's true relation to the sun, not by following a rigid method, but by giving in to "the greater intellectual satisfaction he derived from the celestial panorama as seen from the sun instead of the earth".

Polanyi highlights the role played by assumptions, habit and tradition. The fact that we know more than we can clearly articulate helps contribute to the conclusion that much knowledge is passed on by non-explicit means, for example via apprenticeship, i.e. observing a master, and then practising under the master's guidance.

How Experts Think

An important feature of expert performance is the way in which experts are able to rapidly retrieve complex configurations of information from long-term memory. They recognise situations because they have meaning, echoing Polanyi's view. It is this concern with meaning, and how it attaches to situations, which provides an important link between the individual and social approaches to the development of expertise. Work on 'Skilled Memory' and 'Expertise' by Anders Ericsson and James J. Staszewski confronts the paradox of expertise and claims that people not only acquire content knowledge as they practice cognitive skills, they also develop mechanisms that enable them to use a large and familiar personal knowledge base efficiently.[15]

Artificial knowledge ('expert' computer systems) is typically based on the premise that a repertoire of rules can act as the basis for computer-supported judgement and decision-making. However, there is increasing evidence that expertise does not work in this fashion. Rather, experts recognise situations based on the experience of many prior situations. Consequently, they are able to make rapid decisions in complex and dynamic situations.

THE NEGATIVE EFFECT OF MAKING TACIT KNOWLEDGE MORE EXPLICIT[16]

Ironically, once an expert has unconscious knowledge, asking the expert to make his or her thinking explicit will often cause the expert to pause and return to long 'forgotten' basics.

Asking the expert for the rules he or she is using forces the expert to regress to the level of a beginner and state the rules learned earlier. Instead of using rules they no longer remember, as knowledge system designers assume, the expert is forced to remember rules they no longer use. No amount of rules and facts can adequately capture the deep, embedded knowledge of a true expert.

Memory and Expertise

Carnegie professors William Chase and Herbert Simon, in their studies of how chess is played,[17] found that patterns of information organised in long-term memory 'chunks' helped experts' ability to encode and retain chess patterns. Their research indicated that while all participants retrieved about the same number of chunks, the size of the chunks varied with subjects' prior experience. Experts' chunks contained more individual pieces than those of novices, and it is this capacity that allows experts to quickly recognise and retrieve patterns within their field of expertise. Interestingly, when information outside their usual field is presented, experts' recall is not markedly superior to others.

The key skills involved in developing such long-term memory are:

1. The ability to encode knowledge meaningfully and to build on existing patterns so that the repertoire of skills in increased.
2. The ability to mentally construct frameworks and cues that prompt the memory.
3. The ability, through extended practice, to make long-term memory almost as fast and reliable as short-term memory.

SKILLED MEMORY

Examples of skilled memory described by Ericsson and Staszewski in their study of memory recall[18] include a waiter who could accurately remember up to 20 complete dinner orders by using mnemonics, patterns and spatial relations (position of the person ordering); he would recall all items of a category (e.g. all salad dressings, then all meat types, then all sauces) in a clockwise fashion for all diners. Another example was of a runner who grouped together short random sequences of digits and encoded the groups in terms of their meaning as running times, dates and ages. He was therefore able to recall over 84% of all digit groups presented in a session of 300 digits. His expertise was limited to digits; when a switch from digits to letters of the alphabet was made, he exhibited no transfer – his memory span dropped back to about six consonants.

EXPERTS AND PROBLEM-SOLVING

Research by Chi in 1981[19] showed how experts and novices differ in solving problems. Undergraduates sorted physics problems into categories based upon superficial aspects (e.g. keywords in the problem statement) while the more expert PhD candidates focused on the deeper aspects (i.e. the underlying physics principles needed to resolve the problem).

The Expertise Scale: Marie-Line Germain

While professionals are hired initially for their technical skills (whether in accounting, medicine or other fields), the definition of 'expert' extends to include other factors. Marie-Line Germain has developed a psychometric measure of perception of employee expertise, which she calls the Generalized Expertise Measure (GEM).[20] Her scale contains five objective (evidence-based) expertise items and 10 subjective (self-enhancement) expertise items. In her definition, she summarises these 15 items, and suggest that an **expert**:

1. Has knowledge specific to a field of work.
2. Shows they have the education necessary to be an expert in the field.
3. Has the qualifications required to be an expert in the field.
4. Has been trained in their area of expertise.
5. Can assess whether a work-related situation is important or not.
6. Is ambitious about their work.
7. Is capable of improving themselves.
8. Is 'charismatic' (personable).
9. Can deduce things from work-related situations easily.
10. Is intuitive in their work, bringing implicit or tacit knowledge to bear on tasks. Can judge what abilities are really important in their job.
11. Has sufficient drive.
12. Is self-assured.
13. Has self-confidence.
14. Is outgoing.

The inclusion of intuition and personability may be surprising, but intuition in this case is the application of accumulated expertise (perhaps informal), while self-assurance, confidence and personality help greatly in many professions.

Real experts also have enough advanced knowledge to develop more abstract, high-level perspectives of their concepts or performance; in other words, to develop new theories and practices of how best to work.

The current work era revolves around mental and intellectual activity, as distinct from traditional labour. New ways need to be found to manage expertise, knowledge and innovation.

New Ways to Manage Work in the Modern World of Intellect and Innovation

> *"The intuitive mind is a sacred gift and the rational mind is a faithful servant. We have created a society that honours the servant and has forgotten the gift."*
>
> Albert Einstein

Delving into the origins of *thought* as the fundamental element in knowledge, Otto Scharmer exposes the power of intuition and sensing, especially in a group situation.[21] This, he suggests, can be achieved by being fully 'present' in the moment, working with integrity and trust, in an appropriate setting.

Scharmer proposes a deliberate consciousness and 'collective' leadership. This novel approach is based on the premise that what we pay attention to (and how we pay attention) is the key to what we create.

To avoid remaining stuck in old patterns of acting, Scharmer suggests accessing deeper levels of learning. This increases the likelihood of innovation, he claims, and also promotes a firmer sense of collective purpose. Scharmer's work, code-named 'Theory U', may appear fanciful, but it is well researched and academically accepted by peers such as Peter Senge.

Scharmer's model, shown in the figure below, suggests that this sensing ability is core to developing 'presence', i.e. the ability to be fully 'in the moment', so that new knowledge is created collectively and a common purpose formed. He suggests these measures to promote this kind of sensing ability and collective genius:

- Challenge existing ways of thinking.
- Focus on the current realities.
- Broaden the perspective to nurture new insights.
- Surface key assumptions through deep dialogue.
- Develop common purpose.
- Create new ways of thinking.
- Implement new patterns and activities.
- Create new structures to accommodate changes.

Scharmer's faith in constructive conversation echoes the classic observation that "Where there is much desire to learn, there of necessity will be much arguing, much writing, many opinions; for opinion in good men is but knowledge in the making."[22]

FIVE LEVELS OF CHANGE:
PRESENCING – THE POWER OF DEEP THOUGHT AND CONNECTION

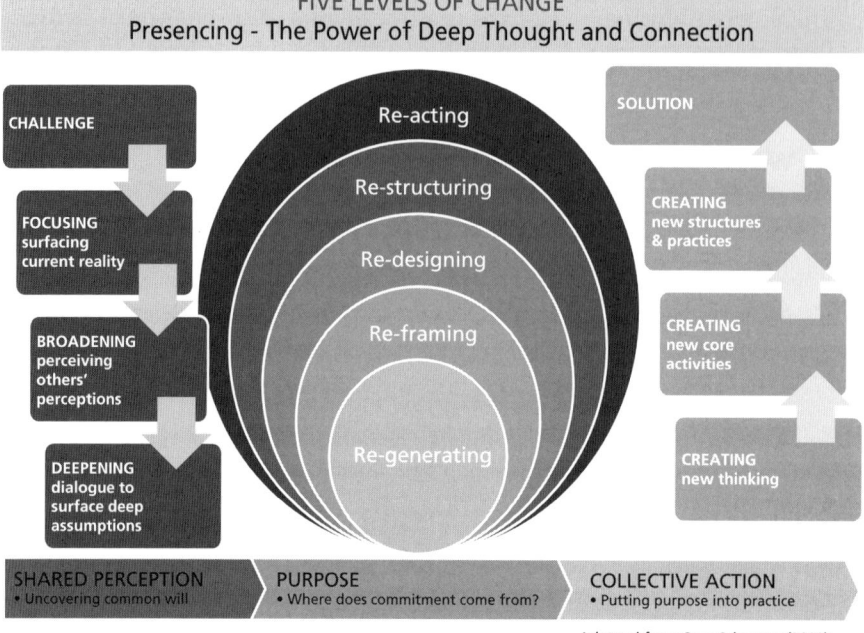

Adapted from Otto Scharmer (2009)

Scharmer uses the above U-shaped model to illustrate the deep dive from surface reality (the apparent facts, for example) down into the territory of hidden assumptions and back up into purposeful actions. This U-shaped curve represents the transition from a single perspective to a richer, collective view, and with it a greater sense of collegiality, all of which promote creativity and innovation, leading to fresher, more imaginative solutions.

R. D. Laing poetically describes how inattention causes us to have 'blind spots':

> The range of what we think and do
> is limited by what we fail to notice.
> And because we fail to notice
> that we fail to notice,
> there is little we can do to change;
> Until we notice
> how failing to notice
> shapes our thoughts and deeds.

Scharmer's theory aims to overcome mental 'blind spots' by increasing attention, deepening dialogue, developing trust and allowing innovation to emerge from this new consciousness. His approach intends to overcome the voices of judgement, cynicism and fear that inhibit our thinking and foster destructive politicking. The graphic below shows these voices overlaid on the earlier U-shaped model:

OVERCOMING THE NEGATIVE VOICES OF CYNICISM, FEAR AND JUDGEMENT

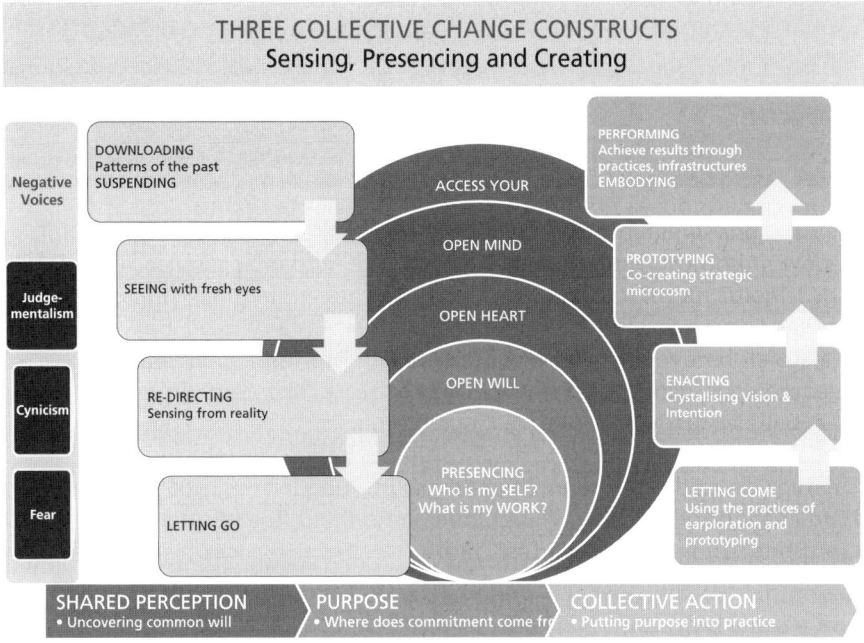

Adapted from Otto Scharmer (2009)

While Scharmer's message is abstract, the actions required are simple to list (even if hard to put into practice):

- Respect colleagues and yourself deeply.
- Demonstrate integrity – 'walk the talk'.
- Listen: really, really listen.
- Immerse yourself deeply enough in the issue so that the solution can be allowed to emerge. Albert Einstein claimed to have immersed himself in the concept of relativity for 14 years – and that his theories could have been formulated by anyone willing to be immersed to such a degree.

While Scharmer is lauded by academics in MIT and Harvard, his approach may need to become more pragmatic. However, a detailed example of developing professional knowledge strategically in a major corporation is provided below.

Innovation and Changing Economic Dynamics

With manufacturing activity and even professional services moving East, the imperative now is innovation and new forms of creation (think of Wikipedia, crowd-sourcing and social networks). In this context, the emphasis shifts to the power of networks of creative people in generating new possibilities.

The chart below illustrates this shift towards innovation and creation: for example, value was created by the mass production of standard products, but this facilitated the shift to lower-wage economies. Western economies shifted then into creating value through services, but now the competitive frontier has shifted again, towards creativity and new forms of value.

Element	Goods	Services	Innovation
Value created by:	Standardised products	Customised services	Experiences
Customer seen as:	Mass market	Mass customisation	Collaborators
Economies:	Scale	Scope	Information
Organisation:	Central, bureaucracy	Local, frontline	Networks
Relationship:	Push product	Pull demand	Partner
Mindset:	Product out	Marketing	Co-creation

This dependency on innovation requires deep exploitation of our mental capabilities. The challenge is to release creativity at both the individual and the network level. Simplistic means (such as brain-storming) are not powerful enough to release the 'tacit' knowledge lying unexplored under the surface. The ideal way is to allow intuition to *emerge*, as described below.

Releasing Tacit Knowledge

The great scientific discoveries since Galileo have been based on deduction and rational analysis, exploring cause and effect, or reducing material to its elemental components. This explicit knowledge has delivered immeasurable benefits. While this 'linear thinking' remains valid today, the difficulty is that complexity (of products, of organisations) has increased exponentially, and that new types of thinking are needed for the management of tacit and latent knowledge ('intuition').

Complexity arises when there are so many interacting variables that cause and effect cannot be linked with any certainty. Such complex situations are 'chaotic', often beyond the capacity of a single mind, and teams of thinkers are required to deal with such complexity. This is analogous to the transition from 'simple' Newtonian physics to the physics of Heisenberg's Uncertainty Principle and Einstein's Relativity – different thought models are needed. While Peter Senge has outlined the elusive 'Fifth Discipline' (personal mastery) required in this new age (see below), he has not proposed practical means of applying his five 'disciplines'. His colleague in MIT, Donald Schön, popularised the term 'reflective practitioner' as a means of bridging the action–learning gap (as a way to combine thought, action and self-awareness).[23] Another MIT colleague, Ed Schein, similarly emphasised this type of 'action-learning' to deal with complexity.[24]

Single-loop Learning

As introduced above, Chris Argyris explains *single-loop learning* as learning from the past. *Double-loop learning*, on the other hand, involves surfacing the underlying assumptions and proposing fresh questions.

Otto Scharmer attempts to go deeper – to learn from the future, so to speak, or access the current tacit knowledge that individuals and groups possess.

This '*learning-from-the-future-as-it-emerges*' involves bringing to the surface tacit knowledge and the release of intuition. It is best attempted when groups are in tune with each other, i.e. when trust is sufficiently high. For this reason, Scharmer calls his approach "presencing" or "social technology", i.e. the participants are fully 'present', attending yet relaxed, insulated from negative and group pressures. Most of us have been in situations where the 'buzz' was tremendous and innovation simply flowed. Scharmer cannot 'prove' this theory, but the phenomenon is clearly observable.

Deepening the Dialogue

The transition to intuition and innovation can be represented as moving from a focus on current reality to a deepening of shared perspectives and real dialogue, as represented in the following figure.

THE TRANSITION TO DEEPER DIALOGUE

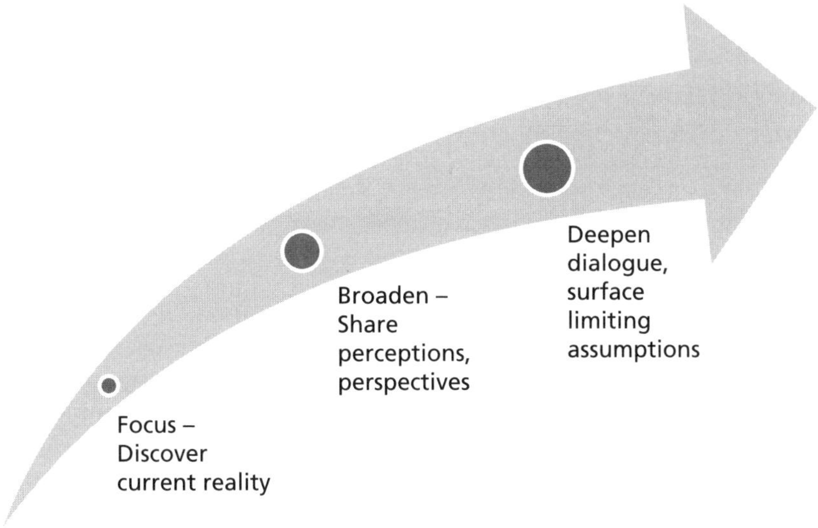

Deepen dialogue, surface limiting assumptions

Broaden – Share perceptions, perspectives

Focus – Discover current reality

With the right conditions and a common purpose ('social presencing'), new patterns of creativity and innovation can be expected to emerge.

During this cycle, negative aspects can interfere with the process: fear, uncertainty, doubt and emotions can intrude (these are the so-called 'voices' of Judgement, Cynicism and Fear). To counter this, Scharmer refers to the need for an open mind, an open heart and an open will.

Intuition: Emerging Knowledge

Scharmer regards tacit knowledge as being already 'embodied', i.e. individuals already have the knowledge, however unconsciously. *Emerging* knowledge (which he calls *'self-transcending'*) is unstructured and latent, but can be caused to emerge in the right conditions. Ikujiro Nonaka similarly regards knowledge as being 'alive', a product of deep, collaborative working relationships. The term used here is the less mystical and more common 'intuition'.

The various basic types of knowledge, and corresponding systems, can be summarised graphically:

TYPES OF KNOWLEDGE

	Explicit Knowledge	**Tacit Knowledge**	**Intuition**
Linear systems	Rational cause and effect	Logical discovery	Not required
Dynamic systems	Systems theory	Multiple trial and error	Not required
Complex systems	Chaos theory	Emergence	Presencing

THE DEC EXAMPLE: PROGRESSIVE THINKING

To illustrate this in practice, consider the evolution of DEC (Digital Equipment Corporation) and its subsequent influence, even after its demise, on many organisations, especially complex or high-tech ones.

DEC was heavily influenced by the benign ethos of its co-founder, Ken Olsen, as well as the chief evangelists of many of the key management movements in business (Schein, Schön, Argyris) in combination with supreme innovators (such as mini-computer pioneer Gordon Bell and Visicalc founder Dan Bricklin).

The culture created was extremely progressive and productive, with a flow of technological and managerial innovations that even today are still being absorbed.

DEC's demise could be simplistically misunderstood as myopia and arrogance. For a better understanding, see Clayton Christensen's book, *The Innovator's Dilemma*,[25] which explains the phenomenon by which successful companies are constrained by their existing investments and then undermined by cheaper new technologies. Think of the development of memory storage devices, from large platters to floppy disks then to hard drives and now solid-state storage.

DEC's progressive approach allowed exceedingly complex systems to emerge (even the overly labyrinthine organisational structure known as the 'matrix'). At heart, DEC was a wonderfully creative and productive environment that collapsed under its own weight, yet did spawn a host of successful former employees. It remains, years later, a catalyst for innovation in Boston in companies such as Bose.

DEC ultimately failed, yet the spirit of DEC lives on today through innumerable offshoots, and a host of new products and services created by former DEC employees: from the Galway operation, 13 new businesses emerged, including one originally founded by myself.

DEC remains the exemplar for leading thinkers on management. The lesson is that openness, inclusion and egalitarianism coupled with high expectations and a fervent culture works spectacularly well, and that the notion of emergence and presence, though hard to verify, is valid, valuable and executable.

The Power of 'Presence' in Creativity and Innovation

Otto Scharmer leads in developing an understanding of the 'deep diving' that is necessary in knowledge creation, especially in team situations. A principal value of his work is in providing a language and a means of understanding the knowledge-creation process and in identifying the various stages in co-creating information.[26] He draws upon a wide array of philosophies in developing his theory (and practice) of 'presencing', meaning the ability to create a context in which the future becomes more visible. The essential elements can be illustrated as shown in the figure below:

Creating New Knowledge

Re-structuring
Surfacing realities
Creating new practices

Re-designing
Broadening perspectives
Creating new structures

Re-framing
Deepening dialogue
Surfacing assumptions
Creating new thinking

Re-generating Purpose
Uncovering common will
Collective action
Putting purpose into practice
Where does deep commitment come from?

DEEPENING THE DIALOGUE FOR GREATER CREATIVITY

Managing in complex situations requires deep understanding of the emerging dynamics, of oneself and of the other players closely involved; much rests on the ability to communicate collectively, and this involves conversational maturity, with the primary stages denoted as shown below:

Presencing Collective creativity Listening from the emerging future Generative flow	**Dialogue** Inquiry, reflection Listening from within Changing your view
Downloading Talking nice Listening, projecting Don't speak your mind	**Debate** Talking tough Listening from outside I am my point of view

The figure above contrasts individualism ('I am my point of view') with collective creativity, and contrasts talking nice (or not speaking up) with genuine dialogue. As with many great theories, the key practices, when distilled to their essence, seem trivial; the notion that the Earth is round does not cause great uproar now, but a few centuries ago it was earth-shattering. It is difficult to over-state the difficulty involved in implementing Scharmer's seemingly simple ideas: few organisations do transcend themselves and get 'into the zone' for any prolonged period. However, the basic principles, as shown below, are easy to understand, if still hard to do:

THE GEARS OF DIALOGUE: OPEN MIND, HEART AND WILL

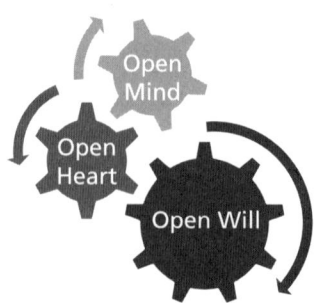

More than concretely doing something, this involves the formation of 'character' and the overcoming the very real and deeply ingrained tendencies to judge, be cynical or be fearful. The *open mind* suspends the voice of unwarranted judgement. The *open heart* silences the voice of cynicism, and the *open will* mutes the voice of fear:

CREATIVITY: SILENCING THE VOICES OF JUDGEMENT, CYNICISM, FEAR

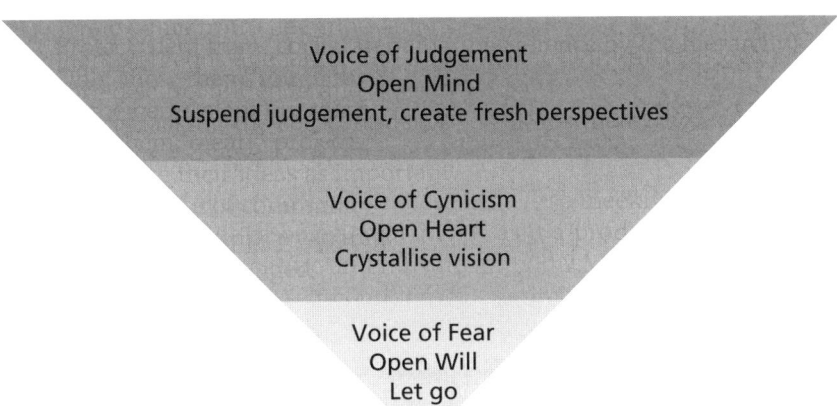

Voice of Judgement
Open Mind
Suspend judgement, create fresh perspectives

Voice of Cynicism
Open Heart
Crystallise vision

Voice of Fear
Open Will
Let go

The process starts with careful initiation to create the conditions for *presencing*: listening attentively, enquiring appreciatively, acknowledging contributions, exploring possibilities, removing barriers to real communication. This then leads to greater collective awareness and openness to new ideas and different perspectives.

THE CREATIVITY ROADMAP

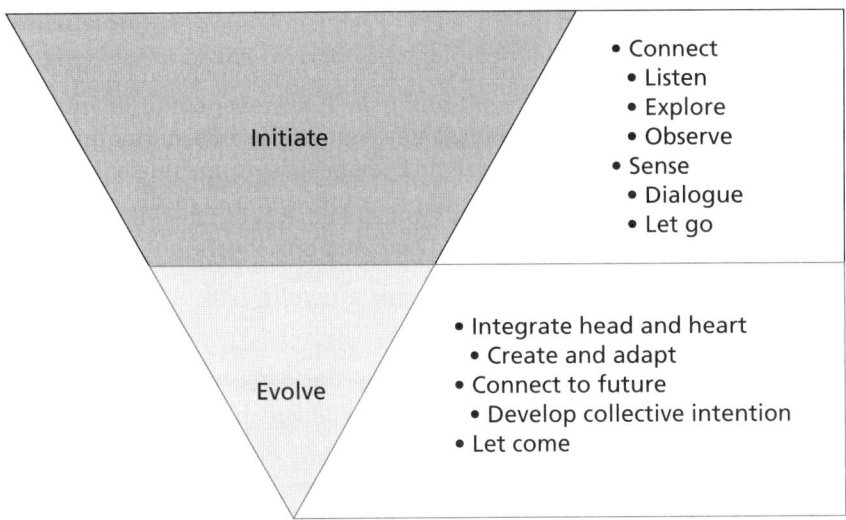

Initiate
• Connect
• Listen
• Explore
• Observe
• Sense
• Dialogue
• Let go

Evolve
• Integrate head and heart
• Create and adapt
• Connect to future
• Develop collective intention
• Let come

New knowledge can then be created 'in the situation', and this helps previously tacit information become more real. For example, new devices, such as iPhones or iPads, emerge first as a concept, a fusion of ideas, a coalescing of different mental models: the more diverse the perspectives, the more radical the new concept. The iPad and iPhone seem 'obvious' mergers of different technologies in retrospect, but they had to bring together different 'worlds', such as telecommunications and computing, music and memory storage.

The Essence of Creation: Coalescing Existing Ideas into New Forms

The creation of something new – a product or service – invariably comes from this coalescence of two or more existing ideas. It is the combining of current ideas into a new form that actually produces innovation. To use some well-known examples, 3M Post-its, the Nintendo Wii and the Apple iPod are fundamentally the combination of pre-existing technologies into wonderful new forms.

INNOVATION AT THE INTERSECTION OF NEW IDEAS

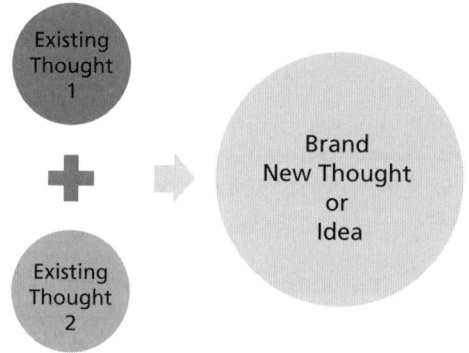

Often, a true innovator has such diverse thoughts and fields of view that he or she can combine existing ideas into a totally new creation. In today's more complex world, this usually takes two or more knowledgeable people to provide sufficient range and depth of ideas and perspectives so that they can meaningfully coalesce into a usable concept or idea.

Knowledge and Creative Spontaneity

Knowledge that lay undiscovered (hidden or dormant) can emerge in conversation (debate or dialogue rather than argument) as the people involved respond to each others' ideas, much in the manner that jazz emerges from players jamming together. Some of this new 'music' (innovation) will be good, some not so good. It is serendipitous, but only to an extent. There are no guarantees but some players will jam better than others, and some combinations will fuse better. It is only 'in the moment' that the new thought emerges. As organisational expert Karl Weick is fond of quipping: "How can I know what I think until I hear what I say?"

The Power of the Moment

Proper conversation forces the succinct expression of often complex ideas. It crystallises thoughts into verbal packets, helping to refine ideas and boil them down to their essence to aid understanding. Just as deadlines usually promote concentrated effort, conversation imposes similar 'punctuation' and demands that ideas be distilled. This distillation clarifies thoughts, not just for the other person, but also for the transmitter. While these can be dismissed as moments of conversation, they actually represent a window into the current state of one's thinking and knowledge accumulated over years.

It is not yet known with precision how a thought actually occurs (although brain monitors can now register specific brain activities); it seems to have no traceable 'history' (i.e. what mental path led to the thought, nor what sparks a novel thought). It is known that certain stimuli (such as a changed perspective or brainstorming) and suitable environments promote 'thinking'. New knowledge 'emerges'; it is spawned rather than constructed.

The emergent (tacit) form of new knowledge naturally makes it difficult to 'manage' in the conventional sense. The best recourse for a manager is to set up the conditions whereby fresh knowledge or expertise can be generated: intuition is not merely a hunch, but the outcome of many strands of thought woven over time, now fused into a new combination.

J. C. Spender has produced an 'epistemology' that categorises knowledge in four quadrants. He regards explicit, individual knowledge as being conscious knowledge. At the other extreme, he notes that the (admittedly rarer) implicit, group knowledge is a kind of collective or social knowledge. This is illustrated in the graphic below, showing the distinction between implicit and explicit knowledge at the individual level and again at the collective (social) level.

Spender's Epistemology[27]

	Individual knowledge	Social knowledge
Explicit knowledge	Conscious	Objectified
Implicit knowledge	Automatic	Collective

Knowledge may start with explicit individual knowledge, but the ideal is collective knowledge (implicit, social or 'team' knowledge).

The hierarchy of knowledge could be expressed as a transition from 'basic' data to 'sublime' wisdom, as illustrated below:

THE HIERARCHY OF KNOWLEDGE

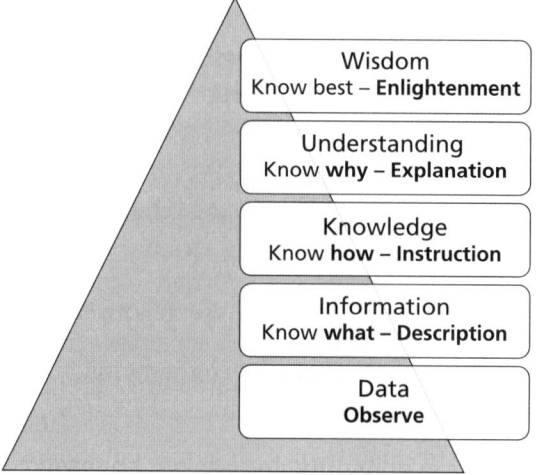

Tacit knowledge has been described as *'know-how'* – as opposed to *'know-what'* (facts), *'know-why'* (science), or *'know-who'* (networking). It involves learning and skill but not in a way that can be written down. Tacit knowledge (as distinct from formalised or explicit knowledge) is knowledge that is difficult to transfer to another person by writing or verbalising it. For example, stating that Manhattan is in New York is explicit knowledge that can be written down, transmitted and understood by a recipient. However, the ability to use algebra, speak a language, or design and use complex equipment requires all sorts of knowledge that is not always known *explicitly*, even by expert practitioners, and which is difficult to explicitly transfer to users.

With tacit knowledge, people are not really aware of the knowledge they possess or how it can be valuable to others. Effective transfer of tacit knowledge generally requires extensive personal contact and trust. Tacit knowledge often consists of habits and culture that we do not recognise in ourselves.

The progression moves from 'knowing what' to 'knowing how' to 'knowing why', followed by a conscious knowing and then, hopefully, mastery:

1. Know what
2. Know how
3. Know why
4. Conscious knowing
5. Mastery.

TACIT KNOWLEDGE – THE STORY OF BESSEMER STEEL

An example of tacit knowledge is the Bessemer steel process. Henry Bessemer sold a patent for his advanced steel-making process and was sued by the purchasers, who could not get it to work. In the end, Bessemer set up his own steel company because he tacitly knew how to do it, but could not convey this implicit knowledge to his patent users. Bessemer Steel went on to become one of the largest steel-making companies in the world.

MORE TACIT KNOWLEDGE – MATSUSHITA AND THE ANCIENT ART OF BAKING BREAD

A second example of tacit knowledge comes from the Matsushita Electric Company and their attempts to capture the nuance of the apparently simple task of baking bread. Just as apprentices learn the craft of their masters through observation, imitation and practice, so do employees of a firm learn new skills through on-the-job training. When Matsushita started developing its automatic home bread-making machine in 1985, an early problem was how to mechanise the dough-kneading process, a process that takes a master baker years of practice to perfect.

To learn this tacit knowledge, a member of the software development team, Ikuko Tanaka, decided to volunteer herself as an apprentice to the head baker of the Osaka International Hotel, who was reputed to produce the area's best bread. After a period of imitation and practice, one day she observed that the baker was not only stretching but also twisting the dough in a particular fashion ("twisting stretch"), which turned out to be the secret for making tasty bread.

The Matsushita home bakery team drew together 11 members from completely different specialisations: product planning, mechanical engineering, control systems, and software development. The "twisting stretch" motion was finally achieved in a prototype after a year of experimentation by the team members, working closely together and combining their explicit knowledge. For example, the engineers added ribs to the inside of the dough case in order to hold the dough better as it is being churned. Another team member suggested a method (later patented) to add yeast at a later stage in the process, thereby preventing the yeast from over-fermenting in high temperatures.

Origins of the Learning Cycle: David Kolb

The dynamics of a 'learning cycle' were described by David Kolb, based on his observations of expert flyers in the Second World War.[28] He noted their ability to prevail by simultaneously being deeply involved in the dog-fight while also detaching themselves so that they had the best aerial view of proceedings. Ron Heifetz later used the phrase 'getting on the balcony' as a metaphor for how those involved in strategising (for instance) should rise above the action and see whatever order there was in the midst of the chaos.[29] Kolb's research showed that pilots who 'learned' in this way had a better chance of survival.

THE BASIC SINGLE-LOOP LEARNING CYCLE

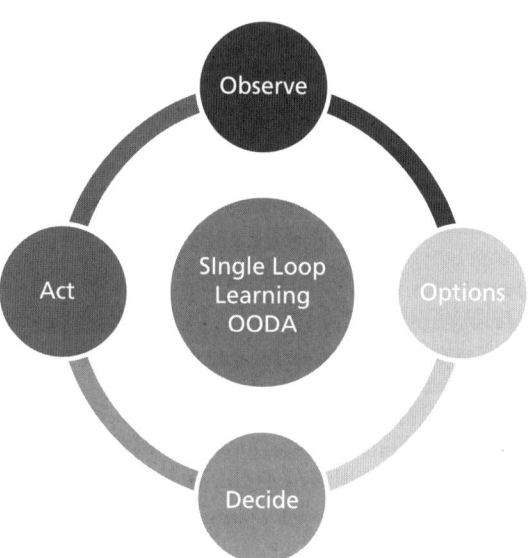

The learning cycle (as explained earlier in this chapter) is a 'single-loop' learning cycle, meaning that its best use is in rectifying a situation (problem-solving) rather than innovating or setting new directions (problem- or opportunity-finding); this is called a 'double-loop' as it breaks out of the single cycle to pose the key question that needs to be asked. For example, to avoid going around in circles, the cycle may need to be broken by asking a different question, setting a new course, or getting on to a different 'balcony'. Russell Ackoff, one of the brightest management specialists of the century, claims (mischievously) that:

> "Our problems arise out of doing the wrong thing righter. The more efficient you are at doing the wrong thing, the wronger you become. It is much better to do the right thing wronger than the wrong thing righter. If you do the right thing wrong and correct it, you get better."[30]

REFRAMING THE ISSUE BY CHANGING THE QUESTION

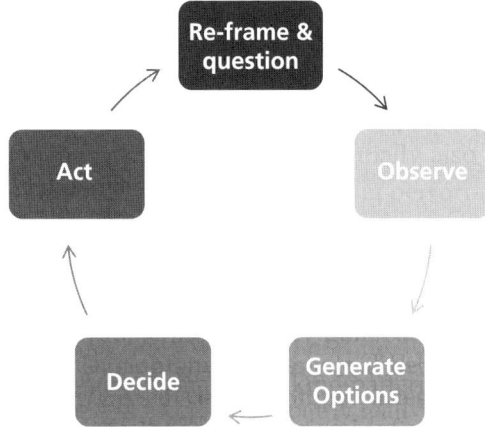

The double-loop helps reveal **how** we learn, whereas the single-loop reveals **what** we have learned.

> *"You can tell whether a man is clever by his answers. You can tell whether a man is wise by his questions."*
>
> Naguib Mahfouz

Learning as a Team or an Organisation

Both the single and double loops originated at the level of the individual: a further challenge is to apply these approaches to groups. If learning and creativity often occur through debate and conversation, some important types of learning can be seen to be *social*. This promises great potential, but also poses significant challenges in getting people to work together, especially if those teams are comprised of diverse personalities or have different mental models. The short answer to these issues, developed further in **Chapter 11**, is the development of trust, encouraged by appreciative enquiry, mutual respect and joint acceptance of high levels of challenge in performance.

Learning in Practice with Real Managers in Complex Situations: Action Learning

The 'action learning' approach described earlier in this chapter is central to the philosophy of the Masters in Management Practice devised by Tony Dromgoole of the IMI in association with Trinity College, Dublin. The programme concerns itself not with the 'dead cases' of a typical MBA, but with complex problems facing participating managers in real time. (The illustrious Henry Mintzberg has strongly commended this subtle approach.[31])

The approach has been seen to work well over an extended time, despite the variety and intractability of some of the issues, and some of the examples used in this book are drawn from this programme.

Learning in Complex Systems: System Dynamics and Systems Thinking

Peter Senge, introduced briefly above, is a pioneer in promoting the idea of the 'learning organisation'. His seminal work, *The Fifth Discipline: The Art and Practice of the Learning Organization,* was published in 1990.[32] In it, Senge defines the 'learning organisation' as one "in which you cannot not learn because learning is so insinuated into the fabric of life".

Senge's work rests on the earlier work of Jay Forrester, an early innovator in computing, who predicted, remarkably, in 1956 that hardware would ultimately be given away to sell associated software and services (this at a time when only major powers could afford the physically massive computers, leading to the infamous forecast that the world market for computers would be confined to four census bureaux). Forrester extended his 'system dynamics' approach to complex problems in economics, and worked with the world's leading nations to successfully develop methods to guide economic recovery.

FORRESTER'S SYNDROMES – PERVERSE OUTCOMES COMMON IN COMPLEX SITUATIONS

Jay Forrester has illustrated how complex problems differ from simple ones. In difficult problems, cause and effect are not directly connected, and consequently the 'solution' can lead to unintended results – the solution can 'backfire'.

Economic policy is notorious for its 'unintended consequences', often backfiring and making matters worse. Forrester recognised the 'causal loops' driving these 'unintended consequences', and Peter Senge later postulated these real, wicked (although quaint-sounding) syndromes:

- The easy way out usually just leads back in.
- Today's problems come from yesterday's solutions (i.e. the failure to find the real root cause).
- The harder you push, the harder the system pushes back (e.g. cutting costs can be expensive).
- Behaviours grow better before they grow worse: you get a temporary boost from short-term measures but as the basic system is not changed, the underlying issues continue to fester.
- The cure can be worse than the disease.
- Dividing an elephant in half does not produce two elephants.

Each wave of apparent progress in organisational learning promised much but generally did not deliver the anticipated benefits. The missing ingredients were subtle human factors concerning trust, politics, recognition, reward and motivation. It took many failed experiments across a range of organisations to realise that:

- The value of soft 'tacit' information was under-appreciated.
- Tacit knowledge could not be transferred by disembodied means (repositories, databases), even if it was heavily incentivised (the incentives simply caused the registering of lots of information of no real value).
- Tacit knowledge could be transferred if the donor was sufficiently recognised and protected (e.g. from being dispensed with as soon as he or she divulged the requested information).
- The exchange of tacit knowledge was rare without these 'social' provisions.

Recent developments, however, such as Web 2.0 and social media, have made the 'learning organisation' a compelling – and feasible – proposition. Success still depends not on technology itself but on overcoming those human factors of earning trust, taming political excess and overcoming thinking ('cognitive') biases.

The concepts proposed here have been piloted with success in large and small organisations. This next section will encapsulate the key learnings. These are simple to understand, but they do require managers to have a willingness to adopt new practices. The good news is that these practices create immediate mutual benefits.

The Manager's Role in the Learning Organisation

The manager's true role in the learning organisation is that of a designer, teacher and steward who can build shared vision and challenge prevailing mental models. The manager, therefore, is not simply a supervisor but is responsible for building organisations where people are continually expanding their capabilities to shape their future – that is, leaders are responsible for learning, at the individual and organisational level.

Similarly, for the key questions, such as what strategy to pursue, the key is learning; as Mintzberg says, it is less about getting the right strategy but fostering strategic *thinking*.[33]

Companies working in volatile markets illustrate this shift from finding 'the one perfect position' to developing organisational agility, i.e. being prepared for a range of envisaged scenarios. Shell, for example, uses the concept of double-loop learning in its credo, "planning as learning".[34] Faced with ongoing unpredictability in world oil markets, Shell's planners realised a shift of their basic task: "We no longer saw our task as producing a documented view of the future business environment five or ten years ahead. Our real target was the microcosm (the 'mental model') of our decision makers."

They realised their fundamental task was fostering organisational learning rather than devising rigid plans, and consequently engaged their managers in dress-rehearsing for the implications of different scenarios. This prepared the organisation for the uncertainties in the environment and embedded the learning process.

The key factor in a learning organisation is *how* organisations mentally process their experiences, *learning* from their experiences rather than being *bound* by them.

The ability of an organisation is not assessed by *what* it knows (that is the product of learning), but rather by *how* it learns – the process of learning.

Creating such a learning organisation requires management practices that are based on the five disciplines: openness, systemic thinking, creativity, a sense of efficacy, and empathy.

SYSTEM RIGIDITY, BUREAUCRACY AND CONSTRAINTS ON ORGANISATIONAL LEARNING

Chris Argyris[35] claims that rigidities in the system of an organisation, such as petty bureaucracy, excessive restrictions and system constraints (perhaps inadvertently imposed by IT) reduce the capacity to change and learn. Invariably, whatever learning is done in an organisation is simple 'single-loop' learning (fixing known problems), and that the "underlying program is not questioned". At best, it is designed to correct errors so that the job gets done within stated parameters, according to Argyris." The trouble arises when the policies are out-dated, or the technology is not effective or where the organisation fails to change as rapidly as the competitive environment. Double-loop, question-oriented learning is needed instead. He states: "Most organizations, often without realizing it, create systems of learning that suppress double loop inquiry and make it very difficult for even a well designed information system to be effective."

SYSTEMS THINKING MADE SIMPLE

Wharton's Professor Russell Ackoff recently used this anecdote to illustrate systems thinking.[36]

The scene is Detroit, at the headquarters of one of the large US car companies. A group of corporate vice presidents is attending a course being given by a distinguished management thinker.

"What you are telling us is great," the VPs say, "but you are talking to the wrong level. You should be speaking to the next tier up."

The next week, working with more senior managers, he hears the same thing. "This is great, but you are talking to the wrong level. You should be speaking with the chief executive."

The week after that, our thinker finally gets in to see the boss. "This is great," the CEO says, "but you should be speaking with my subordinates – I'd need their support in order to do it."

There are two key morals to take from Professor Ackoff's tale: first, do not wait for others in the business to start changing things. Go and do it yourself. But, secondly, never forget that everyone in the business is interconnected, that they are all operating as part of a system, that tinkering with one part of the company is never really enough, and may even make things worse. You need to see the business as a whole, as a complete system, if you want to make lasting improvements to it.
Russell Ackoff had other memorable observations.

- "An organisation that cannot accommodate nonconformity will not be able to retain creative people."
- "Organisations fail more often because of what they have not done than because of what they have done."
- "The less managers expect of their subordinates, the less they get."
- "The only problems that have simple solutions are simple problems. The only managers that have simple problems have simple minds. Problems that arise in organisations are almost always the product of interactions of parts, never the action of a single part. Complex problems do not have simple solutions."

Senge's 'Fifth Discipline': The Art and Practice of the Learning Organisation

As introduced above, Peter Senge advocates using 'systems thinking' (what he calls the 'Fifth Discipline', the one that integrates the first four disciplines) to create learning organisations. The 'Five Disciplines' are:

1. **Personal mastery** Personal mastery is the discipline of continually refining our personal vision and sense of purpose; of developing patience, self-control and self-confidence, and of seeing reality objectively. It is more than competence, and can be regarded as a special kind of proficiency. People with a high level of personal mastery live in a continual learning mode: it is a lifelong discipline. It is a paradoxical combination of humility (prompting the desire to learn) and self-confidence (which facilitates an openness to new experiences).

2. **Mental models** These are what Senge termed the "deeply ingrained assumptions, generalizations, or even pictures and images that influence how we understand the world and how we take action".[37] They resemble what Donald Schön called a professional's 'repertoire'. The nature of assumptions, of course, is that we are often not even aware of them, and so rarely question them, even when they are having a limiting effect. This discipline involves turning the mirror inward and learning to view our mental models of the world and hold them up to scrutiny. It requires a balance of inquiry and advocacy, and making one's thinking open to the influence of others.

3. **Building a shared vision** Senge claims that effective organisations develop the "capacity to hold a shared picture of the future we seek to create" and a compelling vision can have the power to inspire and to promote innovation. It can foster a sense of the long-term, something that is fundamental to the 'fifth discipline'. This discipline of shared vision involves unearthing vivid 'pictures of the future' that engender genuine commitment rather than compliance.

4. **Team learning** Team learning is viewed by Senge as "the process of aligning and developing the capacities of a team to create the results its members truly desire". It builds on personal mastery and shared vision, and this in turn strengthens commitment to act. This discipline of team learning starts with 'dialogue', the capacity of members of a team to suspend assumptions and enter into a genuine 'thinking together'. *Dia-logos* means a free flow of meaning, assisting the discovery of insights not attainable individually. The importance of such dialogue stems from American physicist, David Bohm, who asserted that thought be approached as a collective phenomenon.[38] Dialogue combined with systems thinking, according to Senge, creates a language for dealing with complexity and deep-seated issues.

5. **Systems thinking** Systems thinking involves seeing the whole, not just the component parts in isolation. Systems thinking (rather than the simple cause-and-effect type of problem-solving thinking) is needed to solve complex issues, whether in economics, technology or society. Systems thinking is the crucial Fifth Discipline, as it integrates the other disciplines, making them a coherent body of theory and practice.

For example, short-term improvements often lead to substantial long-term costs: cutting back on research can quickly cut costs but damage the long-term viability of an organisation. Cutting advertising costs may be a short term expediency that leads to ruinous results later.

Senge identifies seven 'disabilities' that inhibit learning, and these provide insight into some of the subtleties that commonly derail progress in organisations:

SEVEN LEARNING DISABILITIES

1. "I am my position." – Not realising your part or purpose in the grander system of the enterprise.
2. "The enemy is out there." The propensity to find someone or something outside ourselves to blame when things go wrong. Not recognising the real enemy is within.
3. The Illusion of Taking Charge – while a positive outlook is generally useful, we nonetheless can scarcely manage ourselves, never mind wider events; in that sense, we have less control than we think.

4. The Fixation of Events – the tendency to see things in the short term. Focusing on events distracts from seeing the longer-term patterns of change that lie behind the event and from understanding the cause of those patterns.
5. The Parable of the Boiled Frog – who didn't feel the gradual heat rise – not being able to assess slow, gradual changes, even when they threaten our survival.
6. The Delusion of Learning from Experience – We often fail to learn unless we pay attention. It could be said that the lesson of history is that we never learn the lesson of history!
7. The Myth of the Management Team – each is an individual.

Senge popularised some of the tenets of systems thinking in his book, *The Fifth Discipline*.[39] These laws reveal much of the irony that bedevils the management of change in organisations, and provide some warnings for those attempting change simplistically. As Law 1 says: "today's problems come from yesterday's solutions":

THE 11 LAWS OF SYSTEMS THINKING

1. Today's problems come from yesterday's (short-term) 'solutions'.
2. The harder you push, the harder the system pushes back (status quo prevails).
3. Behaviour will grow worse before it grows better.
4. The easy way out usually leads back in.
5. The cure can be worse than the disease.
6. Faster is slower (real change can only come slowly).
7. Cause and effect are not closely related in time and space.
8. Small changes can produce big results ... but can be not obvious.
9. You can have your cake and eat it too – but not all at once. Win–win.
10. Dividing an elephant in half does not produce two small elephants.
11. There is no blame – take responsibility, face reality and move on.

Implementing Knowledge and Innovation Management: Guidelines

Knowledge management can be enhanced by such means as discussion forums, 'apprenticeships', corporate libraries, training and mentoring programs. Technologies that enhance knowledge management include databases, expert systems, repositories, decision support systems, groupware and intranets.

A 'push' strategy involves actively managing knowledge by explicitly encoding knowledge into a shared knowledge repository, enabled by a database.

A 'pull' strategy encourages people to make knowledge requests of experts on a particular subject on an as-required basis.

Other means to foster knowledge management in companies include:

- Recognition of the value of knowledge and the people who created it.
- Rewards (as a means of motivating for knowledge sharing).
- Storytelling (as a means of transferring tacit knowledge).
- Cross-project learning.
- During- and after-action reviews.
- Building communities of practice.
- Formalising best practice transfer.
- Systematic evaluation and planning of competences of individuals.
- Work space design to encourage mingling and free association of ideas.
- Assessing and valuing intellectual capital as an invisible asset, like a brand.
- Knowledge brokers who take responsibility for specific topics.
- Social software (wikis, social bookmarking, blogs, etc.).

Organisational Learning: The Social Network

Given the social nature of getting new ideas to emerge, the focus moves beyond the individual to group productivity. Networks drive innovation through genuine collaboration, as evidenced by the findings published in the *Gallup Management Journal* that 76% of engaged employees (but significantly only 21% of actively disengaged staff), strongly agree with the statement: "I have a friend at work who I share new ideas with."[40]

The notion that creativity in today's complex environment is essentially a 'one-man show' is limiting; the generation of creative ideas is mainly a collaborative process rather than an individualistic one. Andrew Hargadon from the University of California claims that inventor Thomas Edison was described in the words of one of his fellow employees as "a collective noun and the work of many men".[41]

Steve Jobs described how confluence and collaboration yield innovation for Apple:

> "Innovation comes from people meeting up in the hallways or calling each other at 10.30 pm with new ideas. It's ad hoc meetings of six people called by someone who thinks he has figured out the coolest new thing ever and wants to know what other people think of his idea."[42]

Thomas Allen of MIT discovered that high performers in R&D report a greater frequency of consultation with colleagues and spend significantly more time in discussions with colleagues than do the lower performers.[43] This brings them in closer touch with new developments in their own and in other fields.

Informal networks can also help solve problems by validating ideas, courses of action, offering critical perspectives and developing fresh solutions. Dealing with creative people can sharpen one's own intellectual abilities.

Close Collaboration among Friends

Robert Kelley from Carnegie Mellon University and Janet Caplan at Bell Labs have revealed how top-performing knowledge workers were able to build highly reliable social ties with colleagues, and when they called someone for advice, they almost always got a quick answer.[44] On the other hand, calls and email messages sent by middle performers often remained unreturned and unanswered. To solve non-trivial, difficult technical problems, knowledge workers cannot just download a ready-made 'solution' from the corporate intranet. They rely not just on a single ad hoc piece of advice but on repeated interactive discussions. Reliable networks, therefore, become vital for problem-solving and work performance.

High levels of mutual responsiveness are a particular feature of social bonds that are emotionally close and trustful; in other words, friendship. Connections to friends have been found to play an essential role for problem-solving in organisational contexts. Karen Jehn from University of Pennsylvania and Pri Shah from Northwestern University have argued, for instance, that friends are able to challenge one another's ideas and manage disagreements in a different way from non-friends, offering more explanations and providing critical feedback in a constructive manner that the receiver is willing to accept.[45]

ENHANCING EMOTIONAL INTELLIGENCE

'Emotional intelligence' is defined by its original researchers[46] as the ability to perceive and express emotion, assimilate emotion in thought, understand and reason with emotion, and regulate emotion in oneself and others.

Time magazine on its cover asked: "What's your EQ? It's not your IQ. It's not even a number. But emotional intelligence might just be the best predictor of success in life, re-defining what it means to be smart."

Daniel Pink, noting the rise in 'intelligence' work, also predicted that the differentiating factor will be the ability to be creative and to communicate with empathy; his forecast already seems to be accurate.

Smart people have already developed a superior capacity to learn; that is not in doubt. However, it has been found that this learning can become narrow, one-dimensional, confined often to the original technical expertise; indeed, smart people can become resistant to learning, either through arrogance, complacency or fear of failure.

A 2005 survey by Booz Allen Hamilton among the top 1,000 global innovation spenders showed that money cannot buy creative results.[47] This survey found no statistical relationship between R&D spending levels and nearly all measures of business success, including sales growth, gross profit, or market capitalisation.

The recognition of informal, interpersonal, human creativity is the start for the development of new ways of thinking. Collegiality cannot be dictated, but it clearly can be encouraged. The research clearly implies that an organisation that lessens malicious politics, antagonism, destructive opposition to ideas and the 'knowledge-hoarding' mentality creates a definite advantage for itself.

THE OTHER SIDE OF FRIENDSHIP

There is a shadow side, even to friendship. As Professor Robert Cialdini[48] says, a major factor in social networks is the 'like me' principle. This works in two ways, he says: we like people who are like us, and we like people who like us. This can potentially lead to groupthink and to people not wanting to rock each other's boats.

Collaborative relationships with smart and creative colleagues enrich the knowledge and strengthen the cognitive abilities of individuals, increasing work performance. Managers who still hang on to the individualistic view of creative performance should re-think. In the past, the aim was to hire the best individuals, but in today's knowledge organisations, this goal expands to hiring and developing the best assembly of talent, and this takes conscious network formation. The nurturing of collegiality across the organisation, small or large, makes best use of the talent and intellect of intelligent performers – and also provides a satisfying, challenging yet supportive work environment of people who like and trust one another.

Getting Professionals to Share

Professionals base much of their reputation on their treasure trove of information. Given the scarcity of information sharing, it would be tempting to think that professionals are not inclined to share information. In fact, even though there is little genuine sharing of information, there is a natural tendency to teach and share: the current 'win–lose' conditions simply act against effective sharing.

People will share – but it depends heavily on the type of information and the rules of engagement, specifically how highly their information is regarded and how much recognition is given in return.

Sharing – Different Types of Information

Information can be categorised into two types – corporate and personal:

1. Corporate information, such as product/service knowledge, reports, accounts, etc., is widely regarded as belonging to the institution, and sharing of this knowledge is considered valid and happens, with varying degrees of compliance.
2. The second type is knowledge generated by the person's own experience and is therefore considered proprietary to that person. This could be a knowledge of how to work around the system, how to effectively

solve certain problems, how to woo certain clients. As such, it is usually tacit knowledge, hard won from personal experience.

Conditions Under Which People Willingly Share Knowledge

The motivation to share is torn between various poles: a natural possessiveness competes with the joys of recognition and of communality; sharing will only take place if there is a regard for the information requested and if there is already a prior relationship that has developed a modicum of trust. There has to be an expectation that the contribution will be acknowledged and perhaps reciprocated at a future date.

According to a recent study by Sara Kiesler, Carnegie Professor of Human Computer Interaction, "Experts will want to contribute to co-workers who need them, who will hear them, who will respect them and who may even thank them."[49]

Using Peer Recognition to Promote Sharing

As this study shows, the primary driver for sharing experiential knowledge is the respect and recognition of peers. It is hard to overestimate the psychic value of peer recognition.

Xerox is justifiably proud of its Eureka website where photocopy repair technicians share 'fixes' they have developed while repairing the copy machines. There is a story about one, the technician who had sent in some fantastic 'fixes' – he was everyone's hero. When he walked into the annual meeting of technicians, his peers jumped up and started clapping and whistling – celebrating both his knowledge and his willingness to share – that's peer recognition!

Recognition means the most to us when it comes from those who really know the subject – who know what they are talking about. It is great to have your boss think you are a top performer, but chances are your boss does not know enough about the technical part of your work to know how good you really are – but your peers do. For a peer to say, "The person that really understands that problem is Pete" is a comment Pete would regard as a sign of respect and one he would value highly.

A professional's identity (who they perceive themselves to be) is closely related to what he or she knows – about leading a team, delivering a project, dealing with investors. People do not give that knowledge away lightly. Before they take the time and trouble to share that knowledge, they need some assurance that the knowledge will be treated with the respect it deserves, and that the recipient actually knows enough to make use of it. This leads to the second reason people share their knowledge – relationships.

Building Relationships

The way a professional can know how someone will treat the precious commodity of her knowledge is to know that person well enough to make that judgement call. Relationships can be built through informal conversations, reading what another has written, working together on a team and so on. If a senior leader is committed to increasing knowledge sharing in his organisation, then focusing on building relationships is the most important thing he can do.

An organisation can foster relationships many ways, but nearly all of them involve people being in *conversation* with each other. It is through conversation that we learn enough about the other to know the depth of their knowledge, where their strengths lie, what interests they have and what they are passionate about.

Success and Delusion among Professionals

> "A man, though wise, should never be ashamed of learning more, and must un-bend his mind."
>
> Sophocles, in *Antigone*

Most professionals have thinking habits and predispositions that inhibit their performance. The optimism and self-confidence of successful people is not always justified but it helps them forge ahead, even in the midst of uncertainty. Self-delusion, while having a positive side, can mean that successful people may be resistant to thinking critically about themselves. Here are three common (and somewhat useful) characteristics of conventionally intelligent (but socially unintelligent) people.

1. **The Winner's Imperative**   They need to win – all the time. Even if is unimportant, they want to win! If it is critical, they definitely want to win. If it is trivial, they still want to win.
2. **One-upmanship**   Many smart people can scarcely resist the urge to reveal their intellectual horsepower. Some just have an over-powering urge to 'improve' other people's ideas. While this might add a small amount of extra value, it can destroy morale.
3. **Winning Battles, Losing Wars** Smart people can presume that intelligence trumps social grace, and may yield to the temptation of putting others down so they themselves rise higher in standing. Criticising others, for example, may be an attempt to show one's intelligence: clever, but not smart, as both victims and onlookers will take a long time to forget the social ineptitude.

Conclusion

In this chapter the nature of intelligence, expertise and innovation has been discussed, with an emphasis on managing knowledge, both tacit and explicit. The true meaning of learning has been explored, particularly in relation to professionals, who may feel obliged to deny that they do not, in fact, know all there is to know. This ultimately led to the types of bias and delusion to which all people, but especially the already successful professional, may fall victim. Strategies and tactics were suggested to promote knowledge management (tacit and explicit) and continuous organisational learning. In the elusive field of innovation (the creation of new knowledge), this led to the introduction of Otto Scharmer's comprehensive 'Theory U', which asserts the power of being really, truly 'present' to develop intuition and creativity.

Because knowledge is so closely tied to identity, it is important that peers view professionals as knowledgeable. One way to demonstrate that is by sharing knowledge. As sharing knowledge is risky, the other person may make a cutting remark about it or indicate that it is not worth listening to. Sharing knowledge is time consuming, because to really respond to another's question or problem requires the time to understand the issue and to explain in sufficient depth. So, we rightly place conditions on sharing in-depth knowledge. The relationships we build with others provide a needed level of confidence that our knowledge will be treated with respect. Knowledge sharing and relationship are coupled.

Rather than management asking how do we incentivise people to share their knowledge, it would be more useful for management to ask how do we develop relationships across the organisation that will set in motion more knowledge sharing?

The principles espoused here arise from many years of experience at the coal-face of innovation in advanced companies: the approach described draws on many sources to help understand – and therefore manage – the intangible tasks so necessary in today's knowledge economy.

In the next chapter Gerry Prendergast provides a detailed case/example of these principles in action. Dr James Sheehan, in **Chapter 4**, discussed his approach to managing peers. It is hoped that this combination of theory and practice will help those leading professionals and other smart people to rise to the challenge of managing in the abstract realms of knowledge and innovation.

ENDNOTES

[1] Ned Herrmann, *The Whole Brain Business Book* (McGraw-Hill, 1996).

[2] Daniel Goleman, *Emotional Intelligence* (Bloomsbury, 1996).

[3] Chris Argyris, "Teaching Smart People How to Learn" (1991) Vol. 69 No. 3 *Harvard Business Review* 54–61.

[4] Robin DiMatteo, "Unleashing Innovation: Health Care Report" *Wall Street Journal* 9 April 2013.

[5] Kurt Von Hammerstein, in Hans Magnus Enzensberger, *The Silences of Hammerstein* (Seagull Books, 2009).

[6] Malcolm Gladwell, *Outliers: The Story of Success* (Little, Brown, 2008).

[7] K. Anders Ericsson "The Role of Deliberate Practice in the Acquisition of Expert Performance" (1993) Vol. 100 No. 3 *Psychological Review* 363–406.

[8] Fred Brooks, *The Mythical Man-Month: Essays on Software Engineering* (Addison Wesley, 1975).

[9] Jane Harper, *Staying Extreme: IBM Internship Manual*, in "The Battle for Talent" by Bill Taylor, HBR Blog, 27 February 2009. http://blogs.hbr.org/2008/02/on-the-battle-for-talent-and-t/

[10] Malcolm Gladwell, "The Talent Myth: Are Smart People Overrated?" *The New Yorker* 22 July 2002.

[11] Daniel Coyle, *The Talent Code* (Bantam, 2009).

[12] Kendra Cherry, "Influence on Intelligence: Twins" (2009) *Cognitive Psychology*.

[13] Peter Senge, *The Fifth Discipline* (Doubleday, 1990).

[14] Michael Polanyi, *The Tacit Dimension* (University of Chicago Press, 1966).

[15] K. Anders Ericsson, Michael J. Prietula and Edward T. Cokely, "The Making of an Expert" (July 2007) Vol. 85 No. 7–8 *Harvard Business Review* 114–121.

[16] K. Anders Ericsson and James J. Staszewski, in David Klahr and Kenneth Kotovsky, *Complex Information Processing: The Impact of Herbert A. Simon* (Lawrence Erlbaum Associates, 1989).

[17] William G. Chase and Herbert A. Simon, in W.G. Chase (ed.), *Visual Information Processing* (Academic Press, 1973).

[18] K. Anders Ericsson *et al.*, "The Making of an Expert" (2007) Vol. 85 No. 7–8 *Harvard Business Review* 114–121.

[19] M.T.H. Chi, Feltovich, P.J. and Glaser, R., "Categorization and Representation of Physics Problems By Experts and Novices", (1981) Vol. 5 *Cognitive Science* 121–152.

[20] Marie-Line Germain, *Generalised Expertise Measure: What Experts Are Not: Factors Identified by Managers as Disqualifiers for Selecting Subordinates for Expert Team Membership* (Academy of Human Resource Conference, February 22–26 2006).

[21] C. Otto Scharmer, *Theory U: Learning from the Future as it Emerges* (Berrett-Koehler, 2009).

[22] John Milton, *A Speech For The Liberty of Unlicensed Printing to the Parliament of England* (Areopagitica, 23 November 1644).

[23] Donald Schön, *The Reflective Practitioner: How Professionals Think in Action* (Basic Books, 1983).

[24] Edgar H. Schein, *Organizational Culture and Leadership* (Jossey-Bass, 1985).

[25] Mark W. Johnson *et al.*, "Reinventing Your Business Model" (December 2008) Vol. 86 No. 12 *Harvard Business Review* 50–59.

[26] C. Otto Scharmer, *Theory U: Learning From the Future as it Emerges* (Berrett-Koehler, 2009).

[27] J.C. Spender and A.G. Scherer, "The Philosophical Foundations of Knowledge Management" (2007) Vol. 14 No. 1 *Organization* 5–28.

[28] David A. Kolb, *Experiential Learning: Experience as the Source of Learning and Development* (Prentice Hall, 1984).

[29] Ron Heifetz, *Leadership without Easy Answers* (Harvard Business School Press, 1994).

[30] Russell Ackoff and Frederick Edmund Emery, *On Purposeful Systems: An Interdisciplinary Analysis of Individual and Social Behavior as a System of Purposeful Events* (Transaction Publishers, 2005).

[31] Henry Mintzberg, *The Rise and Fall of Strategic Planning* (Free Press, 1994).

[32] Peter Senge, *The Fifth Discipline* (Doubleday, 1990).

[33] Henry Mintzberg, *The Rise and Fall of Strategic Planning* (Free Press, 1994).

[34] A. De Geus, "Planning as Learning" (1988) Vol. 66 No. 2 *Harvard Business Review* 70–74.

[35] Chris Argyris, "Teaching Smart People How to Learn" (1991) Vol. 69 No. 3 *Harvard Business Review* 54–61.

[36] Russell Ackoff, *Ackoff's Best: His Classic Writings on Management* (Wiley, 1999).

[37] Peter Senge, *The Fifth Discipline* (Doubleday, 1990).

[38] David Bohm, *Thought as a System* (Routledge, 1992).

[39] Peter Senge, *The Fifth Discipline* (Doubleday, 1990).

[40] Gallup Institute, *Gallup Management Journal* (Gallup Leadership Institute, 2009).

[41] Andrew Hargadon, "When Innovations Meet Institutions: Edison and the Design of The Electric Light" (2001) Vol. 46 No. 3 *Administrative Science Quarterly* 476–501.

[42] Steve Jobs in *Business Week* 25 May 1998.

[43] Thomas Allen, *The Organization and Architecture of Innovation* (Taylor & Francis, 2006).

[44] Robert Kelley and Janet Caplan, "How Bell Labs Creates Star Performers" (1993) Vol. 71 No. 4 *Harvard Business Review* 128–139.

[45] Karen Jehn and Pri Shah, "Interpersonal Relationships and Task Performance: An Examination of Mediating Processes In Friendship and Acquaintance Groups" (1997) Vol. 72 No. 4 *Journal of Personality and Social Psychology* 775–790.

[46] J.D. Mayer *et al.*, "Emotional Intelligence: Theory, Findings and Implications" (2004) Vol. 15 No. 3 *Psychological Inquiry*.

[47] See Barry Jaruzelski, Kevin Dehoff and Rakesh Bordia, "Money Isn't Everything" (2005) Issue 41 *Strategy + Business* (http://www.strategy-business.com/article/05406?pg=all#authors)

[48] Robert Cialdini, *Influence: The Psychology of Persuasion* (HarperCollins, 2009).

[49] David Constant, Lee Sproull and Sara Kiesler, "The Kindness Of Strangers: The usefulness of electronic weak ties for technical advice" (1996) Vol. 7 No. 2 *Organization Science* 119–135.

Chapter 9

Managing Knowledge Worker Productivity in Practice

Gerry Prendergast

I have been impressed with the urgency of doing. Knowing is not enough! We must apply. Being willing is not enough; we must do.

Leonardo da Vinci

Gerry Prendergast, Engineering Director of a large, multinational healthcare subsidiary, has contributed this ground-breaking chapter which charts new territory in leading professionals. A relentless champion of 'total' operational excellence, Gerry pioneered a major change initiative that focused on the development of his engineering unit by managing tacit knowledge and innovation. Gerry and his team took on the formidable challenge of extending world class excellence into the abstract domain of knowledge work. In this chapter, Gerry has outlined that strategic transformation and, particularly, the introduction of a new 'fifth level' in managing knowledge and innovation.

Unleashing Intellectual Potential

The phrase 'the day we stop learning is the day we die' resonates well in a professional environment. This need to continuously learn – and reshape one's thinking – means it is necessary to discover how to obtain the best out of the most important resource in an organisation: the minds of its people.

Managing engineers, as well as other professionals, requires a special approach. Understandably, such people often feel they know more than you, are more intelligent than you and do not want to conform to norms. Sometimes, they do not wish to share knowledge, as it is a way of securing power and gaining a sense of psychological security. However, they usually have an inherent need to demonstrate the power of their knowledge to the group and, ultimately, they have a strong desire to share with the group, creating a powerful nucleus for further bonding and sharing within the group.

In our company (a leading pharmaceutical manufacturer) we have progressed through the four classic stages of evolution in quality and productivity, from basic competence through to 'world class manufacturing', as illustrated below:

FOUR CLASSIC STAGES OF QUALITY EVOLUTION

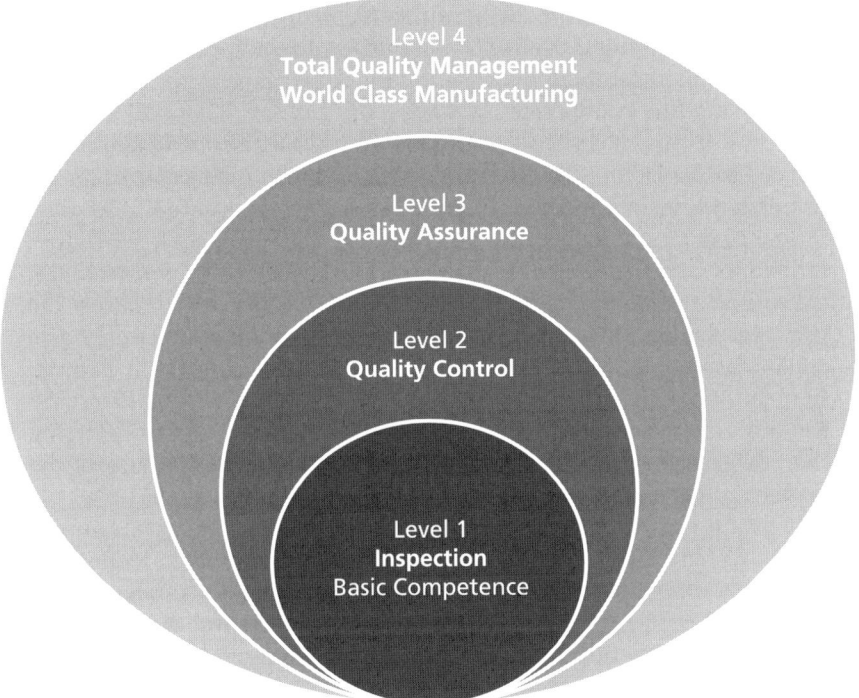

In seeking the next stage of evolution, we came to realise that the key to increasing performance lay in unleashing the intellectual potential of all our employees, but especially staff involved in knowledge work. More specifically, it was in the realisation that we had significant unexplored potential in our engineering staff, who are responsible for the design and functioning of our highly complex operations. Intelligent and driven, they could contribute much more, both individually and as a group. These smart people managed knowledge, engineering expertise, design talent and, indeed, they were primarily responsible for 'planned' innovation, such as the introduction of new methods and machinery.

The 'missing link' in this, we concluded, was not so much the management of the explicit knowledge (which was already well known and codified) but the less explicit knowledge – often called 'acumen', engineering 'prowess' or simply 'expertise'. Despite its elusive and vague nature, we decided to face the need to manage this tacit knowledge; the even greater challenge was to nurture "self-transcending, not-yet-embodied knowledge", as Otto Scharmer phrases it,[1] i.e. creative knowledge.

As discussed in **Chapter 8**, Otto Scharmer explains that purposeful, unscripted dialogue is the crucible for new ideas. It is in this dialogue that innovation frequently occurs. It is through this exchange of ideas in a supportive environment, we have found, that creation emerges.

The age-old apprenticeship system of master and pupil works well in tacit knowledge transfer. However, it is the unwritten expertise or technical know how that is most valuable – and most difficult to unearth and transfer. The important thing to realise is that this wealth of knowledge actually exists, and then act on this realisation by unearthing, tapping into and transferring this knowledge.

At first it can be difficult to understand *self-transcending knowledge*, but when reflecting on a team's discussions, what counts is an understanding of the thought process of each individual and then influencing and shaping that process. The quality of thought shapes innovation and the resultant output is the highest level of performance.

Leading and managing all this is difficult. It is necessary to treat the group as unique, intelligent individuals and yet simultaneously as a collaborative, highly capable, unified team. Achieving the collaboration and the unity is the task of the true leader. It is vital to understand the individual needs and strengths of the various individuals: using the power and capability of the collective team is the true task of the leader.

In dealing with the clever person and the collective group, it is important to recognise that each person may be in a different state of evolution, i.e. a different 'situation' in terms of maturity. It is crucial to recognise and practice situational leadership (see **Chapter 3** for details), to understand the developmental level of the individual and work towards a productive, harmonious relationship, with the outcome being a self-reliant achiever with consistently high performance.

Coaching and mentoring play a huge role in individual development and well-thought-out one-to-ones are indispensible in bringing people along. The true leader will visit the shop floor and the engineering department, talking to people at their workplace. This gives a sense of caring and togetherness, and it breaks down barriers.

We needed to understand the workings of the minds of our engineering people and shape how they think and how they approach their work. How this is done will greatly affect the output of the creative minds working in an organisation. Although self-transcending, creative knowledge is difficult to capture, we felt that there was an imperative to face this challenge.

In knowledge management, the easy part of the job is to collate 'hard' data, such as machine performance; the more difficult job is to manage the implicit, uncodified 'tacit' knowledge. The main mechanism for this is simply meaningful conversation. It is through meaningful conversation, full of debate, discussion and dialogue, that shared meaning arises and innovation emerges.

Real conversation, with its difficulties and tensions, is the crucible from which mutual understanding emerges. Creativity, as discussed in the previous chapter, lies at the intersection of ideas. When ideas collide and fuse, innovation can be sparked. While it sounds simplistic to say that conversation is crucial, real dialogue is actually scarce, as it is fraught with doubts, fears and frustrations. It is difficult, but essential, to manage such conversations so that a real sense of shared understanding and mutual ambition is developed.

The Strategic Framework

Although our division in the company was well established, we had to constantly innovate to ensure our continued survival against international competition. Based on our realisation of the power of conversation, we wanted to weave our new strategy using a deeply interactive, progressive approach. We wanted to incorporate the development of our people into the new strategy, believing that such 'talent management' would be essential in unlocking the creativity needed to drive productivity. We wanted to reach that 'ideal' state where the people and the organisation reach a differentiated level that is better than the competition. Obtaining (and, crucially, acting on) feedback from the individuals and the teams is critical to success and to how to develop knowledge.

Understanding the power of knowledge, harvesting that knowledge and making efficient and effective use of that knowledge can help to create a sustainable competitive advantage.

Harvard Professor Otto Scharmer[2] proposes a distinction between tacit, embodied knowledge and not-yet-embodied, self-transcending knowledge. Throughout the 20th century, industry in the developed economies was transformed from one that largely processed raw materials to one that processes knowledge. The winners will be the "wizards of precognition", those who know where the potential opportunities will emerge. Leaders need a new type of knowledge that allows them to sense, tune into and actualise emerging business opportunities – that is, to tap into the sources of 'not-yet-embodied' knowledge.

Leaders must be able to see the emerging opportunities before they become manifest in the marketplace. This type of knowledge involves more than informed hunches; it is a high-level sense developed from tacit knowledge, based on rational observation, prescience and creation. Steve Jobs typified this depth of immersion, and it helps explain why he had not just one innovation but produced a stream of new ideas over two decades. He also had a breadth of perspective that promoted the productive "collision of ideas"; for example, his interest in font design, art and philosophy merged to form his vision for new ways of working with technology.

Scharmer explains that this ability to sense emerging opportunities is usually associated with artists, not business managers, which is why we need the merging of the logical left- and the creative right-brain capability, sort of a fusion of the arts and the sciences, or the planned and the organic (see **Chapter 8**).

Understanding and Managing the Three Forms of Knowledge

For the purposes of this chapter and discussion, knowledge can be separated into three categories, and the three forms of knowledge – **explicit**, **tacit** and **self-transcending** – are managed differently.

The first form is explicit knowledge, that which can be codified and contained in books and similar media. Because it is already known, this information is relatively easily managed, but because it is commonly available, its value diminishes. With explicit knowledge, we know what we know!

The second form is tacit knowledge, where the knowledge exists, but is hard to specify; for example, how to play winning tennis or how to persuade reluctant buyers. The best exponents know their 'art', but may not be able to articulate it; they don't know what they know! For example, a great tennis player like Raphael Nadal might not necessarily become a great coach, lacking the 'codification' by which he might explain his techniques.

The third form is latent, emergent, embryonic knowledge. This is early stage intuition about what new knowledge might be brought into existence under the right conditions. These are the 'germs' of a good idea, not quite formed, often requiring additional knowledge to become real. These 'seeds' need to germinate and be nurtured. With this type of knowledge, we don't know what we know!

A fourth form of knowledge, not considered further here, is that of the complete unknown, where we don't even know what we don't know! Represented graphically, these four types of knowledge can be shown in quadrants as follows:

FOUR TYPES OF KNOWLEDGE

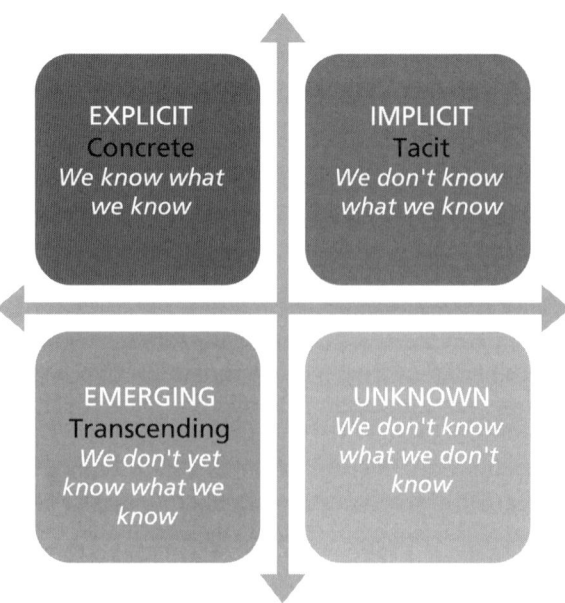

Thus:

- *Explicit knowledge* requires the disciplined storage and retrieval of specific knowledge and information on products, equipment and process.
- *Implicit, tacit knowledge* or *experiential 'know-how'* is more difficult to disseminate and transfer.
- *Emergent, self-transcending knowledge* is that unformed, unstructured and uncodified knowledge generated by intuition, observation, immersion in a problem or the conceptualisation of new possibilities. Clearly, this type of knowledge is impossible to store or archive, but it contains the seeds of new knowledge. As described in **Chapter 8**, under the right conditions and with an appropriate degree of pressure or in a context of trust, this knowledge can be caused to emerge. In the next section, some means of creating the right environment for such crucial conversations and innovations are identified.

Creating the Social Conditions for Innovation

Although our department was already at level 4 (see above), we needed still more innovation to remain competitive. In short, we needed to move into that vague 'transcending' space so that we could garner more creativity in areas such as engineering, but also in the development of a winning strategy.

While we believed that we needed to proceed to the next level, the '5th Level', this was, of course, unknown territory. There were no markers along the path to such levels of innovation, but we sensed that 'crucial conversations' were needed. At the same time, engineers and similar staff were known for their reluctance to immerse themselves in such honest and open conversations. Different departments could be expected to have a 'silo' mentality, when a cross-departmental view would be essential if we were to make significant progress.

For these reasons, we held a series of more-or-less intimate conversations, between individuals and between groups, to get to 'the heart of the matter' and to form the necessary degree of trust – and challenge – for creativity to be sparked and innovations to emerge. These included breakfast meetings, brainstorming sessions, 'think-ins' and formal gatherings. The un-discussable subjects were eventually discussed, and the results were tremendous. A single idea, a surprising notion, or a shared thought can ignite something truly creative with another person, and this proved to be the case, especially given the high intelligence of the engineers and other staff. 'Joining the dots', so to speak, released the enormous accumulated force of the fusion of ideas. This joining of minds created something new, a whole new approach to areas such as strategy and engineering design. The interactions between people created a slew of inventive ideas and alternative concepts, and the blending of old ideas with new thinking was particularly powerful.

In the following sections of this chapter, I will describe how we lifted our performance to the '5th Level', into the realm of 'collective innovation'

STRATEGY ROADMAP: THE JOURNEY TOWARDS EXCELLENCE

in which very significant improvements in effectiveness and efficiency were achieved. Most importantly, this fresh thinking influenced our approach in crafting our strategy, and particularly in harnessing the latent intellectual potential of our people.

Achieving the 5th Level: The Strategy Map

In most organisations today, intellectual capital is the greatest resource. Unfortunately, many organisations spend an inordinate amount of time and effort achieving the best efficiency out of their plant, equipment and systems with means to measure and improve. Rarely is there an effective means of achieving the best efficiency of the thought process, approach and quality of output of knowledge workers. Great attention is paid to upkeep and maintenance of infrastructure and equipment, but rarely to personnel.

Our strategy roadmap, in its raw original form, is shown in the figure below to illustrate the various steps in that progression. Key to this progression were the conversational 'cycles' (as discussed above); these provided the insights that sparked fresh thinking and helped create new ways of manufacturing at higher quality and lower cost, bringing the plant beyond 'Level 4' and positioning it as a thought leader in the wider company, and as a particularly 'smart' plant. Among the innovations were an innovation 'academy', and a customer research centre in which end-user thinking was explored in depth. This was in addition to cost savings of over €3 million, generated by clever engineering of facilities, as well as dozens of smaller incremental improvements. In addition, the fresh injection of creative thought stimulated new possibilities. Staff were encouraged by the realisation that even though the plant was 30 years in existence, innovation was ageless and the journey into new terrain could be exhilarating.

Our aim was not merely to create efficiency of plant, equipment and systems, but to expand with the minds of our people. We did not want to rely on stilted systems, such as annual appraisals, to manage the performance of knowledge workers, but, instead wanted to truly learn about our people and how they thought, as individuals and collectively. By influencing how they think and working to improve the process of knowledge creation, we hoped to increase their effectiveness.

This was achieved through informal and formal discussion. It was assisted by coaching, mentoring and face-to-face meetings. Through dialogue, people learned about themselves and improved the quality of their thought process. These 'pioneering' thoughts led to new ideas, and this in turn sparked fresh thought in the minds of others. Each iteration improved the capability of the individual and team, generating a virtuous and self-replicating cycle.

Through such sharing of knowledge, different levels of discomfort are experienced and, hopefully, can be transcended.

Developing People: Learning from Others

I have witnessed these evolutions in my professional team as I mixed different individuals together into groups to create a variety of dynamics and synergies. One example of this has been in the strategically critical department of new technology. The incumbent Technology Manager was struggling to overcome the complexities of a new process, to bed it down and support manufacturing, while at the same time progressing the aggressive plan for the expansion.

I decided to move the Maintenance Engineering Manager into the team to take responsibility for the operations of the installed lines. As I brought these two senior people together with their teams, I noticed the change in approach of the Technology Manager. Previously, he had a logical, but restricted approach to problem-solving; however, he learned from the achievement of the Maintenance Engineering Manager, and his own performance improved significantly.

Planning the Strategic Shift towards Excellence among Knowledge Professionals

Harvesting, managing and leading the way knowledge can be used provides a powerful platform for strategic development. This following section describes how – and why – our group made the change towards better knowledge management as a strategic platform, starting with the organisational structure, and then moving to achieving higher productivity.

1. Use a Mix of Planned and Organic Change

Jim Collins in *Good to Great*[3] reminds us that "we must get the right people on the bus and then figure out where we are going". In other words, **who** we are takes precedence over **what** we do. That is the surprising first step in the process.

With the right people on board, the right ideas will emerge. The right people, in the right frame of mind will flush out what is wrong, what needs to be done and how to go about it. Models and frameworks help put shape on strategy to achieve a sense of purpose. With the right people, a plan can be formulated to achieve the vision outlined.

The critical thing is to 'get off the fence' and get on with it. Procrastination is a killer!

Once a start is made, the organic activity will emerge. The louder individuals or characters will come to the fore at first with strong ideas and opinions. This must be well managed: it is vital to get into the minds of those others lurking in the dark. After many series of dialogue, those lurking will step out of the shadows, often with profound statements and ideas.

As the activities begin, those with an intuitive mind will display their creativity. It is essential to watch out for this, to grasp and harvest the ideas, to share them with others so that it provokes still more original thinking.

These bursts create momentum and that momentum must be built upon until a 'flywheel effect' emerges. This momentum keeps on gathering energy until breakthrough is achieved.

2. Developing a Viable Vision – Creating a 'Burning Platform'

As soon as I took up my present position I was able to realise, with this fresh perspective, where the gaps were. It had been suggested to me that the culture at our organisation included an underlying assumption that there was a very strong work ethic and a 'can do' attitude. However, some complacency was evident. Staff had accepted a status quo, and thought that the company was isolated from the current economic crisis.

In response, I created a 'burning platform', raising awareness of the potential dangers of losing competitiveness. I then worked with colleagues to fashion a compelling credible vision of the future. I sketched it out on my whiteboard in the office and referred to it at particular times.

As we worked on our strategic cost-reduction programme and talent management, a variety of strains emerged as we worked out what we as a team really wanted to achieve.

3. Handle the 'Messiness'

We challenged ourselves as leaders. Were we doing the right things and was what we were doing making a difference? At our offsite organisational talent review meeting we challenged our own effectiveness through the output of our teams. We rated the performance of our individual team members and other senior management team members critiqued our assessments. At our quarterly offsite meetings we challenged our activities, what we had learned and if we were still going in the right direction. The outcomes were a creation of the spiral of:

- self-transcending knowledge,
- formation of common will,
- shared action (praxis) and
- shared reflection.

This transforms work into shared experience; abstract discussion into shared reflection; and negotiations of objectives into the formation of collective will.

4. Wade in the Swamp but get on the High Ground Occasionally

After 'getting off the fence' and making that start, spurts of activity sprang up throughout the organisation. Those with initiative kicked off programmes in line with the change.

It is of paramount importance to be able to manage these various activities in a way that allows organic development of the work culture. It is necessary to get into the trenches and participate in the 'digging'. It is necessary to 'wade around in the swamp' to get close to the activity and to assess the performance outputs.

One must also be able to get up on the high ground and have a 360 degree view, and deal with any conflict that emerges. In our case, though we started out with a plan, each of the senior management team took their own initiative to drive programmes of change to reflect what we wanted to achieve.

For example, the QA manager initiated a programme to streamline the validations process. This meant that 'lean' efforts started ahead of the mainstream plan. The validation process had been strangling 'agile and rapid' execution, so it was better to allow this critical process to proceed as it would be an important learning in itself and would unearth issues.

5. Strategies Emerge – It's a Long Process

Henry Mintzberg disagrees with Michael Porter's view that strategies are rationally planned and implemented.[4] Mintzberg explains that it is not that simple. However, new ideas emerge as the process travels its journey and this must be taken on board to decide. This is a long process and after each iteration of planning, doing, checking and acting, it is necessary to review and reflect on the outcomes and react to the learnings in order to improve on the next iteration.

6. Leaders must be able to Imagine

Great leaders are great dreamers and relentlessly follow their dreams. Being satisfied with accomplished mediocrity or accepting the status quo is the death knell of any organisation.

Jack Welch believed that General Electric could and must be number one or two within its industry. Bill Gates believed he could build up an empire that would be the greatest software company in the world. Steve Jobs managed to live out his dreams and let nothing get in his way, even the threat of his own mortality.

If we look to the great leaders in history, they were all great believers of what they could achieve. They all possessed great imagination of a better future.

Leaders who do not have vivid imagination and do not follow their dream are rarely truly successful. Great leaders all possess a common goal, with a disciplined and relentless pursuit of excellence.

I struggled somewhat initially in my role to reach a common ground with my senior management peers with respect to the importance of this attribute. We had a corporate expectation of leadership from everyone that filtered down to all levels of the organisation, which was based on the desire to do the right thing and lead by example. We needed to bring this further as senior managers to lead our people to the highest platform. Before too long I was satisfied that technical staff had a good understanding of our 'new' leadership expectations, of reaching that higher level.

7. Managing Knowledge Worker Productivity

In reaching that higher level I found myself with the challenge of managing the 'smarter' people. I had a vision that we as a group could attain Total Excellence by achieving what I call a 'Level 5' in quality of service by the technical group. This echoes Jim Collins's term. He similarly describes the great leaders as having attained "Level 5". These leaders transformed good companies into great companies using, for instance, the 'Hedgehog' concept of defining what they could be best in class at, what they were passionate about, and what drove their 'economic engine'. These same people confronted the brutal facts, got the right people on board, figured out where they were going and in a disciplined manner relentlessly pursued their desired future state.

Gareth Jones[5] writes about the difficulty in managing professionals and other "clever" people, saying:

"These people don't want to be 'managed', and they detest bureaucracy, displaying an outward image of indifference. They know they are smart and they know their self worth. While they scorn corporate titles, they have organisational savvy, and know how to advance their pet projects."

Jones suggests that in managing smart people one needs to give them space, and make the rules flexible:

- Protect them from 'corporate rain' (interference by the hierarchy)
- Only show them 'tough love'
- Be the benevolent guardian
- Give them 'meaty' projects
- Recognise their ideas as important
- Build a sense of community
- Make the workplace exciting
- Keep them challenged
- Cut out bureaucracy.

Clever people create disproportionate value, especially in knowledge intensive organisations like ours.

Chris Argyris[6] suggests that, eventually, the smartest people find it the hardest to learn. The key to success is teaching smart people how to learn. Professionals avoid learning about themselves; they do not want to know what they are doing wrong; and tend not to want to continuously improve. This can be their greatest obstacle to success. They exhibit defensive reasoning; they consider they are too highly educated to require performance management. They rarely experience failure and when they do, they don't know how to deal with it.

Conclusion

Harvesting knowledge is extremely important in today's organisations, but it is difficult to manage. Understanding the value of knowledge is of paramount importance for the progressive leader and turning it into high order value is the stuff of great leaders. This is what can truly differentiate one organisation from its competitors.

The message is to challenge the status quo, even in a relatively successful organisation, with the right people developing a strategic plan, getting it started quickly and allowing the strategy to further emerge, learn and change from each iteration, and managing the thought process of the knowledge workers in order to positively affect the outcomes. Let it be your 'Blue Ocean' strategy, sailing in less contested and less dangerous waters.

On a final note, with regards to myself, I will continue with my own team in the relentless pursuit of Total Excellence in a knowledge environment. I will bring those learnings with me on my journey through life, and share in this brave new world of knowledge.

In the preceding chapters, we have outlined the background to a new approach to achieving excellence, based on the realisation that most work in the modern economy is cognitive and that, unlike other work, there are few means of unleashing this intellectual potential. In this chapter, Gerry Prendergast has described how, in his organisation, substantial gains were made in improving, for example, engineering output, and how this enhanced the division's strategic position and capacity for change. Significantly, while the destination chosen was in uncharted territory, the journey proved exciting and even enjoyable for those involved.

Sincere thanks to Gerry and his colleagues for this very important advance in enhancing a group's intellectual capability and productivity through that "5th Level".

ENDNOTES

[1] C. Otto Scharmer, *Theory U: Learning From the Future as it Emerges* (Berrett-Koehler, 2009).

[2] *Ibid.*

[3] Jim Collins, *Good to Great: Why Some Companies Make the Leap...and Others Don't* (Random House, 2001).

[4] Henry Mintzberg, *The Rise and Fall of Strategic Planning* (Free Press, 1994); Michael E. Porter, "The Five Competitive Forces that Shape Strategy" in *On Competition* (Harvard Business School Press, 2008) pp. 79–93.

[5] Rob Goffee and Gareth Jones, *Why Should Anyone Be Led By You?: What It Takes to be an Authentic Leader* (Harvard Business School Press, 2006).

[6] Chris Argyris, "Teaching Smart People How to Learn" (May–June 1991) Vol. 69 No. 3 *Harvard Business Review* 99–109.

Chapter 10

Managing Different Professions

Being a professional is doing the things you love to do, on the days you don't feel like doing them.

Julius Erving

In this chapter, the management of various types of professional, i.e. from the different professions, is examined, starting with advanced knowledge workers, software developers, then progressing through software engineers, architects, lawyers, surgeons and artists. The chapter also features real-life cases from Nick Koumarianos and Colm Russell, both experienced managers in the technology field, on managing technical staff in practice.

The initial focus is on software development, as this type of complex work involves creativity, collaboration and total immersion: it could even be said to be an emotionally deprived life. (Perhaps Mark Zuckerberg invented Facebook so that he could make friends without actually meeting people?)

Having categorised the various types of work (systematic, creative, judgement, routine), professional activity is further characterised by such factors as deadline orientation, client interfacing and knowledge type. This section of the chapter is indebted to management guru Peter Drucker (who popularised the term 'knowledge worker'), and Larry Prusak and Thomas Davenport (co-authors of *Thinking for a Living*). In this way, we get to 'stand on the shoulders of giants'.

In this chapter we suggest particular ways to manage the intelligent professional, using, for illustration purposes, certain generalisations and stereotypes (without generalisation, there can be no theory). While such stereotyping can descend into caricature, when taken in context stereotypes can provide a means of looking at behaviour in professions that are high-commitment and deadline-driven. Often, the work and the person are inseparable, as is the case with architects, artists, doctors and other vocations.

With knowledge work and innovation so crucial today, it is instructive to note Thomas Davenport's conclusions[1]:

- Knowledge work is extremely diverse, therefore it is necessary to classify the various types of knowledge work and manage them differently.
- There is no universal measure of output, but any measure needs to include both the quantity and quality of work. In other words, 'billable hours' is not a sufficient measure in itself.
- To improve work, it is important to take account of current practice in addition to focusing on redesigned processes.
- While individual information management technology, in the form of powerful laptops, smart phones and other personal computing devices,

is accelerating, there is still a lack of cross-organisation knowledge management.

These are valid conclusions, and Davenport also offers actionable advice. For example, on improving the work process, he advises managers to:

- involve the affected knowledge workers (and professionals) in the design of any new process;
- study the work, paying attention to current as well as future practice;
- understand the context – know why things are done, as well as what is done;
- treat professionals with respect and deference;
- acknowledge the value of experience and tacit knowledge;
- don't just impose your way – consider the concerns of those doing the work.

Peter Drucker posed the following key questions[2]:

- What is a knowledge worker, really?
- How do knowledge workers differ from others, and what does that mean for management?
- Which interventions, measures and experiments in 'knowledge work' are most effective?
- Which are the most important knowledge work processes?
- Which organisational technology is most appropriate to knowledge workers?
- How can knowledge workers' individual capabilities be developed?
- What must be invested in knowledge workers' networks and learning?
- Which physical work environment will help to maximise knowledge workers' performance?
- How are knowledge workers best managed?

In this section, answers to the above questions are offered, with an emphasis on that final question – how best to manage knowledge workers and, by extension, certain types of professional, notably engineers.

Four Types of Knowledge Work

Davenport also formulated a matrix of four knowledge work types, classifying knowledge-intensive processes that range from individual agents to collaborative groups:

DAVENPORT'S FOUR KNOWLEDGE WORK TYPES

1. Integration Model (systematic, repeatable work), as found in the legal profession.
2. Collaboration Model (improvisational work), as found in software engineering.
3. Expert Model (judgement-oriented work), as found in surgery.
4. Transaction Model (rule-based work), as found in some standard types of accountancy.

These four extreme categories are depicted graphically below:

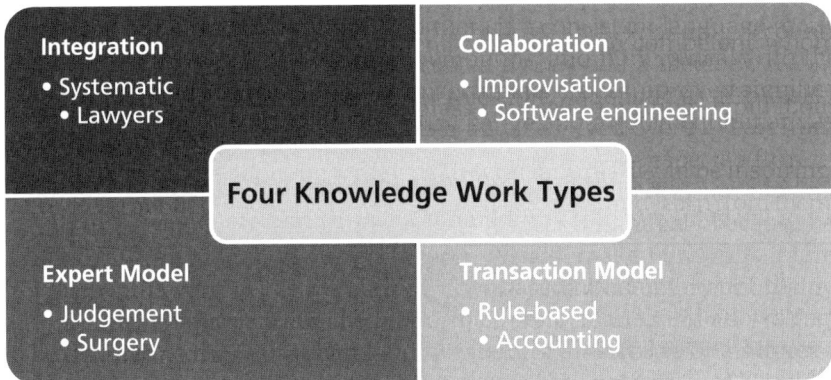

Different kinds of knowledge work require different kinds of knowledge workers. Effective managers are those who get the most appropriate worker in alignment with each task. As Davenport says:

> "A job in which knowledge is created should be treated very differently from one in which it is applied. For example, those who find existing knowledge need to understand knowledge requirements, search for it among multiple sources, and pass it along to the requester or user.
>
> Other workers create new knowledge. Still others ('packagers') put together knowledge created by others. Knowledge workers can also be distinguished by the types of ideas with which they deal. My view, however, is that the organizations that will be most successful in the future will be those in which it's everyone's job to be creating and using both big and small ideas."[3]

High-performance knowledge workers tend to be very effective and efficient experiential learners, seeming "to get more learning out of a single experience and continually updating their skills, expertise, and social awareness as a natural part of their work."[4] This is closely allied to the findings presented in **Chapter 8** on managing knowledge, which showed that achievement depends heavily on action-learning ability, i.e. the ability to reflect critically on events and extract the lessons contained therein. In **Chapter 8**, we highlighted the innovation value of coalescing diverse ideas and of adopting different perspectives, which is a theme that emerges here also. High performers attributed problem-solving abilities to the acquisition of a broad base of knowledge. The high performers Davenport studied "often had unusual, and often somewhat illogical, career paths. However, they repeatedly told us in various ways that these different jobs provided them with unique perspectives and expertise in solving problems." High performers described themselves as "calculated" risk-takers, but "when they do make a decision to pursue a given area of expertise, the high performers invest heavily, and seem to have a 'compass' for personal learning. They often described themselves as highly focused on the domains they have decided to pursue." High performers, having obtained a degree of mastery in one area, seem to be able to use this knowledge with less conscious thought than low performers, and also have a capacity to focus critically on the challenge ahead, 'screening out' irrelevant information.

As will be seen below in the section on software developers, high performers are disproportionately valuable, out-achieving even good performers by orders of magnitude.

The management and fostering of such valuable, and occasionally unorthodox, talent demands a combination of nurturing (to allow the talent to flourish) and setting appropriate challenges (to energise and direct the talent). Hierarchical management, and especially the abuse of rank, will not normally succeed. A manager should focus instead on accommodating high performers' needs (often latent) for important personal relationships, access to critical resources, visible progress and emotional support. Davenport suggests that "perhaps the most important point to consider is the interrelated nature of these practices of the high performer". These points are echoed in the case study below by Colm Russell, who has managed teams of such high performers for a global technology company.

Case Study: Engineers – The Management Challenges by Colm Russell

Colm Russell was an engineering manager with a global telecommunications equipment manufacturer at the time of contributing this piece on managing high-tech engineers. He has since accepted a senior technology management position with the world's leading search engine company. Colm recognises that excellent talent is constantly in demand, reversing the power polarity in more conventional employer–employee relationships.

Professional engineers view themselves as creative beings, designed for a grand purpose and capable of great enterprise.

Their primary expectations include that the company they have joined will provide a well-equipped environment, full support and copious recognition for genuine achievement. In this case study, I present the challenges that are frequently presented to managers of professional engineers, and suggest approaches that one might adopt in addressing each of them.

I believe that high achievers are the backbone to any business. Their retention, creativity and productivity are of paramount importance. As a manager, I may be tempted to resent them as being 'high maintenance' people, but then I will remind myself that they are worth the undoubted managerial effort.

I will start with the challenges presented by the personal development needs of the modern engineer and how to link this with the growth of the organisation. This is then followed by a discussion of the means of developing specific responsibilities and a tangible sense of ownership.

Introducing change is a minefield and often exposes organisational and individual weakness. I will suggest some best practices in change management. I close with the Individual Performance Review – a tedious necessity for many managers, but potentially also a motivational tool for those who manage professionals.

Personal Development

The ability of professional engineers is measured by their efficacy in solving engineering problems, and they gain satisfaction from being immersed in them. During any brief interval between projects, they prepare by analysing gaps in design competencies and assessing their own abilities. Their unfortunate conclusion is often that such preparation is too brief; in fact, it has only served them with a reminder of how much they don't know. Backed into this corner, a manager's best move is to propose the next project – and all the technical challenges it presents.

Career progression in most professional fields involves the assignment of titles, often accompanied by an increase in pay grade and privileges. Such milestones are often light years apart, especially when interspersed with economic slumps and pay freezes. Throughout the interim, other forms of reward and recognition must be deployed. Each step on the path to promotion should be positioned as an opportunity, offered by the organisation, for personal development.

Experience shows that most effective learning is through practical task repetition; an expert will have completed similar tasks at least 10 times and successfully trained at least one colleague to complete the same task: until this point, mastery has not yet been achieved. The advantage of such a model is that it ensures that a professional's need for formal acknowledgement of their expertise may only be satisfied by first addressing the needs of the organisation. The assignment of a trainee to a budding expert is recognition in itself. Training periods should be brief and pertinent. If training is not immediately relevant, its value erodes over a surprisingly short period of time; training that is commissioned for your next project is a wiser investment.

On-the-job training, in my opinion, is the most effective form of development: not only is theory employed, but it is reinforced by demonstrating practical application. More importantly, it demonstrates the process by which it is applied, and the attitude of the high-achieving mentor transmits itself more permanently to the 'apprentice'.

The task as a manager is to reconcile two potentially conflicting agendas: the professional engineer's insatiable appetite for personal development and the needs of the business. One cannot create great engineers; they emerge as a by-product of the state-of-the-art organisation (and challenges) that you are producing. The manager must constantly tie the needs of the business to this development; otherwise it becomes an expensive indulgence rather than a business necessity.

Ownership and Empowerment

Professional staff will ensure that you know of their competence gaps, and they expect you to provide time to address them. They realise that the pace of enterprise is often determined by rising customer expectations and readily accept this reality. They are less tolerant of the weaker links that are allowed develop in some organisations, and the ambitious, clever professional will have long since jumped ship to a more successful project. Clever professionals expect to have clever managers. The good manager must have a kind of peripheral vision achieved via a vibrant network of contacts that provide 'tacit knowledge'.

Introducing Change into Groups

As managers, we initiate change to realign with strategy and to approach optimal operational efficiency. We carry out certain transformations within the confines of our corporate culture and, occasionally, we make changes to modify or rectify this culture. Once the motivation for change is clear and consensus exists across the management team, the collective resolve will ensure implementation. However, in walking this new path, what toes have we stepped on, and who have we left behind? If this question pops up for any of the following forms of transformation, then it is likely that opportunities have been missed:

- technological shift;
- organisational development;
- process change (who does what and how they do it).

Where change is rejected for change's sake, a cultural adversity to change is exposed. In this case, the culture itself must be scrutinised, as it is failing the business. In fact, such a case of rejection is an expressed preference for the culture over the business, and since corporate culture does not generate revenue, the change itself, whether minor or major, has exposed a critical organisational weakness. This degree of conservatism is more often exposed in larger, well-established organisations, and can only be addressed through systematic improvement planning, where all members of the team can expect to receive ownership of changes or improvements in the plan.

Where change exposes insecurities in individuals, it is likely they have identified a threat to their position or status, and such insecurities often manifest themselves as outright rejection or even sabotage to the proposed change. This threat, after it is analysed further and understood better, may then be presented as a benefit or as a consequence of good or bad performance. A benefit can be expressed as a positive reinforcement in performance review; hence, an element of change can be presented as a form of recognition, where it is due. The consequence can be expressed as negative reinforcement or constructive feedback, thus contributing to the performance improvement plan of the individual. In either case, you will have dealt with the uncertainty and transferred potential barriers from change co-ordination into performance-review planning, which is more robust and familiar ground.

The reasons for negative reactions to change among mature professionals are less obvious where rejection is based on a perceived threat to knowledge-based power. When progressive new technologies, such as open systems, replaced legacy systems, for example, many of our engineers did not find the transition easy. At the bottom of the developmental curve, they found their knowledge-based power had been completely eroded, and they were left almost on a par with new graduates, but without the benefit of a more contemporary education in technology.

Despite the difficulties, the high achievers in this group emerged early, forging their way through glass ceilings of technology. Those who make it soar higher as a result. Your role as a manager is to help the engineer/professional maintain his hope in the future while he makes the transition to the new situation.

A collaborative and consultative forum should be a permanent fixture at every level of the organisation. Taking a lead from technical change control boards (which debate product changes, providing a process of presenting change), an organisational change control board can be used to consider lessons learned and new strategic thinking. By using similar language and format, a near identical process of communication, debate and decision-making can be adopted for both technical and organisational change.

Performance Review

The performance review is a vital but unworldly means of assessing performance and of motivating engineers. While it is merely a labour of necessity for many managers, it can be a motivational tool for those who choose to manage professionals professionally. In my view, the key to conducting effective performance reviews is to regard such setpieces as opportunities to coach, cheerlead and develop staff, not just to sit in judgement on them. The real test of whether a performance review has been effective starts with the engineer leaving the review, eyes blazing, fired up for the challenge ahead, more confident and communicative. This 'coaching' perspective changes the encounter from being a classic 'blame-game' to a crucible for enlightenment and motivation.

Conclusion

Engineers are capable of extraordinary achievement – and of being extraordinarily difficult to manage, on occasion. Working with – not against – them is vital; after all, they are simply seeking resources to deliver ever more noteworthy work. Developing a sense of ownership greatly assists communication and shared responsibility. Change should be celebrated as an opportunity for improvement and assigned individual or group ownership; it may then be driven by re-engineering existing cultural norms to meet the needs of each improvement.

Philip Greenspun,[5] entrepreneurial founder of high-tech company ArsDigita, makes similar observations to Davenport: the most desirable, knowledge-oriented culture is characterised by the Five Fs: fast, flexible, focused, friendly, and fun places to work. Greenspun, with enlightened self-interest, provided a successful work environment that he considered was "better than home" for most programmers: more fun, more friendly, more facilities (large-screen TVs, games, ping-pong, etc.) – simply 'cooler'.

Understanding the Different Types of Work Involved

A curious feature of the life of some professions is the degree to which they work alone: the architect works inside his own imagination, the lawyer pores over documents, the surgeon alone wields the scalpel, the artist creates in splendid isolation. Many professionals work in the midst of people, but not *with* them.

Many professionals, such as designers, journalists and engineers, work to strict imposed deadlines, and experience the 'creative treadmill'. Some do work that is complicated but rule-based (such as could be said for some forms of accountancy). Others do complex work, such as psychotherapy, with very many unknowns, subject to judgement and individual interpretation.

Those who manage different professions, therefore, must take account of the particular type of work involved, and decide whether it is, for example, routine or varied, complex or complicated. The table below suggests some key dimensions along each spectrum:

Element	Regular Work	Project
Repetition	Routine	Diverse, project-driven
Work Pattern	Regular	Deadline-driven
Innovation	Low	High
Sociability	Solitary	Group
Direction	Supervised	Autonomous
Type	Simple	Complex
Task Clarity	Clear	Complicated
Predictability	High	Low

For example, software engineering, using some of the categorisations above, is:

- deadline-driven (the window of opportunity closes rapidly);
- highly diverse, requiring constant innovation, new tools and languages;
- complicated, requiring many sub-specialisations;
- complex, with many unknowns, not least user requirements; and
- variable, frequently changing and requiring many sub-specialisations.

While software engineering is a solitary occupation in one sense (hours spent alone programming), it still requires periodic bursts of integration. It is at these interfaces that problems often emerge, based on misunderstandings, incompatible assumptions, different conventions, etc. It is said that the best software is written by a relatively small band of contributors, but, ultimately, every code requires integration of the modules and a degree of collaboration. In that sense, the working life of a software engineer is akin to being in a big city, full of people, but ultimately alone.

This compounds the problem of finding good managers from the ranks of such insulated individuals. A great coder will often not be an effective manager, as the skills are hugely different, one requiring a knowledge mainly of things, the other mainly of people. In addition, the loss (to the management ranks) of that technically able person can be a great waste. The real challenge is in getting ordinary (non-expert) managers to effectively manage extraordinary people. This has been achieved, for instance, in many sports, such as rugby and golf, where the best managers (Alex Ferguson, Arsene Wenger and José Mourinho in soccer, Joe Schmidt in rugby, for example) and coaches (Butch Harmon and Bill Torrance in golf) have been mere journeymen players.

Software development is far from simple and is both complex (involving many unknowns) and complicated (involving many interdependencies). Such a high-pressure and fast-changing type of work demands a special managerial approach. More standard IT infrastructure support-work, in contrast, will have a more regular rhythm and pattern. Management in this case can be more classically conventional.

Managing the talented maverick is a highly skilled art form, especially coping with those 'energy vampires' who can suck the motivational life force from an organisation. For this reason, a section in this chapter is devoted to managing the 'prima donnas' among these mavericks.

Great engineers and other 'techies' add massive value to business and indeed society, but they have the unfortunate reputation of being awkward individuals, nerdish, geeky or renegade. Their undoubted ability and tremendous commitment are sometimes undermined by their paucity of social skills. Often solitary by nature, the challenge for 'techies' and their managers is in how best to utilise their talents. For example, despite his huge technical contribution, even the great Steve Jobs was once forced out of Apple – and not particularly welcomed upon his return.[6] His "arrogance" and "obsessiveness" were considered by observers and some staff to be highly regrettable characteristics, when in fact those seeming excesses of zeal and concern for detail provided him with the motivation to design unimaginably great products. Certainly, it is tempting to acknowledge the wishes of the offended staff and simply dispense with a 'difficult' talent such as Steve Jobs. Though more straightforward, this would not actually be good for the organisation. Those rigid guardians of organisational order have even been known to complain that the 'geeks' are working obsessively deep into the night or that the mission-critical 'nerds' are social misfits. It is simple to trot out the mantra that 'the same rules apply to everyone', but rigid working conditions can hamper creative endeavour. Proper leadership – employing courage, patience and wisdom – can rescue the situation, however. Giving up on such maverick talent seems rational and even prudent. However, a better solution lies in first recognising that the 'geek' is a real human being (often well hidden, admittedly!) and, secondly, recognising that over-indulging them similarly equates to giving up on them.

Managing Interrelated Work: Software Engineering

The world and activity of software engineering offers useful lessons, as it contains particular interrelated dilemmas:

1. The indivisibility of the work means that it is best attempted by an individual or small team, yet because the task at hand is invariably new, large and complex, this is beyond the capabilities of a single individual. Dividing such complex work into pieces of work, creates the second dilemma.
2. The exponential growth of the team-communication overhead: when the task is subdivided, the communication aspects (as the opportunities for misunderstanding) multiply, adding to risk, increasing costs and diluting 'ownership'.

For these reasons, Fred Brooks, IBM 360 designer, declared as far back as the 1960s that a team of just two was the optimal size for software development.[7] Making an integrated whole of individually written pieces of code often proves nearly impossible. In such complex, creative work, conventional, 'rational' management – reducing work to small elements then synthesising them together – is ineffective.

The consequence is that innovative software engineering cannot usually be achieved by large, factory-like teams, each working on a small piece of the problem (the experiment has been tried often across the world, notably by the Japanese, but with poor results everywhere). Instead, it demands massive intelligence combined with heroic effort by a small cadre isolated from daily concerns and freed up from management intrusions and bureaucracy.

In such a context, it is little wonder that the best software engineers evolve by focusing narrowly on technology, with conventional social life being sacrificed: the work becomes both the means of living and an end in itself, giving satisfaction and providing a peer community. Any resulting lack of emotional or social intelligence is therefore understandable: the challenge for managers is to accommodate their special talents and fuse them with the efforts of others without destroying either the organisation or people in the process.

HOW SOFTWARE ENGINEERING DIFFERS FROM MORE CONVENTIONAL PROFESSIONS

- The **talent gap** – the extraordinary degree to which the very best contribute. In software engineering, good programmers are perhaps 10 times more productive than an average programmer, because of their ability to assimilate the available information and synthesise a workable solution, despite the complexities involved. A great programmer can achieve solutions not possible by an army of merely competent engineers, just as one Shakespeare can create more works of genius than a thousand hacks.
- The **technical gap** – Smart engineers will often be more expert than their managers (even when the manager is also a great engineer), at least in the part of the work the engineer has developed.
- The **productivity gap** – caused by pushing great developers into management, and consequently losing that technical talent while gaining only a moderate manager.
- The **management gap** – There is no natural progression from being a great engineer to being a great manager: the skill sets differ widely, and the transitions are often unsuccessful. To compound matters, it is rare that a non-technical manager can understand the issues sufficiently well or gain the respect of his staff. (For exceptions to this 'rule', read the accompanying case study by technology entrepreneur Nick Koumarianos, below.)
- The **measurement gap** – Engineering output is notoriously difficult to measure. The orthodox tally of lines of code per day produced by

> a programmer can even be misleading, as one cannot know whether these lines are useful. In fact, a hallmark of great software engineering is the low code line count, achieved through elegance of design and cleverness of solution.

For many professions, not least software engineering, the following advice applies:

- **Nagging is not managing** Aubrey Daniels in *Bringing out the Best in People* notes: "If we always did what we were told, we would eat only nutritious foods, never drink too much alcohol, and exercise regularly."[8] The effectiveness of written policies and management by nagging is limited. The corollary is that people do what you reward them to do, not what you hope they will do.
- **Remember the achievers as well** It is common, and understandable, to give attention to staff who are falling below expectations, but what about those good people who *are* performing? If you do not grant them positive reinforcement, they may stop going that extra mile for you.
- **Now is a good time to act** The annual review is too infrequent and often too far away to motivate people. Reward good people with frequent smaller bonuses rather than larger but rarer bonuses. Tie it more closely with achievement of specific tasks.
- **Honey catches more bees than vinegar** In the chapter on motivation, we discussed the power of positive reinforcement generally, but especially in creative fields such as software engineering. Praise and recognition need not exclude accountability and high standards. Rather, the combination of a positive 'coaching' approach with an insistence on quality work produces a magical effect.
- **Ownership and output are related** Professionals, and especially engineers, strive to be more knowledgeable than their peers, basing their esteem on who is more up-to-date and who produces more. Autonomy, pride and ownership fuel their motivation. Under these conditions, there is less need for detailed measurement and standards, as the commitment level will cause good engineers to greatly exceed expectations, producing excellent code or designing new products.
- **Building and keeping a good team** Good people like to work with other good people, especially where success depends on the quality of the team and its ability to collaborate. The work of one developer, for example, is passed to another in the team, bugs and all, creating problems for the recipient and, of course, creating the probability of personal resentment.

Case Study: Managing Technical Staff, by Nick Koumarianos

Nick Koumarianos is Managing Director of Softex, a leading information monitoring company. He is also chairman of a number of technology companies, an advisor to high-tech start-ups and very much in demand as an investor. In this section, he imparts some of his accumulated wisdom in managing and mentoring software engineers and other 'techies'.

For someone whose early brush with technology was limited to tinkering with motorcycles, the transition into the world of software and digital telephony was a giant step for me – and a steep learning curve. At this stage, I can probably now admit that I never really mastered this subject but, fortunately, I did learn to gather and keep together a group of colleagues who thrived in that rarefied atmosphere.

I comfort myself with the excuse that the area is so complex and the speed of development so dramatic that nobody really knows it all and, therefore, the ability to attract and retain a good team was actually a vital part of my role. Perhaps because my initial business experience had been in selling, I found that the ability to communicate and to persuade was helpful in managing individuals and groups. If you are out on the road selling, you quickly learn self-management and self-motivation, as you're only as good as yesterday's performance. Nobody is constantly looking over your shoulder, as a supervisor might conventionally do, and whether you sink or swim depends on you alone.

Moving to the subject of engineers and technologists, I remember someone with a sales background once saying to me, "Techies are funny ... but they rarely make you laugh."

One of the dramatic changes I experienced in the communications industry was the transition from crossbar/mechanical through electronic and on into digital technology. The training ground for the industry in those days was usually the incumbent telecom monopoly and, whilst the technical training would have been sound, the work practices left much to be desired. All change was fought strenuously. As in all monopoly situations, especially those involving a vital State-backed utility, a strike could really damage the economy. This frequently resulted in capitulation to demands and low productivity.

Despite a lifetime in the competitive sector, on one occasion I did run an effective monopoly (we liked to pretend that it was only other people who had monopolies, so we described our arrangement as "an exclusive franchise"). When I first arrived, I was a bit perturbed to find our employees describing our customers as "subscribers". It took some time to convert them to the fact that a customer is someone you serve, whereas, it seemed to me, the company attitude was that a subscriber is someone fortunate enough to be allowed to use your facility.

I imagine that in any discussion on managing professionals and smart people there will be a strong common thread, regardless of the discipline, because the basic ingredient is people and, whilst the differences between them are important, the underlying common personality factors are obvious and human.

Those factors combine the basic needs of security of tenure, motivation and stimulation in the work one does, and a reward commensurate with the role. To take these factors individually, it may be that a skilled techie is very employable, mobile and independent, but there are still a significant number who place a real value on security of tenure. At the same time he or she prefers being an individual rather than one of the herd, and to work with flexible, nimble operations.

Where the creative mind is at work, the oxygen that it feeds on is motivation and stimulation. Much of this is based on creativity and the challenge of solving issues and perfecting products and I am often reminded of the importance of regular dialogue on how we're doing and where the opportunities and issues lie. The need to talk is two-sided, but so also is the need to listen! We each have only one mouth but two ears, and it's good to use them in those proportions.

A chairman I once served under had developed a useful style of communication and this involved genuinely listening to the conversation and facilitating dialogue by cleverly making encouraging noises, but using noncommittal terms such as "Really?", "Interesting...", "Dear me... " and "Oh well...". When the informant had finally unburdened himself, the chairman would give him an encouraging pat and say, "Look, you can do it." He would then clear off without actually defining what 'it' was, but he'd heard enough to convince him that the guy knew what he was talking about and could deal with the issue. This, after all, is the executive's job, and not the chairman's. In these cases, the stimulation comes from being given the authority and carrying out the task successfully. I always found that, whether giving or receiving it, encouragement is infectious. Success should be enthusiastically welcomed, and I know how I personally like to get a pat on the back. Equally, I find that congratulating someone else on their success is rewarding.

On the other hand, I have worked alongside managers who adopted the opposite approach and where, out of anything from shyness through indifference, to fear of being asked for a pay rise, they have lacked the simple ability to shake a hand and say, "Well done!"

My wife says I am a study in "learned helplessness" when it comes to the kitchen. Applying this faux helplessness to the management of professionals and other smart people, I have found that, when seeking help on an issue where the professional clearly has the greater knowledge, a bit of flattery can go a long way. Let's be honest and say that we've found that some very bright techies are serious intellectual snobs! An introductory comment along the lines of: "Now, I know you're the world's greatest living expert on this subject, but pretend you're talking to a five-year-old kid because that's about where I am on this," gets the desired result for both parties at the meeting.

The third factor is remuneration commensurate with the role, and this is clearly not an area where one size fits all. Reward packages can be subjective and are often fraught with ego concerns and other emotional matters. They are best tied in with a review process and achievement of objectives, which gives a fair assessment of performance and a chance to communicate on different issues and not just money. Although, I have to say, in my experience, one of the most emotive issues seems to be the company car rather than the salary.

A lesson I learned from my time in the communications equipment business is that the engineers spend far more time in front of the customers than the sales guys do! In addition, the engineer is seen as trustworthy and knowledgeable. The frequency of customers' visits is not always because the equipment is troublesome, but there are constantly product changes or new instruments to be fitted. I was aware that it would benefit the company, and the engineers, if we could train and motivate them to bring back enquiries and leads from their visits with customers, as some already did. I also wanted to give a tangible financial reward, and this was cost-effective, as it was a share of the sales commission.

The scheme was a success, but we found some engineers were just not interested, despite the example of other members of their team making good money. The issues ranged from lack of confidence to inertia to a real distaste for salesmen! The upside was that, eventually, as vacancies in sales arose, we were able to fill them from the ranks of the engineers.

In conclusion, much of the management of smart people involves common sense, but the trick is to remember that common sense in the heat of the moment and apply it fairly. The best managers I have worked alongside have been able to deploy a number of management styles, which were relevant to the situation in which they found themselves. They were fair in their dealings and generous in sharing the credit. These talents enabled them to enjoy their work and succeed in their task, which was 'managing professionals and other smart people'.

Managing Professionals Where the Work and the Person are Inseparable

A feature of many professions is the degree to which the work defines the person. For example, one does not just doctor, one *is* a doctor. Similarly, one *is* a lawyer, not just a knowledge worker doing legal work. Such professionals can often base their self-worth on their expertise and, consequently, can have an unusually high need to defend their ego, becoming defensive, tetchy or arrogant as a result. If the task they are given is below their 'threshold of challenge', they may counteract this by spending months weaving webs of needless complexity into the work, if only to show off or avoid losing face with their peer group. Designers, for instance, if given free rein, will often over-embellish their work. Programmers, as another example, often have a need to demonstrably achieve, and it makes good management sense to simply remove all impediments to such achievement, particularly organisational bureaucracy.

In software engineering, because of the depth of immersion required, success hinges on the degree of commitment in terms of hours spent, effort expended and creative endeavour. As well as appropriate challenge and worthwhile purpose, people like engineers work better in a competitive but emotionally safe and physically comfortable environment, so managers should aim to make the workplace a 'cool' place to be. Google, with their playrooms, free massages, bean bags and top-class equipment, set the gold standard in such enlightened self-interest, and this investment is repaid many times over by increased productivity and innovation.

Architects

To an uncommon degree, the work of architects is characterised by its intensely personal, and often vocational, nature. This can make the leadership and management of architects particularly delicate and intricate. Architects, as a whole, also have a marked tendency to view their work as more art than commercial enterprise, and this further moves the leadership of architects into an aesthetic realm.[9] Furthermore, the volatility of market demand makes the scheduling of architectural work – smoothing the peaks and troughs in demand – difficult.

Despite (or because of) these particular challenges, the architecture profession in general has been slow to embrace a business ethos or to adopt a managerial philosophy. The liberalisation of the market (as happened recently in the UK) was expected to fundamentally change the way architectural firms went about their business. A study by the Royal Institute of British Architects suggested that architects should relinquish "certain cherished but obsolete beliefs" about the nature of their profession and how architects should be managed.[10] The study identified a need for strategic thinking as an important factor in improving the viability of architectural businesses, and indicated that specialisation (a distinctive value proposition or addressing a defined area of work) was the preferred route to commercial and professional success.

A paradox within architectural firms was identified in 1993 by Graham Winch and Eric Schneider:

"Not only is it difficult to anticipate and control workflow and cash flow, the process also involves managing creative professionals who are culturally resistant to being managed. Many architects find the idea of formal planning and adhering to a fixed strategy impractical. This is paradoxical, since architects spend their working lives developing concepts and then detailing plans for their implementation."[11]

Architectural businesses are established to accomplish purposes that cannot be accomplished by an individual alone. While it might be tempting to assume that business goals and individual architect's goals are aligned (as in classical economics and traditional management theories), architects have real needs and aspirations that cannot be readily met in purely economic terms. Architectural businesses have many goals, and profit is not always top of the list.

Strategy and its Effect on the Work in Professional Firms: Architects

The nature of strategy in professional firms can be more easily examined if we take architectural firms as an example. While architecture is showcased here, the same principles generally apply to accountancy, consulting, design and myriad other similar professional service firms. The selection of a strategy then influences the type of work engaged in (innovative work, premium service, for example, or cost-leading delivery), and this in turn affects how professionals should be managed.

Simply put, the architectural practice can be based essentially on delivery, on service or on ideas.

1. **Strong delivery firm**, characterised by a highly efficient service, often to clients seeking more of a product than a customised service.
2. **Strong service firm**, characterised by experienced handling of similar assignments and an ability to deal with changing project conditions, emphasising management processes that co-ordinate multi-discipline talents and services.
3. **Strong ideas firm**, characterised by singular expertise, innovation, or both, on projects of a unique nature – often depending on the working style of the leader.

David Maister, a leading authority on managing professional service firms, similarly urges such firms to focus on brains, experience or cost. He uses the related terms of 'finders', 'minders' and 'grinders' to delineate the different levels of work (see **Chapter 2**).

Each firm also has an underlying *raison d'être*: whether it exists primarily as a commercial business or whether it is primarily concerned with professional fulfilment (the pursuit of architecture for its own sake). It can be said, therefore, that there are two competing philosophies in professional work:

1. **Practice-centred businesses**, where the nature of the professional work is paramount: the architects seek to follow their calling.
2. **Business-centred practices**, engaged in as a means of a livelihood.

This results in six possible strategic positions for any professional firm (in this case architectural), each with different management requirements[12]; the matrix below shows the six strategic positions that can be taken by a professional firm, with the key attributes of each briefly noted:

SIX FUNDAMENTAL TYPES OF PROFESSIONAL FIRM

	Practice-centred	**Profit-centred**
Delivery	Low cost, low profit	Low cost, standardisation
Service	Reliable, market pricing	Value, adaptability
Ideas	Innovation, uniqueness	Premium, branded offer

The Choice of Profit Model

Graham Winch and Eric Schneider[13] (as referred to above) suggest that there are four basic strategic profit models for better-than-average performance in architectural practices.

The first dimension is that of **project complexity**. This measures how demanding the project is, in terms of the sophistication of specification, its size, the rapidity of the work required, or other special client requirements.

The second dimension is the **client's preference for different types of quality work**: whether the client chooses to emphasise the conception of ideas or the implementation of ideas.

These two dimensions therefore lead to **four strategic profit models**, based on quite distinctive competencies:

1. **Strong delivery** – in this strategy, successful practices deliver designs for straightforward building types at relatively low fees, but with ultimately high profitability because of their standardisation and efficiency in the design process.
2. **Strong experience** – in which practices use their depth of experience to meet clients' demanding requirements. This attracts premium fees, because their special expertise achieves unusual value for the client.
3. **Strong ideas** – a particular competence in innovation resulting in premium fees based on their record for original and valuable ideas.
4. **Strong ambition** – an approach favoured by new practices with high ambitions and few clients, charging low fees because of their lack of demonstrated expertise or reputation.

FOUR TYPES OF PROFIT MODEL

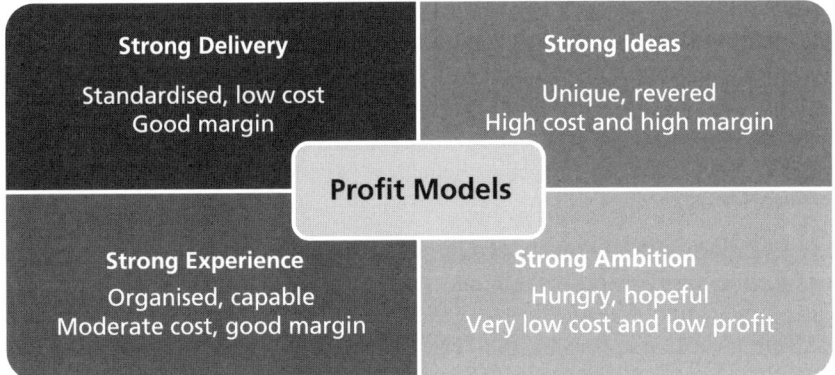

Strong Delivery	**Strong Ideas**
Standardised, low cost Good margin	Unique, revered High cost and high margin
Profit Models	
Strong Experience	**Strong Ambition**
Organised, capable Moderate cost, good margin	Hungry, hopeful Very low cost and low profit

Winch and Schneider suggest that only a few architectural practices develop the distinctive competence to sustain any one of these generic strategies; most, earning average fees, are stuck in the middle, with little to distinguish them from competitors. Those practices which can articulate a clear distinctive competence to potential clients are those most likely to survive.

Their research confirms that the management of architectural practices is not conventional or easy (which, when applied to all professions, is a key message of this book). Perhaps surprisingly to non-architects, the conventional business goal of financial success is often not paramount among the partners in an architectural practice, conflicting with the goal of aesthetic achievement. Architectural practices steer an erratic course between satisfying their creative needs, and the more pragmatic desires of the client. The ingrained ethos of the profession and the esteem of professional peers strongly influence architectural practices. Such considerations apply to most other professions, notably those at the artistic end of the spectrum (such as product designers, engineers and marketers), but also those who chose their profession as a kind of vocation (doctors, nurses, scientists, for example).

The Nature of Professional Firms: Management and the Law Firm[14]

The law is surely one of the oldest and most venerable professions. Lawyers enjoy a high standing in most communities and they play a vital role in the life of any nation. Their training and apprenticeship is long and arduous, with a particular focus on argument, logic and personal detachment. However, this professional formation and the personality traits that help them excel in their profession may, ironically, be the limiting factors in what they can achieve collaboratively, i.e. as a firm or as a team.

The following three factors, arising mainly from their professional development, tend to inhibit the ability of lawyers to think and act collaboratively:

1. professional detachment and high regard for logic and objectivity;
2. distinct preference for eliminating the need for trusting people;
3. disinclination to believe in abstract notions such as organisational culture, corporate values.

Professional Detachment

The era of the mythical, kindly family solicitor has yielded to that of a more dispassionate, driven and impersonal type of lawyer working in ever larger organisations. Lawyers have been trained to deal in logic and to leave their personal feelings at home. It is not that they actively dislike people, of course; just that they can have a tendency, reinforced by their training, to focus on objectivity and the task at hand, not necessarily on client or colleague relationships.

This tendency can become particularly serious when it limits the working of the law firm as a cohesive unit (an increasingly necessary aspect of today's complex legal work) and when it stunts the development of those invaluable 'rainmakers' – the star players – who can draw in the best clients through a combination of expertise and empathy.

These rainmakers understand that clients give business more easily to people they like, and that people respond to (seemingly) being liked. The development of such empathy, based on proven expertise, is the foundation stone in becoming a 'trusted advisor', as detailed in **Chapter 2**. Trusted advisors will have earned the right to high degrees of professional intimacy and to correspondingly more attractive work and higher fees.

This under-appreciation of the value of human relationships can also spread to internal workings, and makes the management of lawyers particularly problematic. Lawyers place high value on their independence and autonomy, and are often reluctant to trust in the judgement of others, particularly where their salaries and fees depend on it. As a result, legal firms develop complicated scorecards to make performance assessment objective.

Such systems, however, are fraught with opportunities to 'game' the system and lead to ever more complex scoring systems. In such circumstances, collegiality can be undermined and team spirit weakened. Genuine loyalty can be displaced by economic concerns, with a decline in team orientation and a rise in contentious behaviour.

Low Trust

A central theme in the formation of lawyers is the development of heightened powers of scrutiny and of foreseeing unfavourable outcomes, no matter how unlikely. Their expertise is in detecting possible legal pitfalls, protecting against opportunistic behaviour in others, and devising contracts that seek to serve their own client exclusively. In short, a good lawyer protects their client from the worst of human behaviour, and such an environment (sceptical, suspicious, adversarial) can easily be replicated in their internal dealings within their own organisations.

Certainly, in management courses of my experience, lawyers have the most difficulty not just in completing group exercises but in agreeing even the objective itself: the tendency is to indulge in point-scoring and in argument for the sake of argument. This preference for individuality acts against almost any collaborative activity: in many cases, lawyers may agree a joint plan at the cognitive level, but at the deeper level may lack real commitment to joint endeavours. Such determined autonomy does not come without a human cost: man, ultimately, is a social animal and performs better in high-trust, high-support working environments. With lawyers reluctant to be 'managed' by others, leadership tends to become autocratic (in order to overcome this reluctance) or pseudo-democratic, with committees established to regulate even minor aspects of management and a false consensus arising. Such artificial consensus can undermine decision-making, especially at the strategic level. Low levels of trust can then generate a kind of shorter term orientation; if staff believe that long-term efforts will not be rewarded, they will focus only on more immediate actions and not invest in strategic organisational development.

Lawyers compete on the basis of their intellect: they will have progressed through a series of very demanding examinations that have tested their cognitive ability, with little emphasis on inter-personal factors. In such conditions, bright legal students can develop 'smart pupil syndrome', becoming resistant to feedback and prone to despondency at any failure, real or perceived. This inhibits the ability to learn from one's experience, and can result in self-absorption and even narcissism.

Low Trust and its Consequences: the 'Tragedy of the Commons'

Trust in a work context cannot simply be declared – it must be forged through repeated successful interaction. A sense of security is needed if trust is to be earned; people must act in accordance with a common set of principles.

Hypocrisy destroys trust: declaring that "our people are our greatest asset", then treating them ruthlessly, irrevocably destroys trust. Creating an organisation based on trust (especially in firms of lawyers trained to be actively distrusting) is a task reminiscent of the labours of Sisyphus, doomed to try to push a giant boulder uphill forever. If an adequate level of trust can be achieved, the benefits are enormous: greater morale, less politicking, less conflict, less sabotage of plans. Trust, and similar values, can act as powerful organisational 'glue', but it takes courage and conviction to act in a principled manner consistently. Self-interest leads to the 'tragedy of the commons' (the depletion of shared resources by individuals acting in rational self-interest, as in overgrazing on common ground).

Some of this short-term orientation can even be ascribed to the common law tradition that is based on actual cases, not principles *per se*. Every case could yield a completely different outcome, depending on a variety of factors, not least the perspective of the deciding judge. The disavowal of principle and this 'case-by-case' mentality can impede progress and slow decisions, making progress uncertain and ponderous.

Organisation Culture, Values and Other "Abstractions"

The propensity to such doubt further reduces the pace of innovation in law firms, as new initiatives, by their very nature, are subject to many unknowable factors. Even the best ideas can be dismissed when subjected to extremes of lawyerly scrutiny or conjecture, using unimaginable scenarios or exaggerated pitfalls. Moreover, given their training in rhetoric and adversarial argument, the debate on new initiatives may resemble gladiatorial intellectual combat among legal proponents than the actual merits of the proposal. As a consequence, law firms may lack strategic differentiation, and default to working harder and longer for less and less hourly competition.

Additionally, law firms may become less than the sum of their individual parts: loose collections of great lawyers as distinct from a great collection of lawyers. They can act as loose confederations if they do not develop the intangible bonds that can glue an organisation together.

Until recently, law firms have flourished, with profits and revenues increasing, though mainly due to the competition between law firms. As clients demand more cross-functional services from lawyers, that will force firms to offer more depth and team-work.

The suggestions given below for transforming law firms are based on the kind of progressive management featured throughout this book, adapted here for the special case of law firms:

- Consciously build trust by developing a corporate culture and proactively developing it.
- Nurture a sense of shared destiny by subscribing to a shared, compelling vision.
- Develop a clear, differentiated strategy – drop the emphasis on simply working harder.
- Recruit with an increased emphasis on personal qualities and organisational 'fit'.
- Encourage collaborative behaviour and promote the value of teamwork.
- Limit the internal debate by acknowledging the role of management and by agreeing to simpler decision-making methods.
- Widen managerial perspective by studying attitudes and practices in other professional occupations.
- Drop the mistaken attitude that every man is an island. Offer training in team development and leadership, and develop a collaborative culture.
- Communicate organisational matters widely and transparently.

In short, adopt the management practices and perspectives promoted in **Chapter 15**.

Managing Surgeons: Lessons for Managers Seeking Control

In **Chapter 4** Dr James Sheehan described his approach to managing doctor peers, and outlined his key principles in managing medical and clinical staff. In this section, another eminent surgeon, Dr Michael Murphy,[15] in an interview with the principal author, points out some crucial and surprising aspects of managing surgeons, namely that they are *already* highly motivated to perform their work, that they are invariably driven to gain the respect of their peers, and that they respond best to a supportive style of leadership that does not seek to punish them.

Classically, a key role of the manager is the motivation of staff; what, though, if the staff are already motivated? Many managers seem unprepared for such a 'gift' and seem to find the need to impose themselves on staff, perhaps as a justification of their position. Consider these observations from this vastly experienced orthopaedic surgeon on what motivates surgeons:

The motivation for surgeons is by and large professional and personal respect and the esteem of their peers; effective management is largely related to managing this drive.

If a manager wants a surgeon to do something, it can best be achieved by the incentive to be the best at something, to have something to speak to his or her peers about at a conference or symposium, e.g. "We are achieving 100% at recording our joint replacements on the joint registry" or "We are compiling figures on all our hip fracture results." For a manager to succeed with a surgeon, he should offer practical and emotional support for the surgeon's own projects, provide back-up staff to record figures, and use those figures to set competition in place between the teams. People will then work harder to outdo their colleagues, and a 'virtuous' circle develops.

No surgeon is interested in the targets of administrative managers: only by blending the two objectives together can output be improved. Alternatively, if the surgeon is asked to meet a target, offer an incentive, such as an extra doctor for the unit or library back-up. Surgeons are highly motivated people, and even a little incentive will produce huge results.

On the other hand, if you want to use the proverbial stick rather than the carrot, good figures can be used to pressurise a surgeon into greater effort: publish each unit's activity, but make sure it is accurate. Some surgeons are motivated by money, and financial incentives can be used to motivate them, but most are very well paid, and money has surprisingly little motivation.

Apart from stroking the surgeon's professional ego, there has to be a realisation that surgery is a very lonely business and things can sometimes go wrong. If you feel you have support when things go wrong, you will buy into the organisation much more and give more, but if you think that at the first sign of a problem you will be hung out to dry, then the instinct will be to hide and do little work so you will have fewer complications.

Traditionally, surgeons have been categorised as aloof, arrogant and stubborn; these characteristics, of course, are precisely those needed to perform difficult, exacting and precise work under enormous pressure, both from a human life-saving view and from a commercial one.

> The best leaders of surgeons are those who can relate to the work, its pressures and the personalities involved, channelling the energy of the surgeon and the team, and by supporting but not overindulging them. Certainly, a technocratic micro-manager will alienate the surgeon and disrupt the work.

Dr Murphy's observations are entirely consistent with the approach advocated throughout this book towards the management and motivation of professionals: such management should be supportive, progressive and individualised to the professional concerned, facilitating rather than commanding.

Managing Creative Professionals: Portrait of the Artist from a Management Perspective

With the increased focus on new product introduction, marketing and web design, there has been a marked rise in the demand for creative people in the commercial world. As mentioned in earlier chapters, these are the vital 'new' professions at the forefront of innovation. While many professions have a creative element, of course, these new professionals or 'smart people' are striving daily for new ideas, and this brings its own pressures in terms of deadline fatigue, creative exhaustion and the equivalent of 'writer's block'. Among the ranks of the creative or artistic professional are product designers (featured also in **Chapter 2**), ad agency 'creatives', graphic artists, marketeers, journalists, copywriters, advertising executives, and legions of different creative people in entertainment and the gaming industry.

It is clear that this creative work differs fundamentally from the type of routine manual work of Frederick Taylor's industrial age, and consequently the management of such people must change correspondingly. This section draws on the surprisingly scant material available on managing creative people, augmented with the author's own experience of working closely over the last three years with companies involved in product design, advertising, web marketing and media. Most striking about these companies is the degree to which they work.

The creative person is perhaps the most difficult to manage by conventional means, as they shun conventional rewards, often claiming a disdain for money, and they do not value greatly the recognition of 'suits' and others outside their peer group. The artistic disposition values purity of thought, elegance of expression, creativity and unconventional approaches. Time is not of the essence for pure artistic types: quality, as they define it, is the prime quality. Concrete action is less favoured than deep reflection. Closure is the enemy of artistic endeavour. The true **artist** seems to believe that leaving matters open-ended allows 'the muse' more time to inform the work. The search for perfection drives out consideration of more commercial concerns. There are, of course, many exceptions to these rather sweeping characterisations: journalists, to mention just one example, are extremely deadline-driven, and all artistic and creative work is subject to commercial pressures and market acceptance, to an unusually high degree.

With the usual levers of management power rendered somewhat irrelevant, how then to manage those increasingly ubiquitous artistic and creative personalities? If they do not value conventional rewards and recognition, how to increase their motivation? If they do not tend to respond to management deadlines, how then to orchestrate their output?

> Take, for example, the case of Evan, a highly intelligent and active graphic designer who branched out into creating and promoting web-based reality campaigns aimed at young women with an interest in fashion and beauty. Evan succeeded in proving the concept behind these online 'pageants' and the enterprise just about covered its costs, with strong commercial support from well-known cosmetic companies. The next phase, to scale up the concept internationally, stalled, as Evan refined the concept ad infinitum, perfecting inconsequential elements. His commercial backers threatened and cajoled him on countless occasions, but still Evan procrastinated. No matter the enticement, incentive or threat, Evan still wouldn't 'let his baby grow up' and the project eventually stalled, even though it was very much in Evan's interest to bring his ideas to a wider audience.

The eventual answer in Evan's case lay in peer pressure: having a series of reviews with fixed deadlines, attended by his artistic peers in the organisation, not just the management crew. Under these circumstances, failure incurs loss of face among those they most respect – their peer network. The abstract nature of artistic or creative work makes the degree of progress hard to measure; for this reason, dividing the work into more discreet portions, if at all possible, and accordingly adding more frequent deadlines helps make progress somewhat visible and more manageable. One reason this works is that, despite their claim that the work itself is the thing, most people with an artistic temperament seek the acclaim of respected peers, and they will therefore strive to avoid such visible failure. For example, a talented designer colleague of mine would endeavour to meet certain public performance dates but otherwise would stray off into other areas, seek out lost causes, join political rallies, or simply dissipate time away: anything bar actually moving a project along. When a real and visible deadline was looming, however, his pace would inevitably speed up, and he would deliver on target.

As another example, take the case of Karl, a highly respected product design leader. Karl was so committed to achieving perfection in his work that it had become almost an obsession. At the same time as being a creative professional, Karl also wanted to be an outstanding leader of his design group and consequently he was always available to other staff. The dilemma for Karl was that he also deeply resented these intrusions into his time, to the extent that his role no longer held any joy for him. In fact, he had become so frustrated that he was constantly pondering leaving the company and retreating up the proverbial mountain for peace and isolation. The solution was rather less drastic: Karl was encouraged to partition his day so that mornings were entirely free of intrusions and administrative work. This provided Karl with the time and space he needed, and matters for both him and the company improved significantly.

A further example, from a high-tech web-marketing agency, concerned Dieter, who was so perfectionist in his approach to recruiting a new hire that it took a full year before he was sufficiently satisfied with the job specification he created to actually interview his first candidate. Needless to say, no candidate matched his exacting specification. Dieter eventually had to be assigned a non-managerial role.

To manage creative, artistic professionals, first recognise that the nature of the work means it will be episodic and unpredictable, hard to forecast, so be tolerant of creatives' idiosyncratic working methods. Allow them maximum flexibility in their work arrangements, such as flexible hours. Nurture the talent, supporting the creative person.

To counterbalance this 'soft' approach, break the tasks into smaller steps and attach a fixed review point deadline to each stage (to steps such as a first draft, an early prototype or product mock-up, etc.). Involve peers to act as an incentive (and apply peer pressure) to meet these deadlines. Some firms even use an informal 'commitment contract' to ensure deadlines are met.

As creative or artistic work is intensely personal, critique the work, but never the person behind it. Adopt a coaching approach to identify creative blockages and highlight possibilities.

Dan Ariely, in his book *The Upside of Irrationality*,[16] looks at the phenomenon of motivation and offers lessons that apply particularly well to creative people. When rewards are too high, especially monetary ones, they actually induce stress (due to loss aversion) and can be counterproductive. As Ariely says, 'social' rewards, such as accolades and other forms of recognition, work better, are less risky and cost less. Finding the purpose or meaning in the work also works well (for creative and artistic work, this can be the sheer beauty or the perfection of it).

As Gareth Jones and Rob Goffee found in their excellent book, *Clever,*[17] those at the leading edge of artistic and creative work have little respect for hierarchies and official titles. Leaders should therefore lead more by influence, and less via their position. They continue to point out the extreme negative effects should these smart professionals become frustrated, demotivated, or feel misled, as they have the capacity to cause enormous damage to an organisation. Goffee and Jones claim that leadership and integrity – a moral compass – is the key: "What determines whether an organization is a hub of clever collaboration or a toxic talent pool? We believe the answer lies with the quality of the leadership and the sense of moral purpose it engenders."

Leaders must therefore have high emotional intelligence and deft soft skills, exercising a light touch, knowing when to show humility or be tough, as the occasion demands. This ability to sense the situation and to "listen to the silences" is crucial. Leaders should "tell them what, but not how", give them space and resources, but also set clear boundaries, protect them from organisational politicking and, above all, talk straight. For some professions, where experimentation is part of the work, the wise but unconventional advice is to encourage failure – in order to maximise learning.

Goffee and Jones propose Arup, Microsoft and Google as examples of how creative work might be better performed in the future in both high-end manufacturing and service organizations in the knowledge economy. They claim that these "clever collectives" are built on "economies of clever" and their competitive advantage relies on diversity of perspective, and task autonomy combined with, paradoxically, excellent collaboration. For this reason, such Clever Collectives mix matrix management with project structures and networks of subcontractors to achieve "co-creation". This requires much "face time" and intensive personal involvement from the leaders. Goffee and Jones conclude that "The most successful organizations in the clever economy exhibit high affinity with clear discipline."

Goffee and Jones stop just short of suggesting some clever clogs need to be treated almost as if they were children, with leaders using their advanced emotional intelligence to counterbalance the sometimes poor social skills of smart people. This analogy is echoed in the earlier section, above, on transactional analysis.

An artist's portfolio defines their work, and they will respond to opportunities to extend that collection. Perhaps surprisingly, many leaders, in my experience, claim that creatives are keener to deepen their expertise in narrow fields rather than widen their portfolio. These leaders claim that artistic and creative workers are ultimately like rock stars, favouring certain milieus, and hoping to achieve fame in this way.

Conclusion

Intelligent and gifted people in all disciplines bring great ideas to life, from new electronic gadgets to medical equipment. These are high-risk achievements, requiring unusual degrees of talent and determination, and they produce huge value, economically and socially. In 2012, Apple made more profits (US $18 billion) than Microsoft, eBay, Google, Yahoo!, Facebook and Amazon combined, and made life a lot of fun for people across the globe with their innovative and sophisticated devices. While many bright people had to collaborate to achieve these extraordinary results, the essential drive and vision came from Steve Jobs, a man often described as impossibly demanding and arrogant.

This chapter has not suggested that such characters be indulged (which is tantamount to 'giving up' on them from a management perspective), nor that a manager should abandon such characters (which is also 'giving up' on them), but to see instead the human trapped inside and release that potential while containing the psychological excess. To do this, one needs to forsake conventional 'management' and practice 'leadership' instead. Create the conditions for success by providing the right working and social environment. Do not stint on positive reinforcement, and use your wisdom in place of corporate policy to shape the right outcomes. The paradox is that only by providing sufficient *challenge* will the best people deliver results, for you as an organisation and for themselves as individuals.

ENDNOTES

[1] Thomas H. Davenport, *Thinking for a Living: How to Get Better Performances and Results from Knowledge Workers* (Harvard Business Press, 2005).

[2] Peter Drucker, *Management Challenges for the 21st Century* (HarperBusiness, 1999).

[3] Thomas H. Davenport, *Thinking for a Living: How to Get Better Performances and Results from Knowledge Workers* (Harvard Business Press, 2005).

[4] *Ibid.*

[5] Philip Greenspun, *Managing Software Engineers* (ArsDigita, 2002).

[6] Joel Siegel, ABC News Report (ABC Corp. Oct 2011).

[7] Fred Brooks, *The Mythical Man-Month: Essays on Software Engineering* (Addison Wesley, 1975).

[8] Aubrey C. Daniels, *Bringing out the Best in People* (McGraw-Hill, 1999).

[9] Royal Institute of British Architects, *The RIBA Business Benchmarking Survey* (RIBA, 2011).

[10] *Ibid.*

[11] Graham Winch and Eric Schneider, "Managing the Knowledge-Based Organization: The Case of Architectural Practice" (1993) Vol. 36 No. 6 *Journal of Management Studies* 923–937.

[12] *Ibid.*

[13] *Ibid.*

[14] See David H. Maister, *Managing the Professional Service Firm* (Harvard Business School Press, 1993).

15 Dr Murphy is a well-respected surgeon, of Irish origin, operating in Manchester for the past two decades, with indepth experience of both public and private health sectors.

16 Dan Ariely, *The Upside of Irrationality: The Unexpected Benefits of Defying Logic* (HarperCollins, 2010).

17 Rob Goffee and Gareth Jones, *Clever: Leading Your Smartest, Most Creative People* (Harvard Business Press, 2009).

Chapter 11

Developing Self-confidence in Professionals: The Power of Self-Talk, Crucial Conversations and Appreciative Enquiry

Irrationally held beliefs may be more harmful than reasoned errors.

T.H. Huxley

Introduction

This book was written to help professionals and other smart people deliver on their full potential by expanding their capabilities to manage themselves and others. Building confidence is crucial to success, and yet the topic has received little research (with the exception of Professor Philip Zimbardo in the US[1]) and is not treated in any depth in management literature. Without self-confidence, there is no foundation for the professional to really flourish: he or she will retain feelings of inadequacy (and may even feel like an imposter) indefinitely, leading to profound disappointment and sadness, often with severe consequences. Strange indeed would be a life without setbacks or disappointment, yet perversely this subject remains somewhat taboo. This chapter, however, draws together different disciplines, such as positive thinking, transactional analysis ('the games people play'), and appreciative enquiry, to allow professionals understand the underlying causes of low self-confidence and consequently how to develop means of developing true self-confidence. Practical advice is given on how to generate authentic self-esteem by accepting and learning from life's inevitable setbacks and disappointments. The chapter specifically indicates how to develop a positive mindset, how to learn to be more optimistic and how to acquire a 'growth' mindset. It also explains how to use the power of constructive conversation and 'appreciative enquiry' to increase self-confidence.

The initial impetus to develop this subject of self-confidence in otherwise capable professionals arose from a fruitless sales trip made by three very smart patent lawyers of my acquaintance. They had attended a major conference abroad, yet came back without generating any significant business prospects. Although each lawyer was extremely high in IQ, they suffered so badly from a lack of self-confidence that none of them spoke to a single delegate at the conference! Lacking the confidence to initiate conversations, they languished mutely for three whole days, before returning shamefacedly without even one new business prospect. Examples of similar self-confidence failings among other intelligent professionals of my acquaintance abound:

- otherwise capable accountants failing to engage with key investors because they lacked the self-confidence to promote their ideas with enough confidence;
- engineers retreating when confronted with the people they disdain, such as marketing executives and almost all similar 'suits', and so failing to generate value from their innovations;
- brilliant surgeons alienating patients and staff with their arrogance and distorted self-confidence; and
- architects lacking the self-confidence to ask for their true worth in fees from clients.

Why did so many smart people like these behave so meekly? Was it a genetic condition, the flipside of being smart? Or was it a product of their training and formation? Was it nature and nurture, or both? More importantly, what might help improve their self-confidence?

In other chapters, we have explored the shadow side of different personality types, such as the introvert's aversion to conversational 'small talk' or the extrovert's tendency to talk before thinking. In this chapter, some of these similar-sounding issues are explored through the lens of self-confidence. After all, if a professional is truly grounded and well-formed as a person, this will be manifest in true confidence: proper regard for oneself and for others. This chapter shows how self-confidence can be developed, starting with an understanding of the origins of low self-esteem and then moving on to interpersonal behaviour.

The foundation of this chapter is the work of Stanford psychologist Philip Zimbardo, with practical applications and special insights from Micheline Egan, an educator from an organisation that deals with teenage depression and who personally specialises in the area of building genuine confidence.

Without confidence, a professional's full potential will not be realised, especially if that professional has to engage with clients, patients, boards of directors, banks or the myriad stakeholders who form important opinions about the message and especially the messenger.

The benefits of true self-confidence include better decision-making, better engagement and enhanced communication in many spheres, from selling one's professional services to imparting financial advice, from caring for patients' well-being to closing business deals.

Enhanced confidence and personal happiness, as we shall see, are closely linked, with wonderful benefits for smart professionals and those who manage them. Developing self-confidence increases inner strength, helping people to become more positive and optimistic, and producing better results. By overcoming limiting beliefs and becoming more self-accepting, a person's attitude improves and anxiety is reduced.

As Micheline Egan expresses it:

"Most of us don't allow our confidence to surface. We think we are impostors, undeserving of our good fortune. Or we allow our inner critic to hold us back. Or, worse still, we listen to the voices of others – real or imagined – that tell us to be quiet and meek because we are not good enough, not worthy of success. Rubbish! Confidence in your abilities is both necessary and accessible. It can be learned, nurtured and enhanced."[2]

Confidence Matters

Confidence is a valuable but elusive quality. Although it is hard to define, and harder still to quantify, we nonetheless believe we can readily detect confidence, or the lack of it, in ourselves and others. Yet, confidence can be manufactured ('faked'), at least in certain situations or for a limited time. Indeed, learning to 'fake' confidence for a while helps break the vicious circle of self-doubt, On the other hand, lack of confidence is not necessarily visible to others, and stilling one's own pounding heart is a good and necessary first step. Confidence really only becomes an issue in the presence of others: making a speech to an empty room is not a challenge. Speaking only to the bedroom mirror involves little tension, but addressing Carnegie Hall can be terrifying, as the risk of reputational damage to one's self-esteem is so great!

Self-confidence depends on the perception both of the individual himself and the 'audience'. False confidence ('bravado') arises when the audience perceives a confidence that the individual does not actually deserve, based on their perceived ability.

Self-confidence is a Natural State

We are not born without confidence. Witness the way babies gaze frankly at people. However, as people grow, and a baby realises it is a being separate from its mother or, invariably, in the early teen years (when identity becomes more important and when the urge for self-direction emerges), confidence can shatter. Shyness then becomes a real issue, and can take time to disappear, if at all. 'Maturity' is the name given to the stage where self-doubt becomes manageable, freeing the 'adult' to act responsibly.

Self-confidence and Shyness

For many people, shyness (one aspect of a lack of self-confidence) remains a significant inhibitor throughout their entire lives. A Stanford University investigation estimates that more than 60% of American people suffer from significant shyness – a figure that might well be exceeded in other cultures.[3] Those most affected, Stanford suggests, are people **whose self-esteem is primarily based on achievement** (rather than a belief that they, in themselves, are worthy).

> While **shyness** resembles introversion, it is fundamentally different. An introvert simply prefers solitary thinking, whereas a shy person avoids congregating out of fear and anxiety.

Even seemingly innocuous teasing of people can trigger long-lasting confidence deficits, especially when delivered by authority figures, such as teachers or parents. The pain of mockery lingers long in the subconscious. Insults can leave permanent psychological scars. This is evident in the many tragic cases of cyber-bullying among teens and indeed the recent prank that resulted in the unfortunate suicide of the Duchess of Cambridge's nurse.

Enhancing self-confidence, then, involves the re-establishment of self-regard, this starts with an appreciation of one's own unique value, and a re-examination of one's limiting beliefs (the unending harmful doubts that trap us in a psychic prison and undermine confidence by inhibiting desired action). There is an aphorism attributed to Henry Ford that captures such self-imposed limitations: "whether you believe you can or believe you can't – you will be right!"

Nelson Mandela, in his 1994 inauguration speech, exhorted the people of South Africa to proceed with confidence in their combined abilities declaring that:

> "Our deepest fear is not that we are inadequate. Our deepest fear is that we are powerful beyond measure. It is our light, not our darkness that most frightens us."

We tend to ask ourselves: who am I to be brilliant, gorgeous, talented, fabulous? Actually, who are you *not* to be?

Self-confidence and Charisma

Charisma can be seen as a self-confidence that transmits itself to an audience. When Bill Clinton, in his prime, addressed even a large audience, many individuals present felt that he was speaking to them personally, even to the extent of making direct eye contact.

In this way, confidence can be seen as the ultimate, cost-free 'win–win', where all involved can benefit and feel uplifted. This charisma, and the related ability to charm, can also be misused, of course, as it was by Hitler in generating his political campaigns.

Self-confidence and Arrogance

While lack of self-confidence is usually passive (one is mainly harming oneself), the opposite side of the confidence coin (such as arrogance) provokes strong personal reactions. Arrogance is based on false pride, and is invariably resisted by those whom it offends; particular contempt (even loathing) is reserved for those deemed 'arrogant'. Conceit, on the other hand, is also a display of pride, but the pride is based on more genuine achievement or some other superiority. Conceit, similarly, can irritate others, but usually to a lesser extent than arrogance.

Arrogance affects others in a fundamental way, by challenging their self-image. The display of arrogance or haughtiness, or an overblown sense of one's worth, can be a very strong irritation as it forces 'odious comparisons' of the respective individual's worth.

Self-confidence and Narcissism

Where the pride is not so overbearing, but still unwarranted, a type of braggart confidence, this, according to emotional intelligence expert Daniel Goleman, is "a narcissistic over-inflation of capabilities".[4] Self-consciousness has similarities to narcissism but is less self-absorbed and, crucially, it involves the *opposite* of self-love.

> *"Shyness has a strange element of narcissism, a belief that how we look, how we perform, is truly important to other people."*
>
> André Dubus

Self-confidence and *Visible* Failure

Lack of self-confidence often stems from a heightened need for achievement. The presence of an audience (of any size – even a single person) raises the stakes, as any failure will be public. When that audience comprises, for example, work colleagues, the need for affiliation is also threatened, exacerbating the situation; loss of face will be accompanied by loss of social standing and the loss of the respect of colleagues. In that sense, lack of self-confidence is rational and understandable: competence in a particular area is indeed required (otherwise it is akin to 'putting lipstick on a pig', as President Obama said when running against Republican candidate Sarah Palin, suggesting that her candidature didn't represent real change, just a cosmetic one). This means that the performance gap between the desired and actual level of performance must be closed. Much of this gap depends on perception: the perfectionist will suffer in this regard, as he or she strives for unusually (even unnecessarily) high standards. In addition, some people will see this performance gap as an unbridgeable chasm, whereas more balanced types might see the gap as a manageable step-up in performance.

Enhancing self-confidence then depends both on altering perception (how the person sees themselves and how they estimate the size of the performance gap) and also on closing **the gap between what a person can truly deliver and what they actually deliver**. It is this underperformance gap that true confidence can close.

MANAGING FAILURE AND DISAPPOINTMENT

Strange indeed would be the life without failure or disappointment, yet there is precious little written about how to manage either. According to leading authority Denis Waitley, in 1990 there were only 16 books in the US Library of Congress explicitly dealing with losing or failure.[5] The subject appears untouchable.

To deal with disappointment, consider these steps:

- Talk about your disappointment with someone competent whom you can trust.
- Don't bottle up your anger: express yourself in writing – spill it out on paper.
- Talk to others about how they dealt with failure – it can be inspiring.
- Read about gifted leaders who suffered setbacks, and learn from them.

Ironically, it is confidence that brings about accomplishment, not the other way around; confidence lifts the platform of performance and allows energy to be directed to the task at hand, not wastefully diverted to one's inner self.

Until recently, I had believed that competence (task performance) would lead to enhanced self-confidence, but I have seen so many high achievers continue to lack confidence that I have come to realise that accomplishment alone does not in itself lead to self-confidence. Accomplishment is necessary for self-confidence, but it is not sufficient: the starting point has to include the simultaneous and deliberate building of confidence. Even seemingly confident achievers, such as senior professionals, frequently suffer from 'imposter syndrome', whereby they feel that they are counterfeit leaders, unworthy of the office.

To a large extent, confidence-building should come first: achievement alone will not inevitably lead to self-confidence, although it helps materially. Improving self-confidence is therefore in some ways a dilemma, and in some ways a vicious circle: reversing this vicious circle is the key to improving confidence. Curiously a little trickery is required to do this: the psyche must be fooled into acting confidently by wearing a **mask** of confidence. This counterfeit confidence spawns achievement (which the sufferer desperately craves, as explained above), leading in turn to more confidence, and then greater achievement: in other words, turning the vicious circle into a virtuous one.

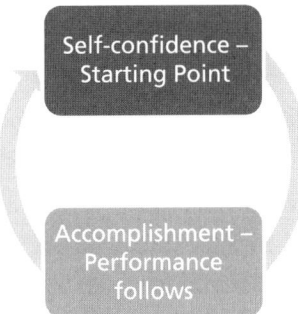

To generate this counterfeit confidence 'kick-start' (and to make the mask believable), the performance gap must be treated like a physical performance gap. In other words, specific steps need to be taken in discreet, identifiable skill areas. This is the 'fitness' approach (based on the principles of improving physical fitness), which seeks to break the vicious circle of low confidence by training the mind into new ways of thinking and of developing better mental habits.

Some tips to improve performance and self-confidence:

- Decide what your true goals are: define success for yourself.
- Note the many, many things for which to be thankful.
- Dwell on your strengths, not your frailties.
- Start to like yourself: give yourself unconditional acceptance.
- Give and receive compliments gracefully.
- Acknowledge your mistakes and move on.
- Take care of your physical appearance. You don't have to be the best looking, just look your best.
- Improve your posture. Stay erect yet relaxed. Walk purposefully. Smile with your eyes.
- Enjoy life's ironies and any humorous aspects.

Developing Self-confidence: The 'Fitness' Approach

The 'fitness' approach treats improving psychological (mental and social) capabilities in the same way as physical training does for the body. Rather than viewing under-confidence as a mushy psychological concept, capability can be systematically improved in this way, by breaking down the elements into discrete steps and practicing those steps until competence is achieved. While it might not work in all cases, this 'mind gym' approach helps one get fitter, mentally. As in a regular gym, fitness is achieved through practice and repetition of discrete activities (such as presenting in public, maintaining a balanced view or dealing with difficult people), making them become automatic and unconscious. (Think of the *Karate Kid*, whose martial arts skills, such as lightning-quick karate chops, are learned by endlessly hand-waxing cars with a circular hand motion – 'wax on, wax off').

Because shyness is so pervasive, this kind of social anxiety may be underestimated, in my opinion. A shy person may similarly use the 'fitness' approach to change behaviour, thinking patterns and attitudes, and to become more skilled at 'emotion regulation' to overcome such shyness. With effort and practice, most people can attain a psychological and social fitness in the same way that most people can attain an improved level of physical fitness.

Research shows that a self-confidence deficit has core components of self-blame, private self-consciousness, shame and resentment.[6] These mental habits operate automatically and often unconsciously. However, through **'mindful awareness'**, it is possible to regulate our attention and emotions. By beginning to notice the mental patterns that cause feelings of anxiety, sufferers can realise the origins of their loss of confidence and begin to work through their anxiety and its causes.

Five Steps to Confidence – the Mental Fitness Performance Cycle: ABCDE

- **Attribution (forget whose fault it is): take the positives, keep perspective**
  Don't wallow in blame, and don't crucify yourself: learn from mistakes, and move on.
- **Behaviour (how well do I act?): enhancing performance**
  Recognise that behaviour can be changed, especially when one becomes aware of one's habitual mental patterns and world-view ('paradigms').
- **Cognition (how well do I think?): the source of thought and subsequent action**
  Identify and change automatic thinking patterns that reduce confidence.
- **Displaying confidence (how do I project a positive attitude?):**
  Project confidence through posture, facial expression, tone and demeanour.
- **Emotion control (what do I feel?): calm your physiological response**
  Emotions evoke a physiological response, such as sweating. Still that inner voice. Know when you are within, or at least close to, your zone of capability.

'Wear the Mask'

Renowned psychologist Philip Zimbardo of Stanford University tells the story of how his little brother, George, was so shy at school that he wore a mask for the first year, only relinquishing it when a clever teacher substituted a different outfit – a costume for the school play.[7] The mask allowed George to avoid identification and provided a safe haven for his young mind; with a mask, he could not 'lose face'.

For professionals, the message is to start to reverse the cycle of under-confidence by wearing the mask or cloak of self-assurance. Dress the part. Know your stuff. Be courteous. Do the simple stuff well. Maintain a tidy appearance. Confidence, says confidence expert Ros Taylor, fundamentally depends on a basic level of accomplishment, "knowing the words to the song" – reaching at least a minimum level of performance in one's particular field, so that confidence is well founded.[8]

Fake it till You Make It: The Pygmalion Effect

The deception involved is not that of other people, but of fooling oneself: using self-deception to silence your doubting inner voice by acting confidently, even if you are not feeling confident. Instead of thinking your way into a new way of acting, this is **'acting' your way into a new way of thinking**. This exploits the inherent connection between mind and body. For example, it is hard to act happy when one is slumped in a downcast position. It is hard to be despondent when one is dancing energetically. Confidence is a kind of 'self-joy' and according to mind guru Tony Buzan, acting joyfully is a rehearsal for real joy.[9]

The 'Pygmalion Effect' causes people to respond to the belief others have in them by increasing their own performance and their own self-belief. It is named after George Bernard Shaw's play, *Pygmalion*, popularised in the film *My Fair Lady*, in which Rex Harrison demonstrated this mirror effect by turning Audrey Hepburn from a flower-seller into a 'duchess'.

The Pygmalion Effect has been demonstrated extensively. For example, teachers who have been told by school authorities, in an extensive US survey, that particular students will be higher performers raise their expectations of these children. The extra belief raises student performance, thereby encouraging the teacher still more; a virtuous circle is created.

Lose the Guilt

The under-confident are 'sure' they are about to fail or be found out in some way; in fact, because many successful professionals acquired their technical expertise with (relative) ease, they often feel like 'imposters', undeserving of their position, bound to be uncovered and shamed. Among CEOs this is so common it has a name: the 'imposter syndrome'. This can undermine their self-confidence, making an already difficult job even more difficult.

Escape the Psychic Prison

Lack of self-confidence may often lie deeply rooted in events long since passed (such as childhood teasing) or parental attitudes (where a child receives attention only for achievement, not for effort). Ironically, the 'mental prison' that results is almost entirely of one's own making and, therefore, can also be de-constructed by oneself. As Nathaniel Hawthorne proclaimed:

> "What other dungeon is so dark as one's heart! What jailer so inexorable as one's self!"

The psychic cell might be taken apart brick by brick (using the fitness approach, gradually gaining little wins), and sometimes a magical 'key' can be found to unlock the psychic door. Often, the key is simply the realisation that change is really possible and that it depends only on oneself.

"A successful man is one who can lay a firm foundation with the bricks that others throw at him."

David Brinkley

Acquire a Growth Mindset

Sometimes, in the best Hollywood tradition, in movies like *The Hudsucker Proxy*, a mentor appears who shows the escape route – and helps the psychic prisoner on his or her way. This mentor can be a friend, colleague, spouse, professional coach, but, in the right context, it can also be a boss or manager. The tragedy is that the under-confident, seeking to hide their 'shame', will not usually ask for this help. A good manager, however, will recognise the condition and point the way forward, quietly supporting, gently affirming, subtly praising and restoring self-belief. It invariably helps the professional to develop a positive 'growth' mindset so that they have an escape route from self-doubt. The opposite approach – undermining, demeaning or intimidating – is a deadly weapon for the psychic sniper or mental bully, and it is a counterproductive approach for a manager.

"There was a very cautious man who never laughed or cried.
He never risked, he never lost, he never won or tried.
And when one day he passed away
His insurance was denied. For since he never really lived,
they claimed he never died"!

Anon

Light at the End of the Tunnel: Positive Thinking

Those afflicted with self-doubt fear that the light at the end of the tunnel is really an oncoming train. Cynics claim that when light can be seen at the end of the tunnel, someone will make more tunnel!

"Our doubts are traitors,
And make us lose the good we oft might win,
By fearing to attempt."

William Shakespeare, *Measure for Measure*

In truth, to escape the psychic prison, the attraction of a valued goal is needed. An objective worthy of the effort needs to be identified. For self-doubters, this could be seeing themselves receiving a professional accolade or a promotion. Such goals provide an outward perspective, focusing on the end result, distracting the mind from its cycle of self-doubt and negativity.

Positive Thinking

Self-doubters believe that the glass is half empty; it is, in fact, also half full. Seen objectively, professionals have large amounts of prestige, power and resources relative to the general population. Not only is their glass half full, but it is a very large glass indeed. Rather than providing satisfaction, however, self-doubting professionals suffer loss aversion; they fear that their hard-earned, half-full glass will get spilled – and probably be spilled by them.

The arrogant hide their fear by denying its possibility, while the under-confident obsess about the possibility of spillage.

Such professionals need to be encouraged to see the logic that their success is well-founded, and they have valuable and enduring qualities – qualities that will help them prevail even if the glass should tumble.

Positive Psychology – Hoax or Hope?

Irrational exuberance, myopia and false optimism can have unwelcome consequences, but what if one's attitude to life did actually presage success or failure? Mindset is defined by the *Oxford English Dictionary* as "an established set of attitudes held by someone". The very word 'mindset' implies that attitudes are pre-set and unalterable, but Stanford Professor Carol Dweck produces convincing evidence that a 'positive' mindset (where failure is used as an opportunity for learning and advancement) is a strong enabler of performance and that one's mental attributes need not be fixed, in fact can be developed.[10]

Lose the Fixed Mindset

While Napoleon Hill (*Think and Grow Rich*[11]) and Norman Vincent Peale (*The Power of Positive Thinking*[12]) have stressed the importance of positive thinking, Carol Dweck's research shows how people can develop fixed mindsets, and the damage this can cause. Dweck describes a '**fixed mindset**' as one in which an individual views their intelligence as pre-determined, a given talent or quality. This can easily be induced when intelligent children are praised for their smartness, rather than for the actual effort they have made. A major consequence is that a person of 'fixed mindset' goes through life avoiding challenge as a means of avoiding failure; failure would mean that the 'innate' quality was not, in fact, present. This loss, to some people of fixed mindset, would be unbearable.

Grow your Mindset

On the other hand, a '**growth mindset**' regards intelligence as being capable of development. It views intelligence as being more fluid, capable of enhancement, simply a work-in-progress, with a real prospect of better performance in the future. This is a much more positive and productive view, avoiding the constant fear of failure, of being discovered as an 'imposter' who was not so smart, after all.

> Socrates argued that knowledge is the sole good, and ignorance the single evil. He also believed individuals should cultivate strong personal character and values.

Self-fulfilling Prophecy

Whether a positive 'growth' mindset can fundamentally change intelligence is still debated; the interesting conclusion is that adopting such a set of attitudes increases the propensity to persevere, despite setbacks, and to experiment more.

Interestingly, though IQ is now used as a quantification of cognitive intelligence, it was introduced as a concept into Parisian schools a century ago precisely because it was believed that intellectual performance could be improved through better teaching methods and a more encouraging school environment. Even a century ago, there was a belief that intelligence was not fixed but could be improved.

> *"If we all did the things we are capable of doing, we would literally astound ourselves."*
>
> Thomas Edison

Praise the Effort Given, not the Given Intelligence

In praising talent ("Gosh, you're smart!"), the person's identity can become synonymous with smartness. They can come to see themselves as being valued only for their intelligence. Carol Dweck advises that it is the work itself that should be praised, not the so-called underlying talent. Praising genuine effort (not tepid attempts or careless failure) can significantly improve the outcome: this is in stark contrast to the 'results only' attitude of those managers who insist, "Bring me solutions, not problems".

Praising effort, rather than innate ability, also protects the recipient from a loss of identity should they under-perform at some future point, as it separates the performance from the person's core identity; this is especially important for smart professionals if their self-regard is based on others' perception of them being inordinately clever.

> *"Confidence comes not from always being right but from not fearing to be wrong."*
> Peter McIntyre

While the approach of praising effort, not talent, is originally centred on young people, it can also be extended to older people. In any case, praising effort, not talent, seems a sound proposition. No one ever failed by striving for constant learning. History is littered with failures who relied on their 'given' talent. Those familiar with Alex Ferguson will know that he is a hugely successful football manager who constantly praises effort, not just talent.

Nurturing Optimism in Professionals

It should also be noted that optimists, because of their more positive dispositions, are not only happier but are even generally more successful. This is not because they are more often correct (in fact, the opposite is true) but because of their *resilience*, their willingness to accept challenge and the greater number of attempts they are inclined to make. Of course, when optimism becomes delusional, rational limits will be exceeded, with potentially disastrous consequences.

Learning Optimism

Martin Seligman, recent President of the American Psychological Society, has been credited with turning psychology from a remedial focus (fixing problems after they arise) to one that emphasises wellness, not illness, and obviating issues before they develop. A seminal moment was the undeniable evidence of a lengthy study by Seligman, which concluded that not only were optimists happier and more productive but that they also lived longer.[13] It is one thing to suspect that the positivity of optimism might be productive and satisfying, but quite another to have it confirmed.

For me, and many others, this landmark result was the spur to consciously learn to be more optimistic, to consciously see the half-full portion of the glass, to have more faith in one's ability and, indeed, more faith in one's colleagues and friends.

This is not a denial of rational thinking nor of prudence, but a conscious attempt to change the nagging voice of self-doubt, to fortify self-belief and be more resilient. Nor is it mindless optimism, but a considered decision to choose the 'high road' of positive thinking rather than descend the 'low road' of needless negativity. Of course, there are many situations where nagging doubts can be a harbinger of danger, but to live with such constant anxiety is debilitating.

> *"Life shrinks or expands in proportion to one's courage."*
>
> Anaïs Nin

Changing Minds

The question that must then be answered is whether one can change one's default pattern of thinking. Martin Seligman points out that habits of thinking need not be permanent: "One of the most significant findings in psychology in the last 20 years is that individuals can choose the way they think."[14] He proposes three aspects of thinking style:

- persistence;
- pervasiveness; and
- personalisation.

In other words:

- how constant;
- how widespread; and
- how self-focused is one's thinking?

Seligman notes that when good things happen to optimists, they build on this emotional boost, believing more good things can happen. Pessimists, on the other hand, attribute their success to mere chance, believing their good luck will be punished sooner or later. This is somewhat akin to the classic Irish response to good weather: "Aye, 'tis fine now – but we'll pay for it later …". Pessimists believe that any success they might enjoy is due to a confluence of external circumstances and, therefore, is likely to be snatched away with the slightest shift in those circumstances.

Cultural conditioning might exacerbate the tendency of pessimists to discount their contribution to success – not giving themselves credit, and certainly not allowing others to give them credit, especially in team situations. Their prevailing mindset is that 'the nail that stands up will be hammered down'.

Conversation and Outlook

One's conversational pattern, and especially one's style of humour, can give an indication of one's degree of optimism or pessimism. Cynical, sardonic or self-deprecating humour may occasionally be socially useful and impressive (similar to the way in which the murkiness of Tolstoy is considered to be deep and meaningful), but as a default pattern, it creates a very negative mindset, as it weakens faith in more positive outcomes. Better to think positively and to believe instead that 'I'm OK, you're OK', and treat setbacks only as speed-bumps on the road to success.[15] Better still, learn to laugh at adversity.

A little self-love talk might help (but do make self-praise a silent courtship!). Knowing that you have a destination ('vision') in mind can help, and don't deny yourself the therapeutic power of a good laugh. As we talk to ourselves all the time, that inner dialogue fundamentally affects our mental well-being: having a positive mindset gives us a better outlook, and having clear goals helps channel our thoughts in a specific direction.

Extroversion and Introversion (Common or Garden Variety)

For the purposes of this discussion, extroversion has the common meaning of being outward-focused: gregarious, animated, assertive. H.J. Eysenck defines it as the "act, state or habit of being predominantly concerned with, and obtaining gratification from, that which is outside the self".[16] This is distinct from the Myers–Briggs view, which holds that extroversion refers to the source of ideas: extroverts generate ideas from the outside domain, whereas introverts locate them internally.

Broadly speaking, life's natural teachers, salespeople and politicians are extroverted, while engineers, accountants, artists, composers and architects tend to be introverts.

Whereas optimism can be learned, extroversion is inherent, according to authoritative studies by H.J. Eysenck.[17] While an extrovert cannot become an introvert, he can still adopt some of the introvert's skills, such as reflection and analysis. The introvert, too, can wear the mask of an extrovert, using a social mask to present ideas more immediately, initiating conversation, connecting with others – at least for limited periods.

Sadly for introverts, their lack of noisiness seems to restrict promotional prospects (in terms of management positions). However, introversion serves well the majority of rationality-based professions, such as accounting and engineering. While extroverts dominate middle-management positions (some studies claim three-quarters of such positions are held by extroverts, even though extroverts are only a relatively small majority in Western society as a whole), the highest echelons, paradoxically, are best peopled with introverts: the extroverts below then tend to compete against each other for the attention of the introvert above, heightening effort and performance. In addition, the more introverted manager tends to have lower ego needs and will consequently be more emotionally stable. For firms of professionals, this can be a tricky conundrum; the firm will want to have enough professionals who are sufficiently extroverted to engage clients, but will want to have management leaders with enough introversion, and lack of ego, so that the business is run sensibly.

> *"Argue for your limitations and, sure enough, they're yours."*
> Richard Bach, *Illusions*

Don't Have a Care

A notorious wag once advised me never to tell anyone my troubles: "80% don't care," he said, "and the other 20% – well, they're quite glad!" Self-doubters and the self-conscious should take note: realise that very few people are paying any attention at all, and act accordingly. At the same time, there are generally more people wishing one well than ill; as in the theatre, the audience wants the actors to perform well, not to fluff their lines. The doubting professional will surely have more friends than enemies, more well-wishers than detractors, and this realisation can provide reassurance.

The Power of Reciprocity: Give Confidence to get Confidence

As Shakespeare wrote, the quality of mercy "is twice blest": it blesses the giver as well as the receiver. So, too, for confidence; helping others become confident helps one become confident also. Helping others in this way shifts the focus away from oneself, and sharpens the lesson. Praise a colleague's effort, send a note of thanks, share a moment of reflection, circulate a helpful book or coach someone lacking in self-confidence, and reap a rich harvest.

Managing the Under-confident Professional

Professionals, with their well-developed intelligence and elevated social status, need a particular form of management, one that is aware of the dynamics at play. In **Chapter 5** we discussed how one style does not, in fact, fit all professionals as they progress through various levels of organisational maturity, from novice to mature contributor.

Games People Play: **Eric Berne and Conversational Transactions**

Analogous to the above progression (from novice to master), and as described in Eric Berne's now classic book, *Games People Play*,[18] is the concept of Parent (boss) and Child (employee), and how both can benefit from a transition to emotionally mature (Adult) roles. In this section, the focus is on the interplay between both parties, which invariably is through dialogue and 'crucial' conversations. The conversations are 'crucial' because they are at the heart of the relationships between people and reveal the various roles being adopted, consciously or otherwise. They are also crucial because such conversations are at the interface between people and therefore can form a kind of battle line: these conversations are essentially 'transactions' between people, and can contain a lot of 'games' whereby people seek to gain advantage or to simply protect their own ego-state.

In the 1993 film *Groundhog Day*, Phil, the character played by Bill Murray, gets stuck in a perpetual loop, each day playing out the same way, until he finally learns not be a self-serving, cynical 'jerk'. It takes many "groundhog days" for Phil to change the inner dialogue tapes playing in his head. Like the character in the film, we all have a tape playing the same message over and over in our heads. This tape insists on playing, even when we want it to stop. It can cause us to engage in repetitive patterns of dialogue and behaviour, even to our own detriment. When we are worried, the tape seems particularly insistent and gets stuck on the same message, just like Phil in *Groundhog Day*.

Worse, it is often not even a tape of our own making, but was produced by the parents or teachers who shaped our formative years. Parents, even when acting in the best interests of their offspring, leave an indelible hallmark on their children, imprinting an enduring view of life and the world that persists at least until the rebellion of adolescence, and often indefinitely. This imprint is a set of standards, telling us what we 'should do', whether it is to be solemn, neat, gregarious, diligent or fun-loving.

Without any awareness, we accept that this parent–child relationship is fundamental (and indeed it is). Our first relationships are in this parent–child (authority–dependant) structure: this is so obvious that it is taken for granted.

At the age of the 'terrible twos', infants come to realise they are not part of their parents, but are separate human beings – with all the terrors that this realisation brings. The teenage years usually bring another rebellion, as the teenager consciously seeks his or her own individual identity, different (often radically) from that of their parents. Where the teenager rebels, the parental imprint is still there, but is rejected by the teenager. Usually, adulthood is eventually achieved, where rational behaviour finally appears. The cycle begins again when the former child becomes a parent, replicating (or reacting against) the template laid down by their own parents.

The parent–child relationship is often mirrored again in the workplace; a traditional authoritarian management style infers that the boss is like the providing parent, and the employee (the subordinate) is the dependent child. Bosses can be dictatorial (like a controlling parent) or benign (like a nurturing parent), but, ultimately, the relationship is still hierarchical. This is the prevalent model at home or work, and one which permeates assumptions about the interaction of people.

There is a third role, however, that is neither a 'child' nor a 'parent': that of the independent 'adult'. 'Adult', in this sense, means a person with a mature, rational, respectful, problem-solving orientation, operating without bias, and psychologically stable. The ideal, at work, is for all parties to act in the adult "ego-state"; however, we can enter a series of transactions in which we are unconscious of the ego-states people are in and with the same 'tape' playing in our heads, over and over.

For example, imagine you are a marketing manager, and you must approach the finance director (FD) about budgeting for a public relations campaign. You believe this is an important investment; the FD may believe it is a frivolous expenditure. Worse, every time you approach the FD, you end up feeling like a child, and leave despondent, even angry. You promise yourself that that won't happen again – but it does. This is your own personal groundhog day.

Both of you are playing your own 'tapes', operating from a certain mindset. The FD, of course, 'controls' the budget and is a serious, qualified professional, suitably dressed in a conservative suit: a 'parent'. You are a creative specialist who has retained a youthful imagination and a trendier dress sense: a 'child'. The conversation, such as it is, goes nowhere, and may even leave a harmful residue of bitterness. The scene is already set to make the next interaction even more rancorous. Both people are operating genuinely, and there is no personality clash, but the parent–child paradigm has nonetheless undermined the transaction. To progress, both need to recognise the unconscious pattern, act as 'adults' and engage in meaningful dialogue about the proposed expenditure. People will still tend to revert to their normal 'type', so continuing efforts need to be made to maintain an 'adult' outlook.

Parent, Adult and Child

We each have internal models of parents, children and also adults, and we play these roles with one another in our relationships. We even do it with ourselves, in our internal conversations. The model below illustrates such 'transactions' between people in their different states (parent, child or adult). The 'parent' (as distinct from the rational 'adult') can be controlling (protecting, issuing warnings, essentially micro-managing) or nurturing (liberating, encouraging). The 'child' adapts to the control at the expense of their personal growth and becomes timid or resentful, or both. The 'natural' child is freer, more creative but may lack self-control. Another form of child may emerge, one that is a 'little professor', seemingly acting like an adult at an overly young age.

TRANSACTIONAL ANALYSIS (ERIC BERNE)

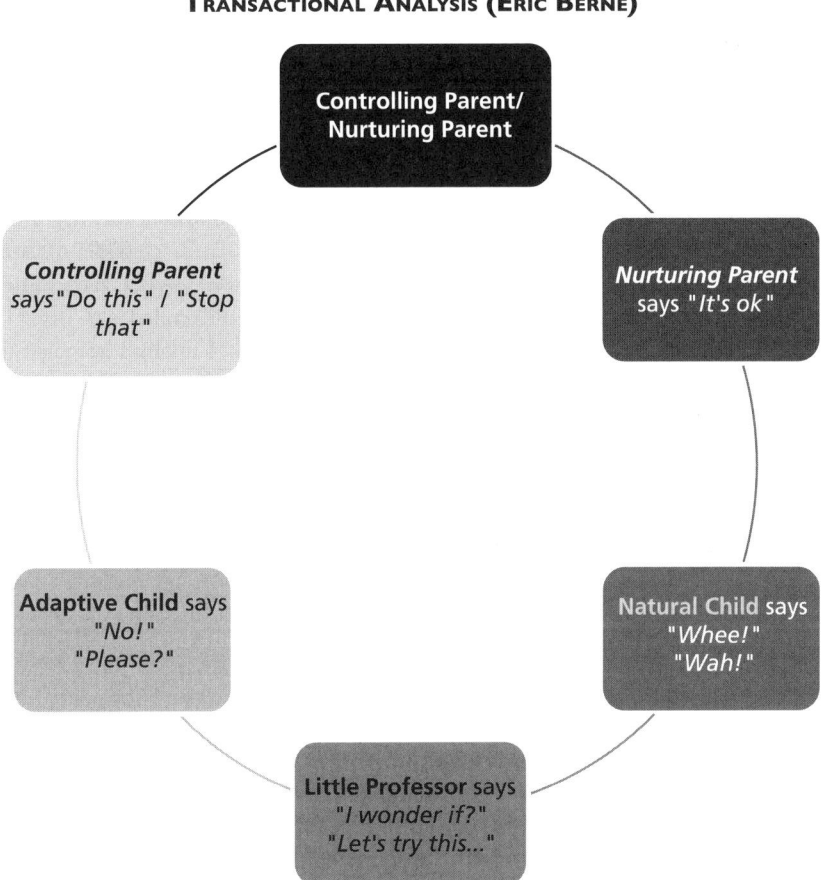

Nurturing or Controlling Parent

Managers can play two forms of 'parent' role in managing professionals:

- The Nurturing Parent is caring and concerned, seeking to keep the Child contented, offering a safe haven and unconditional love to calm the Child's troubles.
- The Controlling (or Critical) Parent, on the other hand, tries to make the Child do as the Parent wants them to do, to help the Child live in this world.

Defining the Adult

The adult is defined as a rational person, who talks reasonably and acts assertively, neither trying to control nor reacting aggressively towards others. The adult is comfortable with his or herself and is close to our 'ideal self'.

Defining the Child

There are three types of child roles we can play (as employees, and indeed as managers):

- The Natural Child is largely unaware of him- or herself, and is characterised by the natural, spontaneous noises they make (gurgles, 'Whee! noises'). They like to play, and are open and vulnerable.
- The Little Professor is the curious and exploring child, who is always trying out new things (often much to their Controlling Parent's annoyance). Together with the Natural Child, they make up the Free Child.
- The Adaptive Child reacts to the world around them, either changing to fit in or, alternatively, rebelling against the world at large.

Understanding Communications: Transactions between 'Adults' and 'Children'

When two people communicate purposely, each interaction is a form of transaction. Many conflict problems come from unsuccessful transactions, as the expected outcomes were not achieved or where the 'games' people played caused frustration or annoyance. Interestingly, each side – even the child – shapes the other and often it is the child, not the parent, who sets the tone of the conversation or transaction.

The Nurturing Parent invokes the Natural Child and the Controlling Parent invokes the Adaptive Child. In fact, strange though it may seem, the reverse is also true: the 'child' invokes a response in the 'parent'. Thus, if I act as an Adaptive Child, I will most likely evoke the Controlling Parent in the other person.

We also play many games between these positions, and there are rituals, from greetings to whole conversations (such as the weather), where we take different positions for different events. These are often 'pre-recorded' as scripts we just play out. They give us a sense of control and identity, and reassure us that all is well in the world. Other, more serious games can be negative and destructive, and unfortunately we can play them more out of a sense of habit ('default thinking') than maliciousness.

Crossed Transactions Cause Conflict

Complementary transactions occur when people in the conversation play the same role or see themselves at the same level (e.g. parent talking to parent, or adult to adult). Here, both are often thinking in the same way, and communication is easier.

Problems frequently occur in crossed transactions, where each person is talking to the other at a different level. The parent is either nurturing or controlling, and often speaks to the child, who is either 'adaptive' or 'natural' in their response. When both people talk as a parent to the other's child, their wires get crossed and conflict results.

The ideal line of communication is the mature and rational Adult–Adult relationship.

Being a Controlling Parent invites the other person to enter into a child state, where they may conform to your demands. There is also a risk that they will be an adaptive 'naughty child' and rebel. They may also take opposing parent or adult states.

Being a Nurturing Parent, or talking at the same level as the other person, acts to create trust.

Watch out for crossed wires; this is where conflict arises. When it happens, first go to the state that the other person is in to talk at the same level. For rational conversation, move yourself and the other person to the adult level.

Decoding the Conversation: Transactional Analysis

Eric Berne, the noted psychiatrist, developed transactional analysis (TA) to understand and improve the conversational patterns of behaviour between people.[19] Transactional analysis is used to decipher 'the games people play' (such as one-upmanship) in these conversational exchanges ('transactions'). The term 'transaction' is used to indicate 'purposeful interactions' rather than chit-chat or small talk. We all play games, to a greater or lesser extent, whether we tend to act as micro-managing 'Controlling Parent' bosses, for example, or as whining, irresponsible prima donna 'children'.

Transactional analysis can help explain those frustrating conversations where the problem (the proverbial 'monkey') always seems to end up on your back, rather than where it belongs. Transactional analysis can help in identifying the underlying pattern of conversations that seem to hit a brick wall, for example, where a friend who asks for your suggestions refutes all of them until it is you who ends up taking responsibility for the task. Consider, for example, how even friends play conversational 'games', in this illustration of the "Yes, but… " game, below:

A friend at work is bemoaning his inability to qualify a potential client in preparation for a sales presentation. You suggest he starts with desk research:

He says, "Yes, but..." and produces a 'reason' why that wouldn't work.
You then suggest getting an intern to do the initial research.
He says, "Yes, but…" and comes up with another 'reason'.
You go on to suggest getting a consultant to provide some insights.
He says, "Yes, but…" and conjures up another way to avoid taking action.

> He continues to reject your suggestions, and eventually inverts the relationship by declaring that,
> "Those suggestions weren't very good, were they?"
>
> The boot has been neatly transferred to the other foot – yours! – and you now relieve the situation by doing the research for him. Game over.

Here, the so-called helpless 'child' has succeeded in making you their 'parent', taking responsibility for the task. His moaning through this 'transaction' has moved the proverbial 'monkey' to your back! Even though he appeared to act as an adult, looking for help, his 'game' all along was to transfer the task to you. You, being 'nice', fell into the trap. You were hooked into this, not just by his gamesmanship but by your persistent need to be helpful.

The 'tape' in your head reminded you of your core value that good people 'help'. In that sense, your strength (impeccable core values) was turned against you, judo-like. On the surface, your friend played the child role before 'switching' to the parent role, making you the victim. He now feels superior, having initiated the 'con', and you probably feel cheated, trapped by your own need to be (or at least to appear to be) helpful. This represents a classic switching of roles where the 'victim/child' entraps you as 'rescuer', becoming the 'persecutor' in the process.

STEPHEN KARPMAN'S RELATIONSHIP TRIANGLE[20]

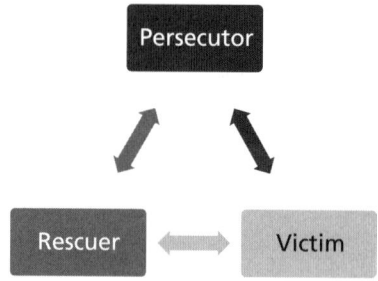

Understanding your Disposition: Life Position

One of the side-benefits of analysing our game playing is that it can actually reveal our disposition or 'life position', i.e. we can recognise the outlook that most corresponds to our ego-state, whether that of parent, child or adult. The ego state might reflect a mature 'adult' outlook on life, for example, or might reflect a self-image as dependent child or as a controlling parent. This is illustrated in the boxes below, where one's position is 'OK' or not (i.e. mature adult). This illustration shows the relationship position between two people, whether they are in the 'OK' position or not.

Life Positions: I'm OK/You're OK – or Not?

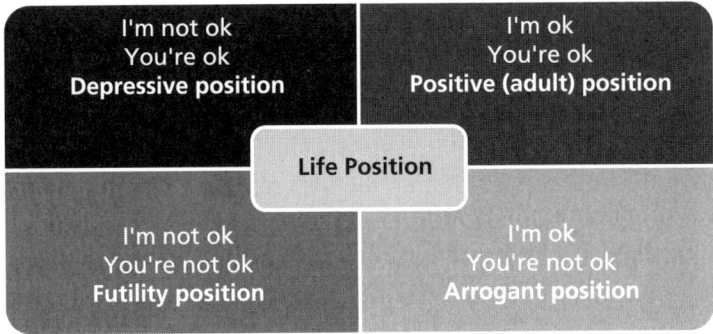

To counteract the 'games people play', consider using the following measures:

- Analyse and understand how games involving you play out. What is the opening gambit or 'trigger'? What is the outcome? What 'switches' are made in the transaction?
- Recognise your needs and how they make you succumb to 'cons' by which the other party dupes you or switches roles. These could be needs for approval, achievement, belonging, to be liked, to be respected, or to be correct. Figure out how you will cope with the disapproval of saying 'no' to a con or a request.
- Stay alert for distortions or denials of reality: the con often begins with a fudging of the facts, a deliberate twisting of reality, the setting of a false premise, or an untested presumption. All of these distortions can disconcert you or make you feel uneasy in some way – and this itself is a warning sign that a con is being attempted.
- Expose the con: state that you believe that games are being played here, and withdraw from the game.
- Be an adult, not a parent: don't provide the con artist with opportunities to reject your reasonable proposals. Instead of saying, "Why don't you…?" say, "And what are you going to do about that?" inviting the other person to make proposals, thereby ending the game-playing.

As shown in the figure above, arrogance is a function of believing that the other person is 'not OK'. Given the professional's long training and undoubted ability, plus the apparent need to be seen to be in charge (e.g. as an accountant, doctor or engineer), it is easy to see how this disposition (mental posture) could occur, and how easy it is to slip further into arrogance, especially given the trappings of a profession (wigs and gowns, jargon, certifications, the trappings of office, etc.).

Dealing with Negative Positions

The quadrants in the figure below show the responses – positive or negative, adult or parenting – of each of the four types of response to the 'child's' whine that "I just can't do this". The top left quadrant responds judgementally, declaring in a negative, controlling way that "you never stop complaining". Note the use of the absolute, judgemental word "never".

The top right quadrant spoils the child by offering to take responsibility: "Let me sort it out for you." The responder's psychological need – in this case, the need to be appreciated – means that he or she is hungry to take the bait.

The bottom left quadrant shows the response of someone who is positive but still controlling, conceding that the task may be 'tricky', but urging the child to try harder.

The final quadrant shows how a positive nurturer would respond, offering help but keeping responsibility in the right place, on the receiver, by asking: "How do you want me to help you?"

DEALING WITH THE DIFFERENT LIFE POSITIONS

I just can't do this... ***You never stop complaining....*** NEGATIVE/ CONTROLLING	I just can't do this... Let me sort it out NEGATIVE/ NURTURING
	Negative Positive	
I just can't do this... Yes, it is tricky, but just try it POSITIVE/ CONTROLLING	I just can't do this... *How do you want me to help you?* POSITIVE/ NURTURING

The top left quadrant is negative and controlling, judgemental, nagging. The top right quadrant is yielding and takes responsibility off the requestor, keeping them in the child mode, spoiling them, and may re-open the *'why don't you/yes, but'* game, as described above. The bottom left quadrant is positive but controlling – a parental state. The bottom right quadrant keeps responsibility on the requestor, where it should be, but offers constructive help and is an adult state.

Knowing your Vulnerabilities: Needs and Principles

Gaining self-confidence involves reaching a higher level of maturity, referred to here as 'adulthood', and conversational transactions play a large part in revealing our life 'positions' in dealing with others. In these transactions, the game-player seeks to hook their 'target' by getting them to respond in accordance with their principles and set values. For example, you have a core value of being reasonable; you are likely to maintain this posture and uphold this value, even if the other person is acting unreasonably, i.e. mischievously or malignantly. In extended variations, the principle is maintained, even in the face of severe provocation, i.e. it is now a battle of wills to show I am a superior person to you.

Similarly, the need to be (or to be seen to be) helpful can descend into a primeval contest of wills, in which the overly 'helpful' person aims to make the other 'grateful'. Such a need for gratitude can be exploited thoroughly by the person who plays games; many people have deep needs for gratitude, even wallowing in self-pity for 'unappreciated martyrdom'.

Sometimes it is the felt need to avoid, for example, awkward silences that triggers a stream of *'why don't you'* suggestions. These well-meaning suggestions can easily rebound, as explained earlier, loading the originator with a formidable to-do list.

To overcome these felt needs, it is useful to question one's flawed assumptions, rigid imperatives and dogmatic beliefs, asking if such fixed views make the game an inevitable loss for oneself. One method of doing this is to use reason (rational thinking, facts and logic) to anchor the 'con' artist by grounding him or her in some reality.

Don't Play Games – Especially if Winning is not a Possibility

Sometimes, maintaining our needs (e.g. for approval, harmony, consistency) can doom us to occupy the same losing role indefinitely. For example, the need to 'be a good wife' can lead a woman to become a human doormat indefinitely. Similarly, the need to 'be a good friend' can trap one in 'damned if you do, damned if you don't' situations, where no friendly act is ever good enough. For example, a colleague might refuse one's offer of a quiet chat about problems at work, only to get annoyed later because the issue is not brought up for discussion. In a similar manner, a colleague might spurn the suggestion to get involved in a new hill-walking group, for instance, but then makes you pay a heavy price later when you actually cross the mountains with new friends – and without him.

Changing the Conversation and Improving Self-confidence through Appreciative Inquiry

A further means of developing self-confidence is to engage in a positive form of conversation known as 'appreciative enquiry', which is a constantly open, affirmative and therefore 'appreciative' approach to conversation and discussion. It is a mode of debate (as opposed to heated argument or bickering) where proposals are 'appreciated' and developed. The spirit is one of enquiry, rather than challenge or confrontation for its own sake.

The idea behind this approach is to keep discussion on track – not to be derailed by games or ego. It espouses respect, good listening and patience to enquire appreciatively into a proposer's arguments. It is the opposite of game playing, replacing the show-stopping word 'but' with the continuity of 'and'.

Appreciative inquiry operates from a mental platform of strength. It avoids self-defensiveness and fosters positive relationships by building on the unique potential of the individuals and groups involved. This positive philosophy can enhance an individual's self-confidence and can similarly increase an organisation's capacity for collaboration and change.

Although appreciative inquiry is essentially a philosophy, rather than a rigid methodology, it uses a cycle of four processes on which to focus:

1. **DISCOVERY:** the identification of organisational processes that work well.

2. **DREAM:** the envisioning of processes that would work well in the future.

3. **DESIGN:** planning and prioritising processes that would work well.

4. **DELIVERY:** the implementation (execution) of the finally agreed proposal.

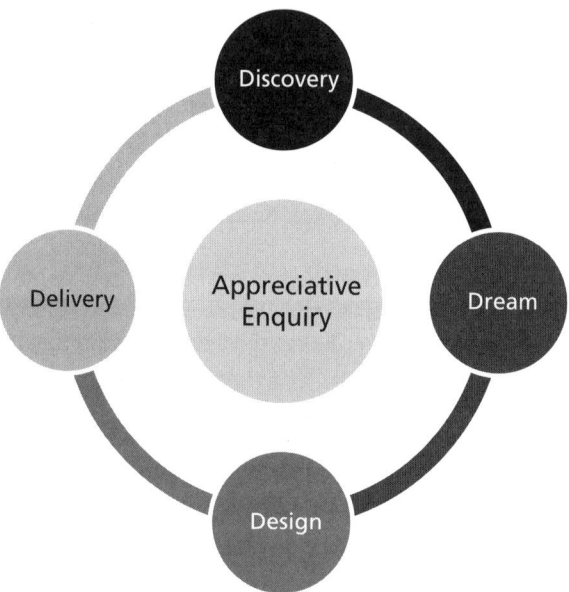

The idea is to focus on the positive and build organisations around what works, rather than trying to fix what does not. Appreciative inquiry is a particular form of deliberate, ongoing improvement and is rooted in a conscious attempt to create a positive mindset in individuals and in organisations, starting with the building block of organisational life: crucial conversations. Individuals who can analyse conversational 'transactions' can then avoid getting stuck endlessly in the same mental ruts, and can become 'adult' in their relationships. This, naturally, builds confidence. If organisations can achieve such maturity, the whole culture becomes transformed. Appreciative enquiry is then a means to develop a positive disposition, to engage in progressive dialogue by seeking to build on strengths rather than focus on the inevitable negative points. Simply put, it is a way to see that the glass is half full, rather than half empty.

In that sense, it provides a 'win–win' outlook, in which all sides are "ok". It is, of course, a method that is free-of-cost and works well in releasing the human potential of individuals and organisations.

For example, many lawyers do outstanding work, but can't work well with their colleagues. Some lawyers weave a tight argument, but can't settle a case. Others are only interested in winning, no matter what the cost. Many of these otherwise successful professionals would benefit from using appreciative inquiry.

Appreciative enquiry focuses on possibilities, not problems, which sounds easy, but it does require a shift from the more typical negative, problem-centred approach to bringing about change, in individuals or organisations. Appreciative enquiry helps people discover what is working, so that they can do more of it. It is inquiry-based on positive questions, assuming the best in people. In appreciative enquiry, a clear topic is chosen, and constructive questions are developed. Individuals are urged to tap into positive achievements and stories that inspire. The process doesn't ignore problems – it just approaches them from the positive side: what is working rather than what is **not** working. It can be used in a conversation or at a strategic planning conference, with two people or many more.

Appreciative enquiry builds on several assumptions, including:

- Our goals help guide us.
- The very act of asking questions of an individual or group influences them.
- We already have the resources we need: what we want already exists in ourselves, whether we realise it or not.

The first step is to choose a topic that sets a positive tone. Start with a constructive, 'appreciative' enquiry that focuses on what is working and build on that. Ask, for example, what is satisfying about working here, or what drew you to working here, or what you value in this profession. This should frame the ensuing conversation positively and generate attractive possibilities.

Here are some examples of questions aimed at bringing change around employee satisfaction:

- What drew you to this firm?
- Describe a situation in which you felt that you received exceptional mentoring.
- Relate your most meaningful experience in working here.
- What is good about your firm's culture?
- What is the most meaningful feedback you've received as a [lawyer]?
- When did you feel most recognised for your work?
- How did you feel when you were expressly valued by a client?
- Describe a shift in your thinking that gives you hope for yourself, firm, or community.

Always, whatever the topic, group or individual, look for patterns in the response. Pay attention to the attitudes of the responders, both at the time they respond and later. Notice the changes that start to take place, the shift in thinking based on the enquiry and the positivity of the conversation.

Appreciative inquiry is an affirmative approach to individual and organisational development. It springs from possibilities and from hope, and works with two people or with many thousands. Structured correctly, everyone gets to be heard, and it is a great joy to be truly listened to. It brings out the best in us.

Suspend judgement; experiment with appreciative enquiry. Keep in mind the words of Gandhi, an attorney himself: "Be the change you want to see in the world."

Conclusion

Perhaps, building self-confidence is the simplest and yet most rewarding route in developing professionals: it requires little psychological analysis, the steps are very practical and the results can often be immediate and substantial.

As in the case of my smart legal friends who came back across the Atlantic with absolutely no new client contacts, it may well be a vital addition to their professional capability, turning that undoubted mental prowess into useful work, with significant economic and professional rewards.

The singular drive that invariably accompanies professional achievement can inhibit attempts in other areas (such as networking or otherwise 'selling' services). As Nicola Davila refers to this need for preservation of self-esteem among professionals: "Being right is one more good reason for not succeeding."[21] It is important to note that confidence comes not from always being right but from not fearing being wrong.

Perhaps Mark Twain was correct when he claimed that "thousands of geniuses live and die undiscovered – either by themselves or by others"; and as a manager of smart people, it is surely a privilege to help develop this genius. Like Shakespeare's "quality of mercy", developing confidence is "twice-blessed": it blesses both the giver and the receiver. If one works on developing others' confidence, the insights for oneself can be illuminating and rewarding. It also creates an onus that one should practice what one preaches.

A further bonus of developing confidence is that it is a pre-requisite for achievement and, in turn, nothing builds self-esteem and self-confidence like accomplishment. As Edmund Hillary put it: "It is not the mountain we conquer but ourselves."

This chapter has covered a wide terrain in order to develop an understanding of the underlying reasons smart people can lack confidence and to explain what practical measures can be taken. Starting with positive thinking, the chapter moved on to transactional analysis ('the games people play'), before showing how 'appreciative enquiry' can shape a positive mindset. Self-confidence manifests itself in a bolder attitude to life, and becomes evident through more assertive conversation and a more joyful approach to work and life.

The final word in this chapter will rest with Henry Haskins, who said in his book, *Meditations in Wall St.*: "What lies behind us and what lies before us are tiny matters compared to what lies within us."[22]

ENDNOTES

[1] Philip Zimbardo, *Psychology and Life* (17th ed., Allyn & Bacon Publishing, 2005).

[2] Micheline Egan, "Simply Confidence" (Thesis Paper, Dublin: IMI, 2010).

[3] Philip Zimbardo, *The Power And Pathology of Imprisonment*, Congressional Record, Serial No. 15, 1971-10-25, (US Government Printing Office, 1971).

[4] Daniel Goleman, *Emotional Intelligence* (Bloomsbury, 1996).

[5] Denis Waitley, *The Pyschology of Winning* (Berkley, 1996).

[6] Daniel Goleman, *Emotional Intelligence* (Bloomsbury, 1996).

[7] Philip Zimbardo, *The Lucifer Effect: Understanding How Good People Turn Evil* (Random House, 2008).

[8] Ros Taylor, *Confidence In Just 7 Days* (Vermillion (BBC), 2001).

[9] Tony Buzan, *Make the Most of Your Mind* (Touchstone, 1984).

[10] Carol Dweck, *Mindset: The New Psychology of Success* (Random House, 2006).

[11] Napoleon Hill, *Think and Grow Rich* (Ralston, 1953).

[12] Norman Vincent Peale, *The Power of Positive Thinking* (Ballantine Books, 1996).

[13] Martin Seligman, *Learned Optimism* (Knopf, 1991).

[14] *Ibid.*

[15] See Thomas Harris, *I'm OK – You're OK* (HarperCollins, 2004).

[16] Hans Eysenck, *Genius: The Natural History of Creativity* (Cambridge University Press, 1995).

[17] *Ibid.*

[18] *Ibid.*

[19] *Ibid.*

[20] Stephen Karpman, "Fairy Tales and Script Drama Analysis" (1968) Vol. 7 (26) *Transactional Analysis Bulletin* 39–43.

[21] Nicolas Gomez Davila and Franco Volpi, *Escolios A Un Texto Implicito: Obra Completa* (Villegas Editores, 2005).

[22] Henry Haskins, *Meditations in Wall St.* (William Morrow, 1940).

Chapter 12

Managing Professionals through Emotional Intelligence

Dr Mary Collins and Dermot Duff

All learning has an emotional base.

Plato

The essential difference between emotion and reason is that emotion leads to action, while reason leads to conclusion.

Donald Gaine, neurologist

Introduction

Today, the complex world of professional work requires unprecedented levels of collaboration and interaction between people (effectively, social interaction). More than ever, social and emotional intelligence are vital for cohesion and for organisational well-being. In this chapter, these 'intelligences' are explored – critically – with practical suggestions made for their application.

Emotional Intelligence (EI) is the ability to perceive, control and evaluate emotions. EI is not the polar opposite of conventional intelligence, not the triumph of 'heart over head'. Rather, it is the coalescence of both, with prodigious results. John Mayer, a pioneer in the area of emotional intelligence, asserts with some validity that: "People high in emotional intelligence are expected to progress more quickly through the abilities designated and to master more of them."[1] It also emerges that people who can master optimism (one of the characteristics of emotional intelligence) and maintain a good mood are better at inductive reasoning and creative problem-solving. Similarly, developing self-knowledge and experiencing one's self in a conscious manner is a vital part of learning.

It is estimated that 20% of a person's success is based on what is normally considered intelligence: the ability to learn, understand and reason (the components of the well-known intelligence quotient (IQ)). The other 80% is based on the ability to understand ourselves and interact with people, i.e. emotional intelligence (EI). An article in *Fortune* magazine, "Why CEOs Fail", highlighted qualities that characterise effective leaders, with EI traits such as integrity, maturity, business acumen and social skills leading the list.[2] Yet, according to Professor David Kirch of Ohio University, employers seem to hire accountants based primarily on grade-point average, an IQ-related measure, and a relatively short interview.[3]

Man: An Emotional Animal?

Some decades ago Dale Carnegie, a recognised master of influence and persuasion, said:

> "When dealing with people, let us remember we are not dealing with creatures of logic. We are dealing with creatures of emotion, creatures bustling with prejudices and motivated by pride and vanity."[4]

Economists used to assume that man was a rational animal, but even they have come to realise that people often simply 'rationalise', justifying non-rational purchases with a flawed after-the-fact logic. For example, a man buying an expensive car for ego reasons might justify his decision by quoting its technical specifications, but really it is in defence of a 'trophy purchase'. People offer 'rational' justifications, but many important decisions (such as buying a house or choosing a school for your son or daughter) are rooted in primal emotions.

Many psychologists insist that people are fundamentally emotional, driven by *wants* more than *needs*, and that we are not inherently logical, but merely use logic as a means to an end. In any case, it would seem that we are at least social animals, drawn together not just to collaborate to achieve goals but by the need for social – and emotional – engagement.

Joshua Freedman, author of *At the Heart of Leadership* and advisor in emotional intelligence to the US Navy, defines emotional intelligence as a way of recognising, understanding and choosing how we think, feel and act.[5] Emotional intelligence shapes our interactions with others and our understanding of ourselves. It defines how and what we learn; it allows us to set priorities and determines the majority of our daily actions. Freedman suggests that EI is responsible for as much as 80% of the 'success' in our lives. Peter Salovey and John Mayer define emotional intelligence as a subset of social intelligence, which involves the ability to monitor one's own and others' feelings and emotions, to discriminate among them and to use this information to guide one's thinking and actions.[6]

The first step on the path to greater social and emotional intelligence starts with self-awareness, and both professionals and their managers can benefit greatly from EI, easing the strains that inevitably occur when people interact. Emotional intelligence involves the management of oneself, one's interaction with others, one's tolerance for stress and 'impulse control', as well as developing optimism, flexibility and, ultimately, self-fulfilment.

(**Note**: this chapter can be read independently, or the interested reader can also refer to **Chapters 4, 5, 7** and **13**, on leadership, personality, motivation and coaching respectively.)

In this chapter we introduce some relatively straightforward means to improve this ability to process emotional information (especially the perception, assimilation, understanding and management of emotion). Before doing so, we can examine some criticism of the theories around emotional intelligence, especially how EI can be improved, to consider if it is warranted.

Some Criticisms of Emotional Intelligence Theories

Psychologist Hans Eysenck has criticised "the fundamental absurdity of the tendency to class almost any type of behaviour as an 'intelligence'".[7] Others, such as Frank Landy, similarly claim that the concept of emotional intelligence adds little to the explanation – and especially the prediction – of some common outcomes claimed by its advocates: "EI compared with a measure of abstract intelligence but not with a personality measure, or with a measure of academic intelligence."[8] Emotional intelligence measures and personality measures may correlate because they **both** relate to personality traits, specifically to neuroticism and extroversion (see **Chapter 5**). Other critics, such as R.D. Roberts, suggest that emotional intelligence is based simply on conformity to social norms, not on any innate ability.[9] The implication by such critics is that EI is simply a new clustering of personality traits. In practice, however, EI is proving both popular and effective in improving skills in leadership, conflict management, personal and team development, etc. Because it offers simple, clear instructions, behavioural change is more readily achieved than with other, personality-based models.

The Curse of Emotion

Professor John Antonakis claims that an *excess* of emotional awareness may prevent leaders from operating rationally and inhibit hard decision-making.[10] He calls this the "curse of emotion". If a leader is overly sensitive to their own and others' emotional states, they may have difficulty making decisions that would produce an emotional burden for them or their followers. In other words, overly sensitive leaders might shirk hard decisions to avoid hurting colleagues emotionally.

Emotional Intelligence

Intelligence, without grace or charm, may enable a person to qualify for their profession, but it will not usually be sufficient for real career success or life satisfaction. Above a certain threshold (claimed by Daniel Goleman to be a moderately high IQ of 105), it appears that additional intelligence has no significant further effect on success, while emotional intelligence does.[11]

> *"Research shows us convincingly that EQ (Emotional Intelligence Quotient) is more important than IQ (Cognitive Intelligence Quotient) in almost every role and many times more important in leadership roles. This finding is accentuated as we move from the control philosophy of the industrial age to an empowering release philosophy of the knowledge worker age."*
>
> Stephen R. Covey[12]

A BRIEF HISTORY OF EMOTIONAL INTELLIGENCE

While it has long been recognised that 'social intelligence' (the ability to get along with other people) is important for career and life success, the first writers to formalise this were David Wechsler and the renowned Abraham Maslow, who described how people can build emotional strength.[13] Howard Gardner, renowned US psychologist and author of *Frames of Mind*, articulated the idea of multiple forms of intelligence.[14] The curiously named Wayne Payne introduced the term 'emotional intelligence' in his doctoral dissertation in 1985.[15] The term 'emotional quotient' is claimed by Reuven Bar-On,[16] while psychologists Peter Salovey and John Mayer published a landmark article, "Emotional Intelligence",[17] and the central conclusions were later popularised by science writer Daniel Goleman in his book, *Emotional Intelligence: Why It Can Matter More Than IQ*.[18]

While some may dispute the very concept of emotional intelligence, there is no denying that the ability to 'read' (and respond to) facial expressions and other non-verbal communications greatly increases one's success in interacting with people. Similarly, while the office 'jerk' eventually gets found out, people truly come to love those who treat them with grace and respect. Call it 'bedside manner' or 'a way with clients', there is real value in being able to interpret and respond to the non-verbal signs that underpin 70% of human communication. In other words, emotional intelligence allows you to hear that which is not being said verbally, and also to decide if, on 'face value', what is being communicated is valid, i.e. is the projected message accurate and real, or are there hidden meanings or deceptions? The human face is not just a dumb display terminal; it is an active interface in the emotional process. As Malcolm Gladwell says, "the face is not a secondary billboard for our internal feelings. It is an equal partner in the emotional process."[19] For example, when a person is lying, they may construct a story that is logically consistent, but their body language (nervous tics, strained facial expression, awkward posture, averted gaze) sends out messages that let the aware listener deduce that a deception is being attempted.

Emotions at Work

Emotions are intrinsically linked to energy. Negative emotions dissipate energy – we can all relate to the tight knot in the stomach that comes with anger and resentment. We also know the excitement and even the adrenaline rush of being involved in a successful bid or presentation. Emotions can have a huge impact on our working life. There are insensitive managers who try to bulldoze staff with a firm 'stick approach', who believe that steady criticism and fear are the levers for higher performance. Being badly treated by such a manager can arouse reactions of anger, antagonism, fear, desire for revenge, and a general feeling of ill will and resentment. The manager may be behaving this way because this is the school of management that he or she has experienced in the past. Once emotionally unintelligent behaviour sets in, a downward spiral of low morale, avoidance and negative politics evolves. A positive, successful work environment is not compatible with knotted stomachs and anxious looks over the shoulder.

> *"People high in Emotional Intelligence will build real social fabric within an organisation, and between the organisation and those it serves; whereas those low in EI may tend to create problems for the organisation through their individual behaviours."*
>
> John Mayer, Peter Salovey and David Caruso[20]

So, what is 'Emotional Intelligence'?

> *"It is very important to understand that emotional intelligence is not the opposite of intelligence, it is not the triumph of heart over head – it is the unique intersection of both."*
>
> John Mayer and David Caruso[21]

As outlined above, the concept of emotional intelligence was initially developed by psychologists John Mayer of the University of New Hampshire, and Peter Salovey of Yale. Psychologist Reuven Bar-On worked independently on a similar concept he called 'emotional quotient', and it was he who first coined the term 'EQ' in the early 1980s.

The subject was then popularised by Daniel Goleman, a science journalist and psychologist, in his 1996 bestselling book *Emotional Intelligence: Why It Can Matter More Than IQ*[22] and in follow-on articles in the *Harvard Business Review*.[23] Goleman found that emotionally intelligent people finish first by almost every standard used to measure business success. He defined emotional intelligence as "the capacity for recognising our own feelings and those of others, for motivating ourselves, and for managing emotions well, in ourselves and in our relationships."[24]

Salovey and Mayer, for their part, had defined "emotional intelligence as a subset of social intelligence; it involves the ability to monitor one's own and others' feelings and emotions, to discriminate among them and to use this information to guide one's thinking and actions."[25]

Organisations are now realising that EI is the engine for building strong client relationships, having successful, collaborative teams and empowering talented staff. Dr Martyn Newman, author of *Emotional Capitalists: The New Leaders*, cites extensive research he has conducted into what differentiates good, from truly exceptional leaders.[26] Good IQ is important and always will be; however,

Newman's research shows how a combination of strong IQ and cognitive and emotional intelligence really sets leaders apart in terms of performance. Good leadership generates emotions like trust and confidence, which in turn create good relationships; together, these build real commercial value.

While 'traditional' IQ tends to peak at around 18 years of age and is quite an innate ability, EI can be successfully developed through coaching and training to enhance skill in the deficient domains. People with high EI cope well with their own emotions, and notice and respond appropriately to the emotions of other people. This makes it easier to harness their potential and, thereby, the potential of the organisation.

> *"Emotional intelligence can be both misunderstood and misrepresented. But the bottom line is that the manager who can think about emotions accurately, and clearly, may often be better able to anticipate, cope with – and effectively manage – change."*
>
> John Mayer and David Caruso[27]

BRANCHES OF EMOTIONAL INTELLIGENCE

Peter Salovey and John Mayer delineate four different factors in emotional intelligence: the perception of emotion, the ability to reason using emotions, the ability to understand emotion and the ability to manage emotions.

- **Perceiving Emotions** The first step in understanding emotions is to accurately perceive them, and this might require understanding the non-verbal signals, such as body language and facial expressions, that reveal a person's underlying emotions.
- **Reasoning with Emotions** The second step involves consciously using emotions to foster deeper thinking and cognition. Paying attention to emotions can tell us what our underlying, unspoken concerns are, and where our heartfelt priorities lie. That knot in the stomach is a gut reaction that may well be processing tacit danger signals.
- **Understanding Emotions** Emotions need interpretation: a colleague's silence may be mere reflection or might be a prelude to an emotional outburst; knowing the person well enough, psychologically speaking, can help you tell the difference. In that regard, knowing the person's 'type', as explained in **Chapter 5**, can aid this interpretation: the natural extrovert, on this occasion, may well just be pausing for reflection, or this unusual silence might indicate extreme frustration that is about to boil over.
- **Managing Emotions** The ability to regulate one's response is a vital aspect of emotional intelligence. Responding appropriately to the emotions of oneself and of others is the acid test of managing emotions.

Applying the Components of Emotional Intelligence

Emotional intelligence is more than being happy or sad; it is the ability to effectively express and manage one's emotions (intrapersonal) and relationships with others (interpersonal). As shown in the following graphic, the journey to improved emotional intelligence starts with increased self-awareness and self-confidence (see also **Chapter 11**). This then facilitates one's self-management (self-control, adaptability, achievement drive) and one's ability to empathise and be of some service (social awareness). With these enhancements, one's ability to inspire and develop others is improved: one can become more of a transformational leader (see also **Chapter 3**).

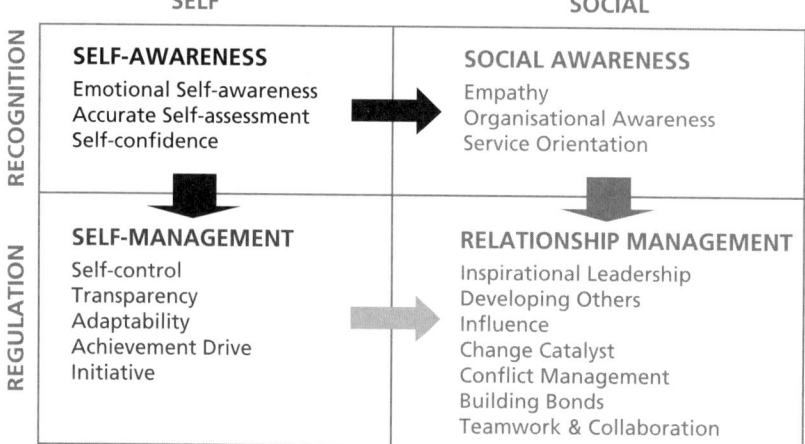

EMOTIONAL INTELLIGENCE AND THE PATHWAY TO LEADERSHIP

The above graphic shows the general pathway to enhancing one's emotional intelligence. To help apply this in practice, it is helpful to note the five central 'domains' (categories) to improving one's emotional intelligence, starting with the intrapersonal 'domain', as shown. These domains then break down into a number of more specific 'competences', such as self-awareness, self-regard, assertiveness or independence.

Domain	Component
Intrapersonal	Self-regard, self-awareness, assertiveness, independence, self-actualisation
Interpersonal	Empathy, connecting with others, motivation
Stress management	Stress tolerance, coping under pressure, impulse control
Adaptability	Testing for reality, flexibility, problem-solving
General mood	Optimism, happiness

1. Self-awareness

This refers to understanding one's own emotions (emotional self-awareness), knowing one's strengths and limits (self-assessment) and having self-confidence. In a large-scale study Daniel Goleman conducted of CEOs globally, self-awareness was found to be the top trait of the most successful leaders.[28] This 'success' was measured not just in terms of financial success but also overall satisfaction in the areas of health, emotional well-being and relationships. Interestingly, when a gender analysis was undertaken, women CEOs scored significantly higher than their male counterparts.

> For many 'smart people' **self-awareness** can be an important area for development. Take the example of a really bright lawyer in a leading MBA school presenting to her class. She simply will not/cannot pick up the clues from her classmates that her presentation is too long. She is quite single-minded in her need to drive the project and bristles at any criticism. This emotionally unintelligent behaviour drives her other team members to despair. Even if she had just relayed back to her team what they were saying, it would have helped: "So, what you're saying is ... the presentation needs fewer slides?" Or even a nod of acknowledgement: "Yep, I hear you." Actually, a smile would have done wonders!

2. Self-management

Self-management essentially involves the management of one's emotions; keeping disruptive emotions and impulses under control. Leaders who practice self-management tend to be optimistic in nature. They demonstrate integrity or consistency between their values, emotions and behaviour. There was a case a number of years ago of a senior board member in a large FMCG organisation who was so annoyed after a particular board meeting, where he was severely criticised, that he threw a photocopier down a flight of stairs – an example of a lack of self-control in action!

> *"People in good moods are better at inductive reasoning and creative problem-solving."*
>
> James Pennebaker[29]

3. Social Awareness

This dimension of emotional intelligence centres on showing empathy to others in an authentic way – really understanding others' perspectives or mental models, i.e. their 'framework of the world'. There is a focus on recognising and meeting follower, client or customer needs, and having a strong awareness of political relationships within an organisation.

4. Relationship Management

The final dimension in emotionally intelligent leadership refers to the leader's ability to inspire, guide and motivate with a compelling vision. It also refers to developing others through feedback and guidance. Teamwork and collaboration are key elements of this in action in the workplace.

> *"Strategically, relationships are at the heart of effective working partnerships; the best relationships are founded on the perception of equality and a mutually positive purpose. Connecting with people is easier if you focus on the commonalities rather than traditional differentiators such as status, power or hierarchy."*
>
> Martyn Newman[30]

EMOTIONAL INTELLIGENCE – A QUICK SELF-ASSESSMENT

You can make a quick measure of your own EI by reflecting on these questions:

- Are you aware of the subtleties of your own feelings?
- Do you usually know what other people are feeling, even if they do not say so?
- Does your awareness of others give you feelings of compassion for them?
- Are you resilient in the face of adversity and try to maintain a positive outlook?
- When you are angry, can you make your needs known in a way that resolves rather than exacerbates the situation?
- Can you create and maintain strong relationships?
- Are you flexible and adaptable during times of change?
- Can you use your feelings to help you reach decisions in your life?

People with high EI will tend to answer 'Yes' to these questions. However, it is worth noting that this is only a 'self-view'; to get real value and understanding, invite others to give you feedback, or use a formal 360-degree process with a qualified coach.

Emotional Intelligence in Organisations

A large professional services firm decided to introduce an emotional intelligence 360–degree feedback tool for managers in response to capability gaps in the area of empathy and motivating staff. The managing partner at the time wanted to highlight any potential issues earlier in people's careers and provide focused coaching on developing these areas to ensure fully-rounded leaders in the organisation. Despite initial resistance, the EI approach is now part of the organisation's culture, and there is a consistent language in use to help express the nuances of different emotions, and how to deal with them. Team morale and the overall "emotional climate" have improved significantly, and consequently it is easier to effect change and implement initiatives.

Developing Emotional Intelligence

> *"Every experience is a positive experience if I view it as an opportunity for growth and self-mastery, it will help me to control my emotions, thereby building my emotional capital."*
>
> Martyn Newman[31]

Here are some practical strategies to improve your levels of EI in a simple and time-effective way:

Self-awareness is at the core of EI; if a person is not aware of the impact of their own emotions (on themselves and others), it is almost impossible to demonstrate the other EI traits in an authentic way.

There are many 'profiling' tools on the market to aid in the journey of self-understanding and awareness. Among the most popular, and frequently used, in leadership development is the Myers–Briggs Type Indicator (MBTI) – see also **Chapter 5**.

It can be a very worthwhile exercise for all people managers to go through the MBTI process; to learn about their own preference styles (in terms of personality indicator) and equally to understand their least preferred areas. Such self-knowledge in terms of personal awareness also builds the capacity to understand, and notice, one's likely impact on others. The limitation to this, and other self-profiling tools, is that it is a 'self-view' only, which may not be an accurate reflection of how the individual is perceived.

To address this gap, '360-degree feedback' processes, if handled correctly, can be a powerful way to allow people to gauge their impact on others. This can be as simple as asking a number of people for feedback. More effectively, however, the use of a confidential, online feedback system, linked to the core competencies of the organisation, can be developed. Again, many large professional services firms now use 'upward feedback' as a metric in managers' performance management schemes.

Empathy Once regarded as an innate ability, this capacity can be developed by individuals over time, if the desire is real. The key skill with empathy is 'active listening'; taking a real and genuine interest in the person you are dealing with. This can be as simple as asking 'how was your weekend?' on a Monday morning.

It is important to try to get to know the individual in a holistic way, as colleagues do not leave their non-business life issues at the office door. Often, indeed, this can be simply done by reserving one-to-one meeting time with the individual to allow them to share what is going on for them.

The '70/30' listening/speaking rule of thumb comes into play here, however. As in coaching, the manager should only speak about 30% of the time and spend the remainder of the time actively listening – not always easy for smart people!

Self-control of one's emotions is crucially important to maintain in the workplace. Can you recognise when you are getting 'wound up', and control that impulse?

When you start noticing agitation, stress or upset, it is crucial to have personal strategies to cope with it. For some people, this will be as simple as taking a few deep breaths to compose themselves. For others, it may require leaving the building for some fresh air and headspace. More 'extroverted' types may need to have a good rant – with a trusted confidante – to let the steam off.

Optimism is probably one of the more intractable EI competencies to work on, but it too can be developed over time. Do you see the glass as half full or half empty? As discussed in **Chapter 11**, we know that successful leaders are more optimistic in nature. It is important to try to see the positives in situations and to be resilient in the face of adversity and change.

Rather than dwelling on the negativity of a situation, try to be constructive and have a plan of action to improve it. To encourage a positive disposition, note the recent research by Dr Martin Seligman, father of the positive psychology movement. His findings show that an optimistic disposition produces a longer and happier life (see also **Chapter 11**).[32]

> "I am personally convinced that one person can be a change catalyst, a 'transformer' in any situation, any organization. Such an individual is yeast that can leaven an entire loaf. It requires vision, initiative, patience, respect, persistence, courage, and faith to be a transforming leader."
>
> Stephen R. Covey[33]

The Language of Emotions

Having a language to articulate emotions is useful for understanding them. As Albert Einstein said:

> "Few people are capable of expressing with equanimity opinions which differ from the prejudices of their social environment. Most people are even incapable of forming such opinions."

Becoming emotionally 'articulate' (i.e. having an adequate command of the language of emotions) is clearly important. Some emotions are easier to deal with than others; most people can sympathise with a friend's suffering, but it takes an especially fine nature to rejoice in a friend's success – and even more in that of a rival.

The Potentially Distorting Effect of Power – and Intelligence

As discussed above, smart people have sufficient IQ for an intellectual challenge, but above a certain threshold, emotional intelligence counts for much more than intellectual capability. This would seem especially true in today's world, where the sophisticated tasks undertaken by many professionals require specialists of many kinds to collaborate, especially where innovation is an imperative. In this environment, social and emotional skills are particularly important, yet there have been, until recently, few clear ways to improve these invisible 'soft' skills. This is regrettable, because the absence of emotional intelligence can render a work situation 'toxic', perhaps dominated by a bully, for example, when the real need is to foster productive relationships.

While Robert Sutton's infamous "no asshole" rule is gaining a lot of traction (see below), questions nevertheless remain about superstars such as Steve Jobs who ruled partly through terror: was he successful because of his extreme tendencies, or in spite of them? Would emotional intelligence have dimmed his drive or vision, or would it have helped him reach new heights of achievement?

The answer may lie in the distinction between inspiration and perspiration: emotional intelligence is more likely to produce inspiration, whereas fear and bullying may produce the perspiration (effort) needed to attend to the level of perfectionism and detail required to achieve Jobs's vision. In either case, it is hard to dispute that emotional intelligence (or simply courtesy, manners and respect) will assuredly help most professionals, especially those where human interaction is required (in other words, almost all professions!).

Zero Tolerance?

Professor Robert ('Bob') Sutton of Stanford University, a prolific writer and eminent researcher with a reputation for cutting through nonsense, has raised the temperature of the debate by decreeing the "no asshole" rule.[34] While the term may be offensive, his point is that obnoxious behaviour should not be tolerated. He claims that 'jerks' who burn through assistants or inflame colleagues are never worth keeping, as they destroy the social fabric of an organisation. Some pragmatic managers make a merely financial calculation to decide what course of action to take: fire the 'jerks' or endure their obnoxiousness simply in pursuit of economic returns. The view in this book is that most of these vile characters are redeemable, except for those with deep pathological issues. Most can be helped by revealing their blind spots to them (or releasing hidden talents) or through better management.

The discriminating factor lies in the 'jerk's' motivation: Steve Jobs was motivated to "make a dent in the universe", an outwardly directed aim (even if it could be claimed that there is no such thing as altruism or unselfish motivation), whereas Bernard Madoff, the Enron gang and countless dictators were driven by a self-centred egotism and greed.

Just as power exaggerates elements of personality, the professional's cloak of expertise, authority and academic distinction can serve to isolate him or her from the feedback necessary to promote realism and empathy. The professional may have such a highly developed intellectual capacity that it diminishes the need to use other faculties. Those unfortunate enough to be deprived of their eyesight often develop other senses, such as better hearing, to compensate. The smart person, by contrast, may come to over-rely on mental acuity at the expense of emotional intelligence, limiting their success and happiness, and damaging relationships with colleagues and clients. Furthermore, there is a widespread assumption that cleverness is linked with a sharp tongue or critical manner.

At the same time, it is of course possible in some roles, especially in management, to operate purely on the level of charm, but ultimately the vacuous will be revealed as empty containers – and discarded. The goal is to combine content with charm, to merge prowess with personal ability, and have winners, rather than losers, jerks or non-entities, as illustrated below:

	Low EI	**High EI**
High Achievement	JERK – dangerous position	WINNER – unassailable position
Low Achievement	LOSER – untenable position	CHARLATAN – undetected position

Emotional Cases

The following are disguised but true examples of low emotional intelligence at work.

Brutal Bruce Bruce was an educated boss who prided himself on his cognitive intelligence. Lily, his much-admired marketing executive, had been laid low for a year, devastated by the loss in childbirth of her son. In that time, none of the 'intelligent' professionals in her consultancy firm had sent her any but the most cursory notes. Lily was still unsure of her ability to cope when she finally re-entered the office, only to be embraced by Bruce, her manager, who hugged her closely, saying "Lily, Lily, Lily … I am so glad to see you … *Let me tell you about the terrible year I have been having!*" Lily was stunned, but Bruce was completely oblivious to this, and out went any shred of respect Lily had for Bruce, an emotionally inept and self-obsessed manager.

One-up Wally Gary had been asked by a colleague about his expedition to the Carpathian Mountains. He had just finished relating his dangerous encounter with brown bears in Romania, when Wally's ego (his need to be always seen to be one-up) prompted him to jump in with an even better tale. He stole Gary's thunder with his (wholly imaginary) tale of wrestling with even more dangerous bears in the wild snows of Alaska. The conversation died, and with it another piece of One-up Wally's credibility.

Mr Wonderful Maurice was a self-declared 'treasure', and we were lucky to have his companionship, as he frequently told us. No cloud ever crossed Maurice's horizon, self-deprecation was an unknown visitor, and everything in Maurice's garden was rosy, or soon would be. In short, Maurice was 'Mr Wonderful' – a name he bestowed upon himself. After all, he was wonderful, and it would be a shame not to declare it, wouldn't it?

Delusional Des, the Conversation Killer Des was a serial failure in his other university roles – so now, with one final chance, he redoubled his self-promoting efforts, digging ever-deeper holes for himself, and epitomising the definition of madness: doing the same thing over and over, and expecting different results. Des turned every conversation into a monologue about himself, and showed his arcane but useless knowledge at every chance, heedless of the numbing effect of his chatter and digressions. Des eventually ran out of road, and was asked to leave the university, an unprecedented occurrence.

Narky Ned, the Legal Eagle The legal team had laboured long into the night to meet the deadline for an important international client. Justly proud of their endeavour, they presented an impeccable case for the partner's review. Narky Ned, the partner in question, was an inveterate crank and ignored the quality of their work and the earnestness of their endeavour, focusing instead on the pickiest of detail – the quality of the vellum. Running out of paper in the dead of night, the team had used expensive, high-grade paper. Narky Ned had hit a new low, and eventually the stunned silence gave way to mutterings of discontent, with the group vowing never again to work late. Ned later justified his criticism by pointing to the "fact" that his criticism was indeed "accurate", but ignoring the value of being "approximately right" rather than "precisely wrong".

Perfect Pete Pete was a perfectionist, and assumed all his colleagues should be too. There were no limits to his pursuit of perfection, no matter how trivial the work or its priority. As Pete debated just how many angels could dance on the head of a pin, metaphorically speaking, he failed to notice the frustration of his fellow professionals, who were keen to return to higher priorities. Enough wasn't enough for Pete, and he routinely took work home, devoting many unnecessary hours to 'gilding the lily'. Eventually, no colleagues would work with him, and he became an 'individual contributor', left to wonder how such devotion to perfection could possibly backfire.

Lax Larry Larry was hired as a business development director at a large professional services company. In the interview process, he showed strong values, seemingly aligned with the firm's own values. He had a high sense of community and teamwork and looked particularly strong in his ability to engage with others. His warmth was the deciding factor with the interview board. An emotional intelligence assessment indicated his scores were normal for the population, but one high score stood out: independence. The panel considered this to be a positive indicator, as Larry would need to venture abroad and travel widely on his own. Larry was hired, and quickly engaged with his own business development team, as well as the management team. However, before long, a rift between Larry and the managing partner became evident. The root cause was the managing partner's desire to have tightly controlled processes. Larry, on the other hand, felt he 'knew his game' and paid lip service to his boss's desire for standardisation. Sadly for Larry, a longer-than-expected lead time in landing new business made him vulnerable. Larry continued to resist challenges to his independence and had to leave the firm "by mutual agreement". High independence may be a good thing for a particular role, but runs counter to a firm's prevailing culture!

This last example reveals how EI can be used (and misused) in interview situations, and how even basic coaching or better management might have prevented Larry and the company parting ways, to the detriment of both parties. A tragedy is where a major cause is lost for a minor reason and, in this sense, Larry's loss is indeed tragic. Intelligent people, especially those with drive and a strong task focus, suffer similar tragic consequences. These consequences can often be avoided by understanding the nature of the person and by developing their emotional intelligence.

Sally Forth Take, for example, the case of Sally Forth, a highly productive analyst, very capable and driven. Her focus on the task, as distinct from any emphasis on building relationships, made her unpopular. Her brusque style (a result of the single-minded focus on achieving tasks) made her unpopular with her less productive colleagues – and even with management, who encountered only her demanding style and earnestness. When the opportunity occurred to meet the MD, Sally didn't hesitate to launch a barrage of well-meaning criticisms concerning the project and unfinished tasks. Her interest was in getting the project back on track. She harangued the MD, urging her to sort out the malingerers, and telling her what she "should" and "must" do. The MD knew of Sally's dedication and her sterling efforts, but the MD could not stomach this barrage. The meeting broke down in acrimony. Both sides were damaged, and it took the intervention of a more emotionally intelligent intermediary to rectify matters. (**Chapter 13** describes how to coach in such situations.)

How to Increase Emotional Intelligence in Professionals

Daniel Goleman emphasises that it's not a matter of "IQ versus emotional intelligence" – both have significance: "IQ tells you what level of cognitive complexity a person can manage in their job: you need high levels for top management, the professions, the sciences, while lower levels work fine in lower echelons. Emotional Intelligence (EI) sets apart which leaders, professionals, or scientists will be the best leaders."[35] Emotional intelligence is not the polar opposite of intelligence, nor is it the triumph of the heart over the head – it is the unique intersection of both intelligences.

Goleman explains what professionals can do to become more self-aware. Emotional intelligence competencies are learnable abilities, like emotional self-control. A professional can build on underlying EI components, such as self-management, and an effective way to develop self-awareness is to get constructive feedback from people one trusts to evaluate one's EI competencies. Goleman's landmark *Harvard Business Review* article identifies three abilities that distinguish the best leaders[36]:

1. self-awareness, which lets one knows one's own strengths and limits and also guides one's ethical "radar";
2. self-management, which lets you lead yourself effectively;
3. empathy, which lets you relate to and read other people more accurately.

All these abilities come together in the act of leadership.

According to Goleman, psychology is important in understanding the needs of employees and clients. For employees, how a leader makes them feel plays a large role in their level of motivation and commitment, and even nudges their brain in or out of the productive zone for the cognitive abilities they bring to the job. For clients, how they feel about their interactions with the people in the organisation determines how they feel about the company as a whole.

Conversely, losing control of one's unwanted emotions can make the manager and the professional ineffective; as the classic scholar Epictetus said: "Any person capable of angering you becomes your master." Emotions are not easily disguised, and people can read each other with ease. As Malcolm Gladwell says:"The face is not a secondary billboard for our internal feelings. It is an equal partner in the emotional process."[37]

Writer and civil rights activist Audre Lorde claims that "Our feelings are our most genuine paths to knowledge."[38] With knowledge so central to the professional's career, this is a warning worth heeding, even if it cannot be scientifically proven. As Karen Stone McCown *et al.* write: "Experiencing one's self in a conscious manner – that is, gaining self-knowledge – is an integral part of learning."[39] Mayer and Salovey similarly claim that: "People high in emotional intelligence are expected to progress more quickly through the abilities designated and to master more of them."[40]

> *"Experience is not what happens to you – it's how you interpret what happens to you."*
>
> Aldous Huxley

While we cannot really control what happens to us, we can try to control our reactions, and thereby re-frame the situation to our benefit. Self-improvement champion Dale Carnegie was echoing the wisdom of the ages when he pointed out that fear is based on our *perception* of fear: "You can conquer almost any fear if you will only make up your mind to do so. For remember, fear doesn't exist anywhere except in the mind."[41]

Daniel Goleman argues that if you can't manage yourself, you won't be able to manage someone else. In many ways, the ability to manage oneself – to have self-awareness and self-regulation – is the basis for managing others.

> *"Better keep yourself clean and bright; you are the window through which you must see the world."*
>
> George Bernard Shaw

Professionals, unfairly or otherwise, have a reputation of seeing themselves as superior in many respects to the layman. Nathaniel Branden suggests a way forward for any such professionals: "Persons of high self-esteem are not driven to make themselves superior to others; they do not seek to prove their value by measuring themselves against a comparative standard. Their joy is being who they are, not in being better than someone else."[42]

Emotional Intelligence and Different Professions

Steven Stein and his collaborator Howard Book conducted many substantial studies on emotional intelligence and different professions, with initially surprising findings.[43] For example, they found that 'star' fighter pilots in the US Navy (think *Top Gun*) scored high in emotional intelligence, and were especially impressive in their lack of arrogance, over-confidence or blind faith in their own abilities. Because they knew they were good, it seems, they had no need to exaggerate. These 'top guns' also rated highly in reality-testing (the objective evaluation of situations and oneself) and in impulse control, vital attributes of emotional intelligence that can make the difference in combat.

Tim Turner, quoted by Stein, discovered that the distinguishing factor of star police leaders was social responsibility (the ability to see the greater good).[44] Other defining factors, in order, were: problem-solving (defining the problems, generating solutions and acting on them), self-actualisation (ambitious goal-setting) and interpersonal relationships (an expected outcome of high emotional intelligence, of course).

Irene Taylor discovered that star litigators in Canada, rather than being "pit bull" types, were sensitive, private introverts. They were "fiercely independent self-starters", but were driven by social responsibility rather than money.[45] Taylor also found that top deal-makers in the legal profession had high levels of self-awareness, really knowing their strengths and weaknesses. They also had high "raw intelligence", a very strong drive to succeed and emotional intelligence scores that were well above average.

Dr Dana Ackley's research has discovered that the defining factors for dentists running a practice were emotional self-awareness, reality-testing, assertiveness and self-actualisation. Interestingly, her study of physicians found that doctors and their patients (the general population) had similar scores on EI, and that patients rated more highly doctors whom they perceived to be "happy"; it would seem that the old adage of "behaviour breeds behaviour" is correct.

Furthermore, a major study of school principals in the US revealed that the better ones scored higher on self-awareness, self-actualisation, empathy, interpersonal relationships, flexibility, problem-solving and impulse control.[46] A study of star salespeople by Stein found similar characteristics.[47]

The Center for Creative Leadership, a highly respected US organisation, found that emotional intelligence accounted for approximately 28% of leadership performance. To become a better leader, focus on four pillars:

1. Be centred and grounded: stay stable, keep in touch with reality, know your strengths and weaknesses, balance your work and personal life – manage the tensions.
2. Take action: use EI to reduce your tendency to procrastinate, for example. Know the typical barriers to action in yourself (e.g. over-analysis) or others (e.g. lack of assertiveness).
3. Have a participatory management style: simply include others in your decision-making. You can still make the final decision, but let it be based on inputs from others. This is especially true in managing professionals and other smart people, who have the ability to make a contribution and who expect to do so. Every leader has two ears and one mouth, and should use them in those proportions!
4. Be tough-minded: use EI to avoid making poor decisions – have empathy (not just sympathy), and keep the greater good and end goal in mind.

Emotional Intelligence Factors and Work Success for Different Professions

Steven Stein and his colleagues assessed the EI and self-rated work success of 4,888 professionals of various types in North America.[48] While the findings are based on estimates, the sample size suggests that these findings can provide useful guidelines, if read in context. For example, one might expect high-performing engineers to be better at reality-testing than low-performers, but it turns out that almost all of the engineers score highly in reality-testing, so that itself is not a defining factor. Rather, it is other skills, such as self-actualisation, happiness, optimism, empathy and inter-personal relationships that make the defining difference: in other words, it is the engineer who can combine technical skills with these emotional and social abilities who succeeds the most. Accountants are often caricatured as cool and conservative: the most valuable retain their accounting skills and enhance their ability in interpersonal relationships and emotional self-awareness.

Emotional intelligence, unlike some other forms of intelligence, can actually be improved significantly (principally through self-awareness and consequent action, such as developing impulse control or listening skills). In fact, EI usually increases with age ('maturity'), by about 1% per decade, from age 25 to 65, according to Stein, and this process can be heightened or accelerated. Developing both sides of the person (left and right brain) in this way is critical to achieving high performance, and especially in turning 'geeks' into 'stars'. It is, of course, a goal of this book, to help professionals to maximise their potential by releasing the power of their multiple intelligences, not just their raw cognitive ability. As the research discussed here shows, this has the wonderful benefit of also improving levels of happiness and self-actualisation ('becoming their best self') in professionals and other smart people.

DIFFERENT PROFESSIONS AND MOST SIGNIFICANT FACTORS IN WORK SUCCESS

Occupation/Profession	Emotional Intelligence Factors
Overall	Self-actualisation
	Happiness
	Optimism
	Self-regard
	Assertiveness
Accountants	Problem-solving
	Interpersonal relationships
	Happiness
	Self-regard
	Emotional self-awareness
Engineers	Self-actualisation
	Happiness
	Optimism
	Empathy
	Interpersonal relationships
Lawyers	Self-actualisation
	Happiness
	Stress tolerance
	Assertiveness
	Social responsibility
Physicians/Surgeons	Independence
	Stress tolerance
	Empathy
	Impulse control
	Flexibility

(Continued)

Occupation/Profession	Emotional Intelligence Factors
Psychologists	Reality testing
	Independence
	Happiness
	Stress tolerance
	Flexibility
Management consultants	Assertiveness
	Emotional self-awareness
	Reality-testing
	Self-actualisation
	Happiness
Marketing Professionals	Optimism
	Reality testing
	Independence
	Impulse control
	Social responsibility
Senior managers	Self-regard
	Happiness
	Interpersonal relationships
	Reality-testing
	Self-actualisation
Salespeople – Insurance	Assertiveness
	Self-regard
	Happiness
	Stress tolerance
	Self-actualisation
Graphic designers	Flexibility
	Self-actualisation
Nurses	Self-actualisation
	Independence

"Science has learned that if you are tuned out of your own emotions, you will be poor at reading them in other people. And if you can't fine-tune your own actions – keeping yourself from blowing up or falling to pieces, marshalling positive drives – you'll be poor at handling the people you deal with. Star leaders are stars at leading themselves, first."

Peter Salovey, President, Yale University

Conclusion

All information to the brain comes through our senses and when this information is accompanied by overwhelming emotion or stress, instinct can take over the ability to act rationally: people will be limited to a primitive flight, fight or freeze response. To choose the right course of action, you need to be able to bring emotions into balance at will.

Memory is also strongly linked to emotion. By learning to use the emotional part of the brain as well as the rational, a professional will not only expand the range of available choices in responding to an event, but will also factor emotional memory into that decision-making, helping prevent making the same mistakes again. This is especially important in dealing with people, as it is hard for a professional to recover from real or implied emotional transgressions, such as personal slights, outbursts of temper or social gaffes.

The deepest human connections are formed not through cool logic but through warm emotions. Logic need not exclude emotion, but should work with it in a conscious way. Effective leaders are masters of all the classical elements of rhetoric, as explained by Aristotle many centuries ago:

> "You can reach people through *logos* or logic, by appealing to their sense of what is rational. You can use *pathos*, appealing to their emotions, or you can make an argument based on their sense of values or *ethos*."[49]

Professionals, with their gift of intellectual intelligence, have an invaluable opportunity – and a compelling need – to add to their emotional intelligence. Indeed, it is argued here that their progress beyond standard professional competence into the higher echelons of many professions depends much more on emotional intelligence than on cognitive ability.

The wonderful discovery is that developing EI not only enhances the professional's happiness but is also professionally rewarding. As one becomes more self-aware and empathetic, clients and colleagues respond in kind, setting off a rewarding spiral of happiness and professional achievement. In many ways, the science attaching itself to emotional intelligence reaffirms ancient wisdoms that happiness begets happiness and that happiness cannot be pursued – it must *ensue*. The smart professional will first look in the mirror, and start the journey to personal and professional happiness by first knowing themselves better. As Jean de la Fontaine said in 1679: "He who knows the universe and does not know himself knows nothing."

ENDNOTES

[1] Peter Salovey and John D. Mayer, "Emotional intelligence" (1990) 9(3) *Imagination, Cognition, and Personality* 185–211.
[2] Ram Charan and Geoffrey Colvin, "Why CEOs Fail" *Fortune Magazine*, 21 June 1999.
[3] David Kirch, "Better Profits through Better People: The Benefits of Emotional Intelligence in Accounting Firms" (August 2001) *The CPA Journal* 60–61.

[4] Dale Carnegie, *How to Win Friends and Influence People* (Simon & Schuster, 1981).

[5] Joshua Freedman, *At the Heart of Leadership: How to Get Results with Emotional Intelligence* (Six Seconds Publishing, 2007).

[6] John D. Mayer, Peter Salovey and David Caruso, *Emotional Intelligence Tests* (Multi-Health Systems, 2002).

[7] Hans Eysenck, with L.J. Kamin, *Intelligence: The Battle for the Mind* (Wiley, 1981); published in the US as *The Intelligence Controversy*.

[8] F.J. Landy, "Some historical and scientific issues related to research on emotional intelligence" (2005) Vol. 26 lssue 4 *Journal of Organizational Behavior* 411–424.

[9] G. Matthews, M. Zeidner, R.D. Roberts, *Emotional Intelligence: Science and Myth* (MIT Press, 2004).

[10] John Antonakis, N.M. Ashkanasy, M. Dasborough, "Does leadership need emotional intelligence?" (2009) 20(2) *The Leadership Quarterly* 247–261.

[11] Daniel Goleman, *Emotional Intelligence: Why It Can Matter More than IQ* (Bantam 1995).

[12] Stephen R. Covey, *The Speed of Trust* (Free Press/Simon & Schuster, 2006).

[13] David Wechsler, "Non-intellective factors in general intelligence"(1940) 37 *Psychological Bulletin* 444–445.

[14] Howard Gardner, *Frames of Mind* (Basic Books, 1983).

[15] Wayne Payne, "A study of emotion: developing emotional intelligence; self-integration; relating to fear, pain and desire (theory, structure of reality, problem-solving, contraction/expansion, tuning in/coming out/letting go)" (doctoral dissertation, University of Cincinnati, OH., 1984).

[16] Reuven Bar-On, *Bar-On Emotional Quotient EQ-I Inventory Technical Manual* (Multi-Health Systems, 1997).

[17] Peter Salovey and John D. Mayer, "Emotional intelligence"(1990) 9(3) *Imagination, Cognition, and Personality* 185–211.

[18] Daniel Goleman, *Emotional Intelligence: Why It Can Matter More Than IQ* (Bantam, 1995).

[19] Malcolm Gladwell, *Blink: The Power of Thinking without Thinking* (Penguin Books, 2006).

[20] John D. Mayer, Peter Salovey and David Caruso, *Emotional Intelligence Tests* (Multi-Health Systems, 2002).

[21] *Ibid.*

[22] Daniel Goleman, *Emotional Intelligence: Why It Can Matter More Than IQ* (Bantam, 1995).

[23] Daniel Goleman, R. Boyatzis and A. McKee, *Primal Leadership: Realizing the Power of Emotional Intelligence* (Harvard Business School Press, 2002).

[24] Daniel Goleman, *Emotional Intelligence: Why It Can Matter More than IQ* (Bantam, 1995).

[25] Peter Salovey and John D. Mayer, "Emotional intelligence"(1990) 9(3) *Imagination, Cognition, and Personality* 185–211.

[26] Martyn Newman, *Emotional Capitalists: The New Leaders* (Wiley, 2007).

[27] John D. Mayer, Peter Salovey and David Caruso, *Emotional Intelligence Tests* (Multi-Health Systems, 2002).

[28] Daniel Goleman, *Emotional Intelligence: Why It Can Matter More than IQ* (Bantam, 1995).

[29] James Pennebaker, *Emotion, Disclosure, and Health* (American Psychological Association, 1995).

[30] Martyn Newman, *Emotional Capitalists: The New Leaders* (Wiley, 2007).

[31] *Ibid.*

[32] Martin Seligman, *Learned Optimism: How to Change Your Mind and Your Life* (Knopf, 1991).

[33] Stephen R. Covey, *The Speed of Trust* (Free Press/Simon & Schuster, 2006).

[34] Robert Sutton, *The No Asshole Rule: Building a Civilized Workplace and Surviving One That Isn't* (Warner, 2007).

[35] Daniel Goleman, *Emotional Intelligence: Why It Can Matter More Than IQ* (Bantam, 1995).

[36] Daniel Goleman, "Leadership That Gets Results" (March–April, 2000) *Harvard Business Review* 78–80.

[37] Malcolm Gladwell, *Blink: the Power of Thinking without Thinking* (Little, Brown, 2005).

[38] Audre Lorde, *Sister, Outsider: Essays and Poems* (Random House, 2011).

[39] Karen Stone McCown *et al.*, *Self-Science: The Emotional Intelligence Curriculum* (Six Seconds, 1988).

[40] Peter Salovey and John D. Mayer, "Emotional intelligence" (1990) 9(3) *Imagination, Cognition, and Personality* 185–211.

[41] Dale Carnegie, *How to Win Friends and Influence People* (Simon & Schuster, 1981).

[42] Nathaniel Branden, *Honouring the Self: The Psychology of Self-Esteem* (Bantam, 1985).

[43] Steven J. Stein and Howard E. Book, *The EQ Edge* (Wiley, 2006).

[44] Timothy Turner, "Identifying Emotional Intelligence Competencies Differentiating FBI National Academy Graduates" (unpublished dissertation, University of Virginia, 2006).

[45] Irene Taylor, "Canada's Top 25 Litigators" (July/August 2002) *Lexpert Journal* 64–89.

[46] Robert H. Bardach, "Leading Schools with Emotional Intelligence: A Study of the Degree of Emotional Intelligence" (unpublished dissertation, 2008).

[47] Steven J. Stein, *Make Your Workplace Great: The 7 Keys to an Emotionally Intelligent Workplace* (Wiley, 2007).

[48] *Ibid.*

[49] Alan G. Gross and Arthur E. Walzer, *Re-reading Aristotle's Rhetoric* (Southern Illinois University Press, 2000).

Chapter 13

Coaching and Mentoring Professionals at Work

Hannah Carney and Dermot Duff

The real voyage of discovery consists not in seeking new lands but in seeing with new eyes.

Marcel Proust

Introduction

While high-achieving professionals can certainly think for themselves, they still need help in dealing with intellectual 'blind spots' and 'emotional' issues. It is at certain crucial moments – career transitions, turning points, interpersonal conflicts, unexpected failures, client encounters, etc – that they can be helped either to take the correct turn at the fork in the road or gain enough self-belief to meet new challenges, such as business development, public speaking, client engagement, or adopting new technologies.

This chapter, written with Hannah Carney of Hannah Carney & Associates, focuses on developing professionals' potential through coaching, through mentoring, management, and fundamentally through meaningful conversations. Highly qualified in this area, and formerly a partner in a leading law firm, Hannah explains her approach as a means of helping talented professionals flourish.

Following on from leadership development, as discussed in **Chapter 3**, the emphasis here is on practical means of mentoring and coaching to unleash (or rediscover) inner drive and latent talent. A separate chapter has been dedicated to building self-confidence in professionals (see **Chapter 11**).

A good manager (or mentor or coach) will make professional staff see *what they can be* rather than what they are now. A good manager must see people in terms of their future potential, not their past performance. Additionally, a good manager will pose powerful questions that provoke insight, enthusiasm, discovery and action. Managing in this sense is about 'partnering' in a process that should be thought-provoking and creative, and that inspires them to maximise their own potential.

Despite the enormous benefits of coaching, some managers are reluctant to forsake their conventional supervisory role and intrude into what they perceive as 'personal' space. Many claim they simply do not have the time for such coaching. However, managing without coaching or mentoring is simply business administration; it is not effective management at all. While coaching or mentoring can, and should, happen within agreed boundaries, being 'safe' rather than 'intrusive', time spent in coaching will invariably be well spent, avoiding a host of downstream issues. It will often also provide tremendous satisfaction to the manager/coach and to the client/professional. Moments of authentic engagement developed through trust and respect can illuminate a career, placing milestones on life's journey.

Put more simply, it's good to talk, and often the mere opportunity to share doubts or express hopes makes issues evaporate.

For professionals who are 'difficult' to deal with, encouragement may be found in Steve Jobs's observation that it is often the 'difficult' staff who "make a dent in the Universe":

> "Here's to the crazy ones, the misfits, the rebels, the troublemakers, the round pegs in square holes, the ones who see differently. They are not fond of rules. Because they are the ones crazy enough to think they can change the world, they are often the ones who do!"[1]

The Heart of the Matter: Crucial Conversations – Coaching and Mentoring

Whether coaching, mentoring or managing professionals, real dialogue is essential: the interface between people occurs during those 'crucial conversations' that ultimately lead to success or failure. Crucial conversations help people get to the heart of the matter and understand the fundamental, often obscured, deeper causes. In other chapters, the role of personality in such conversations has been explored, and approaches such as transactional analysis suggested as means of having more productive dialogue. In this chapter, this approach is taken further, by using coaching and mentoring techniques and process to enhance the performance of professionals. In that context, the intervention can be provided by an external professional coach or by the professional's manager, subject to certain conditions, as below. While we define here the difference between coaching and mentoring, the essential point is that positively framed 'crucial conversations' make the critical difference for professionals and their organisations.

The word 'mentor' has some of its origins in Greek Mythology. Before setting out on his epic journey, Odysseus entrusts the education of his son, Telemachus, to his old and faithful friend, Mentor:

"For you I have some good news – if only you will accept it ..."

"Oh Stranger," heedful Telemachus replied, "Indeed I will. You've counselled me with so much kindness; like a father to a son; I won't forget a word."[2]

Mentoring

Over the years, the term 'mentor' has gradually become associated with the idea of **a more experienced person acting as a guide to a younger**

or less-experienced person. As renowned authority David Clutterbuck expresses it:

> "The Mentor helps the Mentee 'step outside the box' of his/her job and personal circumstances so that they can look at it together. It is like standing in front of a mirror with someone else, who can help you see things that have become too familiar for you to notice."[3]

Coaching

A 'coach', by contrast, will generally not advise directly and will often not even be a subject-matter expert. The term 'coach' is derived from the French word "to transport or carry", and similarly infers helping a person to get to their desired destination by finding their own solutions.

Coaching is a broad-based, one-to-one development relationship. For the purposes of this chapter, it is *that part of a relationship in which one person is primarily dedicated to serving the long-term development of effectiveness and self-generation in the other*. The chapter is written to support anyone, regardless of profession, who is supporting the development and leadership of others, whether as a coach, mentor, a manager, or consultant.

In any of the relationships described here, the coaching process can take place in informal interactions – say, meeting by the water cooler for a brief exchange. The descriptions of the coaching and mentoring process in this chapter, however, will be based on the assumption that most 'high-level' coaching takes place in conversations that are dedicated to that purpose. The model presented, then, is one that will guide any professional in structuring conversations dedicated to the development of others.

The most challenging of the specific situations discussed here involves conversations within a supervisory relationship, where both parties must be able to move the authority differences to the background in order to maintain a clear focus on the goals and needs of the client.

Getting Behind the Labels: Mentoring Versus Coaching

While mentoring and coaching skills overlap, there are some key differences to bear in mind, as shown in the following figure:

MENTORING VERSUS COACHING[4]

Mentoring	Coaching
• Generally an ongoing relationship is required by the mentee.	• Relationship generally for a set duration.
• Meetings can be informal and as required by the mentee in terms of advice and guidance.	• Short-term and focused on specific development areas/issues.
• Takes a long-term and broader view of the person.	• Generally more structured, with scheduled and regular meetings.

Mentoring	Coaching
• Mentor is usually more experienced than the mentee and can bring that experience to bear by way of suggestive direction. In this way, knowledge and experience can be passed on and 'doors helped open' to out-of-reach opportunities.	• Coaching does not require the coach to have direct experience of their client's occupational role, unless the coaching is specific and skills-focused.
• Focus on career, professional and personal development.	• Focus is generally on development/issues at work.
• Agenda is set by the mentee, with the mentor providing support and guidance to prepare them for future roles.	• Coaching is, in general, non-directive and the client discovers their own answers and solutions.
• Mentoring revolves more around developing the mentee professionally.	• The agenda is focused on achieving specific, immediate goals.
	• Coaching revolves generally around specific situations, development areas and issues.

Effective mentoring crosses over with coaching in terms of facilitative and conversational skills; however, a mentor focuses on the longer term with their mentee, in addition to immediate skills development and/or problem-solving. While clearly the mentor is not a 'friend' (although friendship and mutual respect is hugely important), to ensure they remain independent and objective, clear professional and ethical boundaries (similar to actual contracts) are essential to have in place.

Timothy Gallwey's 1974 book, *The Inner Game of Tennis*,[5] laid the formal foundations for executive coaching. He astutely noted that, in tennis, "the opponent in one's own head is more formidable than the one on the other side of the net". Psychologists and coaches are now common in sport, and many, such as Bob Rotella, mind-coach to champion golfers like Phil Mickelson and Padraig Harrington, enjoy worldwide acclaim. Curiously, the world of business has been slower to accept the benefits of coaching until recently, but now executive coaching is no longer seen as frivolous or superfluous. In executive coaching, Graham Alexander, Jonathon Passmore, John Whitmore, David Clutterbuck, Doug Silsbee, David Lassiter, Nancy Kline and Peter Hawkins are among the leading authorities, and this book is indebted to them for their contributions.

The good news for managers attempting to coach or mentor staff is that they can continue to 'be themselves' (in fact, they must remain authentic): the real need, when coaching or mentoring, is to develop listening and questioning skills, and to generate sufficiently deep reserves of personal calm and optimism. To get the best out of people, one must first believe that the best is in there somewhere. It can be helpful to accept philosopher (and holocaust survivor) Viktor Frankl's assertion that: "Man's search for meaning is the primary motivation in his life and not a secondary rationalization of instinctual drives."[6]

At the same time, as well as being empathetic and optimistic, a coach/mentor must provide a reality check and help set appropriate challenges and accountability. It is not a matter of simply being 'nice'. As Tim Gallwey has explained, "the opponent who stretches you is really your friend: someone who taps the ball back to you provides little help."[7]

Much successful coaching or mentoring depends on creating a heightened level of awareness and a fundamental core of trust and safety. An attitude of blame cannot enter the relationship. Blame generally evokes defensiveness, and defensiveness reduces awareness: this is not usually helpful in any way.

Preparing to Coach or Mentor: Achieving a Heightened Mindfulness/Presence

Mindfulness is the state of being aware of our own sensations, thoughts, feelings and judgements. As we become more self-aware, we learn to identify and acknowledge our own habits of mind and so prevent ourselves from becoming trapped by them; as we see and accept them, they tend to dissipate, giving us a clearer view of what is around us.

All human experience comprises three levels: cognitive, emotional and sensational. When we bring our attention into the granular experience of each of these levels, we become more alive, more sensitive, and better able to identify our habits and unconscious tendencies as they arise.

Our habits are held in place by attachments and aversions. We can sense these within us and learn to intervene with our habits before they lead to behaviours that undermine our goals. We can recognise certain habits that impede our mindfulness as coaches or mentors: self-judgement, social identity, projections, emotional triggers, routines, distractions and expert mind. Learning to recognise these through self-awareness and self-monitoring is essential.

Mindful self-awareness is the essential starting point in coaching or mentoring well. This heightened consciousness provides the best platform from which to coach or mentor others. It is unbiased by our own agendas. It allows us to be aware of the nuances of the other person. It is open-minded and accepting. In preparation for coaching or mentoring, we can cultivate mindfulness through:

- *Self-observation of our habits and tendencies*, becoming intimately familiar with how they arise, and thus able to intervene with ourselves to choose a more effective response. Self-observation is critical in building sustainable change and furthers this through a learning rather than a performance agenda.
- *Other practices,* such as meditation, centering ourselves (*simply existing, now*), physical and creative activities, experiencing nature.
- *Committing to our own learning process,* such that we are in the learning business ourselves. If we want to coach others, it is wise to be coached ourselves.
- *Building our own accountability* so the people we are coaching or mentoring can be assured of our qualities as coaches/mentors.

Opening the Psychological Window

Simply put, a prime function of coaching, mentoring or indeed managing is to help the professional see 'the man in the mirror', any 'blind spots' or, more especially, any unrealised areas of potential. This is sometimes referred to as opening the 'JoHari' window, so that one can see the blind spot that is in plain view to all – except oneself. In this model, there are four windows: the blind spot 'window' is where others can readily see you as you are, but you cannot see the full picture – some spots are blind to you. However, a good coach or mentor can help open this window and reveal, in a constructive way, that which has been hidden from you, perhaps because of an aspect of your personality or simply lack of self-awareness. The hidden window frame is your private space, with elements known only to you, not others. The final window frames are self-evident, where all is visible or, alternatively, unknown.

A prime use of the JoHari window is to selectively and judiciously open the windows, revealing something of ourselves, so that we deepen the relationship and build trust. In this case, the main use is to open the window and shed light on blind spots.

THE JoHARI WINDOW

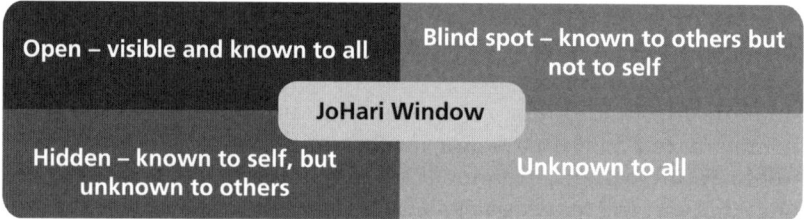

Establishing Context: Today Management and Coaching are Interlinked

Traditionally, management had a dominant role at work, and could specify the necessary work. This was the industrial era of Frederick Taylor's 'Scientific Management', and was successful in managing standardised, physical work. As work became less physical and more cognitive, this approach gave way to the more participative 'Human Relations Model', pioneered as a result of the Hawthorne experiments, which showed that workers respond better to participative styles of management. This, in turn, was supplanted in many industries by Japanese-style 'world class' total quality management, with its emphasis on teamwork and continuous process improvement. With the increasing need for innovation and change, Peter Senge's 'Open Systems Model' (see the section on the Learning Organisation in **Chapter 8**) shaped much of the current approach to management, emphasising shared destiny, proactive transformation, innovation and collaboration. These various models of management are illustrated below:

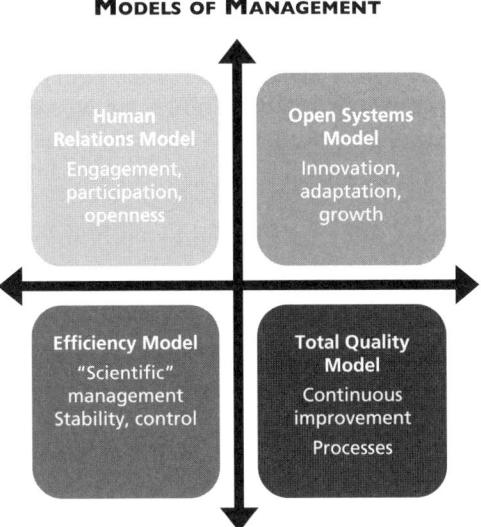

MODELS OF MANAGEMENT

The manager today is expected to be an innovator, power broker, producer, visionary, co-ordinator, monitor and, indeed, facilitator or mentor. All of this requires a huge breadth and depth of skills, as portrayed below:

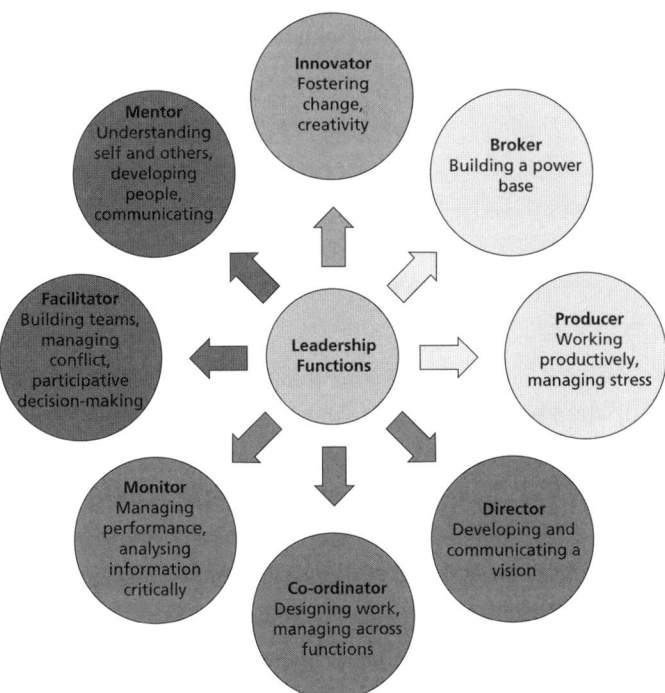

THE MANY LEADERSHIP FUNCTIONS OF A MANAGER TODAY

The manager, therefore, must have many skills and attributes, especially in leading professionals and other smart people. However, any attribute carried to excess can then become a liability. Having excess commitment, for instance, can turn one's zeal into fanaticism. The diagram below is intended to illustrate how, for example, initially positive values can harden into rigid dogmatism on the one hand, or slide into chaos on the other. Similarly, one's motivating values can sometimes produce apathy in others, or even outright belligerence. For example, the value of discipline helps ensure that tasks get implemented, and those who hold that value will be motivated accordingly. However, if discipline is enforced rigorously on others, they will not usually find that value of discipline motivating. Rather, they could well find themselves indifferent to it, or even rebel against it. On the other dimension, while discipline avoids chaos, an excess of discipline will harden into rigidity or dogma.

WHEN VALUES DISTORT INTO LIABILITIES:
THE EXAMPLE OF EXCESSIVE DISCIPLINE

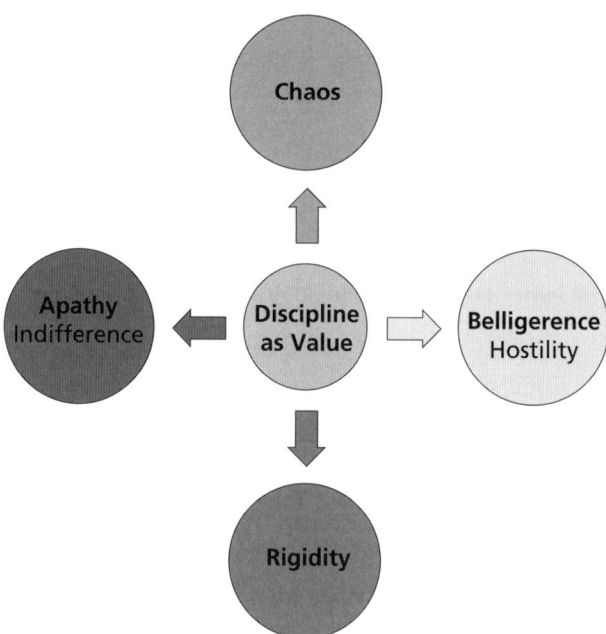

Similarly, regarding leadership effectiveness, it can be inferred that excessive preoccupation with innovation, for example, can be wasteful. Over-concern with coaching or mentoring can engender soft-heartedness, or at least the perception of such.

Whether coaching, mentoring or managing, all involve helping people realise their potential by seeing their blind spots and to recognise when their strengths become liabilities. The accountant who must always be 'right' and can find no place in the balance sheet for 'human capital' may provide a technically correct service, but may be limited in effectiveness as an executive or manager. The lawyer who indulges his or her professional scepticism stifles progress. The engineer who will only attend to the latest in technology wastes resources and neglects present reality. In that sense, managing, mentoring and coaching are all mainly concerned with issues of perception, confidence and emotion, rather than simple cognitive ability.

Commencing the Process: Creating a Thinking Environment – The Kline Method of Attentive Listening

For better decisions in a coaching or mentoring relationship, especially in unclear situations – perhaps where an analysis of the situation is difficult, or where complexity is obscuring the reality of the moment – a deep approach may be needed. This is particularly true if one hopes to get real commitment to the agreed actions and the prospect of a 'shift' in behaviour or performance. Deep discussion is needed to realise the underlying *assumptions* (particularly those self-limiting assumptions that inhibit action) and to evoke personal commitment by the professional to a challenging goal or behavioural shift.

A relatively simple approach, originally developed by Nancy Kline, has proven effective, both in one-to-one and group sessions.[8] Though simple in concept ('listen attentively'), it is difficult in practice. This is because there is a common tendency to fill conversational voids and to be seen to make one's mark by making a 'contribution' to the conversation (often in the form of an interruption, and invariably as we prepare our own response or riposte). Professionals who are habitually engaged in advisory or directive behaviours need to be very aware of this when commencing a coaching or mentoring process. The Kline style of attentive listening is also helpful in demonstrating respect for people.

Kline's premise is that the quality of the decisions we make and all of the results we get are founded on the quality of the thinking we do first. To get better results, take time to create the conditions to enable us to do the highest quality thinking. It is always a 'cumulative experience'.

KLINE'S TEN COMPONENTS OF A THINKING ENVIRONMENT

- Attention – Listening with respect and without interruption.
- Incisive questions – Probing and removing flawed assumptions that limit ability to think clearly and creatively.
- Ease – Offering freedom from internal rush or urgency (or embarrassment).
- Appreciation – Demonstrating acknowledgement of a person's qualities or contribution.
- Encouragement – Giving courage to generate ideas, especially by moving beyond internal competition.
- Equality – Providing equal opportunity to all, treating each as thinking peers.
- Feelings – Allowing sufficient emotional release to restore thinking.
- Information – Supplying the facts. Dismantling denial.
- Diversity – Welcoming divergent thinking and diverse identities.
- Place – Creating a physical environment that tells people: they matter.

The three *fundamental* tenets of these 10 Components are:

- Giving Attention,
- Creating Ease,
- Affording Equality.

In Particular Coaching/Mentoring: 'Crucial Conversations'

Giving Attention Distractions are everywhere; temptation to lose attention abounds. And yet we know that focusing on what someone is saying is the key to meaningful discussion and to successful decisions. Nothing is more distracting than knowing that someone is not focused on what we're saying. Typically, as someone is talking, we are rehearsing ahead of time what we will say or pretending to be intrigued while actually just waiting to get our own point across. However, investing those extra seconds (and minutes, if necessary) make a real difference: "listening to ignite the mind" (as Nancy Kline says) can kick-start great interventions.

Creating Ease Allowing people uninterrupted time to share their thoughts (and stay with those thoughts, even in moments of awkward silence) lets their thinking to go further. This seems easy, until you think of the eye-contact avoidance that accompanies the 30-second journey in a hotel lift or the seemingly interminable two seconds between traffic lights going green and the car ahead moving!

Affording Equality Each individual must be given dignity and respect. Treating people 'equally' is often confused with treating people 'as all the same'; equality and equalness are very different concepts.

To apply the Kline principles in a group or individual setting, here are some simple steps to better "coaching" of professionals who are having difficulty reaching their potential:

- Set up the conversation or meeting in a way that is consistent with as many of the 10 Kline components as possible (especially the three foundational principles).
- Start with a well-crafted question (whether it's structuring your agenda with a question or posting a question for the group or individual to work on). Why? Because questions stimulate thinking.
- Set up a positive and appreciative environment, e.g. simply by asking what's going well or framing a question positively (e.g. what would enhance our client service? Rather than: what are the issues with our client service?). We know from research that more of the brain functions in the presence of positive focus and praise than problems focus and criticism. Experience shows this creates generative thinking.

It sounds straightforward – and it is. There's an art to doing it really well and that only comes with practice.

COACHING GROUPS: THE **CLEAR** CONVERSATION MODEL

Professor Peter Hawkins is an organisational strategist and team coach, and author of *Leadership Team Coaching*.[9] I have watched him heal a very dysfunctional consulting firm, full of otherwise smart professionals. Noting the road blocks, he looked for ways to unblock critical conversations, using the 'CLEAR' model. CLEAR is an acronym and it is based on the learning model described in **Chapter 5**:

C what's the contract for the conversation? In other words, what commitments are both parties making with regard to the quality and sincerity of the engagement?

L is about listening, really listening, without interruptions or judgement.

E stands for exploring, but also evidence – what's the data available to support positions taken and opinions ventured?

A is for action and accountability – the outcome of the conversation.

R is about reflecting on the experience and learning from it.

In this opening section, the fundamentals of coaching and mentoring (and related areas of management) have been described, with approaches and component elements outlined. In the remainder of this chapter, Hannah Carney, originally a partner in a large law firm and now an executive coach, outlines her approach to coaching/mentoring and shares some of her practical experience in coaching and mentoring professionals.

The question of how best to enable professionals to think differently has been an ongoing theme in Hannah's professional career, in which she moved from the technical practice of litigation law into the more intangible area of leadership and team development. Having trained in coaching and mentoring (and experienced the processes from both sides of the table), she has come to appreciate that both coaching and mentoring must be non-directive and experiential, as well as client-focused, with an 'inside out' approach, enabling the client to find their own solutions. To get the best results, either process needs to be positioned and implemented on a cumulative basis to enable progress, accountability and positive momentum. Her focus currently is in helping senior professionals, especially legal and accounting partners, achieve their potential and lead fulfilled lives, professionally and personally.

HOW TO COACH OR MENTOR PROFESSIONALS

By Hannah Carney

For much of my career as a lawyer and executive coach, I have wrestled with the idea of how best to truly enable people (especially those smart professionals who have a well-developed capacity to think for themselves) to think differently, creatively and effectively. How, indeed, to get such people to think differently in situations of challenge, difficulty and complexity? And not just to 'think' but to act and behave differently, possibly even becoming fundamentally different.

Professionals most often need support when faced with career or personal transitions, and the list below highlights some of the most common situations:

- very demanding client expectations;
- team leadership challenges, especially dealing with conflict, stress or 'difficult' people;
- partnership break-up;
- joining a partnership as a lateral hire;
- promotion and otherwise 'moving to the next level';
- team and performance management;
- internal organisational politics;
- redundancy and other career transitions.

When professionals seek help or guidance from a coach or mentor, what are they really looking for? Yes, they want the 'top tips' and the 'tools', but the real issue is what will be the catalyst that ignites the shift or change? What is it that connects with the professional's experience, thinking and being that will enable the start of transformation?

The fundamentals that provide a strong foundation for coaching, mentoring and similar work are as follows:

- the ability to create a safe environment that facilitates dialogue;
- good questioning and understanding;
- an attitude of active and genuine interest, curiosity and concern;
- the art of deep listening to the experience of the other;
- the ability to use the 'power' of silence to allow messages sink in or deep understanding to emerge;
- the ability to be truly attentive and present in the whole experience;
- empathy and compassion.

Mapping the Professional Career Journey

If we take a helicopter-style overview (a 'balcony perspective') of any professional's career progression, it becomes evident, as with any life journey, that there are usually well-defined stages and 'cycles'. It can be useful to be aware of these typical stages in order to deal with issues of career transition, and to proactively manage one's career – common issues that arise in coaching and mentoring relationships.

In recent years, professional life has become more complicated and uncertain. Modern organisations and partnerships no longer offer lifetime employment – and neither do graduates wish to stay in any one company for very long. Straightforward ladders of career progression are no longer evident.

Client demands, expectations and business pressures have increased, but client loyalty has decreased. Competitiveness, conflict and change are all very real features of professional life.

Careers, therefore, need to be 'self-managing', with professionals actively considering their own 'personal brand and value proposition', i.e. what it is that they contribute to their organisation. Professionals need to think actively, carefully and independently about:

- their own overall career development and strategy, with the requisite amount of flexibility;
- connecting with and establishing their own stakeholders and trusted advisors;
- an individual sense of clarity around personal and professional values and purpose; and
- energy and productivity – achieving effective results: being able to understand and manage themselves, including their own capacity and contribution, in a balanced and more focused way.

Every professional career journey will, of course, be unique, influenced by factors both within and outside of the individual's control. To actively manage both career development and progression, it is useful to have a form of 'map' giving a view of the classic stages, as shown below. This may assist in understanding what can impact and shape individual career paths.

CLASSIC STAGES IN PROFESSIONAL CAREERS

While the development of any professional is based primarily upon the development of technical competence, there are also some general discernible career stages:

Experimentation Early graduate stages of qualification and traineeships provide the opportunity for experimentation and clarification of the question: who am I in the world of work?

Accumulation As experience accumulates, in early to mid-career, a professional's credibility and value increases as their expertise, track record, portfolio of clients and work experience grows.

Leadership The paradox of dependency dictates that results and profitability are more effectively achieved through working with others at all levels. As promotion to manager, team leader and partner occurs, the rate of development of technical expertise slows; the accumulation of experience, value and wisdom continues. The skills of effectively managing the capability and performance of team members become essential. Rather than IQ and intellect, it is EI, emotional intelligence, that is most important.

Core Areas of Professional Focus

An effective mentoring or coaching process for professionals can often be structured around the following core areas of common focus:

- **Developing the Relationship** Focus on personal effectiveness: their 'self-brand' and personal 'value proposition'; their expertise and confidence; their skills, style and self-development; how they are managing, sustaining and resourcing themselves within their own circumstances or role.
- **Internal Focus** How their role fits into the organisational framework: performance and contribution; how internal team and peer relationships are developing; how the individual is developing within the internal team; how broader key relationships within their internal market are being developed.
- **External Focus** How the individual is developing their value proposition with the external market: clients, stakeholders, intermediaries, patients and wider business world.
- **Personal vision or ambition** Understanding and developing their own personal 'picture of success'.
- **Progress and Problems** The current reality: how the individual is making progress within his or her role or situation; what strengths are assisting progress; what are the challenges; the difficulties, obstacles or problems being encountered.
- **Resolution**   How to find or create different solutions, really assess what is within one's control and experiment with new skills, style and approaches; reflect and reprioritise.

Creating the Time and Space to Think Differently

Often when people look back at turning points in their professional lives, they remember the significant things said to them. More often, however, they remember not just the words that were spoken but also the *experience* of having someone support, encourage and challenge them through tough times. People remember those who stood by them – physically and metaphorically. Supportive coaches (or indeed managers or mentors, of course) do this by being really 'present', by truly listening, by understanding deeply what might be going on, by encouraging and enabling them to actively find their own solutions and, as appropriate, challenge them to find their innate resilience and capacity. Some of the results of being 'totally present' in this way are manifest in these actual comments from my clients:

> "It was by far the most sensible conversation I have had in my three years in this role; very clear, understood the realities really quickly, very practical."

> "I was able to have the conversations that I needed to have to clarify expectations. I gradually developed better boundaries and stopped getting 'sucked into' the dynamics that were going on. I just felt much stronger and less exhausted. It definitely helped me become more effective in managing myself – and then being more productive."

> "I always felt encouraged; sometimes it was nothing specific – I just felt listened to and renewed in my own energy. Basically, it helped 'get me out

of my own head' and to continue to believe that I could effectively deliver the managing partner role, *my way*."

"Just from talking things through I felt much more able, and confident, to be me; to trust myself and my own judgement. The conversations helped me not be overwhelmed by what I perceived to be 'expected'."

"Looking at problems in a different way – and talking them through in confidence – helped me see how I could break them down, not just for me, but in the context of the whole team."

"I learned a lot. Mainly about myself."

"I hadn't thought about my situation in the way we discussed; looking at how other people might be experiencing *me* did make me consider things differently. I now realise I need to consistently look at what I need to do differently in that context."

"I began to value myself again; I started to 'get on' with things rather than feeling 'stuck'."

"My confidence was very low. I actually felt I was caught in a shattering experience and felt panicky but I couldn't let anyone know that ... In reflecting on what I am really good at, I did find a new sense of energy and self-belief."

These comments highlight some of the different experiences from professionals of all levels and types.

Clearly, even just truly listening and 'being present' can be a tremendous help for people, and in this chapter on mentoring/coaching for managers, the focus is specifically on how to create a safe and secure environment in which to have ongoing private coaching conversations that lead to meaningful development.

How to Discover What's Really Going On

High-achieving professionals can think for themselves and usually work out their own solutions. However, when consistently demanding challenges, situations and dynamics arise, the situation changes, and even the best professionals may need support and a safe, contained space.

In supporting such people, it is important to realise what the challenges and dilemmas really are, and what inhibits their progress. It is vital to uncover what really is limiting the effectiveness and 'interfering' with the potential of otherwise achieving professionals. The conversation should discover what are the opportunities for improvement, both for the individuals and for their organisations.

> **Mentoring or coaching can be an empowering experience.** It is not meant to be an experience of being told what to do, or reliving the mentor's experience, or of receiving compulsory advice. Rather, it provides an opportunity to step back, create thinking space, actively think about career progression, solve problems, meet challenges, create opportunities, create new ideas, build confidence, or just keep making progress.

Successful coaching/mentoring can be the difference in a person's career between making mistakes and strategically avoiding them; between getting off to a good start, and stumbling at the gate. For the coaches or mentors, it can be an opportunity to review, and refresh, a professional perspective, whilst gaining the satisfaction of guiding and enabling others to achieve professional success. The 'soft' people skills and attributes required to be an effective mentor or coach, however, can be very different to those 'hard' skills that have brought a senior professional success.

The foundation blocks for an effective partnership and process are:

- a positive, meaningful and relevant relationship, which focuses on what the professional needs and what will be most useful to the professional;
- a respectful and non-judgemental interaction: a generative space being created to listen, for both parties to listen and to think differently;
- the internal 'self-resourcing' of the professional: the courage and capacity to notice and develop their own professional style, build their sense of confidence to take different actions and to achieve results;
- flexibility, safety, feedback and trust – so that both can discuss what's working well and what's not, and keep the relationship moving forward.

What to Expect from Each Other?

> *"If you talk to a man in a language he understands – that goes to his head. If you talk to him in his own language – that goes to his heart."*
>
> Nelson Mandela

The relationship between coach/mentor and coachee/mentee rests on trust. However, trust needs to be supported by clear terms of reference, informally or otherwise, to deepen understanding, clarify boundaries and to have resolution mechanisms, should the relationship stall or even turn sour. Mentees/coaches need their mentors/coaches to:

- understand their reality, context and challenges;
- give them space – not overcrowd or overwhelm them;
- be real, practical and sensible;
- show empathy and authentic understanding;
- listen well, and be encouraging;
- help them to actively think – clear their heads of negativity, look at risks and options, help them realise they have their own solutions;
- value them – let them see what they are doing well;
- be clear about progress and barriers;
- help them feel they are progressing and that they are supported.

Mentors and coaches, too, will have expectations and needs of their own in the relationship. They may be busy practitioners or consultants – their time is valuable. These factors need to be carefully thought about and discussed in an open, candid and realistic way before initiating the real conversations.

Mentors and coaches also gain from these relationships, and here are some different aspects they have highlighted to me:

"Interesting how 'just being there' in difficult times was enough (for the mentee)."

"The opportunity to share perspectives and learning was in itself a lesson for me."

"Seeing someone walk out the door knowing, and believing, they can move things on themselves, that is very satisfying in itself."

"It is possibly the most meaningful contribution I can make – I really enjoy the experience."

"Mentoring causes me to continually reflect upon myself."

"I find it very hard not to advise or give my solution immediately."

Practically Speaking

When embarking on a coaching or mentoring process and relationship, it is important to bear in mind and discuss:

- the initial purpose and focus: being clear as to the initial priorities;
- mutual expectations: what you both need and expect from each other;
- boundaries/limitations: what you are both comfortable to discuss;
- confidentiality: this is essential, for both parties;
- meetings: scheduling and arranging (including cancellation);
- how to deal with any misunderstandings: discuss the openness required;
- how both sides should give and receive feedback;
- reviewing points periodically and on a cumulative basis.

Session Content

Clearly, professionals may bring any range of situations/issues into the confidentiality of the conversation and process space. These may well include:

- career progression: getting started, ongoing performance;
- promotion or decisions to leave or make other changes;
- workplace relationships;
- team dynamics;
- performance management;
- misunderstandings and conflict;
- managing both 'upwards' and 'downwards' in the organisation;
- perceived bullying and aggression;
- issues around client interactions and new business development;
- dealing with difficult issues or relationships;
- business or financial issues;
- self-awareness: learning about their own professional and management style;
- dealing with pressure, expectations, stress/burnout: workload/balance.

Important Prior Considerations

Both mentors/coaches and mentees/coachees have important questions to ask themselves in advance of beginning the process and partnership, examples of which (in a mentoring relationship) are shown below[10]:

Mentor Considerations/ Questions	Mentee Considerations/ Questions
• How much time do I actually have to devote to this process? • What are my expectations of my mentee? • Am I comfortable with the areas of focus, expertise and priority being identified? • Is my mentee clear about why they want mentoring and its relevance to their career/situation? • Has my mentee demonstrated some focus and success in their career to date (regardless of stage, i.e. newly qualified)? • What is my likely mentoring style? • Am I clear on my own boundaries, our contact terms and that mentoring is the appropriate intervention/process?	• How can I get the most from this support? • What is the area of focus/priority and learning that is most important for my development or my situation? • How will I prepare for the sessions? • Do I have practical examples of the areas that I want to develop? • What is my learning style, and how will that inform my approach and our discussions?

During the Session: How to Establish What's Really Going on

When matters are 'on track', events usually progress naturally and well. It is, however, when uncertainty, change or dissatisfaction occur that the need to keep things in perspective becomes acute. As with changes in any part of life, developing and creating alternate, realistic and purposeful strategies can be essential.

To sustain capacity for personal change in professionals, a resilient and optimistic attitude is required. Developing resilience can mean searching for, and finding, the answers inside oneself, and this can take some time to evolve. A listening and experienced ear can be a wonderful help. The mentor should focus on 'attending to' the dilemmas, challenges and solutions of the mentee, with a combination of compassion, understanding, creativity and practical suggestions.

Presented below are a number of disguised cameo cases, drawn from my actual experiences, in order to provide insight into real situations. The names and circumstances have been changed, of course, to preserve client confidentiality, the cornerstone of any such relationship.

THE CASE OF THE DRIVEN ACCOUNTANT: PERCEPTION AND REALITY

Peter is the managing partner of a progressive and expanding accountancy firm. Over the course of his career, he has had a meteoric rise in industry and worked in a variety of roles internationally as a specialist tax advisor. He set up his own practice, and it evolved over 12 years from a two-person partnership to a multi-disciplinary, well-respected firm.

Peter is entrepreneurial; he moves at speed both in decision-making and in personal interaction. His clients respect him hugely because he is experienced, courageous and direct. He can make hard calls. More junior professionals enjoy working with him because he is highly experienced and determined.

Peter is, however, mercurial. He can be short-tempered and arrogant. He constantly interrupts, he forgets people's names, and his management style has been described as 'dictatorial'. As a result, the firm has had retention issues, and staff turnover has become a problem. To combat this, the practice had hired expensive, niche specialists as part of an expansion strategy. However, this was ultimately unsuccessful due to the specialists' ongoing differences of opinion and clashes with Peter. He has also found himself increasingly in conflict with one of the junior partners with whom he works closely, and who is 'mercurial' in the same way as Peter.

In Peter's direct team, and across the firm, there has been a growing sense of 'us and them'. Feedback gathered in a firm-wide survey indicated that the junior practitioners do not feel respected, listened to or valued. A decrease in levels of trust and communication as the firm expanded was cited repeatedly.

One particular 'blow out' with a junior partner caused the senior partners to discuss interventions to develop the organisation. Peter indicated that he was primarily interested in 360-degree feedback and in having an external coach help him focus on his own leadership capacity. He sought feedback from both his partners, a number of junior professionals and from his personal assistant, as to his leadership capacity and style.

Conversations and Process

The benefit of a psychometric profile (in this case, a leadership 'emotional capital' profile, with feedback from a number of people in Peter's organisation) is that it presents data for discussion. In addition to increasing self-awareness, it can provide a valuable basis for future-focused skills development.

Peter was interested in the differences that appeared across the 10 competency areas profiled between his own rating (self) and the quantitative ratings from his colleagues. The biggest differential appeared in the area of self-confidence. His rating indicated his assessment for this competency was 'development need', a surprisingly low figure. Conversely, Peter's peers and colleagues rated this competency highly as a 'signature strength', indicating their experience of his 'confidence'.

Having remarked on this difference, Peter then read the qualitative feedback commentary from his colleagues. This reflected that his strong 'signature strength' was actually taken to excess and had become an 'Achilles' heel' or blind spot. It was clear from some of the commentary that while his colleagues' experience of his confidence was mainly positive, it could also be one of overweening ego and tight control.

However, in reflecting on the very positive comments about his technical excellence, his innate kindness, his genuine interest in others and his compassion (when he had time to take an interest in others), Peter's eyes filled with tears. He expressed the view that while his technical competence had clearly brought him to the top of his game in terms of being an expert practitioner, managing a firm, looking after clients and, particularly, working with peers demanded a whole different kind of energy.

"I don't actually feel confident," he commented. "I really hate conflict; I worry a lot about how to manage internal differences and different personalities. I do question myself and my own judgement in relationships. I know I often speak before I think. I actually do feel out of my depth quite often – but I can't let anyone know. I'm managing partner: it's my name over the door. Sport and family help but, to be honest, it's not enough. I'm consistently tired; I often feel overwhelmed, but I find it hard to 'let go' of control. I don't honestly think my colleagues know what my vision is for the firm – I'm not sure if I know myself. To be honest, I think I've forgotten what I am good at."

Outcomes and Reflections

Having reflected on his contribution to the firm and his enjoyment of the work, Peter set some professional and personal goals. He decided to delegate more authority and work more closely with his 'natural successor'.

Over a 12-month period, the coaching conversations evolved. (Note: as highlighted earlier, the quality of such coaching sessions or 'conversations' is crucial to the success of any such coaching, mentoring or management intervention.) The conversations on 'skills' were coaching in nature: helping Peter try different ways, experimenting with methods of dealing with people and noting what happened – for himself and for others. The conversations on his career development were mentoring in nature, guided by the experience of his mentor's career journey in a major partnership. In overall terms, Peter said the conversations helped him to slow down, and he felt supported. As trust grew, he felt more confident in trying different ways of doing things.

He found it useful to reflect upon how difficult this was and the expectations he had of himself, and others. He also realised the value of 'small things' – remembering people's names, asking questions, taking a genuine interest in his colleagues, saying 'thank you' and expressing appreciation when appropriate – and the difference they made.

As the mentoring/coaching sessions progressed, Peter raised 'delegation' as an issue, identifying it as something he struggled with. He was coached through delegation as a process and framework involving not just 'direction' but effective positioning, involvement, setting of accountability and encouragement. He began to understand different levels of listening and the whole communication process – including body language. Peter learned to pause and to stop talking – difficult for an extroverted personality. He began to listen, and in a different way. He began to understand what empathy really means. He began to notice the experience of others.

Peter later raised 'influencing peers' as another issue he was struggling with. He began to notice the difference that not having to 'have his way' all the time made. He tried different negotiation strategies with different personalities. He realised the impact of his high level of competitive drive – an attribute that had served him well since boyhood, and continued to do so. He began to find himself better able to 'flex his style'.

Peter then identified 'effective succession planning' as another issue of concern. He later came to realise that in this issue there was a hidden opportunity to improve his organisation. He worked through, in private, the kinds of conversations that he wanted to have with others. He began to look across the partnership and think about collaborating more strategically to leverage strengths. The partnership had never formally set 'business goals'. Rather than present his own strategic plan, Peter instead began to develop discussions with his partners about an outline 'framework for progress'. The ongoing conversation between the partners then took on a different momentum: rather than the 'circular' conversations previously experienced, the partners began to indicate their desire to take on areas of responsibility.

Outside of the firm, Peter dedicated more time, together with his wife, to the charitable causes that he was involved with internationally, and that gave him real pleasure. Within 18 months he had also taken up both cycling and triathlon training. In Peter's view, nothing had changed dramatically or immediately, but over time he began to notice both 'internal' and 'external' changes.

The feedback from the profiling exercise (mentioned earlier) was startling to him, and 'stopped him in his tracks'. He came to understand that his own internal struggle and lack of self-value was contributing to a negative 'spiral effect', which had a significant effect on his role – and his impact on others.

The Case of the Team that Wasn't:
What brings a Team Together Can Pull it Apart

Ewan trained in a large corporate law firm, rotating between practice groups. He spent his first two years of qualification in the litigation area. A high-achieving sportsperson, he was regarded as having very high potential. He was technically strong, 'quick on the uptake' and combined a very relaxed interpersonal style with strong team management skills. He demonstrated a high level of personal authenticity, to which both peers and clients responded. Two years after qualifying, he moved to a regional firm where he very successfully developed a niche practice and a strong client base over a period of 10 years.

He was then approached by his former firm to rejoin as a partner in his specialist area. They asked him to lead the existing team, as the incumbent partner was taking early retirement for health reasons. Ewan was somewhat reluctant to make the move because he valued both his own autonomy within his current practice and the very high level of client connection he had developed there. The regional practice was a more traditional practice, with a strong familial culture.

Nevertheless, the opportunity to both broaden his range of skills and experience and to offer a more extensive service to his existing clients, and potential clients, from within a progressive corporate environment was very attractive. His wife was also supportive and keen for the move, as she also had her own professional opportunities to pursue.

Six months into his new role, Ewan was struggling. This was not due to his level of enjoyment of the new environment, or because of the extent or range of his work and client connection, but rather with the management difficulties he was experiencing from some of his senior associates.

Two of the senior associates had joined the firm within the previous five years, one from another city firm and one returning from overseas. It was very apparent that both were technically very strong, clearly ambitious and felt (respectively) that they had an entitlement to promotion. Each was unhappy that Ewan's position had been filled externally. Over the previous two years, they had had a number of disagreements and were noted within the firm for being competitive with each other.

Externally, and on the surface of the group, all appeared to be fine; however, in team discussions, in work allocation and in general interactions, the dynamic in the group was highly tense. Ewan felt like he was 'walking on egg shells'; even small issues felt 'explosive'.

Conversation and Process

Ewan and I, as his external coach, began our coaching and mentoring 'conversations' with a very useful overview by Ewan, not just of the factual scenario but the effect it was having on him personally. He felt drained, exhausted and, as he described, "spinning". He had made a very significant move, but each day he was internally questioning both his own judgement and wisdom. He also felt that he was in a constantly reactive state: "I felt really edgy, like I was constantly being baited; I kept expecting to be ambushed. I felt manipulated. I wasn't sure how long I could control my temper."

The first part of the work was to create a space where Ewan could effectively gather his own thoughts and, over a number of sessions, develop and focus and on his short- and medium-term goals. He felt "sucked into the dynamics" of what appeared to be really latent conflict with those two senior partners, rather than being able to establish with any directness his vision for the team's success. There was clearly, once again, both an internal and external aspect to the work.

Ewan needed to reach back into his own experience and really remember why he had been promoted to the position of partner and team leader. Gathering his internal self-belief and confidence – and holding on to it – was, he realised, essential.

He also realised that, whilst he needed to understand his team members' perspectives and their disappointments, part of his role was to help them realise in what areas they may not be delivering as effectively as they could be. He had had feedback from other partners on the team's performance and he could see, in terms of client handling and influencing, where both partners could improve their performance. Rather than viewing his team members as adversaries, he began to identify opportunities where he could positively influence them with the benefit of his client relationship management skills.

Outcomes and Reflections

Taking a step back from his situation, along with the benefit of a confidential and safe coaching relationship, helped Ewan to develop a very business-focused framework and to envision a picture of success for the team that could be achieved over the next six to 12 months. Following a number of useful conversations with colleagues and fellow partners within the practice, and in particular getting to understand the managing partner's perspective, Ewan became much clearer in his own mind in terms of what his 'picture of success' for the team could be, across core delivery areas.

Each of the team members were different, and he carefully planned, in the privacy of his coaching sessions, his approach to discussions with each. He needed to take into account their different personalities, strengths, objectives and areas for improvement. He developed, in advance, a framework approach for the discussion with each, thinking carefully about the best outcomes for the individual.

Having successfully positioned a team initiative, Ewan then felt able to plan an offsite business planning session for the team. Prior to the process, he worked hard to engage his team in the planning. Their input, views and ideas were actively gathered across all areas of the team's activities, both internally and externally focused.

The benefit of listening to them in a structured business context helped Ewan. This was both on the offsite occasion, and for individual one-to-one follow-up discussions regarding contribution, performance and career development. During the external session, they looked at, as a team, what they truly valued about their professional area and approach. They became clearer on what they, both as individuals and as a team, do well. They discussed openly how they could deal more effectively with disagreement and differences. Ultimately, they developed a charter of rules, behaviours and goals that would bring them forward – noting also what was not acceptable and where they would not waste time and effort.

Ewan's reflection on the coaching sessions and their outcomes was that, "They calmed me down." He began to really realise that he still had what it was that had made him so successful, both technically and as a trusted partner to his clients, in his former firm – and as the captain of his sports team.

He realised that his fears in relation to his sense of adequacy had combined with his team members' sense of disappointment and frustration at their lack of promotion to generate a very negative 'mood and atmosphere' within the team:

> "It constantly felt like 'shadow boxing'. Once we really got the discussion going, and particularly in the facilitated day, we got some of the 'elephants onto the table'. Then we started to make progress."

While very hard work, and particularly when he still had a very full case/client portfolio, Ewan realised that once he gave himself his own authority and developed a structured framework for the team, where they could see both their own progression and the team's progression, his team members felt both positive and involved.

Ewan's final realisation was that it was a continuing work in progress:

> "It did take a while. However, once I felt the situation was manageable, it helped me 'move my thinking along' more quickly. Things began to move and fall into place – in actual fact, I began to value myself and my own vision for the team quite quickly. I started to 'get on' with things rather than feeling 'panicked and stuck'."

Conclusion (to Chapter)

Early approaches to management were best suited to repetitive, factory-style operations; the modern era, with its emphasis on innovation and change, requires a more progressive and collaborative approach. This is particularly important for today's professionals, who are not immune to these global forces and who generally benefit from a supportive, yet challenging, approach. In that context, the best management style has a coaching and mentoring element, as distinct from the more conventional emphasis on strict supervision. Professionals, as has been shown here and elsewhere throughout this book, seek mastery of their trade, appropriate autonomy in their work and a sense of real purpose in their work life. Coaching (and the related activity of mentoring) can provide the self-belief, personal insight and encouragement to help professionals flourish, for the benefit of the professionals themselves and their organisations.

In this chapter, the essentials of coaching and mentoring (whether performed by the manager or an external provider) have been delineated, with guidance given on the practical steps involved. Classic, and real, situations have been described by **Hannah Carney**, who has also provided two relevant cameo cases. The chapter opened by indicating how to have those 'crucial conversations' that can lead to success in one's profession, and in life generally.

Interested readers will find closely related material in the chapters on leadership, on building confidence in professionals, on understanding personality types, and on action learning. The following chapter on emotional intelligence and self-awareness is most especially relevant.

ENDNOTES

[1] Steve Jobs, "Foreword" *Think Different* (Internal Apple publication, commemorating the first year of the advertising campaign with that slogan, 1998).

[2] Homer, *The Odyssey*. Trans. by Robert Fagles. Introduction by Bernard Knox (Penguin Books, 1994) p. 13.

[3] David Clutterbuck and David Megginson, *Mentoring Executives & Directors* (Butterworth-Heinemann, 1999).

[4] David Clutterbuck, *Everyone Needs a Mentor* (CIPD, 2004).

[5] W. Timothy Gallwey, *The Inner Game of Tennis* (Random House, 1974).

[6] Viktor E. Frankl, *Man's Search for Meaning: An Introduction to Logotherapy* (Beacon Press, 1964).

[7] John Whitmore, *Coaching for Performance* (Nicholas Brealey Publishing, 2002), p. 12, quoting W. Timothy Gallwey, *The Inner Game of Tennis* (Random House, 1994).

[8] Nancy Kline, *Time to Think: Listening to Ignite the Human Mind* (Cassell, 1999).

[9] Peter Hawkins, *Leadership Team Coaching* (Wiley, 2012).

[10] David Clutterbuck, *Everyone Needs a Mentor* (CIPD, 2004).

Chapter 14

Managing Senior Professionals: An Insider's View

Mary Goulding

What you do speaks so loudly that I cannot hear what you say.

Ralph W. Emerson

Mary Goulding, a strategic business consultant and executive coach, has managed professionals in many different capacities over the past 20 years. In this chapter, she applies this wealth of experience to managing smart people in general, but especially those in senior roles in organisations. This personal account provides real insights and practical advice on how to deal with four common types of smart – but difficult – performers.

Introduction

I have partnered in business with them; I have sat on boards with them; I have managed them in my own company and in others' companies; I have coached them as owners of their own businesses; and I have interviewed workforces led by them. This chapter is about my experiences of managing smart professionals in senior technical and management roles.

I believe the key common factor with these professional, clever people is that they are often good at managing their work in their expert field but are poor at managing the business and poor at managing the people. They put such high value on their expert knowledge (which drives them to become expert in the first place) that they do not value managing people or putting appropriate systems and procedures in place to support the business. This can result in a lack of respect for those people in the organisation who are doing these perceived 'lowly' administrative or non-technical tasks, which in turn can cause friction, upset and disruption.

The irony is that these professional, clever people actually cannot excel alone. They need to feed off other people to thrive and survive. They most certainly need to be 'managed', perhaps without them even realising it.

This chapter describes four types of senior professional (managing or technical directors), and how to manage them. These four types are drawn from my direct experiences of:

- Managing people as their managing director – where 'managing' is not about managing fixed tasks, but quite often is the management of

technical people's insecurities in order to create an environment for them in which they can flourish and excel, enabling their expert knowledge and skills to be maximised for the good of the business.
- Managing people as a business consultant and coach – where 'managing' is about helping owners/managing directors to:
  - achieve their goals;
  - understand their strengths and weaknesses;
  - become aware of their blocking factors;
  - understand areas for learning and development;
  - develop their leadership and management style;
  - be more accountable; and
  - maximise their potential.

In the examples below, I have highlighted four frequently encountered dysfunctional 'types', and suggested ways in which to improve their management ability:

- Type 1: The Busy MD – Efficient Individual, Ineffective Manager
- Type 2: The Controlling MD – Ineffective Individual, Ineffective Manager
- Type 3: The MD who Does Not Know How to be an MD
- Type 4: The (Technically) Clever Prima Donna.

Type 1: The Busy MD – Efficient Individual, Ineffective Manager

The Busy MD is excellent in his expert area, and his key focus is on winning and working on projects for clients. He is quick-thinking and tends to be impatient with staff he perceives as being a number of steps behind him. His focus is on the project work staff are doing, rather than on the staff as people. For example, he would not bother with superficial talk about what staff did at the weekend or just asking them how they are doing over a cup of coffee. He perceives that giving staff this non-project-oriented time is a waste of time! It does not achieve results. He wants staff to be busy, because that means they are completing more projects and making more money for the company.

Staff can therefore feel undervalued, not respected and even used, because of this denial of the human aspects.

It is either naïve or unduly idealistic to believe that staff, even technical staff, will work well in an emotional vacuum or can be relied upon to perform specified tasks in isolation, devoid of social or motivational needs.

In the cameo case below, I was asked to coach the MD, an excellent technical achiever who gave no consideration to anything but the task element of the work: this is akin to wanting only the harvest, without planting seeds.

Cameo Case Example 1: The Busy MD

A successful company, in business for over eight years with a staff of nearly 30, provided professional services to large corporate clients. The MD and all staff (except two) were professionals with specialised skills focused on delivering projects to clients.

The first thing I noticed when I visited this company (in my role as coach to the MD) was that I was not offered tea or coffee – either on arrival or at any stage during my full morning session. This was the first indicator of the type of task culture within the company.

On getting a better understanding of the company, it became clear that:

- The MD was very task-oriented, and her motivation was to 'keep busy' doing as much work as possible for as many clients as possible.
- She said 'yes' to all work requests, regardless of resources. Staff would just have to work longer hours!
- Staff performance was only measured on delivery of projects to clients, and staff had to work overtime.
- The MD did not see value in the people-related or procedural side of leadership and management; therefore, her managers in turn always put such tasks to the bottom of their priority list.
- Staff turnover was very high, indicative of a resulting lack of commitment from employees.
- There was serious inefficiency due to a lack of proper management and processes.
- The MD did not have a vision for the business and had no long-term goals or strategy and, therefore, was unclear about the direction of the business.

No-one on the management team had management experience or training. The MD 'delegated' (as she thought) management tasks to members of the management team and then absolved herself of the responsibility. For example, she would ask them to 'hire in more resources', or 'furnish the visitors' room' or 'write content for the website', but then she would land them with another project with a tight deadline that was 'top priority'.

She did not hold them accountable for these management tasks, but grumbled about them not being done. Of course, the management team were always too busy on projects to carry them out. They knew that once they were busy on projects, the MD would be happy. Why would they spend time working in areas that were not valued by the MD?

In turn, the MD found it difficult to manage challenging or difficult relationships and to deal with face-to-face confrontation, so she stuck her 'head in the sand' rather than challenging her managers and holding them accountable.

The MD was very keen to quickly put a solution in place so she could get on with her business, and suggested a manager with appropriate management experience be recruited who could manage all of these issues and get rid of the headaches they were causing her. The MD also believed that if she could get more staff, the management team would have more time to do management tasks, and many of her problems would be solved. Simply adding a new manager in this way would not change the fundamental problem, and would probably confuse and compound matters by blurring the lines of authority and adding to overhead costs, as is now explained.

Managing the Busy MD

In this case, the MD needed to understand what she would potentially lose if she did not address these crucial issues correctly. She needed to be challenged regarding her leadership and management of the business. A forum was required in which she would be held accountable, for example, to a board or advisory committee.

It was important for the MD to understand that this was a process that would involve a change in the culture of the company, and this change would have to come from the top (i.e. the MD). The MD struggled with her desire to get to the end point as quickly as possible – she didn't like a procedural approach, and didn't see the value in it. In her view, it was simply all about results.

The MD had to see the value in 'management' before her staff would see the importance of it. It was crucial that she recognise her leadership style and learn how to improve the leadership of her staff. She needed to see that this was not a 'quick fix' solution that wouldn't require her involvement or any change on her part. It was clear to me that if she had more staff, she would simply take on more project work, rather than allowing for 'management time', which would not be revenue-earning time. She also had to get 'buy in' from her management team before they would invest time in non-project-related tasks. If a new manager was simply hired at this point and forced to work in isolation, without the full and proper support of both the MD and her management team, he or she would not succeed.

A number of strategy sessions were held with the MD and key members of the management team to collectively explore the vision, long-term goals, business offering and strategic objectives of the company. This process was also used to involve key people in the future development of the business and to help them understand key success factors and the part they could play moving forward to ensure success. This also helped to get buy-in from all concerned parties regarding the importance of people management and quality procedures, and to agree a solution that would have the mandate from all the key people.

The MD was challenged to:

- face up to her own limitations and weaknesses;
- understand her leadership style and specific areas for development and learning, to bring about better, improved leadership; and

- take overall responsibility for the culture and poor management within the company and learn ways to deal with it better.

She began to understand the importance of investing in people. She set up sub-committees for different aspects of the business, e.g. to run social events, to look at improving overall quality and to enhance the office environment. She learned about the strategic planning process and how her organisational model fit into this process, thereby allowing her to set long-term goals, strategic objectives and priorities for her business. She learned the importance of communication in business, and started one-to-one weekly meetings with key managers. She learned to gain control of her future, her company and her people, and she continues to develop her people, relationship-building and influencing skills. Additionally, she learned to involve the key people at senior management level in setting overall company objectives and taking responsibility for achieving them.

The result of all this was:

- a management team driving and managing the business collectively with a common agenda, rather than the MD on her own managing individual teams who were, in effect, competing against each other;
- accountability of each manager to a group;
- clearer direction and focus, which helped to set the right priorities;
- decisions being made by the group and acted on quickly, rather than getting stuck in the communications bottleneck trying to access the Busy MD;
- less dependency on the MD;
- improved quality of work;
- a greater allocation of time by the management team for people management, which meant people were more effective, better trained and learned from their mistakes;
- a better team spirit among the staff, with more social interaction and fun;
- a greater sharing of knowledge and resources; and
- better communication between managers and staff.

Case Summary

In summary, these changes resulted in a huge change in the culture and effectiveness of the company. Staff began to feel more involved and valued, and even had some fun! And the management team continued to progress and drive through management objectives and tasks despite the ongoing tendency of the MD to keep 'busy' on projects!

Type 2: The Controlling MD – Ineffective Individual, Ineffective Manager

The Controlling MD thinks people are trying to undermine him and that they do not respect him when, in reality, people are afraid of him. So, he ends up having 'yes people' working for him.

If someone challenges his thinking or disagrees with him, he is too insecure to deal with it. He thinks it is him as a person that is being criticised, and he gets emotional and upset, sometimes to the extent that he cannot speak and has to leave the room for fear of 'losing it'. He just cannot seem to separate the issue at hand from the person presenting it.

Sometimes the Controlling MD can favour the underdog and 'stick up for them'. However, if he thinks someone is getting too confident and taking initiative, he quickly beats them back down. He thinks that people should know their place, and they need to be put back in their box from time to time so that they always know who the 'boss' is.

The Controlling MD tends to have a poor communication style in that he does not convey clear messages. He 'beats about the bush', leaving room for different interpretations. He is not clear in his communication about what deliverables he wants, when he wants them and who should do them. And, quite often, he thinks that he has said something to somebody when he has not – he has only thought it, and said it in his head! This leads to many frustrations and misunderstandings.

CAMEO CASE 2: THE CONTROLLING MD

One such example of a controlling-type MD was in a company providing professional specialist contracting services, which had a core team based in the office, with a further 200 or so people working outside the office on client sites. Again, the MD was an expert and well-known in his field, but he seemed to have huge difficulties delegating and getting key staff to take responsibility.

On reviewing the company, it became clear that the MD got upset very easily and took things personally. It was very difficult for staff to discuss or argue a point of view with him about any aspect of the business that differed from his own perspective, as he would perceive this as an attack on him personally. His immediate reaction would be: "Who do they think they are?" or "How dare they – why don't they show me the respect I deserve?"

Poor communication was causing many problems. For example, at one meeting I attended, the MD was discussing a particular issue and gave a vague description about a possible solution, typically 'beating about the bush'. People left the meeting not really knowing if there was an agreed course of action or whether any of them should be doing anything, and they were afraid to ask or to take initiative. So no-one did anything! Subsequently, the MD got very annoyed (and upset) when he checked up to see the state of progress and realised that nothing had been done. His reaction was: "People don't listen to me; they don't do what I ask them to do, which implies they don't respect me. They are not reliable, and they will not take responsibility. Everyone has to be hand-held by me!" As a result, the MD believed he was the only one who could make things happen and that nothing proceeded without him. This, of course, is a nice reinforcement for him and makes him feel important and 'the boss'.

The truth of the matter is that he wants:

- to be in control;
- to be pulling all the strings;
- to start and stop things at his will, and without explanation;
- everything and every decision to go by him first; and
- to know about everything that is going on.

This is what gives him power and makes him the boss. So, he does not want someone else to start taking control, to start taking initiative, to start taking responsibility, because then he will feel he is losing control. He does not want anyone else to know the complete picture, but it is very difficult for his staff to make the right decisions if they don't know the complete picture.

All of this makes for a working environment in which people are fearful of:

- stepping out of line;
- saying anything that may cause upset; or
- taking any initiative or action without the approval of the MD.

People are walking on 'eggshells'. They do what they are told to do and nothing more. This is not an environment that encourages creativity, self-responsibility and self-development. It does not bring out the best in people. To the contrary, it causes people to operate out of fear and takes responsibility away from them, making them appear almost childlike and immature – a culture that, as always, comes from the top (i.e. from the MD). The MD, through his management style, is creating a self-fulfilling prophecy, inducing people into a state of dependency – a kind of "learned helplessness" – that reinforces the ego of the boss, and perpetuates itself.

Guidelines for Managing the Controlling MD

To improve managerial effectiveness, this controlling type of MD needs instead to have independent advisors or external directors to guide and discipline him. These may be financial accountants, technical experts, management consultants, business advisors or business coaches. The advisors need to have the skills and experience to 'manage' this type of individual, given his controlling style. Not every advisor is suited to this type of client. Curiously, in my experience, this type of MD is very good at sourcing the right type of advisors.

The MD will be more respectful of his advisors and listen to their views and perspectives. The advisors can act with maturity, responsibility, initiative and belief in his or her own abilities and decision-making skills without 'fear of the boss', unlike the staff. The MD respects this and can develop his management ability, with the help of his advisors. Also, he is paying for a service and expects to get a good return on it.

For those people working within the company, they need to stick by the rules, know their place at all times, be respectful and be prepared. They need to gather all the facts before a meeting with the MD, anticipate questions he may ask and be armed with the answers. Then they will gradually gain his respect and trust. Once they get this, the Controlling MD will show great loyalty, albeit he will still get upset.

In this case, I coached the MD by:

- giving him feedback from staff interviews about key issues from their perspective (which indirectly led to discussions around his leadership/management style);
- training him in how to manage managers;
- attending meetings and giving him feedback on his communication style and interaction with others, and teaching him better communication techniques; and
- role-playing with him on how to react in certain situations and how to deal with his emotional responses.

This resulted in him delegating specific areas of responsibility to key managers and allowing them to meet as a management team, without him being present, to agree actions and review progress. The MD received a status report subsequent to the meeting, at which point he then gave his input, giving key managers the opportunity to take more responsibility and start to think more for themselves (without the physical presence of the Controlling MD). They could openly discuss and argue points with each other and then propose possible solutions in writing. They could note areas where they required clarification from the MD, guidance regarding priorities and approval for taking action. The MD had time after reviewing the status report to decide on how he would react, rather than reacting impulsively (and emotionally) as he would do if he were in attendance at the meeting.

Controlling MD – Case Summary

The MD became more aware of his style of communication and the impact it had on others. He began to better understand his thought patterns and the resulting assumptions he made, which were leading him to behave in a certain way. He learned ways to stop these thought patterns and do a reality check, which in turn led to more effective behaviours.

Interestingly, the key managers moved from a situation where they constantly complained about the boss, to a situation where they were giving out about each other. As more responsibility began to shift to the key managers, some took greater responsibility on their shoulders than others, and this resulted in them watching each other carefully and taking under-performers to task – all part of learning to grow up, and of growing the company rather than stifling it under the suffocating control of the MD.

Type 3: The MD Who Does Not Know How to be an MD

In many company start-ups, one individual has an idea for a product or a service in their expert area, whether it be a software product, an IT service, a medical product, or a professional service, such as engineering, architectural, etc. The individual's focus is on developing the product or service offering, but he has no knowledge or experience of what's involved in developing other aspects of the business. He tends to stay within his comfort zone, using his expert skills to further fine-tune his product or service before it is released to the world. In the meantime, no-one knows the product or service exists, no customers have been lined up and there is no money to pay for additional resources or sales and marketing activities. In essence, there is no business plan. If he is lucky and gets some help along the way, he may start to build up a customer base and hire staff on the back of resulting revenues. However, some MDs continue to focus on development and delivery of the product or service, rather than on 'managing the business', and this causes the company to stall in its development.

Cameo Case 3: The MD Who Does Not Know How to be an MD

One such client example of mine was a training company with 10 employees, providing health and safety training.

The MD was spending much of her time out of the office training the clients herself. This was her area of expertise and what she felt most comfortable doing. After a few sessions, it became clear that when the MD was in the office, she didn't know what to do. She didn't know how to manage her business, so she booked herself back out training clients again. This was difficult for her to admit; in fact, she hadn't quite realised that this was the case until we talked it through. It also became clear that she had personal goals which she wanted to align with the business.

Managing the MD Who Does Not Know How to be an MD

I asked the MD to go through the following:

- a life-planning exercise, which she did with her partner to set life goals over an agreed timeframe;
- a business-planning exercise to set business goals that were aligned with her life goals;
- review her customer base/services and revenues to identify which customers were profitable to serve, and then to put an appropriate sales strategy in place;
- staff and management issues; and
- gaps in systems and procedures.

In addition, she worked with a financial advisor to understand her finances better and the management of her cash flow.

The MD learned about strategic thinking and the business-planning process. She learned about the different aspects of running a business, as well as acting in the role of MD. She learned how to integrate her personal goals with her business goals. She learned how to do a cost–benefit analysis and assess the value of her services and customers. She worked through her sales strategy and prepared a sales plan to achieve targets. She also learned how to manage her finances better. This all resulted in a well-thought-out business plan, starting with a clear mission statement and ending with an action plan to achieve goals.

Case Summary

As a result, the MD now knew what she needed to do back in the office to manage her business more effectively. In other words, she now knew how to be an MD! She could clearly see the benefit of utilising her time to do this rather than booking herself out with clients yet again. She became a leader – steering the company in the right direction, and ensuring the right things were being done – and a manager – ensuring things were being done right. She employed more people to do the training she had been doing previously. She increased her revenues and profit, and she quickly started to achieve her personal goals as well.

Type 4: The Clever Prima Donna

I think we all know, or have had experience of, the Clever Prima Donna! I have managed a few in my time and describe below a 'typical' Prima Donna. This is the technical genius within the company, who has probably been with the company since it started, so is likely to be a director, but does not easily fit into the confines of the organisational structure that has necessarily developed as the company has grown.

The Typical Prima Donna

The Clever Prima Donna:

- is an expert in his field;
- can get through a huge workload;
- can contribute hugely to a business (in fact, he can be the unique selling point (USP) of the business);
- can be very charming, positive and good fun; and
- can 'wow' customers with his knowledge and problem-solving skills.

The clever prima donna's technical knowledge can make the above contributions if (and only if!) a number of factors are right. Despite delivering such huge benefits, if he allows his ego to dominate him, he can become a prima donna, being at times:

- disruptive;
- non-communicative;
- unco-operative and unreasonable;
- emotional;
- demanding;
- negative; and
- critical, finding problems and reasons why work cannot be done.

He can have a very strong presence and so his mood is very visible, seeping through the rest of the organisation. This means there can be great, up-beat, high days and terrible, down-beat, low days.

The Clever Prima Donna:

- Needs a lot of managing, though he doesn't think so. As he is excellent at his job (from a task/project perspective), and he places little or no value on anything else, he doesn't see what has to be managed.
- Needs to feed off others in order to flourish. He cannot do it on his own. This 'feeding off' can take many forms, including 'dumping stuff' onto his manager – the prima donna never accepts responsibility. In his view, it is always someone else's fault! Unfortunately, this 'dumping' might satisfy the prima donna's need for attention but it leaves the manager with many problems to be solved. The manager can get drained by these emotional intrusions, while conversely the Prima Donna gets to feeling a lot better.
- Is respected and liked by his team (who can learn much from him). However, the Prima Donna is not respectful himself and does not follow rules. In fact, he enjoys breaking them. He quite often will not 'play ball' or will fail to turn up for a meeting without a reason – or apology. He either feels "it is just a waste of time" (for example, if the issue is an administration or people issue), or believes "no decisions will be made because the real decision-maker is not there!" And sometimes he's right!
- Does not stick to reporting lines and boundaries. He will often decide to go directly to the MD, instead of his manager. Even if his manager is good with people, the Prima Donna will typically undermine him, and be very disruptive.

- Can get twisted views of situations (sometimes to suit his particular agenda). He can be paranoid and does not like to be left out of the loop. He can build a relatively minor issue up in his head to a much bigger issue, go totally off track with it, and then explode with rage. He also has a very strong sense of fairness and gets very upset if he perceives unfairness towards him or, indeed, towards a member of his team.
- Tends to storm into his manager's office and demand things which can be unreasonable or even whacky. This is usually as a result of some issue he has been worrying about since waking at 5am. He will arrive at his version of a solution to the problem (usually one which creates more problems than it solves!) and then demand that his needs be met. It can be easy to get caught up in a heated discussion about his demand or the viability of the solution, so here are some suggestions that I have found useful in dealing with the Prima Donna.

Guidelines for Managing the Clever Prima Donna

The only person who can manage the Prima Donna is the 'boss' (i.e. the MD), whose job it is, in as much as possible, to create and manage an environment in which the Prima Donna can flourish. This requires a lot of energy and is more about managing the Prima Donna's moods, concerns and insecurities, than about managing his work. If he is in the right frame of mind, then great work will follow. The key, as explained below, is to reduce, over time, the irrationality of the Prima Donna's behaviour by first defusing his attention-seeking outbursts and injecting balance into his demands.

1. **Empathic Listening** If the Prima Donna comes storming into your office, avoid any temptation to arbitrarily dismiss him (or something similar). Remember, you are the manager, and this is about you managing his insecurities – this is not a battle of egos. So, stay grounded. Avoid getting into a row about the solution/demand being made. Instead, allow him to 'let off steam' and give him space to say (or shout!) whatever is on his mind. You cannot reason with someone who is feeling emotional. So, stay with the emotions for a while; listen to him; let him know you understand how he is feeling by reflecting his feelings back to him. Stephen R. Covey refers to this as "empathic listening" and suggests that we "seek first to understand, then to be understood".[1]

EXAMPLE: THE PRIMA DONNA AND EMPATHIC LISTENING

Prima Donna: "I've had it with this project; it sucks! I'm finished with it, so count me out."
Manager: "So, you're feeling frustrated about this project?"
Prima Donna: "Yes, I am; the deadlines are ridiculous. It's just a waste of time, and it's only going to get worse."

Manager: "You're worried it won't get finished on time, and it's not going to get any better?"

Prima Donna: "Yeah, we just don't have enough resources, and they keep changing the goalposts. It's completely impractical to expect us to work day and night for them."

Manager: "You feel it's unfair of them to change the scope of the project and still have it finished on time?"

Prima Donna: "Yes, it's totally out of order. If they change their requirements, they should get a new delivery date. And they should be charged more."

Manager: "They should get a new proposal based on their new requirements?"

Prima Donna: "Absolutely, and it should cater for an extra person on the project if we want to have a realistic delivery time."

Manager: "You need more people?"

The Prima Donna is now more logical and has worked through his emotions, so both he and the manager are looking at the problem from the same side and can look at finding the right solution.

2. **Problem-solving** After you have given him this space in which to vent his emotions (allowed him 'psychological air', so to speak), you can then start to problem solve and influence. Logic and emotion do not co-exist. If he responds logically, you can ask questions, give advice and seek a solution. If he responds emotionally, you go back to empathic listening, and stop probing. When you get to the problem-solving stage, you should backtrack to understand what the real issue or problem is, asking questions such as:

   - "OK, what exactly is the problem here; what are you concerned about?"
   - "How is it a problem for you? Or for others?"
   - "Why is it a problem?"

   When the underlying issue is uncovered, it might simply be a misunderstanding or a miscommunication, and may just require clarification or reassurance. If it is a real issue (as distinct from an issue that exists only in the Prima Donna's mind), then look at alternative solutions, e.g. "How can we solve this?" "What are the options?" "Is there another way?" "What exactly will be solved if we do this?"

3. **Regular One-to-one Communication** As his manager, you should have regular communication with the Prima Donna to:

   - keep his perspective on the right track;
   - let him air his concerns and get issues out in the open as soon as possible in order to nip them in the bud;
   - clarify misunderstandings;

- reassure him and calm his insecurities; and
- keep him in the loop.

You should explain important issues to the Prima Donna, ask for his input, and get him 'on side' for any resulting course of action, in advance of any group meetings. He will feel included, 'in the know', and will have a better understanding of the value attached to the issue and its importance to you, the MD. This will make for better co-operation, as and when required.

4. **Reduce Dependency** This is easier said than done. Reducing the dependency on the Prima Donna may make him feel more insecure and, hence, more disruptive. You need him on side; you need to convince him of the benefits of training up members of his team. They may never be as good or as talented or as knowledgeable as the Prima Donna, but they can keep the show running, if needs be. This team should then be encouraged to document what they can, rather than keeping knowledge in their heads, thereby further reducing the dependency.

Finally, the clever Prima Donna is unpredictable, and just when you think everything is running smoothly, he may erupt again with yet another issue, or else go into non-communicative mode for no apparent reason. If this happens, it is important not to let him distract you from focusing on achieving the company's key objectives. You should not 'absorb' his negativity. If he is too disruptive or high maintenance, ask yourself, "Is he worth it?"

But remember, this Prima Donna is like a rough diamond. As his manager, you have to take the rough with the smooth. If you can manage the rough, and filter its impact as much as you can from the rest of the staff and the company, the brilliant gem will emerge and make your business uniquely shine and sparkle!

Conclusion

Each of the types described here suffer from a limitation that can be lifted through awareness, education or emotional development. The Busy MD has a naive belief that talent will blossom without being nurtured, and must learn to accept that people will always have emotional needs. The Controlling MD operates with an insecure mindset, and contrives a 'learned helplessness' in staff, heaping pressure on the MD as well as feeding his weak ego. Such an MD can retreat from their need to control by progressively taking steps to delegate more. Adding independent advisors or external directors can add the necessary rigour to decisions by challenging the MD constructively. With the third type, the solution (management training) is relatively simple, and involves a shift in internal attitudes or behaviours.

Managing the Prima Donna is an art in itself, requiring patience and skill: further help can be found throughout this book, but special attention is drawn to **Chapter 13** on coaching (as this is essentially the manager acting as coach to the Prima Donna), developing self-confidence in professionals (see **Chapter 11**), leadership (see **Chapters 3** and **4**), and transactional analysis (as the Prima Donna is playing games, acting as a child, and using the 'gimmicks' described in the section on managing conversation). The chapter on personality types (see **Chapter 5**) should also prove useful, notably the use of personality profiles (such as the DISC profiler). This profiler not only indicates the underlying 'drives' and 'fears' of different types but also helps predict the likely behaviour patterns; if, for example, the dominant type of Prima Donna doesn't get his way, he will sulk. If sulking does not achieve his aims, he could actually sabotage the project or even organisation.) The section in that chapter on dealing with difficult people was included with types such as the Prima Donna in mind.

ENDNOTES

[1] Stephen R. Covey, *The Seven Habits of Highly Effective People* (Simon & Schuster, 1989).

Chapter 15

Managing Professionals and Other Smart People: A User's Guide

None of the books I have written matter in the long run. All that matters is how you touch people. That's what I want to have done. Insights last, theories don't.

Peter Drucker

In this final chapter, the key lessons of this book are brought together as a practical guide to managing professional people and organisations.

Finding the Time: Manage Better by Managing Less

Perhaps the biggest dilemma facing any manager of professionals is how to find the time to actually manage, i.e. to schedule the work, coach individuals, shepherd the team, develop the strategy and increase profitability. There is, additionally, a more fundamental dilemma: how much management is enough? Managing people conventionally is expensive and time consuming, especially given the consequent loss of fee income or 'production' time when a senior professional assumes the role of manager. Perhaps, therefore, there should be no specific management effort at all. On the other hand, with no management effort, decline or chaos might ensue. Resolving this dilemma is a make-or-break issue for many professional firms. The answer lies in having management principles, not rigid rules or dogma, that promote self-management in professionals and other staff.

Take, for example, the case of Vivian, an ambitious and able accountant who started his own practice to serve high-potential start-ups as their outsourced chief financial officer. Facing the usual early-stage pressures on cash flow, Vivian grabbed almost any business he could and gradually expanded his practice to include a dozen other accountants. Overwhelmed with office management duties as well as his client work, Vivian chose Lily to take over some routine duties. An excellent accountant, charming with people, Lily was a natural for this new role. However, some staff bristled at now being managed by someone other than the firm's founder.

Upon promotion, Lily was told she could give up some of her client work, but in practice her new role simply added to her former accounting responsibilities; indeed, as she was now a manager, her sense of duty encouraged her to absorb any unexpected work and deal with client emergencies.

Vivian, too, had difficulty relinquishing control: after all, he was the boss, so he never really dropped his managerial involvement. This led to serious frustration for all concerned. It also impacted on the bottom line, with lower productivity and the additional cost of "managing" people. After a year of long days and short tempers, Lily quit. Her departure disconcerted the remaining staff, and many left as a direct consequence.

Vivian himself was disappointed, as he had 'helped' Lily by sharing the management burden with her. Worse, he had lost some self-confidence and wondered what he should do next time: it seemed he was damned if he did (hire a manager) and damned if he didn't. Determined to succeed, Vivian appointed an advisory board and resolved to take their advice, summarised as follows:

Commit to hiring a manager only when it makes clear economic sense. Vivian realised that a certain amount of management was a necessary cost of doing business: the real cost was a trade-off between the expense of giving time (one's own or a Lily's) to manage staff and the actual return in productivity from that management effort. Below a certain number, Vivian could and should perform the management tasks. If these were to consume 20% of his time (a day a week, costing €20,000 in 'lost' fees), he would need to see just a 5% improvement in productivity among his 10 staff.

This was the economic breakeven number that allowed Vivian to estimate the actual financial value of management, and to quantify how much time should be dedicated to supervising and coaching staff. As staff numbers increased, this number should rise proportionately: he should devote additional management time (his own, or Lily's) incrementally as staff expanded. This led him to limit management effort to a certain proportional range that was affordable. Moreover, he quickly realised that good management was an investment that paid dividends.

What, then, do good managers do that bad managers don't do?

Less is More, When it Comes to Management

In the example above, Vivian came to realise that the management equation had another dimension: he could minimise management time if he could maximise staff's ability to self-manage. In other words, if staff were developed into top performers, they would be self-managing: professional, capable of acting independently and in the best interests of the firm. The need for 'management' would decrease accordingly. He set about developing staff with great purpose, identifying professional and personal areas for improvement.

Taking the time to talk to each of his staff in turn, he came to understand their personalities, their ambitions and even the difficulties they were having in producing their best work (for more on this, see **Chapter 5** on personality types and **Chapters 6** and **7** on motivation).

Informed by these conversations, Vivian began to delegate properly (see the section on situational leadership in **Chapter 7**, or the version shown below).

SITUATIONAL LEADERSHIP: MANAGE ACCORDING TO THE SITUATION AND STAGE OF DEVELOPMENT

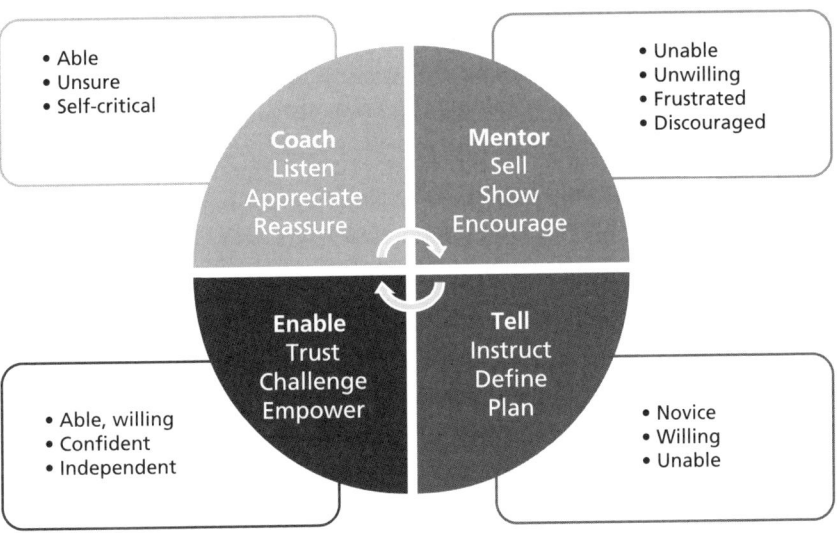

Staff responded in kind, and they were glad to give extra discretionary effort in response. This kind of communicative action – a dialogue that is well-grounded in rationality – is a powerful tool in generating and executing strategy. Lack of substantive reasoning, ignoring the broader strategic and human questions, is myopic, rather like rearranging the deckchairs on the *Titanic*.

> *"The most effective way for firms to remain competitive is to hire smart people and let them talk to each other."*
>
> Thomas H. Davenport and Laurence Prusak[1]

As well as providing opportunities for growth, such delegation gave Vivian the opportunity to coach staff 'in the actual moment'. Sometimes, he coached technical skills or accounting interpretations, but more often it was interpersonal skills, dealing with clients, handling banking relationships, negotiating deals or other 'soft' issues (see **Chapter 11** on building self-confidence in professionals, and **Chapter 13** on coaching).

Business blossomed – as did the staff, none more so than Vivian himself, who appreciated the difference he now was making in the working lives of his "colleagues" (as he now called them). The extra income was no less appreciated!

Although not quite "making a dent in the universe", to use Steve Jobs's exhortation, there was a clear rise in staff morale and in client satisfaction: the phenomenon of reciprocity ("good behaviour (in staff) breeds good behaviour (in clients)") was in evidence. Clients were happier to deal with smiling faces, and the improved service (proactive advice, quicker report completion, closer client engagement) was helping them get beyond the start-up phase.

Almost without his realising it, Vivian's strategy was paying off. In the coaching sessions, he realised that communication was a two-way process, and that staff were looking for direction about what way he wanted the firm to head: should they stay as a standard accounting firm or should they offer something a little bit different? If special, what skills would they need, and how could they get them? How quickly did he want the firm to grow – if at all, especially given the previous disappointment? What would this mean in terms of career opportunities for them? Vivian decided to revisit his strategy (see **Chapter 2** for more on strategy), this time involving his staff.

His starting point was *who* they were, not so much *what* they did, i.e. he matched the market need (for value-added accounting) with their personal ambitions, professional skills and individual motivations. To quote Steve Jobs again: "Don't be trapped by dogma, which is living with the results of other people's thinking. Don't let the noise of others' opinions drown out your own inner voice. And most important, have the courage to follow your heart and intuition. They somehow already know what you truly want to become."[2] (For more on this, see **Chapter 3** on leadership.) Remember that **performance = ability x motivation**, and tapping into the professional's inherent drive can unleash tremendous productivity and creativity.

CHOOSING THE RIGHT STYLE IN MANAGING PROFESSIONALS

Treat All Equally – But Not the Same

Many managers mistakenly believe that having a single style is optimum: that this promotes consistency and fairness. Some of these managers will favour a modern, consensual style, but, referring back to situational leadership (see **Chapter 3**), it can be seen that a directive style is preferable with, for example, a novice. Seeking consensus in such situations is folly, and does a disservice to the newcomer seeking direction. Conversely, micro-managing the experienced campaigner will be counter-productive: the effective manager chooses the right style for the right occasion. She treats everybody equally – but not the same.

Sharpening the Strategic Vision

In our example, Vivian realised he would have to sharpen his vision for the firm, and that all his people could – and should – contribute to its fine-tuning. After all, if it was just *his* strategy, why should they go that extra distance?

It took a few sessions before staff opened up to this new-found opportunity – but eventually the ideas tumbled out. Naturally, commitment to executing the strategy also soared as people came to appreciate they had a shared organisational destiny. "You get what you focus on": strategic vision really matters. The starting point for achievement is a focus on the goal: it would seem correct to say that one only gets what one focuses on. Similarly, research has shown that simply having a specific, smart goal is a significant determinant of increased performance in professionals and others.[3]

Vivian found that answering three fundamental strategic questions (see below) clarified his own thinking. It also allowed him recognise what kinds of people and types of talent he would need. The staff similarly appreciated the sharper focus on specific categories of client, as this would reduce frustration – and loss of profit – that come with chasing the 'wrong' clients.

Three fundamental – and difficult – strategic questions:

- Who will we serve, and who will we not?
- What will we offer, and what will we not?
- With whom will we compete?

Vivian used a diagram like the one below to indicate the firm's competitive advantage, i.e. the area where the firm would have a distinct, profitable value proposition that served specific, significant client needs:

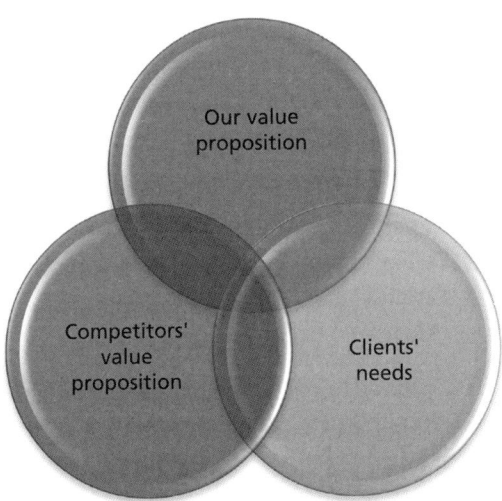

In this diagram, the unique value proposition lies in the segment where clients have a real and substantial need that we can meet but that competitors can't.

Note that there are still significant unmet client needs (signified by the bottom right segment) that no competitor is currently meeting: these are potential business opportunities – strategic "arcs of opportunity", which Vivian then explored.

He found that professionals, particularly, can get blinkered by organisational paradigms, bounding their scope unnecessarily and limiting their ability to think outside the box, thereby missing interesting opportunities for profit and development. Intellectual curiosity is a vital ingredient in uncovering such possibilities. Later sections in this chapter offer advice on how to stimulate ideas and promote innovation.

The Case of Carol: Win-Win by Reviving her Career

Despite the improvement in communication induced by their involvement in strategy formulation, some of Vivian's people were stumbling. Carol, for instance, had been hired to add extra experience to Vivian's workforce, but she didn't show real drive to get tasks completed. A pleasant professional, she allowed her concentration be diluted through an over-concern for other people at the expense of the task at hand. Her passion really lay in relating to people. Initially, Vivian ignored the festering situation, then later reacted with disciplinary 'performance management' sessions, none of which led to sustained improvement, as the fundamental personality issue was not being addressed. Vivian resolved to remove Carol from the payroll, until the Board suggested using a more empathetic coaching approach, getting to know what motivated Carol – what made her 'tick'.

Carol revealed that she needed a different kind of challenge and wanted also to interface more with people. She was even willing to reduce her salary to achieve those aims (see the sections on dealing with difficult people and in the use of psychometric tools, such as DISC, in **Chapter 5**). The solution emerged: Vivian needed someone who would take the risk of starting a new line of business (providing in-depth, personalised financial analysis – a strategic arc, as noted above), and Carol's rapport with people and deep experience could be ideal.

Energised by this challenge, Carol succeeded spectacularly, creating a valuable new business stream – as well as rescuing her own career and her self-esteem. Vivian welcomed this new business development, and also enjoyed seeing Carol newly enthused. For him, this was a defining moment, a revelation. By tapping more into a person's make-up, he was matching the person to the job, and reaping the rewards. He now was *managing less, but managing better*. Carol was now self-motivated and self-starting, needing little direction. (For more, refer to the section on situational leadership and motivation in **Chapter 7**.)

Vivian reflected on how unsatisfactory his earlier, traditional approach to "performance management" was. He now realised that performance management was entirely personal, and that the true goal was not to pass judgement on a person but to light their inner fire and give them the self-belief that they could succeed. Rather than leave a performance management session downhearted and despondent, **the goal is to have those eyes shining with enthusiasm, self-confident, and committed to the cause, rather than merely compliant**.

Smarter Working

Vivian now recognised that 'try harder' was fine as an exhortation, but not strategically effective. As quality expert Edwards Deming has noted *"Everyone is already doing their best"*,[4] and a change from the target-driven treadmill approach (see figure below) was needed.

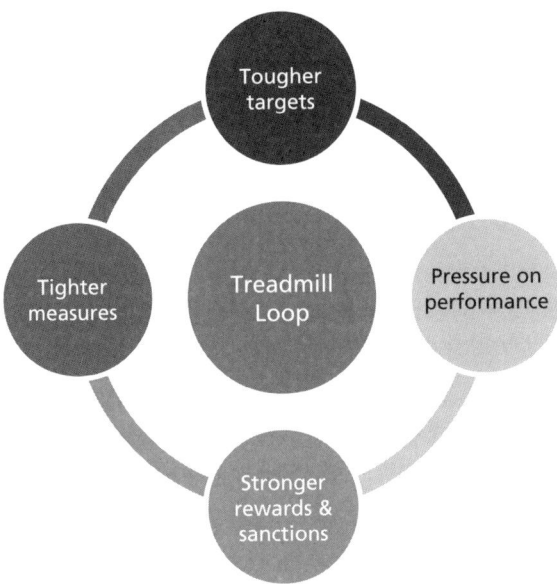

Vivian was shifting the firm towards a smarter "learning" loop, where the goal is development and ongoing improvement (as explained in detail in **Chapter 8**), and illustrated here in summary form:

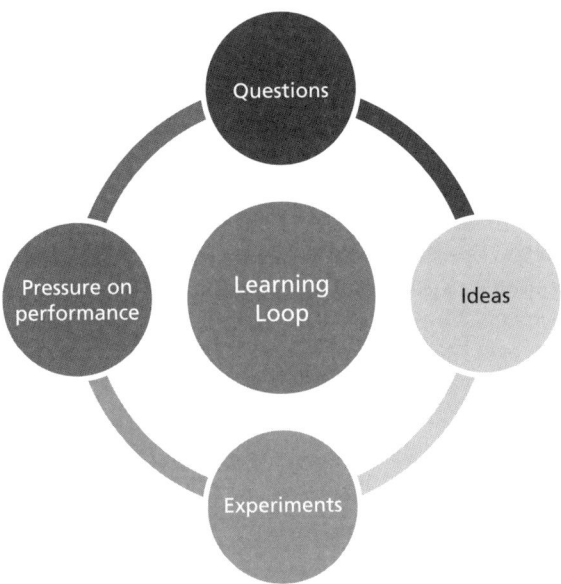

Working smarter is vital in the new economy: the nuanced, tacit knowledge of staff is a critical competitive edge. Valuable, rare or inimitable knowledge is crucial to success, especially in "knowledge firms" such as Vivian's. Knowledge may indeed be the most strategically important of the firm's resources. "The foundation of industrial economies has shifted from natural resources to intellectual assets."[5] The central competitive dimension that firms must know how to do is to create and transfer knowledge efficiently within an organisation.[6]

Performance Management: a Necessary Evil?

> *"Some managers have a genius for castrating their people."*
>
> David Ogilvy

The concept of performance management is straightforward, and it is hard to argue against it, until one notes the distress and counter-productive outcomes that frequently ensue. Invariably, such sessions have a judgemental approach, causing great tension and much 'game-playing'. Renowned conductor Benjamin Zander overcomes the problem by giving everybody an "A" grade, before the season even begins! This sets expectations high, and he finds that players continually strive to retain that "A" grade. He says: "you know if you are doing well if you look into their eyes – the eyes never lie. If the eyes are shining, then I know I am being an effective leader."[7] His orchestra, in turn, says that Benjamin Zander "makes you better than you ever thought possible". This is the essence of good leadership.

Zander urges bosses to know their people as individuals – their fears, hopes and aspirations. His mantra is to make one-to-one conversations a non-negotiable fact of orchestral life: such conversations are crucial to success and should not be deferred. (For more on managing conversations, see **Chapter 12** on emotional intelligence and **Chapter 13** on transactional analysis.) Having that 'little chat' with someone about a shortfall in performance should be timely and specific: many managers find it helpful to follow the 'SIP' formula, starting by showing respect and first asking 'permission' to give feedback:

S: Start with the Specific Situation: start with the assumption that the person operated in good faith and was trying their best. Recognise the positive aspects. Deal only with what you observed or know for sure, e.g. "I didn't get the new proposal document from you until 5.30 pm."

I: Inquire, Impact and Importance: inquire if that is factually correct. Explain the significance of this delay, for example, and its impact.

P: Performance Promise: the goal is to improve performance, so ask for a 'Performance Promise', for example, that such a delay will not occur again.

If the performance shortfall then re-occurs, repeat this formula, but introduce a sanction, such as a 'ticking-off' or even a verbal warning for more serious breaches.

Professional Work is Intensely Personal

From our example, Vivian realised just how surprisingly personal is the world of the accountant, especially when the emphasis shifts, as it did for Carol, from routine accounting services to deeper involvement with the client as a "trusted advisor". (**Chapter 2** discusses this progression up the value curve from arm's length service to closer involvement with the client's core needs.)

The profession and the person are indistinguishable: one *is* a doctor, lawyer, accountant, architect, and so on. There is a close identity with one's profession: one's work and self overlap. The work of the professional is individual and very personal, in the sense that one's value is wrapped up in one's work. This is particularly true for doctors, architects, designers and others whose work is subject to constant observation: it is even true for engineers, software developers, accountants and other professions where the work is less intimate but has significant impact for the client. While many professions tend to ignore this personal aspect, it is well to remember that inside every professional and other smart person is a human being waiting to get out: that nerdy, introspective software developer may not want to be noticed, but he doesn't want to be ignored either. Tapping that inner potential unblocks the inner drive and liberates the creativity trapped inside.

The matrix below attempts to classify how 'personal' the work is for the professional along the vertical dimension and for the client on the horizontal dimension. For example, the work of the accountant, designer or software developer is very personal to him or her, but not usually personal for the (corporate) client. On the other hand, the work of a medical doctor is very personal for both the patient and the doctor.

THE PERSONAL NATURE OF PROFESSIONAL WORK

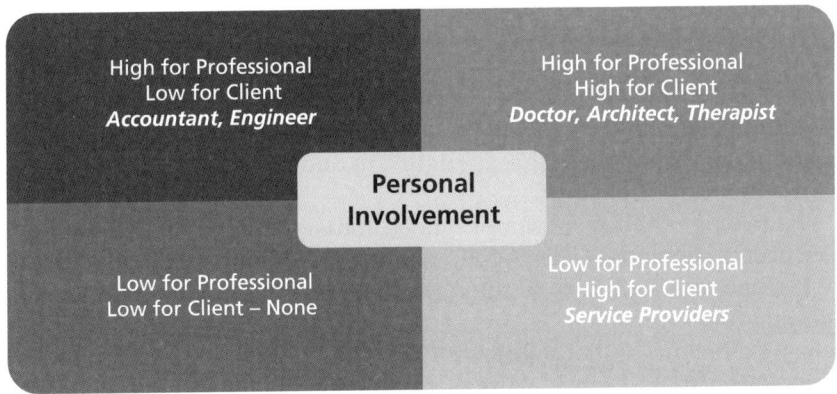

The matrix below gives an additional way of seeing the essence of different professions, and hence managing each professional appropriately, particularly in regard to emotional intensity. In this categorisation, accounting, for example, is considered to be knowledge intensive; one still rises or falls in one's career depending on the level of application of that knowledge, making accountancy very personal in a sense.

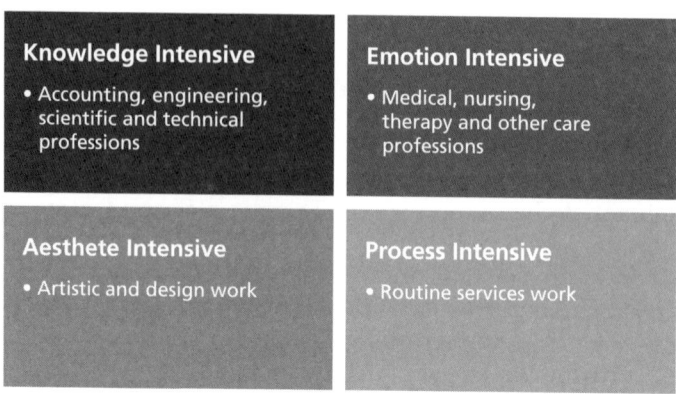

Different types of professional work require a matching managerial approach, and it can be helpful to consider the type of 'intensity' involved in the work. Running an advertising agency, for instance, according to the legendary David Ogilvy, "requires midnight oil, salesmanship of the highest order, a deep keel, guts, thrust, and a genius for sustaining the morale of men and women who work in a continuous state of anxiety."[8] In similar vein, Dr William Menninger has said that "The executive is probably a father figure. To be a good father, whether it is to his children or associates, requires that he be understanding, that he be considerate, and that he be human enough to be affectionate."[9] In the language of transactional analysis (see **Chapter 13**), the best fathers are adults who "nurture" rather than "control".

The Power of Innovation

There is no strategic advantage in being identical to competitors: indeed, being better is fine, but ideally the professional might aspire to being special in a particularly meaningful way: one doesn't want to just be the best at what one does, one wants to be unique. The essence of strategy is successful innovation: "Discovery consists in seeing what everyone has seen and thinking what nobody has thought", to quote Albert Szent-Gyorgy, the noted American biochemist.

Vivian's moment of epiphany echoes management savant Russell Ackoff's observation that "The righter we do the wrong thing, the wronger we become. It is better to do the right thing wrong, than the wrong thing right."

Being different – in the right way – leads to strategic advantage. The irony in managing professionals, such as accountants, is that a narrow focus on profit limits one's perspective and therefore misses the opportunity to realise potential. As famed macro-economist Professor Michael Porter says the pursuit of a successful strategy depends on "the courage to be different". Being neither low cost nor undifferentiated leads to a situation where an organisation is 'stuck in the middle', neither one thing nor another. The "gale of creative destruction",[10] to use Joseph Schumpeter's term, keeps blowing businesses away, and constant reinvention is needed, even in the most venerable of professions.

Counterintuitively, managing costs directly cause overall costs to rise, because managers are looking at the wrong thing. But if they manage value to the customer, they cause costs to fall, because they are no longer paying to provide what the customer doesn't want. Success, in other words, is measured by added value, not profit, and in our example Vivian was pleased he had extended his portfolio, courtesy of Carol's renewed energy and ambition.

Pull, Don't Push

Vivian's strategy, accordingly, was to bring reality and business sense to conventional accounting of the more limited kind. He also realised that targets were all well and good, but that real motivation came from meeting a need rather than an arbitrary target. Viktor Frankl captures the counterintuitive nature of achieving success:

> "Don't aim for success – the more you aim at it and make it a target, the more you are going to miss it. For success, like happiness, cannot be pursued: it must ensue, and it only does so as the unintended side effect of one's surrender to a person other than oneself. Happiness must happen, and the same holds for success: you have to let it happen by not caring about it."[11]

This could be called *the oblique rule*. Companies that set out to maximise profits end up, on average, being less profitable than those with visionary goals, according to renowned researcher Jim Collins. His extensive study, *Good to Great*, revealed that companies that set out to maximise profits exclusively, generally end up being substantially less profitable than those whose starting point was more 'visionary', i.e. had a greater sense of mission in meeting a real need.[12] To paraphrase London Business School's Jules Goddard, cash flow is a consequence of strategy, not its justification.[13]

Aristotle similarly observed that people often have similar end-goals but disagree about the means of achieving these goals, and it is the means that actually matter more: "When we deliberate, it is about means, not ends". To extend this point, it is our reasoning (in the strategic sense) that matters: Antoine de St Exupéry, author of *The Little Prince*, and quoted by Jules Goddard, wrote that: "What sets us against each other is not our aims – they all come to the same thing – but our methods, which are the fruit of our varied reasoning."

Manage your Relationships, not your People: the Enemy is Within

The importance of managing staff proactively cannot be overstated. As Donald Sull, a real-world strategist, says: "Companies fall prey to active inertia – responding to even the most disruptive market shifts by accelerating activities that succeeded in the past. The internal enemies are complacency and myopia".[14]

Factors external to the organisation – such as economic downturns and geo-political events – account for fewer than 20% of "stall" points; the majority of failures are due to internal causes, of which the omission of an emphasis on innovation is critical.[15]

For accountants, their usual time horizon, because of the nature of their work, is the recent past. This proclivity acts against a strategic stance: similarly, the orientation of a natural sales person is short-term, while the true strategic leader has a much longer time horizon. In facilitating corporate strategy-making, I have found it essential to recognise the implications of this, and work to extend and widen the habitual time horizons of accountants, salespeople and others. Similarly, the accountant's starting point in strategy is the annual planning cycle or budget, whereas it will be more productive to aim for innovation and insights – ideas that draw the response: "I wish I'd thought of that". According to productivity expert W. Edwards Deming, managing by numerical goals is an attempt to manage without knowledge of what to do.[16] (For more on this, see **Chapter 4** on leadership, and the contribution of pioneering surgeon Dr James Sheehan.)

Stimulating People's Ideas

Jules Goddard[17] offers the following framework for having ideas, explaining that ideas emerge from adopting these different perspectives – especially that of the artist, who has the patience to allow ideas "emerge" (see **Chapter 8** on the learning organisation for more on this concept).

DIFFERENT PERSPECTIVES: WAYS OF STIMULATING IDEAS

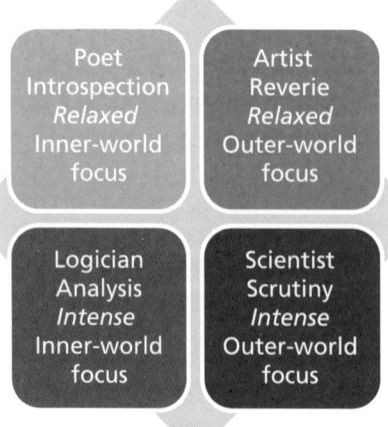

Poet Introspection *Relaxed* Inner-world focus	Artist Reverie *Relaxed* Outer-world focus
Logician Analysis *Intense* Inner-world focus	Scientist Scrutiny *Intense* Outer-world focus

Profit, Promotion and the Professional

The economic viability and strategic future of the professional firm, such as an accountancy practice, depends on the 'shape' of the firm, i.e. the ratio of junior to senior staff determines whether the work is sufficiently leveraged (using enough juniors successfully) or is top heavy with experienced, high-earning senior staff. The 'economic number' reflects the span of control, and effectively determines the career promotional opportunities. For a standard practice, the shape might be wide (a span of 1: 10), as illustrated below.

The Shape of the Staff Pyramid: Profit and Promotion

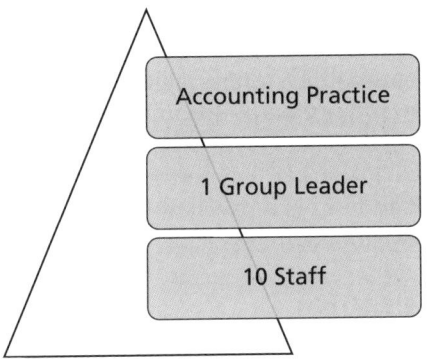

The shape for a more customised, project-based firm, such as a management consultancy, would be narrower, as the number of specialists that could be effectively managed (coached) is less, perhaps six or so:

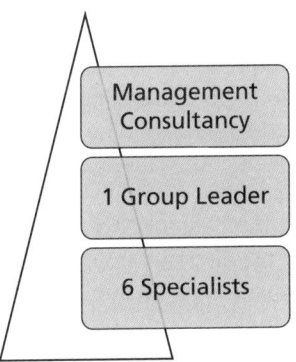

The proportions of this organisational triangle determine both the promotion opportunities (one-in-10 versus one-in-six), and the need to recruit new hires to replace promoted staff and to compensate for staff leaving because they were passed over for promotion or otherwise felt compelled to resign. In other words, with a span of 10, typically one-third of staff would need to be replaced every few years; a McKinsey-style 'up-or-out' promotion policy would increase that number significantly, from approximately three to six.

In a management consultancy, it means that the full complement of staff would be replaced every few years – even though the expertise is highly specialised for particular brain-work.

The **nature of the work**, the **degree of specialisation** and the **promotion policy** (up-or-out versus organic development) has profound influences on the recruitment strategy and the remuneration practices. The 'better' firms make a virtue of the aggressiveness of their up-or-out policy, by making membership a privilege, heavily immersing new recruits and turning departees into advocates for the mother-firm, as McKinsey famously do.

There is no perceived shame in leaving such firms after a few years: the training and apprenticeship provided is so rich that these 'exiles' become highly prized candidates. Furthermore, the exiles retain a love for the home firm, and are a rich source of new business. Even though, from our example, Vivian's firm was small, he appreciated the significance of the triangle, adopting a McKinsey promotion philosophy, and endeavouring to develop his staff to such a level that they were highly valued – either to him, or, failing that, to the external market, where they would carry his firm's DNA. (For more on explicit and implicit psychological contracts with staff, see also **Chapter 6** by Dr Mary Collins.)

Autonomy and Delegation

With the realisation that *at least* one-third of his staff would have to be systematically replaced every few years (and significantly more if the organisation expanded – and still more again to replace staff who leave for myriad other reasons), Vivian turned his attention to the talent pipeline: he was competing with other firms for good professional people. He could, of course, attract these people on a mercenary level by paying above market rates for them, but that would be both unwise and unsustainable.

As a new firm, Vivian couldn't offer the prestige, evident career path or security of more established firms to attract the best people. Instead, he turned necessity into a virtue, recruiting those who had made it to the final stages of recruitment with the big firms, but who had not been successful. He decided to target these good people, who were motivated by their rejection and wanted to succeed. Not mavericks, but clever people with seeming 'deficiencies', they would glory in conquering new frontiers. Vivian's staff became crusaders, unafraid to be first in their field with new technology and with fresh attitudes. They didn't just accept delegation, they craved and demanded it! Though Vivian's management skills were tested to the extreme, he learned that he didn't have to know all the answers, he just had to share his passion for the work and demonstrate his belief in his people, helping them when they fell down, and sharing in their agony of doubt and the ecstasy of triumph. (For more on the underlying psychological contract, read Dr Mary Collins's thoughts in **Chapter 6**.)

Hiring and Firing Smart People

The inimitable David Ogilvy, doyen of the advertising world (think of the TV series *Mad Men*), offers pointed advice on hiring smart people – creative directors, in this case.[18] He says that there are five kinds of creative director:

1. those sound on strategy, but dull on execution;
2. good managers who don't make waves – and don't produce brilliant campaigns;
3. duds!
4. the genius who is a lousy leader;
5. *Trumpeter Swans* who combine personal genius with inspiring leadership.

These 'Trumpeter Swans', Ogilvy says, are rare birds indeed. High-calibre brains, he claims, stem from having intense curiosity, deepened 'common sense', learned wisdom, vivid imagination and boundless literacy (similar to the attributes of the 'Transformational Leader', discussed in **Chapter 3** on leadership).

David Ogilvy's advice on how to deal with office "politicians":

- Fire the worst of them, even just as a lesson to the others!
- When someone denounces a rival, summon the rival and get the denouncer to repeat the accusation directly to him.
- Crusade against email and memo warfare: make people settle rows face to face.
- Start a lunch club: it turns enemies into friends.
- Be fair and don't play politics yourself: if you play the art of *divide et impera*, the organisation will implode.
- Sustain unremitting pressure for high professional standards.
- Hard work never killed anybody: people die of boredom and disease. There is nothing like the all-night push to raise morale. Just be sure to be *on the bridge* in any storm.
- The best leaders are apt to be found among those executives who have a strong component of unorthodoxy in their characters. Instead of resisting innovation, they symbolise it, and companies cannot grow without innovation.
- Never summon people to your office. It frightens them. Go to their office. Don't be an invisible hermit.[19]

No Sand, No Pearl: Flawed Leaders, Great Leadership

Great leaders almost always exude quiet self-confidence. They are never petty, not buck-passers. They pick themselves up after defeat. They are fanatical about their work. They don't have a crippling need to be liked by everyone. They grasp nettles. They can also often have their flaws. David Ogilvy noted how an early advertising pioneer, Albert Lasker, loathed committees, refused to use phones and, idiosyncratically, drove a yellow Rolls Royce. Another, Stanley Resor, was austere, dignified, despised hierarchies, banned job descriptions, yet hired many professors into his firm. For Ogilvy, the common factor among the greats is energy, passion and resilience.[20] Ogilvy himself was noted for his candour and insight: he famously declared that "People don't read ads. They read what interests them, and sometimes that happens to be an ad."

The brightest stars cast the sharpest shadows and every coin has a flip side. The truly effective manager sees any hidden potential and turns perceived 'flaws' into catalysts for change.

Patrick McKenna, close associate of David Maister (see **Chapter 2**), offers the following advice on how to add value as a leader of professionals:

- Create energy in the organisation (echoes here of David Ogilvy).
- Be a perpetual font of encouragement, chief critic and cheerleader.
- Be a source of creative ideas – stimulate creativity in others.
- Be available to listen: act as a sounding board, help people think through their issues.
- Be a good role model: set high standards, for yourself and others, with no hypocrisy.
- Espouse teamwork, develop a common purpose, break down barriers between people.
- Build relationships, infect people with enthusiasm, allow people to try different things, do what you say you will, give credit where it is due, be a conscience when self-discipline fails.
- Take work seriously, but yourself less so!
- Develop people: coach them, ask what is it they want to do that would make them distinctive and more valuable, what is their biggest dream and greatest source of pride.[21]

Managing the Prima Donna, and Other 'Difficult' Types

Just as it is the sand that generates enough friction or irritation in the oyster to produce the pearl, it is often the personality or character 'flaw' that is the genesis of high achievement in professionals. While that 'flaw' is often the source of the drive behind outstanding performance, it invariably comes with a high price, both for the organisation and for the individual. The firm benefits from the talent and dedication of the high achiever, but has to bear the emotional and financial cost of any disruptive consequences. The manager of the high-achieving but, for example, stubborn, excitable, demanding or reclusive professional bears a particular responsibility and opportunity simultaneously. The world of sport, to provide popular examples, is rife with driven achievers, narcissists and rebels. Readers of **Chapter 5** should be able to match these types with high-achievers such as Roy Keane, Cristiano Ronaldo and Carlos Tevez.

The first key to managing 'difficult' people is to realise their 'flaw' is simply their dominant characteristic, taken to excess. For example, the perfectionist is driven to make sure that no criticism can arise, and this perfectionism initially produces acclaimed results, which facilitates even greater perfectionism and possibly a kind of addiction to such acclaimed success, until the tendency becomes an obsession. Eventually, not only does the perfectionism become counter-productive, but in mid-life the perfectionist can come to question their very purpose in life.

The second key consideration is to realise that the more difficult types have unusually deep fears: the more aggressive types (see **Chapter 7** on motivation, especially the section on DISC) fear that the world is hostile and try to overcome their environment. The more passive types have a similar fear, but try to control their own environment. On the other hand, some types believe the world is benign and either seek to enjoy it or to 'not rock the boat'. A brief illustration of one set of different types is shown below, with the excessive tendencies (the 'difficult' behaviours) shown in italics.

DIFFICULT BEHAVIOUR TYPES

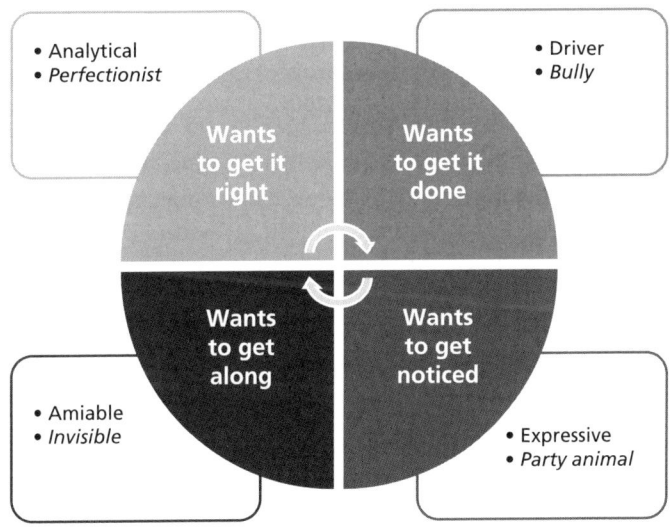

Each of the four extreme types distrust each other: the dominant type despises the passivity of those 'indolent' types who never make waves, and vice versa. The prima donna (whether male or female) is seeking attention, while the control freak is trying to limit the probability that things will go from bad to worse. The steady type wants things to stay as they are and will often make a good team player, avoiding conflict. The dominant type might want to lead, and can often be a good individual contributor, but impossible to work with and actually a poor leader of others.

Recognising these different types, and their fears and dispositions, is the basis of managing 'difficult' types effectively:

1. Try to place them in the right roles, e.g. asking the dominant type to lead the way in an export market, letting the socially active type take a business networking role, giving the steady type a role that requires harmony, or putting the control freak into a regulatory compliance role. (For more on this, see **Chapter 5** or refer to the Personality/Profession grids below.)
2. Understand – and appreciate – their fears, as these are what produced the talent in the first place. Recognise that their disruptive behaviour is simply virtue taken to excess, or a distorted view of reality.
3. Consider the underlying motivation driving the need, and what will make the professional satisfied.
4. Develop together a fulfilling long-term vision or a compelling goal to channel future behaviour: give them a worthwhile destination and a roadmap to get there. If possible, centre this on a client-oriented goal, such as developing new services.
5. Expect relapses, as they are struggling with deeply embedded beliefs and motivations.

To deal with the prima donna, for example, give them attention but show them you understand their fears and motivation. Eventually, go so far as to let them know what 'game' is being played, and make their constructive behaviour part of the deal: in other words, promise them more attention if they play a 'good' (constructive) game rather than a 'bad' (destructive) game. When you catch them doing something 'good', praise them: this, of course, applies to everybody you manage.

Similarly, Marcus Buckingham points out the negative aspects of different thinking styles: for example, the thinking, reflective type can lapse into navel-gazing and get locked in internal post-mortems, the controlling perfectionist can get 'paralysed' in analysis, while the active type can tend to engage in perpetual fire-fighting.[22]

EXCESSES OF THINKING STYLES

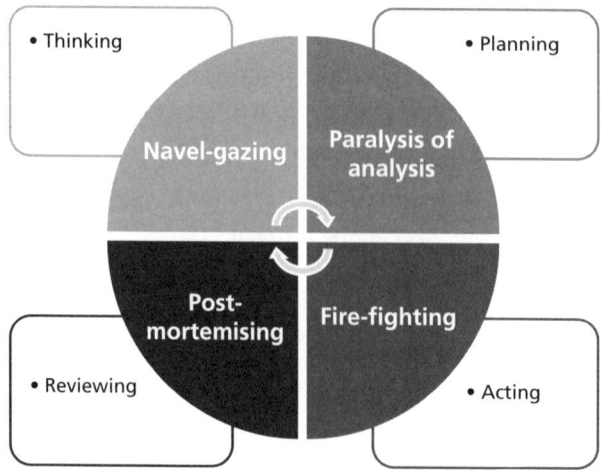

> "By three methods we may learn wisdom: first, by reflection, which is noblest; second, by imitation, which is easiest; and third, by experience, which is the bitterest."
>
> Confucius

David Perkins lists eight deadly sins of the 'stupid' smart person[23]:

- impulsiveness (doing something rash),
- neglect (ignoring something important),
- procrastination (actively avoiding something important),
- vacillation (dithering),
- backsliding (capitulating to habit),
- indulgence (allowing oneself to fall into excess),
- overdoing (like indulgence, but with positive things), and
- walking the edge (tempting fate).

Such personality-based dysfunctions have been addressed throughout this book.

People assume learning comes naturally, especially to 'smart' people. In listening to someone in conversation, it could be assumed that one simply absorbs what they are saying, but in reality you will be judging and categorising. The more experienced professional may even have all sorts of opinions that refute the ideas being expressed. Lifelong learning means working hard to stay open-minded. The need for learning is endless, and new ideas will help keep you engaged and relevant. Listen intently: quieten the little voice that keeps talking when you are meant to be listening to someone else. Stay curious: Professor Simon Mosey of Nottingham University Business School says that the essence of creativity lies in staying curious.[24] Innovation occurs when ideas collide and coalesce. So, probe the issues, ask the pertinent question, and stay curious.

Personality and Profession: Reprise

As with personality, no single style suits every situation: the secret is to be able to deploy the right style at the right time. As a reminder (see **Chapter 7** for more detailed explanations), below are two matrices showing the stereotypical associations between personality type and occupation. The first matrix is a general overview, and the second is a more detailed view, based on Myers–Briggs types. For example, as a brief reminder, the top right-hand quadrant shows the rational, abstract thinking types: whether they are then stereotypically suited to 'Field Marshall' or 'Mastermind' roles hinges on whether they are mentally organised and whether they are inclined to extroversion or introversion. If these rational, abstract thinkers are extroverted and flexible, they are likely to suit innovation roles; if they are introverted, on the other hand, they may be naturally inclined, all things being equal, to 'Architect' roles.

The 'Artisan' roles are based on the grounded, flexible nature of the corresponding personality types. The 'Guardian' types are similarly grounded but less inclined to show flexibility. Finally, the 'Idealists' are abstract thinkers with a people-focus: they may be inclined to teaching, if they are expressive (extroverted) types, or to healing roles if they are introverted.

MATRIX 1: PERSONALITY TYPE AND OCCUPATIONAL INCLINATION

ARTISAN	Grounded, Flexible and	RATIONAL	Abstract thinker, Rational and ....
Promoter	Extroverted, rational	Field Marshall	Extroverted, organised
Crafter	Introverted, rational	Mastermind	Introverted, organised
Performer	Extroverted, people	Inventor	Extroverted, flexible
Composer	Introverted, people	Architect	Introverted, flexible
GUARDIAN	**Grounded, Organised and ...**	**IDEALIST**	**Abstract thinker, People-oriented and ...**
Supervisor	Extroverted, Rational	Teacher	Extroverted, organised
Inspector	Introverted, Rational	Counsellor/ Guide	Introverted, organised
Provider	Extroverted, People	Champion	Extroverted, flexible
Protector	Introverted, People	Healer	Introverted, flexible

In the second matrix, the various types are related to the Myers–Briggs types discussed in **Chapter 7**. Once again, these are classic or stereotypical "types" and should be interpreted as generalised indications, not firm rules. This matrix also shows the extreme of each quadrant, e.g. the top right-hand quadrant is labelled "Visionary" because of the propensity for abstract thought and a tendency to optimism. The top left "Valuing" quadrant, by contrast, is based on similar thinking style but has the "ideas" element replaced with a greater 'people' orientation.

MATRIX 2: MYERS–BRIGGS PERSONALITY TYPES AND OCCUPATIONS

NF	Possible				**NT**

NF
Valuing
Manifesting universal values

NT
Visioning
Pulling people with ideas
to an optimistic future

Personal

Logical

ENFJ Teacher	**INFJ** Counsellor	**INFJ** Mastermind	**ENTJ** Field Marshall
ENFP Champion	**INFP** Healer	**INTP** Architect	**ENTP** Inventor
ESFP Performer	**ISFP** Composer	**ISTP** Operator	**ESTP** Promoter
ESFJ Provider	**ISFJ** Protector	**ISTJ** Inspector	**ESTJ** Supervisor

SF
Relating
Including and building
trustworthiness

Present

SF
Directing
Action from a strategic
perspective

Conclusion

The world of work has changed from physical to mental work, and this has prompted the need for a way of managing that recognises the new realities of managing smart, specialised people. Change is the new constant and innovation is a pre-requisite to staying competitive. Managing has now, by necessity, become less about supervision and more about enabling the conditions in which knowledge productivity and creativity occur. Motivating today's professionals depends on encouraging autonomy, fostering professional mastery and aligning individual goals with overall organisational purpose, as explained in **Chapter 7**. Increasing specialisation and extended training can narrow the professional's focus, limit perspective and restrict psychological growth.

This book recognises the value of intelligence in people and suggests ways to extend the professional's range of 'intelligences', particularly emotional and social intelligence. It has not laboured the definitional semantics of words like 'intelligent' or 'smart': the definitions differ radically from region to region. In Ireland and the UK the term 'smart' can have an undertone of undesirable cockiness, while in the US it is an undiluted compliment.

Moreover, with some justification, valuing intelligence in people is regarded by some as being disrespectful to those excluded from such exalted classification: such critics favour an entirely egalitarian view of people.

An aim of this book has been to raise awareness in managers of the centrality of personality ('type') in broadening the professional's range of styles and increasing the use of different 'intelligences' (such as emotional intelligence) to achieve a professional's full potential. This is similar in concept to the way in which a good 'bedside manner' improves the life of the patient and the medical professional alike.

Conversely, highly intelligent people, especially if they have very defined personality types and are driven by their need for achievement, can become 'difficult' to manage. Harvard's Chris Argyris, as mentioned in **Chapter 8**, explains how fear of losing their status as high achievers ironically undermines their ability to learn. The CEO of Monitor, a premier strategy consultancy formed by Harvard gurus, similarly tells how his belief in raw IQ nearly undid his company:

> "Our belief was to hire super smart consultants because, thanks to their great intellect, they will be able to learn best and fastest. In fact, we had a thoroughly obnoxious catchphrase – stupid is forever – that I am very embarrassed ever existed, and repeating it here is part of my penance for once holding the view. Its (deeply flawed) logic was that you could teach someone all the interpersonal skills necessary as long as they were really smart. But if they weren't really smart to begin with, there was nothing you could do ... Having great respect for Baker Scholars (the top 5% of the Harvard Business School class), we hired as many of them as we could. But they didn't work out nearly as well as we expected, and some flamed out pretty spectacularly. As is often the case, we attributed that to flawed execution of a fundamentally awesome theory – we had just hired the wrong super smart people.
>
> Then I read Chapter 8 of *Teaching Smart People How to Learn* which argued trenchantly and compellingly that really smart people have the hardest time learning. They are so very smart that they are also very 'brittle', to use Argyris's descriptor. When something goes wrong, rather than reflect on what they might have done to contribute to the error, they look entirely outside themselves for the causes and blame outside forces – irrational clients, impossible time pressure, lack of adequate resources, shifts beyond their control. Rather than learn from error, they doom themselves to repeat them. Before reading the article, I would have been inclined to finish that last sentence with 'despite being so very smart.' After the article, my conclusion was '*because* they are so very smart.' I personally changed my philosophy and worried a lot more about 'smart is forever' than the opposite, and we changed how we recruited and developed ever after."[25]

"The greatest danger in times of turbulence is not the turbulence; it is to act with yesterday's logic."

Peter Drucker

Perhaps surprisingly, researchers have concluded that bright girls are more prone than boys to regard intelligence as a fixed entity, and this view inhibits their learning: they say that more often than not, bright girls believe that their abilities are innate and unchangeable, while bright boys believe that they can develop ability through effort and practice.[26] **Chapter 11**, on building self-confidence in professionals, and **Chapter 13**, on coaching, may help develop an attitude that believes learning is always possible.

Personality plays a large part in the selection of a profession: the introvert may be drawn to an accounting career, for example, and this preference can become exaggerated over time, especially if the person, consciously or otherwise, adopts the persona of the 'true' accountant: cool, quiet and conservative. Conversely, those with the intelligence to 'crunch the numbers', but without the right personality, will find a career in accountancy hard to sustain indefinitely: the analogy is a right-handed person doing something left-handed – fine for a while, but unsustainable in the longer term. The disaffected person will migrate to other roles, better suited to their personality.

Those who feel trapped in the wrong role may eventually find this mismatch unbearable, with tragic consequences. Specialist professions, such as dentistry, suffer particularly in that regard. This book suggests using a wider range of styles from time-to-time so that analytical left- and creative right-brain activities are better harnessed: living constantly outside one's natural state, however, is not recommended.

A great many business sectors are animated by the new economics, and the reward for managing knowledge astutely has been substantially enhanced. In this new world, harnessing the knowledge of the whole organisation is the key factor in success, and creativity is the imperative. Knowledge, if applied well, may indeed be the most valuable asset an organisation has.

The professions themselves have changed and become less stable and predictable. The most valuable professionals now are those who have alloyed technical expertise with empathy, combining hard *and* soft skills. This combination need not be maintained indefinitely, but it is an invaluable asset at crucial periods. The dilemma that leaders of all kinds must resolve is how to foster internal stability (in individuals and whole organisations) in order to pursue constant progress. The alchemy of blending analytical skills and creative ability is still an art form, but the best managers create the conditions that make such a duality possible. It is hoped that this book will help and inspire those who have the responsibility – and privilege – of leading those talented people who can make a difference to the world.

KEY THINGS TO REMEMBER IN MANAGING PROFESSIONALS AND OTHER SMART PEOPLE

- Professionals are sufficiently different to merit special attention in how best to manage them.
- Professions differ greatly in nature, from the analytical professions (such as accounting) through the caring/curing professions (such as found in medicine) and on to the imaginative and creative professions (such as architecture and design).
- Autonomy, mastery and purpose are central to the motivation and development of professionals. The old philosophy of 'carrots and sticks' is redundant here.

- The rate of development and of promotion opportunities for professionals depends greatly on the strategy of the organisation (which sets out the type of work attempted, from routine to leading edge) and the organisation design (which determines the shape of the organisation and hence the opportunities for growth and promotion).
- The inspirational power of authentic leadership, as presented in **Chapter 4** by Dr Jimmy Sheehan, an entrepreneurial pioneer in orthopaedic surgery, engineering and management.
- The determining effect of personality on decision-making and career choice.
- The dramatically different motivational drivers of different personality types, and the consequences for those who manage them.
- The root causes and personality aspects that make some smart people 'difficult' to manage.
- The well-spring of innovation: curiosity and the capturing of ideas.
- The power of the psychological contract, explicit or otherwise, in managing professionals.
- The utility of an effective HR strategy in managing today's professionals (see **Chapter 6** by Dr Mary Collins).
- The nuances in managing different professions, from engineers to accountants and surgeons.
- The value of coaching professionals (see **Chapter 13**) and of building self-confidence (see **Chapter 11**).
- Finally, the central tenet is that progress depends on deliberate learning, and individuals and organisations can reach the magical next level of innovation and knowledge productivity through collaborative effort and intuition. **The prerequisite to this is simply being one's authentic self, tutored by experience and a regard for others**.

ENDNOTES

[1] Thomas Davenport and Laurence Prusak, *Working Knowledge: How Organizations Manage What They Know* (Harvard Business School Press, 1988) p. 88.

[2] Steve Jobs, CEO of Apple Computer and of Pixar Animation Studios, Commencement address at Stanford University on June 12, 2005.

[3] Edwin Locke and Gary Latham, *Theory of Goal Setting and Task Performance* (Prentice-Hall, 1990).

[4] W. Edwards Deming, *Out of the Crisis* (MIT Press, 1986).

[5] Morten T. Hansen, Nitin Nohria, Thomas Tierney, *What's Your Strategy for Managing Knowledge?* (Harvard Business School Press, 1999) p. 109.

[6] Bruce Kogut and Ugo Zander, "Knowledge of the Firm, Combinative Capabilities, and the Replication of Technology" (1992) (3:3) *Organization Science* 384.

[7] Nancy Duarte, *Resonate: Present Visual Stories that Tranform Audiences* (Wiley, 2010) p. 48.

[8] David Ogilvy, *The Unpublished David Ogilvy* (Sidgwick & Jackson, 1988).

[9] Dr William Menninger quoted in A.C. Houts, "Fifty Years of Psychiatric Nomenclature: Reflections on the 1943 War Department Technical Bulletin, Medical 203" (2002) 56 (7) *Journal of Clinical Psychology* 935–967.

[10] Joseph Schumpeter, *The Theory of Economic Development: an Inquiry into Profits, Capital, Credit, Interest and the Business Cycle*, translated from the German by Redvers Opie (Oxford University Press, 1961).

[11] Viktor E. Frankl, *Man's Search for Meaning: An Introduction to Logotherapy* (Beacon Press, 1964).

[12] Jim Collins, *Good to Great: Why Some Companies Make the Leap ... and Others Don't* (HarperCollins, 2001).

[13] Jules Goddard and Tony Eccles, *Uncommon Sense, Common Nonsense: Why some Organisations Consistently Outperform Others* (Profile Books, 2013).

[14] Donald Sull, *The Upside of Turbulence* (HarperCollins, 2009).

[15] Donald Sull, *The Upside of Turbulence* (HarperCollins, 2009).

[16] W. Edwards Deming, *Out of the Crisis* (MIT Press, 1986).

[17] Jules Goddard and Tony Eccles, *Uncommon Sense, Common Nonsense: Why some Organisations Consistently Outperform Others* (Profile Books, 2013).

[18] David Ogilvy, *The Unpublished David Ogilvy* (Sidgwick & Jackson, 1988).

[19] *Ibid.*

[20] *Ibid.*

[21] Patrick McKenna, *First Among Equals* (Free Press/Simon & Schuster, 2002).

[22] Marcus Buckingham and Curt Coffman, *First, Break All the Rules* (Simon & Schuster, 1999).

[23] David N. Perkins in Robert J. Sternberg, *Why Smart People Can Be So Stupid* (Yale Press, 2002).

[24] Simon Mosey, *Ingenuity in Practice* (University of Nottingham Business School Press, 2011).

[25] Roger Martin, Harvard Business School, Blog, accessed 17 October 2012.

[26] Dr Heidi Grant Halvorson, *Succeed: How We Can Reach Our Goals* (Hudson Street Press, 2012).

Index